Volume Two
by Choi Kyung-ah

English Adaptation
by Sarah Dyer

Los Angeles • Tokyo • London

MANGA

.HACK//LEGEND OF THE TWILIGHT
@LARGE
ABENOBASHI
A.I. LOVE YOU
AI YORI AOSHI
ANGELIC LAYER
ARM OF KANNON
BABY BIRTH
BATTLE ROYALE
BATTLE VIXENS
BRAIN POWERED
BRIGADOON
B'TX
CANDIDATE FOR GODDESS, THE
CARDCAPTOR SAKURA
CARDCAPTOR SAKURA - MASTER OF THE CLOW
CHOBITS
CHRONICLES OF THE CURSED SWORD
CLAMP SCHOOL DETECTIVES
CLOVER
COMIC PARTY
CONFIDENTIAL CONFESSIONS
CORRECTOR YUI
COWBOY BEBOP
COWBOY BEBOP: SHOOTING STAR
CRESCENT MOON
CULDCEPT
CYBORG 009
D.N. ANGEL
DEMON DIARY
DEMON ORORON, THE
DEUS VITAE
DIGIMON
DIGIMON ZERO TWO
DIGIMON TAMERS
DOLL
DRAGON HUNTER
DRAGON KNIGHTS
DREAM SAGA
DUKLYON: CLAMP SCHOOL DEFENDERS
ERICA SAKURAZAWA COLLECTED WORKS
EERIE QUEERIE!
ET CETERA
ETERNITY
EVIL'S RETURN
FAERIES' LANDING
FAKE
FLCL
FORBIDDEN DANCE
FRUITS BASKET
G GUNDAM
GATE KEEPERS

GETBACKERS
GIRL GOT GAME
GRAVITATION
GTO
GUNDAM SEED ASTRAY
GUNDAM WING
GUNDAM WING: BATTLEFIELD OF PACIFISTS
GUNDAM WING: ENDLESS WALTZ
GUNDAM WING: THE LAST OUTPOST (G-UNIT)
HAPPY MANIA
HARLEM BEAT
I.N.V.U.
IMMORTAL RAIN
INITIAL D
ISLAND
JING: KING OF BANDITS
JULINE
KARE KANO
KILL ME, KISS ME
KINDAICHI CASE FILES, THE
KING OF HELL
KODOCHA: SANA'S STAGE
LAMENT OF THE LAMB
LES BIJOUX
LEGEND OF CHUN HYANG, THE
LOVE HINA
LUPIN III
MAGIC KNIGHT RAYEARTH I
MAGIC KNIGHT RAYEARTH II
MAHOROMATIC: AUTOMATIC MAIDEN
MAN OF MANY FACES
MARMALADE BOY
MARS
MINK
MIRACLE GIRLS
MIYUKI-CHAN IN WONDERLAND
MODEL
ONE
PARADISE KISS
PARASYTE
PEACH GIRL
PEACH GIRL: CHANGE OF HEART
PET SHOP OF HORRORS
PITA-TEN
PLANET LADDER
PLANETES
PRIEST
PRINCESS AI
PSYCHIC ACADEMY
RAGNAROK
RAVE MASTER
REALITY CHECK
REBIRTH

01.09.04T

ALSO AVAILABLE FROM  TOKYOPOP®

Translator - Jennifer Hahm
English Adaptation - Sarah Dyer
Copy Editor - Troy Lewter
Retouch and Lettering - Christina R. Siri
Cover Layout - Anna Kernbaum
Graphic Designer - Deron Bennett

Editor - Bryce P. Coleman
Managing Editor - Jill Freshney
Production Coordinator - Antonio DePietro
Production Managers - Jennifer Miller, Mutsumi Miyazaki
Art Director - Matt Alford
Editorial Director - Jeremy Ross
VP of Production - Ron Klamert
President & C.O.O. - John Parker
Publisher & C.E.O. - Stuart Levy

Email: editor@TOKYOPOP.com
Come visit us online at www.TOKYOPOP.com

A TOKYOPOP® Manga

TOKYOPOP Inc.
5900 Wilshire Blvd. Suite 2000
Los Angeles, CA 90036

Snow Drop Vol. 2

ISBN: 1-59182-685-3

First TOKYOPOP printing: March 2004

10 9 8 7 6 5 4 3 2 1
Printed in the USA

Previously in

Snow Drop

Wealthy but emotionally fragile So-Na is trying to reintegrate into high school. Luckily for her, her best friend, the outrageous Ha-Da, will be going back as well. But when a handsome and enigmatic young model named Hae-Gi also enrolls, emotions and competitive natures run rampant. As reclusive as Hae-Gi is, there's a definite connection between him and So-Na—something that doesn't sit well with Ha-Da, who takes an immediate dislike to the attention-grabbing new student.

C·O·N·T·E·N·T·S

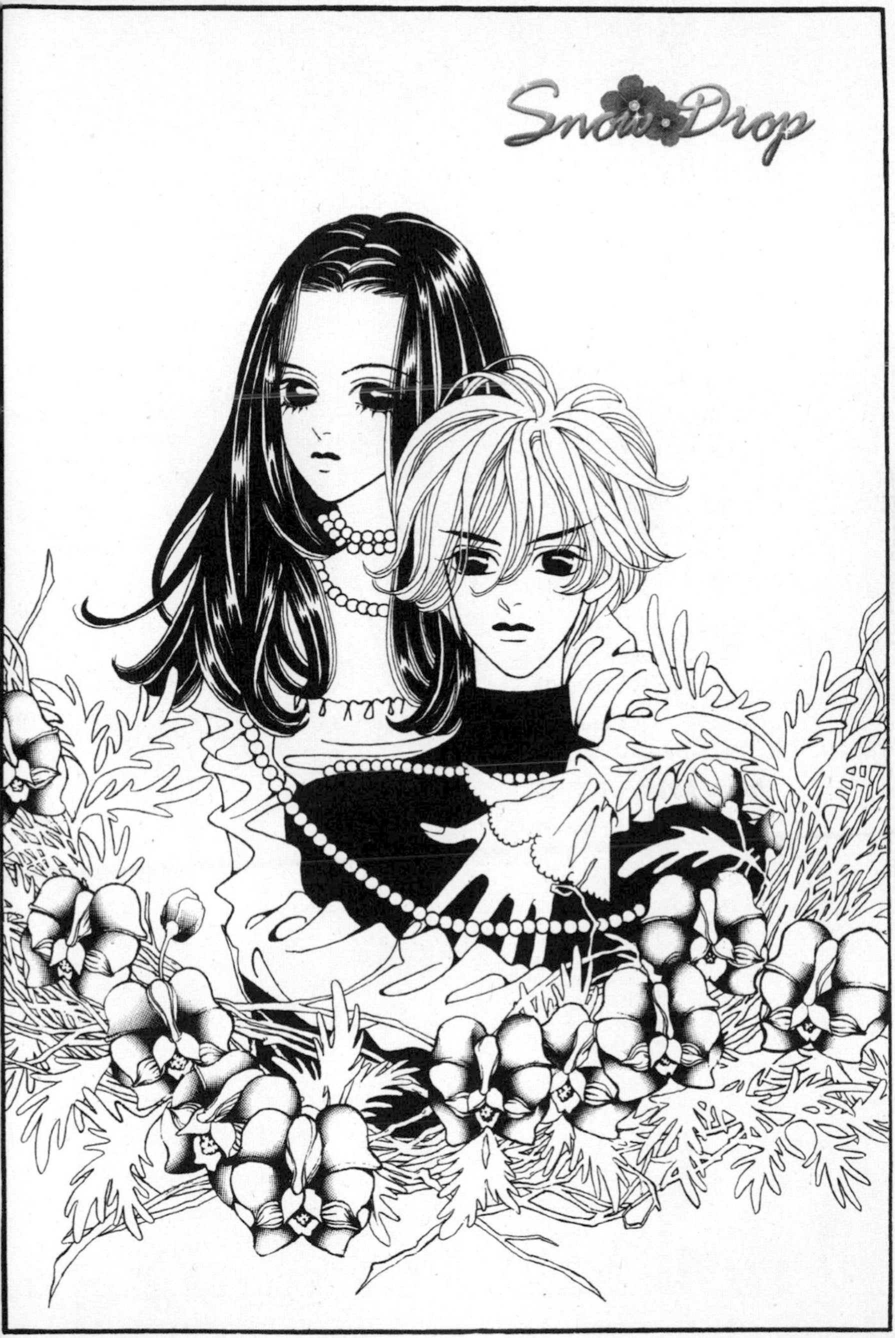
Snow Drop

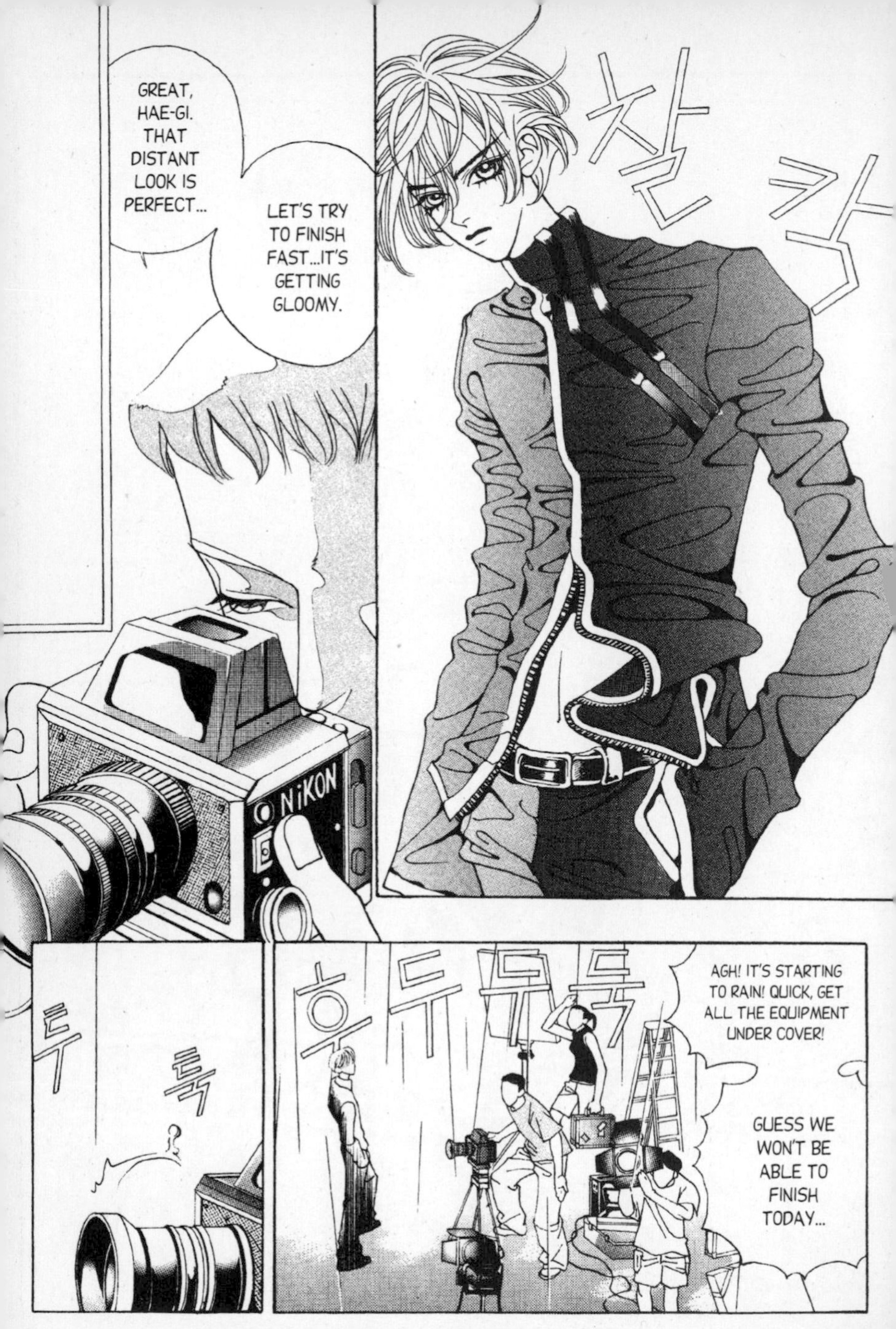
GREAT, HAE-GI. THAT DISTANT LOOK IS PERFECT...
LET'S TRY TO FINISH FAST...IT'S GETTING GLOOMY.
NiKON
찰칵
투
툭
?
후두두둑
AGH! IT'S STARTING TO RAIN! QUICK, GET ALL THE EQUIPMENT UNDER COVER!
GUESS WE WON'T BE ABLE TO FINISH TODAY...

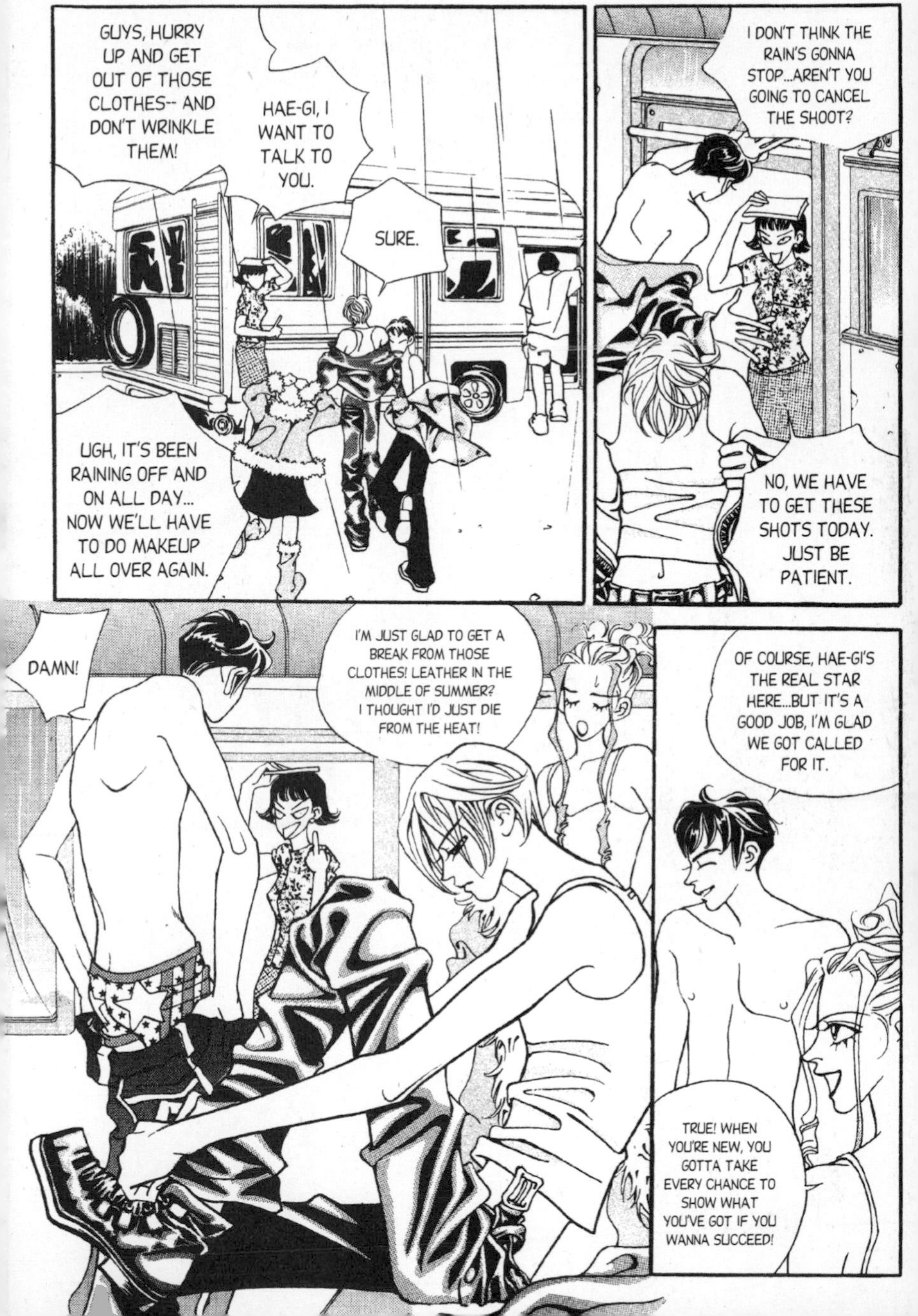
GUYS, HURRY UP AND GET OUT OF THOSE CLOTHES-- AND DON'T WRINKLE THEM!
HAE-GI, I WANT TO TALK TO YOU.
SURE.
UGH, IT'S BEEN RAINING OFF AND ON ALL DAY... NOW WE'LL HAVE TO DO MAKEUP ALL OVER AGAIN.
I DON'T THINK THE RAIN'S GONNA STOP...AREN'T YOU GOING TO CANCEL THE SHOOT?
NO, WE HAVE TO GET THESE SHOTS TODAY. JUST BE PATIENT.
DAMN!
I'M JUST GLAD TO GET A BREAK FROM THOSE CLOTHES! LEATHER IN THE MIDDLE OF SUMMER? I THOUGHT I'D JUST DIE FROM THE HEAT!
OF COURSE, HAE-GI'S THE REAL STAR HERE...BUT IT'S A GOOD JOB, I'M GLAD WE GOT CALLED FOR IT.
TRUE! WHEN YOU'RE NEW, YOU GOTTA TAKE EVERY CHANCE TO SHOW WHAT YOU'VE GOT IF YOU WANNA SUCCEED!

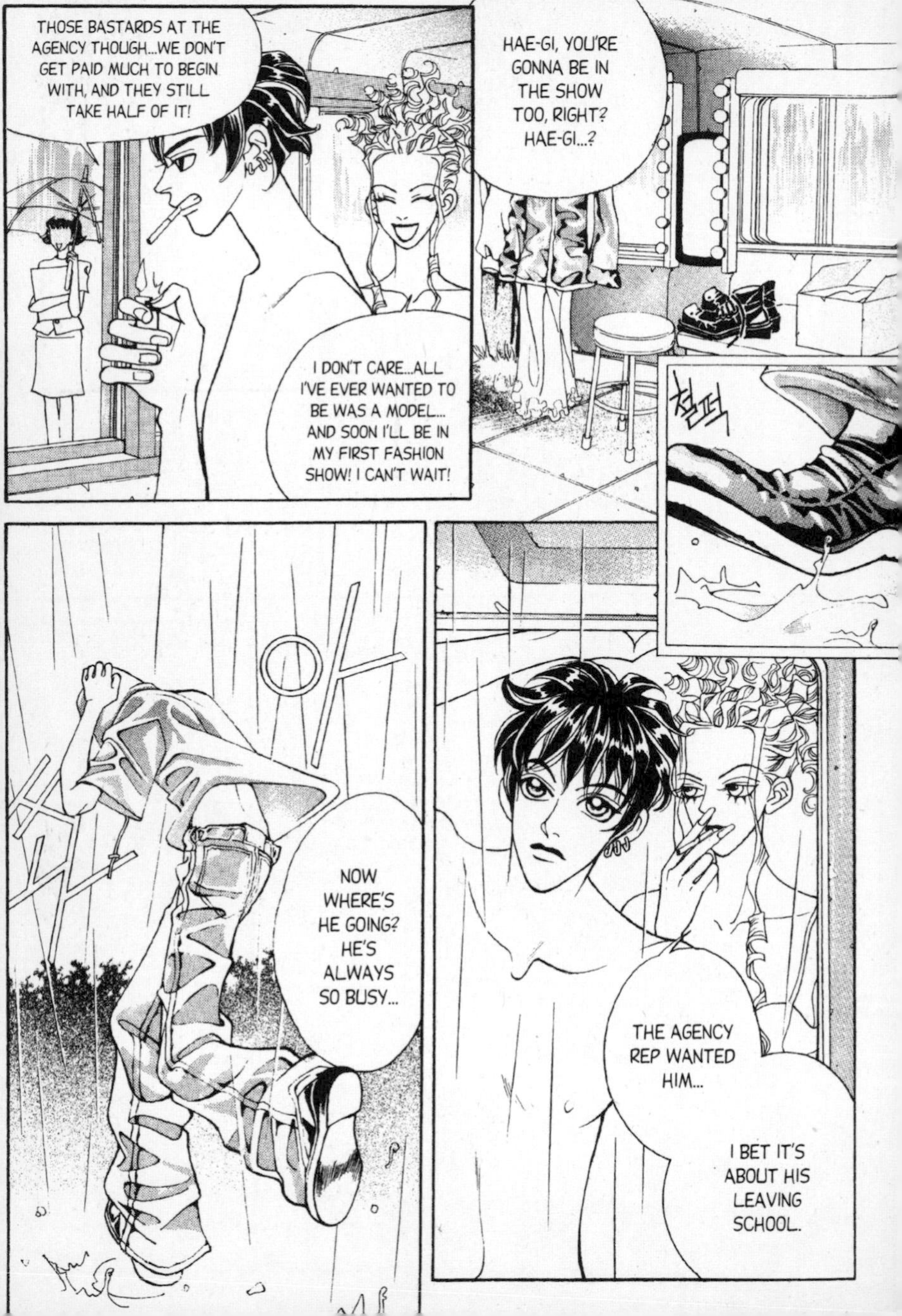
THOSE BASTARDS AT THE AGENCY THOUGH...WE DON'T GET PAID MUCH TO BEGIN WITH, AND THEY STILL TAKE HALF OF IT!
I DON'T CARE...ALL I'VE EVER WANTED TO BE WAS A MODEL... AND SOON I'LL BE IN MY FIRST FASHION SHOW! I CAN'T WAIT!
HAE-GI, YOU'RE GONNA BE IN THE SHOW TOO, RIGHT? HAE-GI...?
NOW WHERE'S HE GOING? HE'S ALWAYS SO BUSY...
THE AGENCY REP WANTED HIM...
I BET IT'S ABOUT HIS LEAVING SCHOOL.

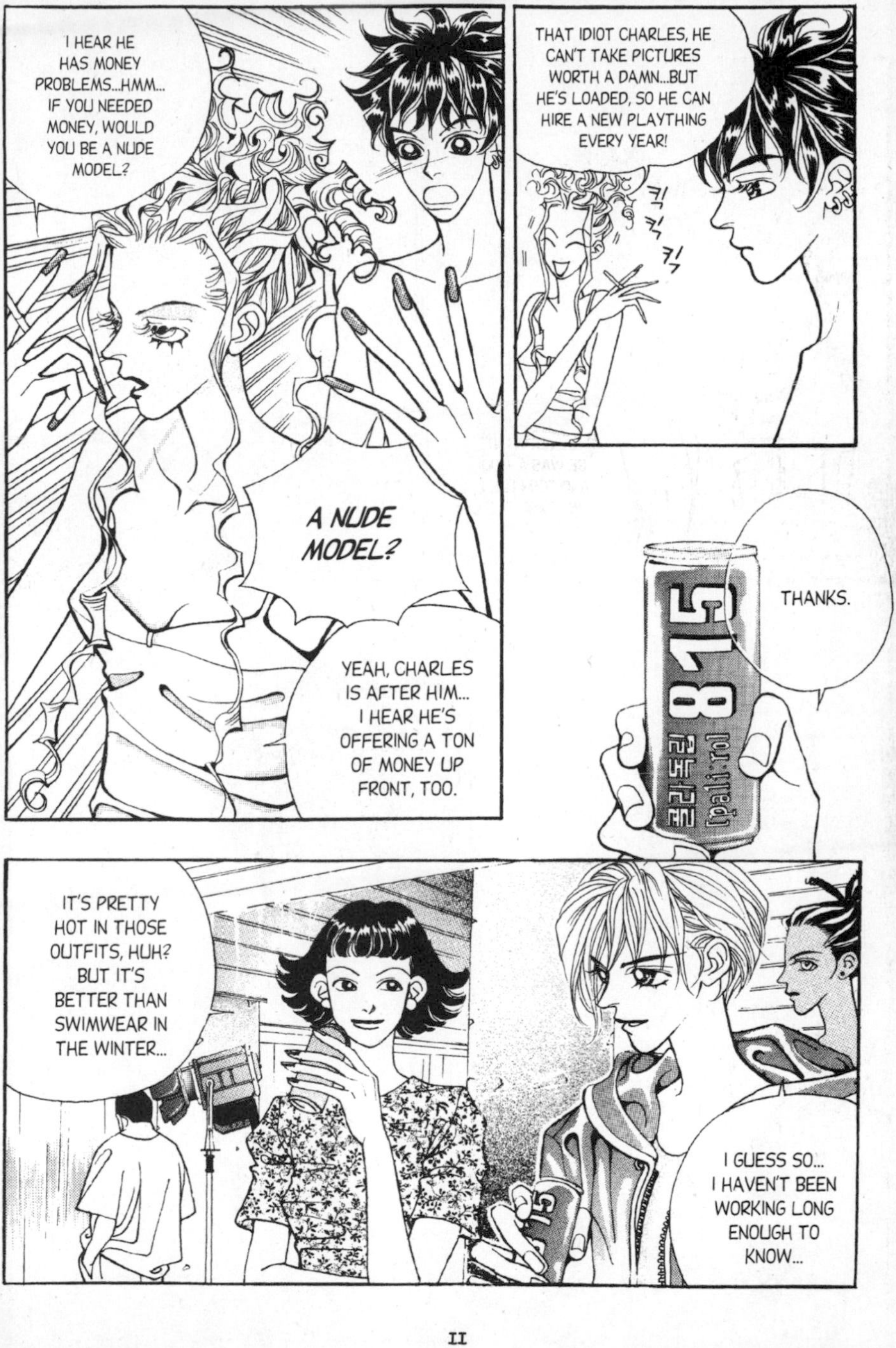
I HEAR HE HAS MONEY PROBLEMS...HMM... IF YOU NEEDED MONEY, WOULD YOU BE A NUDE MODEL?
A NUDE MODEL?
YEAH, CHARLES IS AFTER HIM... I HEAR HE'S OFFERING A TON OF MONEY UP FRONT, TOO.
THAT IDIOT CHARLES, HE CAN'T TAKE PICTURES WORTH A DAMN...BUT HE'S LOADED, SO HE CAN HIRE A NEW PLAYTHING EVERY YEAR!
킥
킥
킥
815
THANKS.
IT'S PRETTY HOT IN THOSE OUTFITS, HUH? BUT IT'S BETTER THAN SWIMWEAR IN THE WINTER...
I GUESS SO... I HAVEN'T BEEN WORKING LONG ENOUGH TO KNOW...

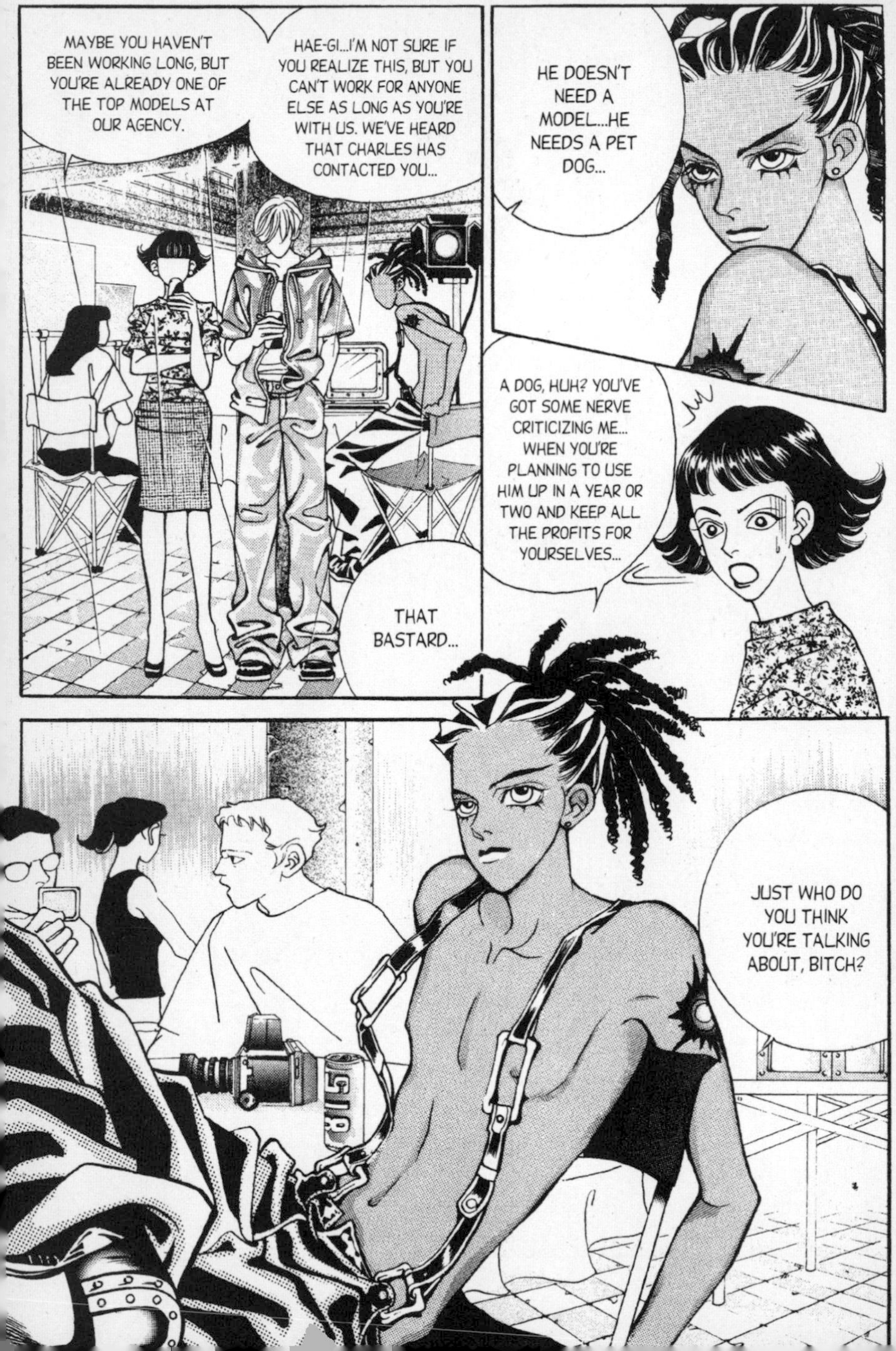
MAYBE YOU HAVEN'T BEEN WORKING LONG, BUT YOU'RE ALREADY ONE OF THE TOP MODELS AT OUR AGENCY.
HAE-GI...I'M NOT SURE IF YOU REALIZE THIS, BUT YOU CAN'T WORK FOR ANYONE ELSE AS LONG AS YOU'RE WITH US. WE'VE HEARD THAT CHARLES HAS CONTACTED YOU...
HE DOESN'T NEED A MODEL...HE NEEDS A PET DOG...
A DOG, HUH? YOU'VE GOT SOME NERVE CRITICIZING ME... WHEN YOU'RE PLANNING TO USE HIM UP IN A YEAR OR TWO AND KEEP ALL THE PROFITS FOR YOURSELVES...
THAT BASTARD...
JUST WHO DO YOU THINK YOU'RE TALKING ABOUT, BITCH?

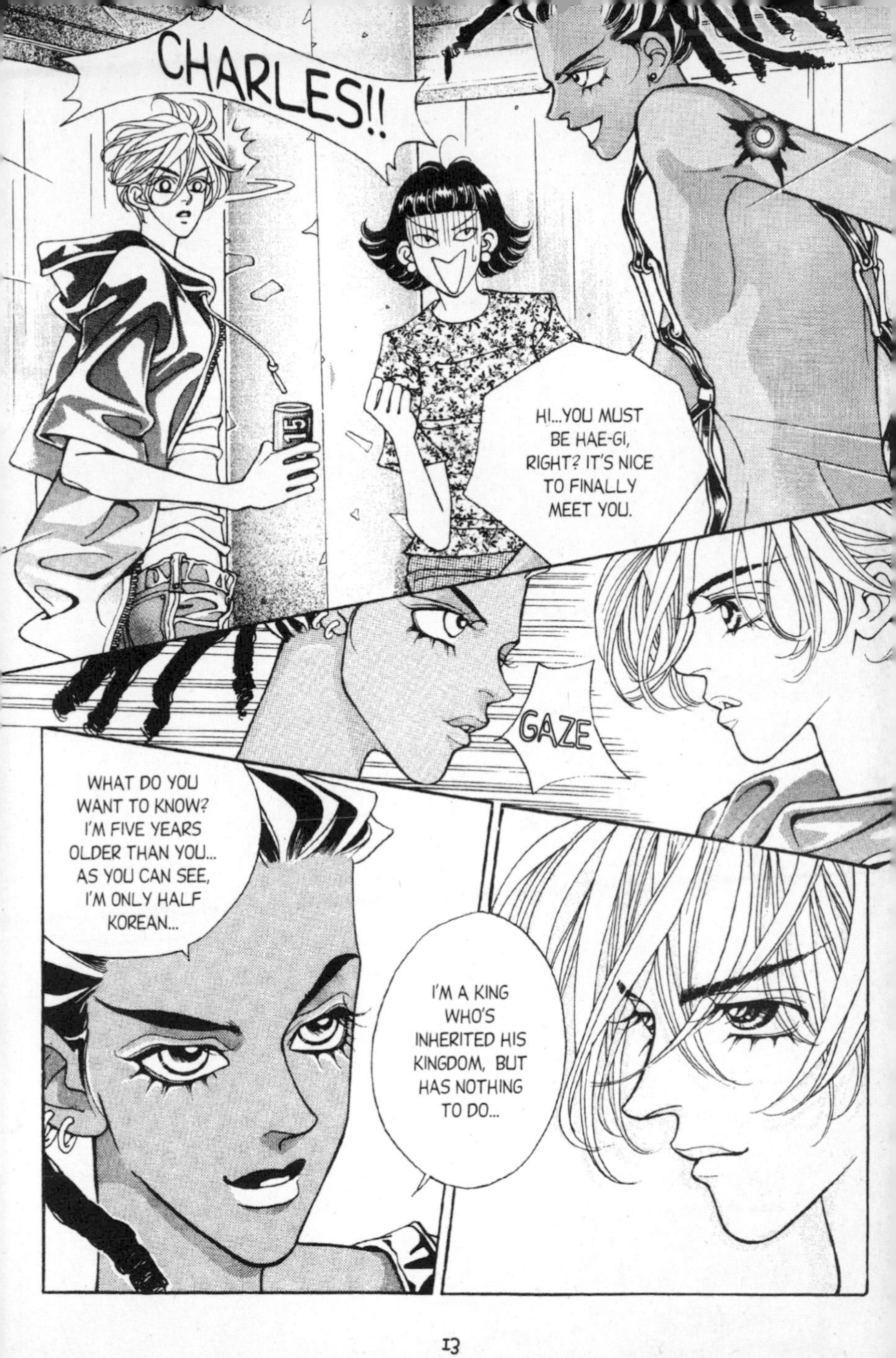
CHARLES!!
HI...YOU MUST BE HAE-GI, RIGHT? IT'S NICE TO FINALLY MEET YOU.
GAZE
WHAT DO YOU WANT TO KNOW? I'M FIVE YEARS OLDER THAN YOU... AS YOU CAN SEE, I'M ONLY HALF KOREAN...
I'M A KING WHO'S INHERITED HIS KINGDOM, BUT HAS NOTHING TO DO...

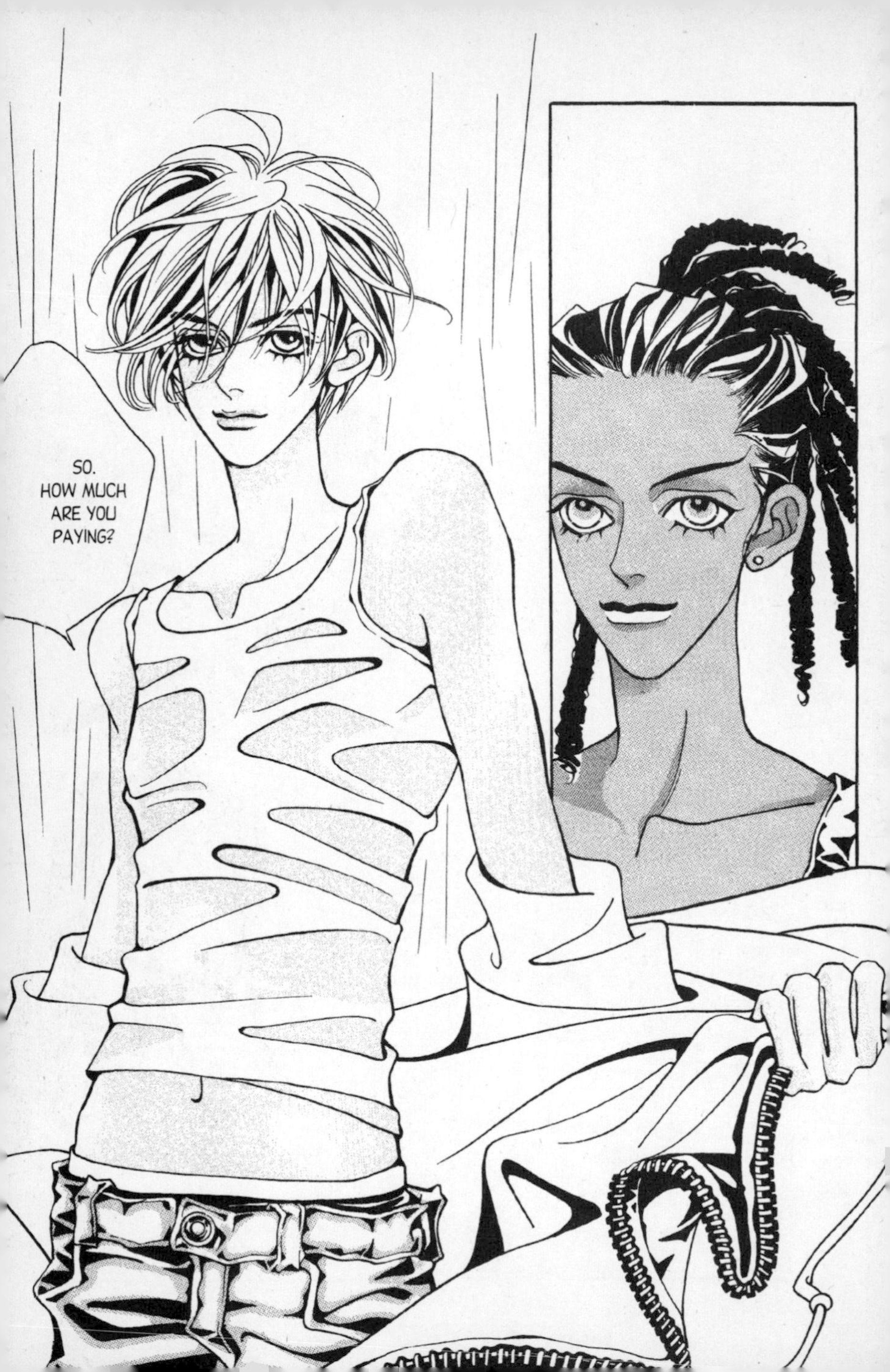
SO. HOW MUCH ARE YOU PAYING?

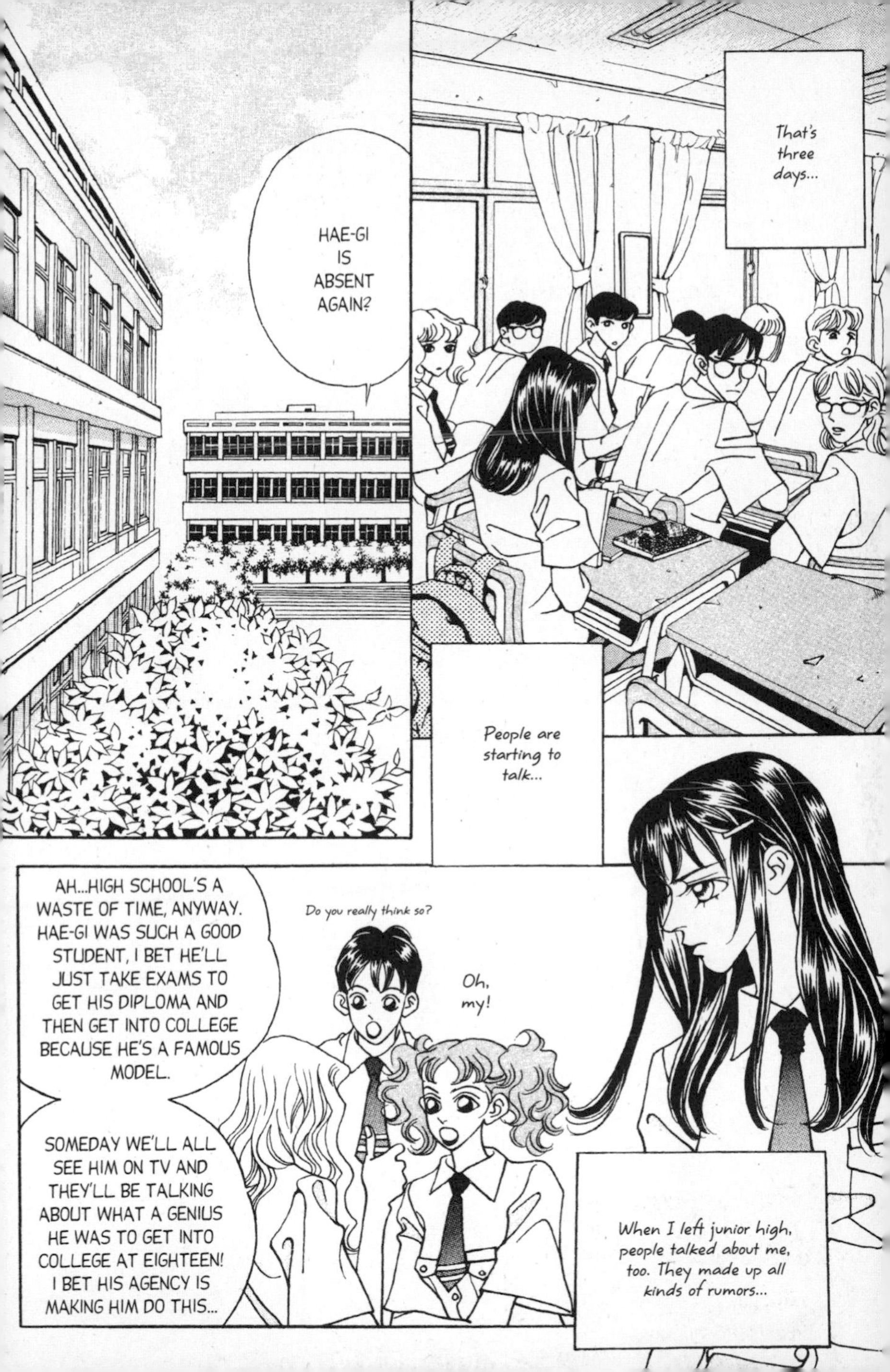
HAE-GI IS ABSENT AGAIN?
That's three days...
People are starting to talk...
AH...HIGH SCHOOL'S A WASTE OF TIME, ANYWAY. HAE-GI WAS SUCH A GOOD STUDENT, I BET HE'LL JUST TAKE EXAMS TO GET HIS DIPLOMA AND THEN GET INTO COLLEGE BECAUSE HE'S A FAMOUS MODEL.
SOMEDAY WE'LL ALL SEE HIM ON TV AND THEY'LL BE TALKING ABOUT WHAT A GENIUS HE WAS TO GET INTO COLLEGE AT EIGHTEEN! I BET HIS AGENCY IS MAKING HIM DO THIS...
Do you really think so?
Oh, my!
When I left junior high, people talked about me, too. They made up all kinds of rumors...

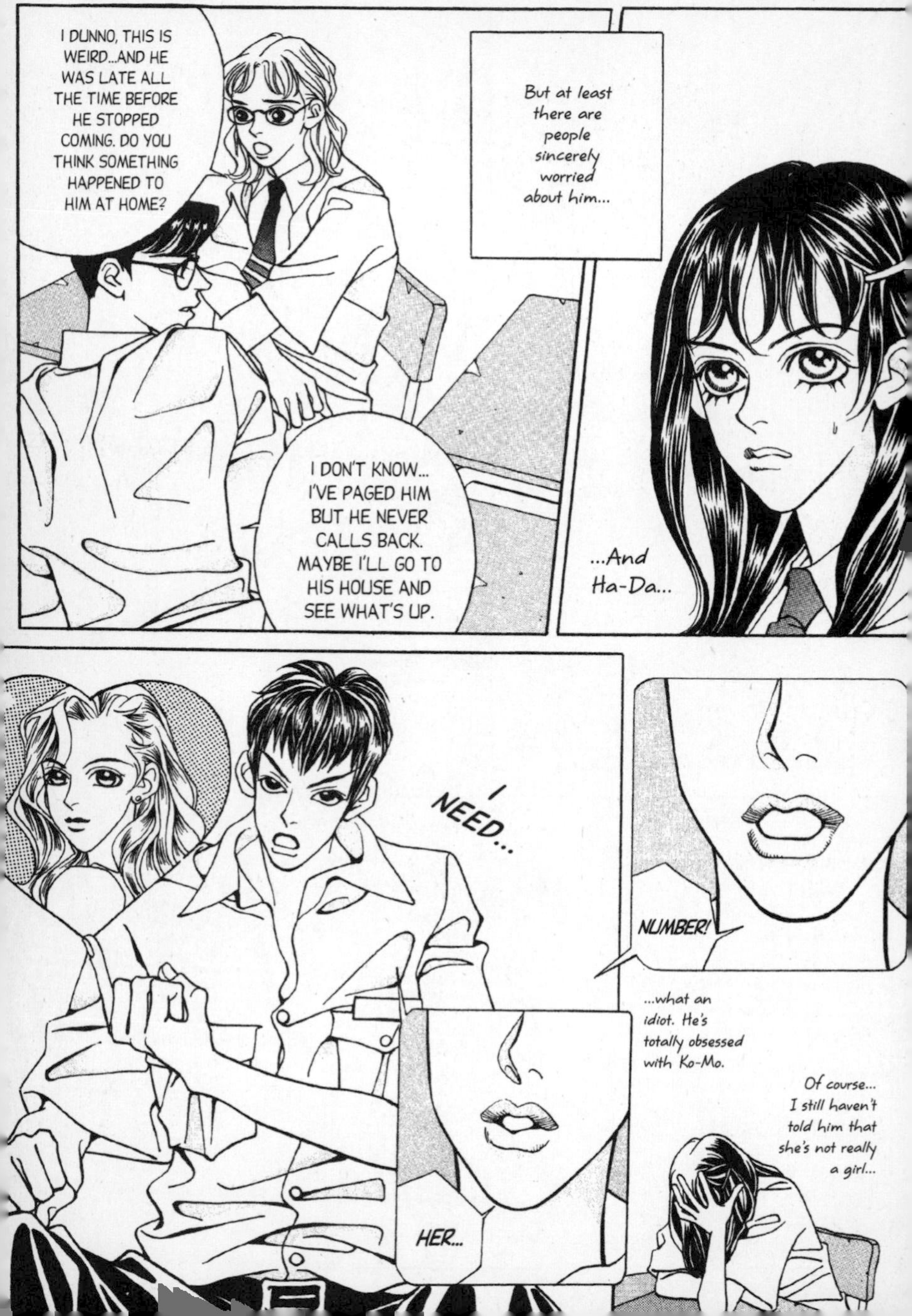
I DUNNO, THIS IS WEIRD...AND HE WAS LATE ALL THE TIME BEFORE HE STOPPED COMING. DO YOU THINK SOMETHING HAPPENED TO HIM AT HOME?
I DON'T KNOW... I'VE PAGED HIM BUT HE NEVER CALLS BACK. MAYBE I'LL GO TO HIS HOUSE AND SEE WHAT'S UP.
But at least there are people sincerely worried about him...
...And Ha-Da...
I NEED...
NUMBER!
HER...
...what an idiot. He's totally obsessed with Ko-Mo.
Of course... I still haven't told him that she's not really a girl...

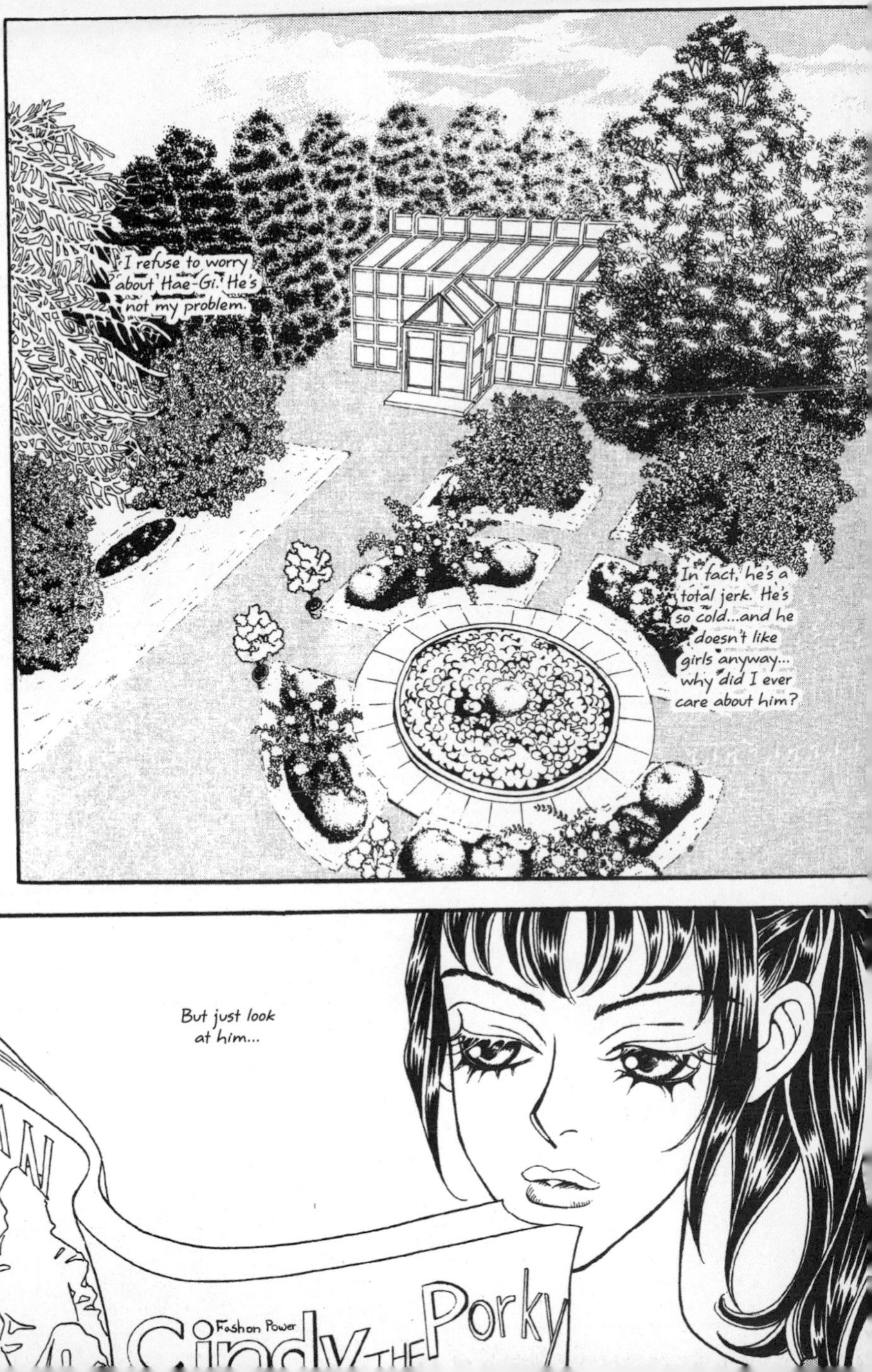
I refuse to worry about Hae-Gi. He's not my problem.
In fact, he's a total jerk. He's so cold...and he doesn't like girls anyway... why did I ever care about him?
But just look at him...
Fashion Power
Porky

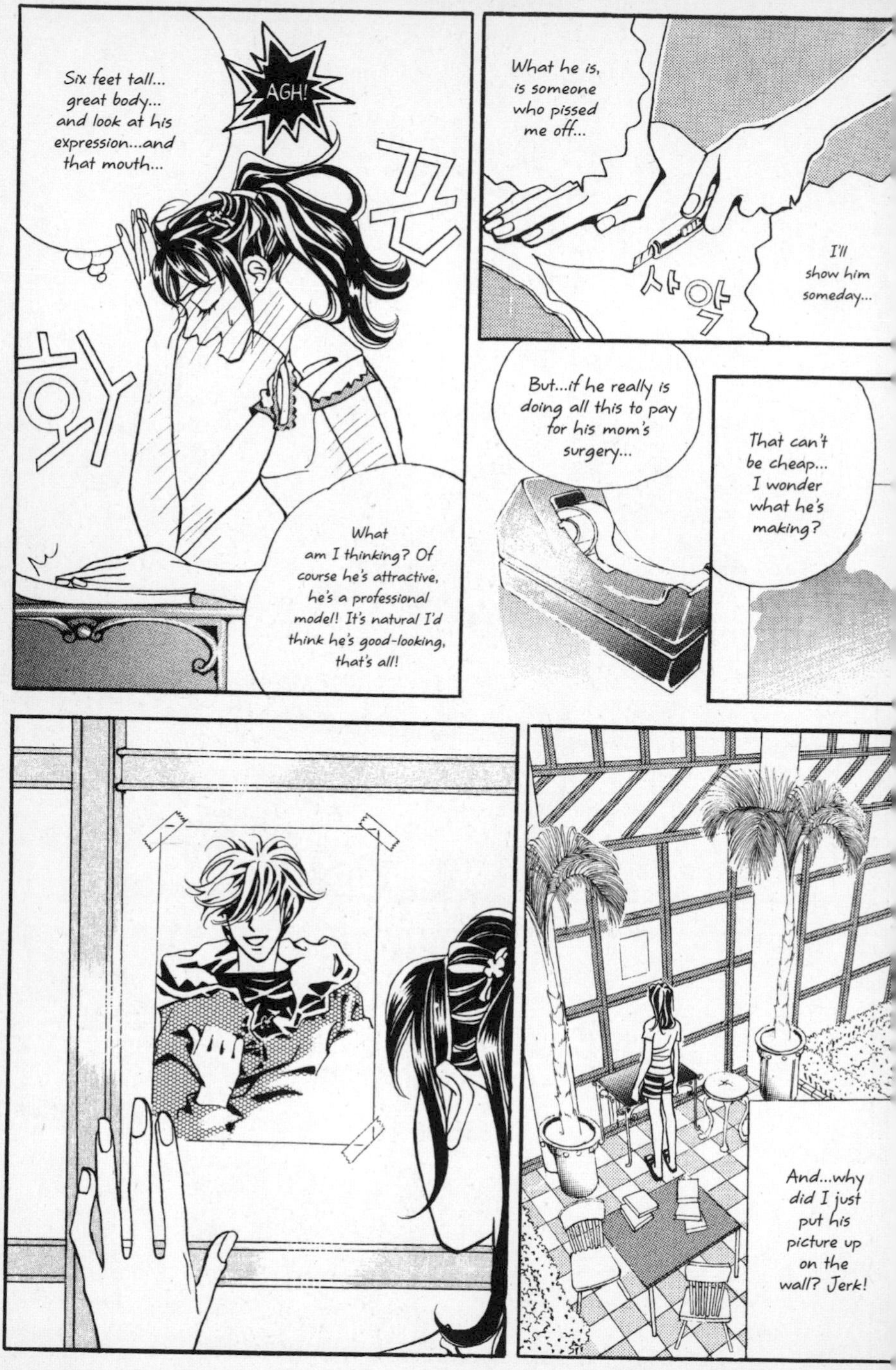
Six feet tall... great body... and look at his expression...and that mouth...
AGH!
What am I thinking? Of course he's attractive, he's a professional model!! It's natural I'd think he's good-looking, that's all!
What he is, is someone who pissed me off...
I'll show him someday...
But...if he really is doing all this to pay for his mom's surgery...
That can't be cheap... I wonder what he's making?
And...why did I just put his picture up on the wall? Jerk!

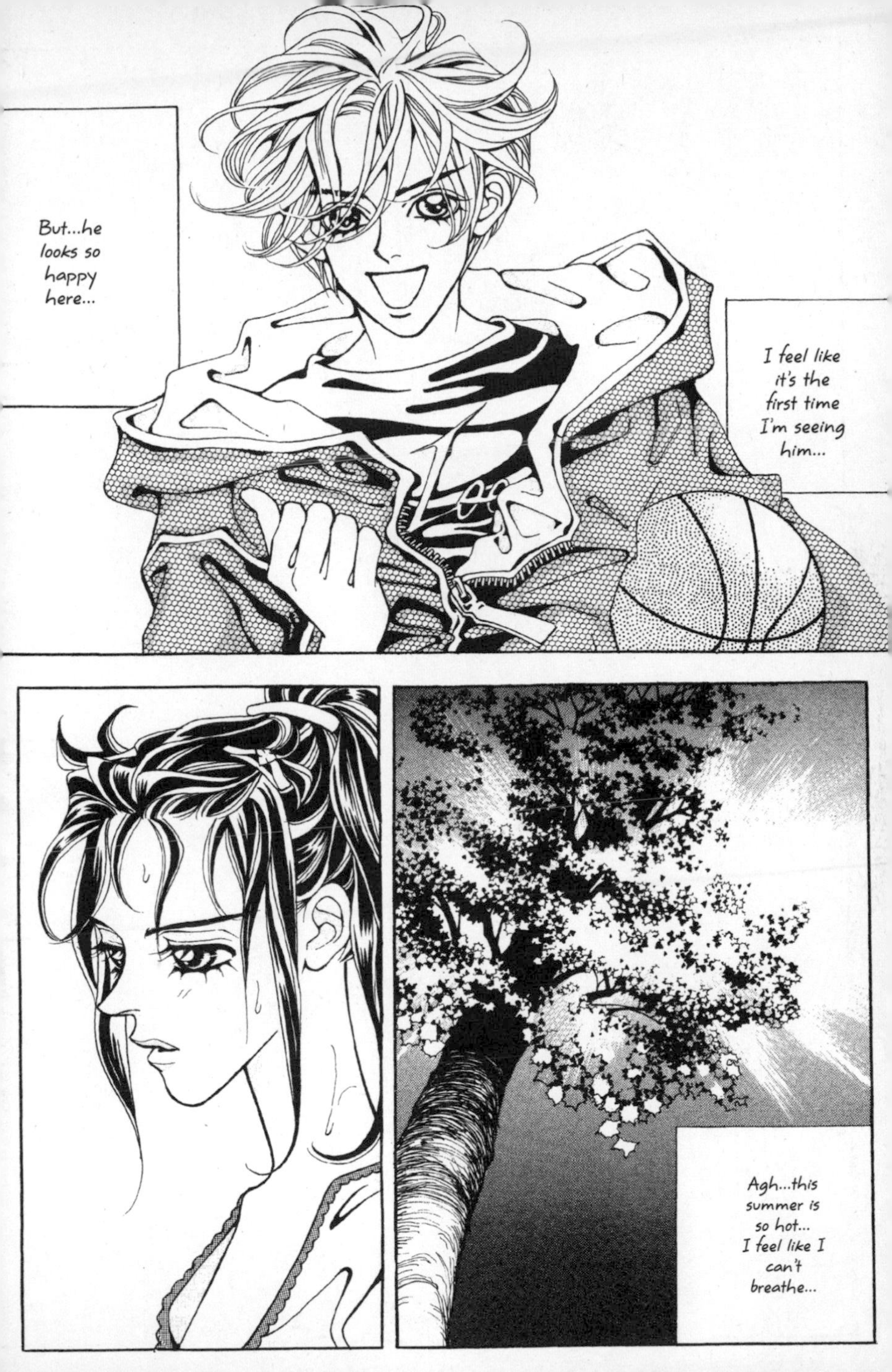
But...he looks so happy here...
I feel like it's the first time I'm seeing him...
Agh...this summer is so hot... I feel like I can't breathe...

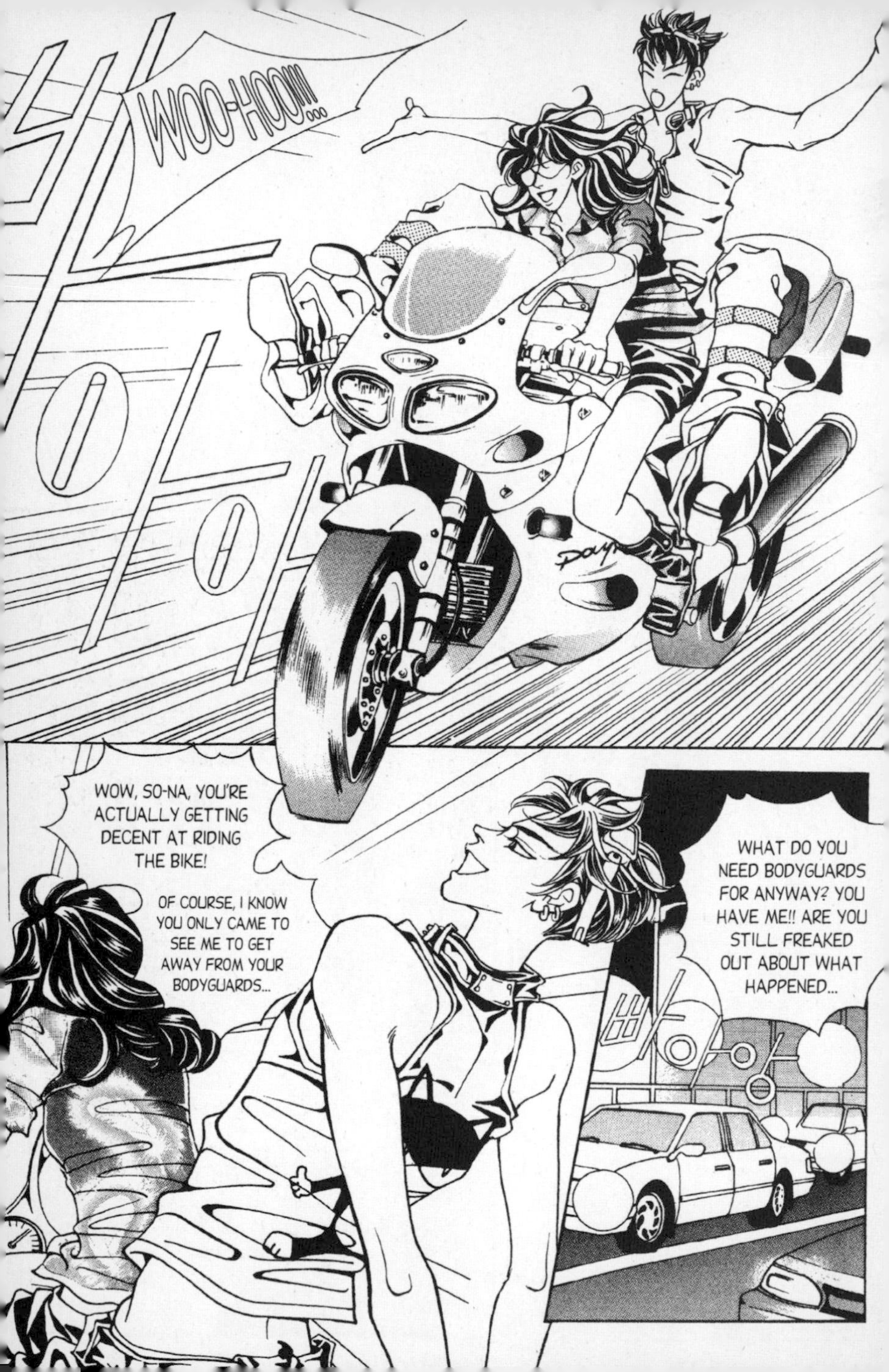
WOO-HOO!!!...
WOW, SO-NA, YOU'RE ACTUALLY GETTING DECENT AT RIDING THE BIKE!
OF COURSE, I KNOW YOU ONLY CAME TO SEE ME TO GET AWAY FROM YOUR BODYGUARDS...
WHAT DO YOU NEED BODYGUARDS FOR ANYWAY? YOU HAVE ME!! ARE YOU STILL FREAKED OUT ABOUT WHAT HAPPENED...

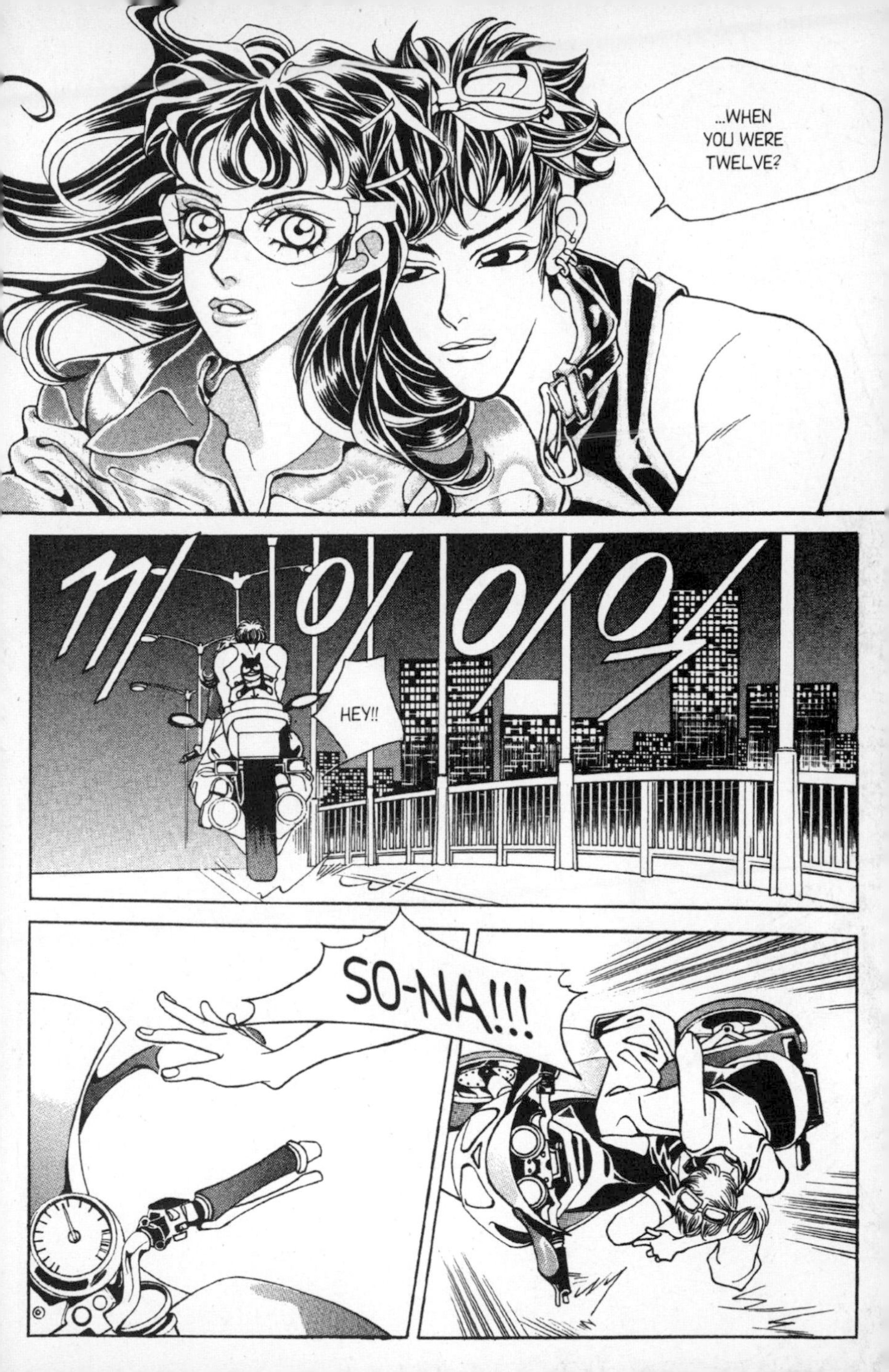
...WHEN YOU WERE TWELVE?
HEY!!
SO-NA!!!

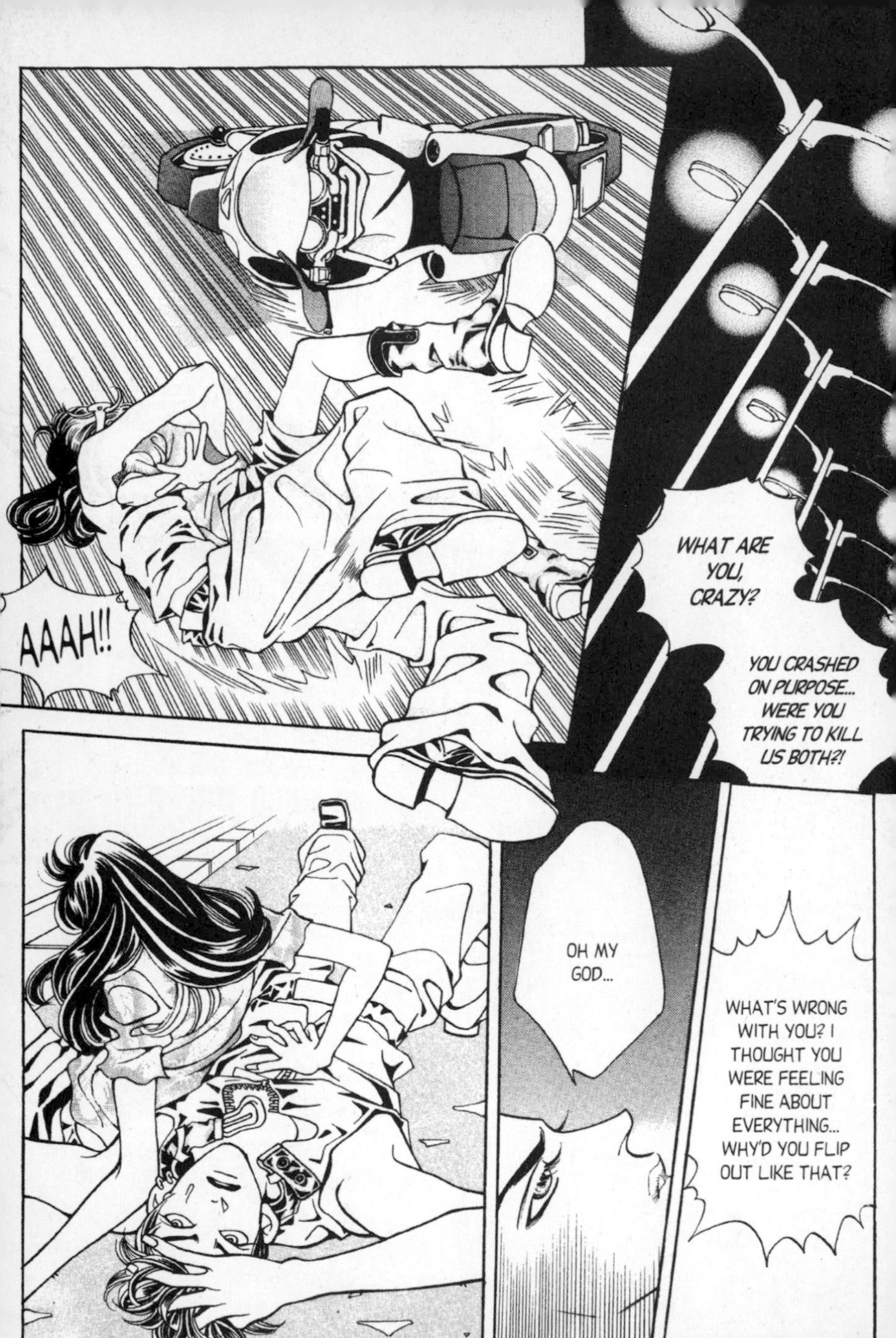
AAAH!!
WHAT ARE YOU, CRAZY?
YOU CRASHED ON PURPOSE... WERE YOU TRYING TO KILL US BOTH?!
OH MY GOD...
WHAT'S WRONG WITH YOU? I THOUGHT YOU WERE FEELING FINE ABOUT EVERYTHING... WHY'D YOU FLIP OUT LIKE THAT?

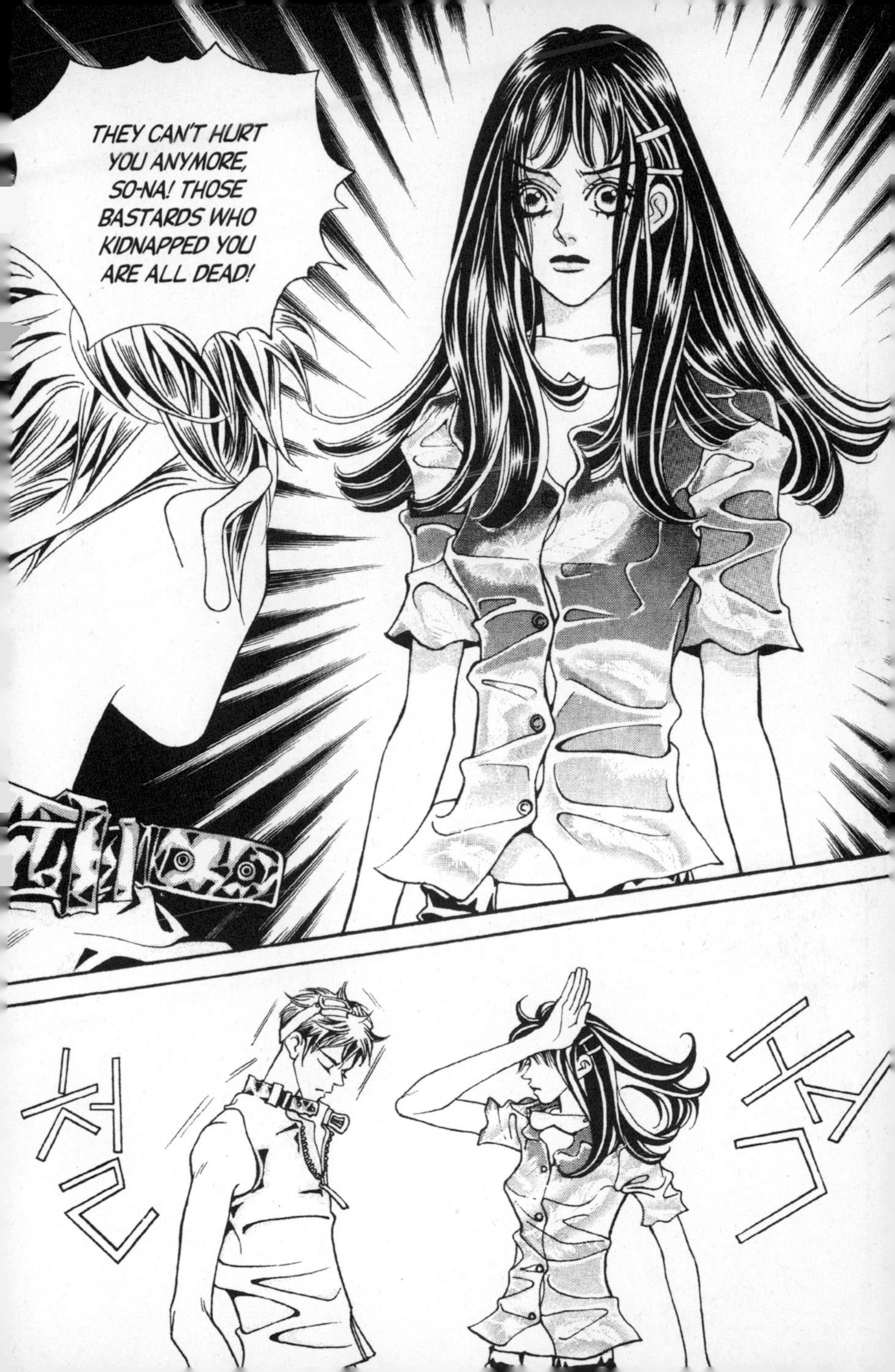
THEY CAN'T HURT YOU ANYMORE, SO-NA! THOSE BASTARDS WHO KIDNAPPED YOU ARE ALL DEAD!

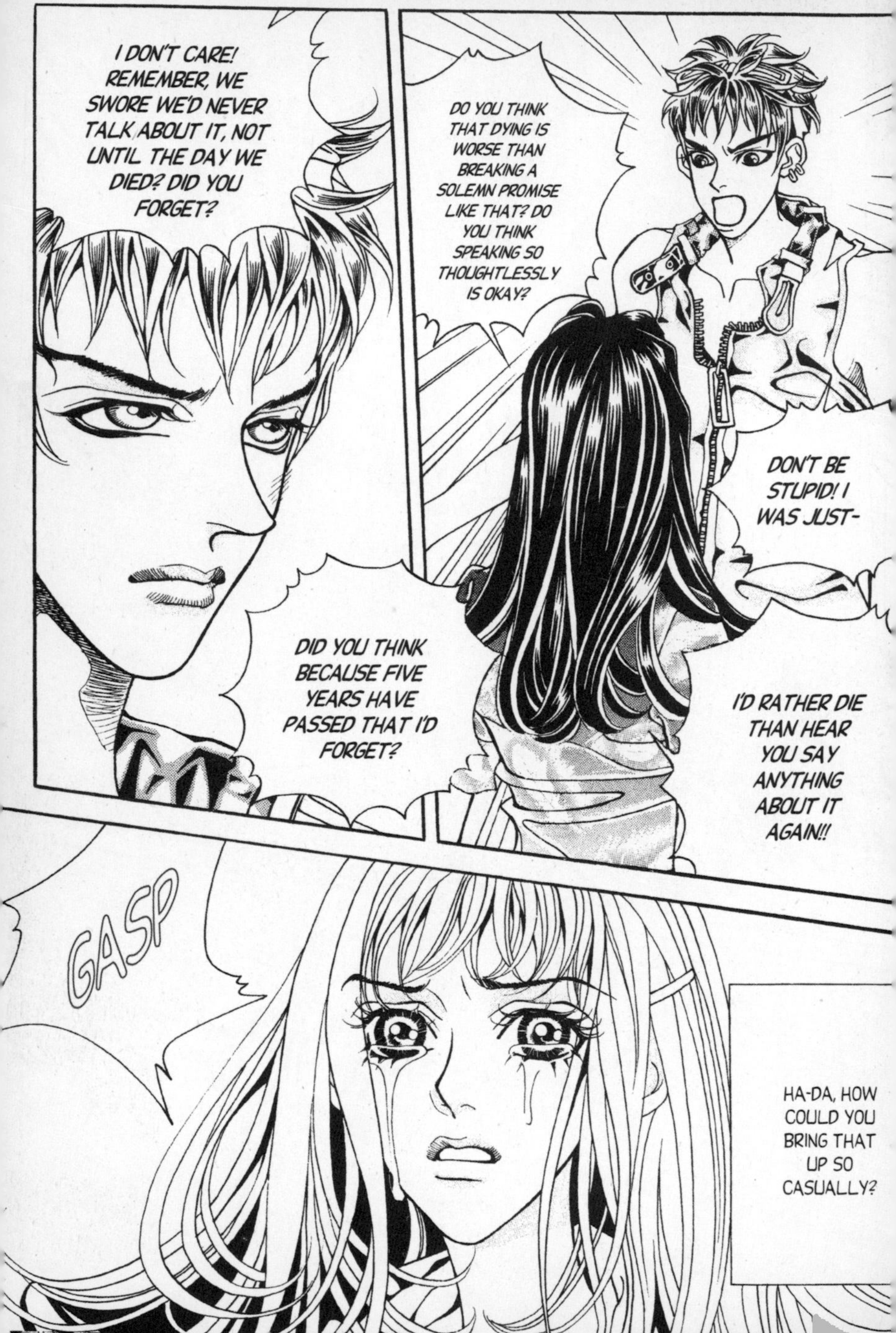
I DON'T CARE! REMEMBER, WE SWORE WE'D NEVER TALK ABOUT IT, NOT UNTIL THE DAY WE DIED? DID YOU FORGET?
DID YOU THINK BECAUSE FIVE YEARS HAVE PASSED THAT I'D FORGET?
DO YOU THINK THAT DYING IS WORSE THAN BREAKING A SOLEMN PROMISE LIKE THAT? DO YOU THINK SPEAKING SO THOUGHTLESSLY IS OKAY?
DON'T BE STUPID! I WAS JUST-
I'D RATHER DIE THAN HEAR YOU SAY ANYTHING ABOUT IT AGAIN!!
GASP
HA-DA, HOW COULD YOU BRING THAT UP SO CASUALLY?

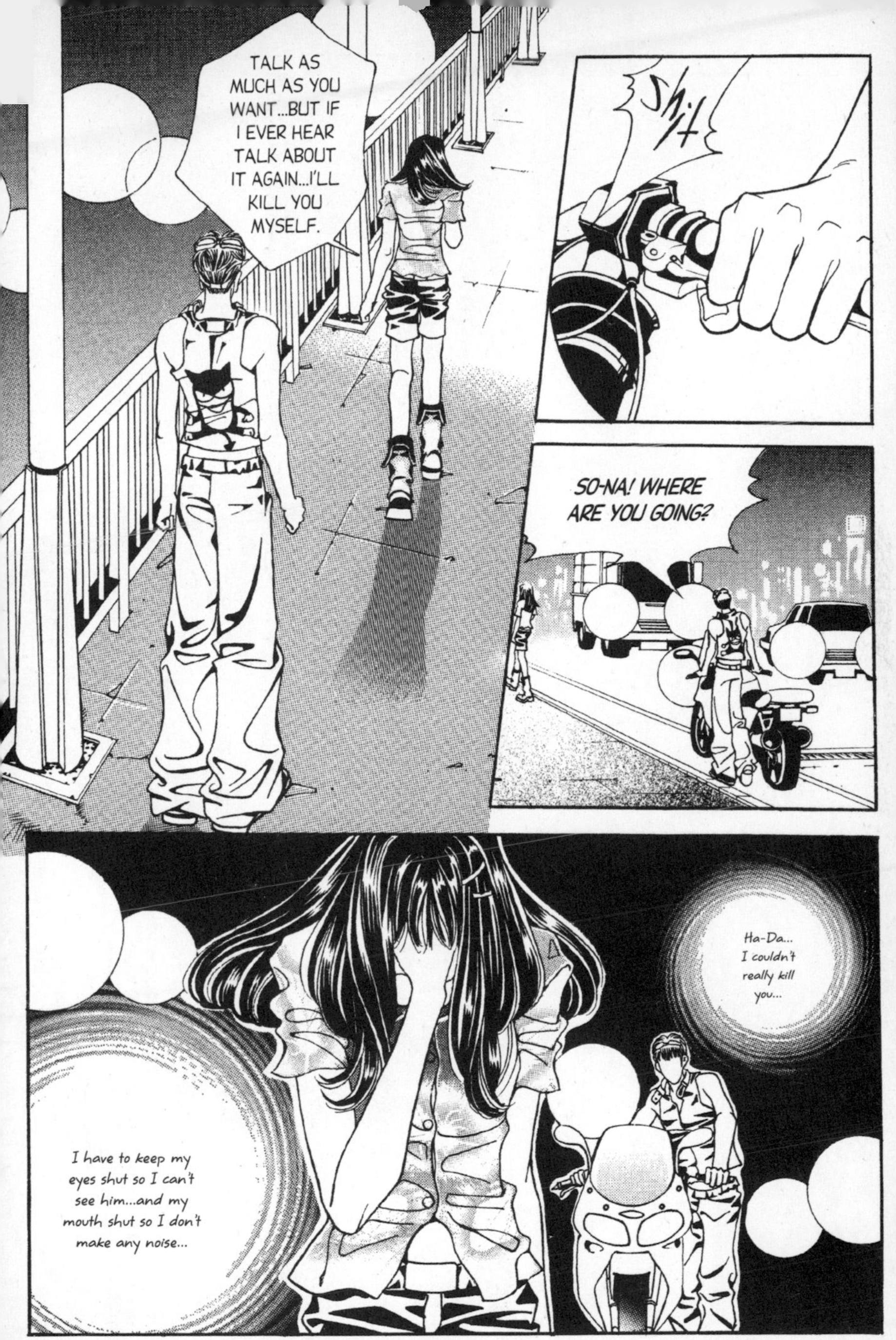
TALK AS MUCH AS YOU WANT...BUT IF I EVER HEAR TALK ABOUT IT AGAIN...I'LL KILL YOU MYSELF.
Sh!t
SO-NA! WHERE ARE YOU GOING?
I have to keep my eyes shut so I can't see him...and my mouth shut so I don't make any noise...
Ha-Da... I couldn't really kill you...

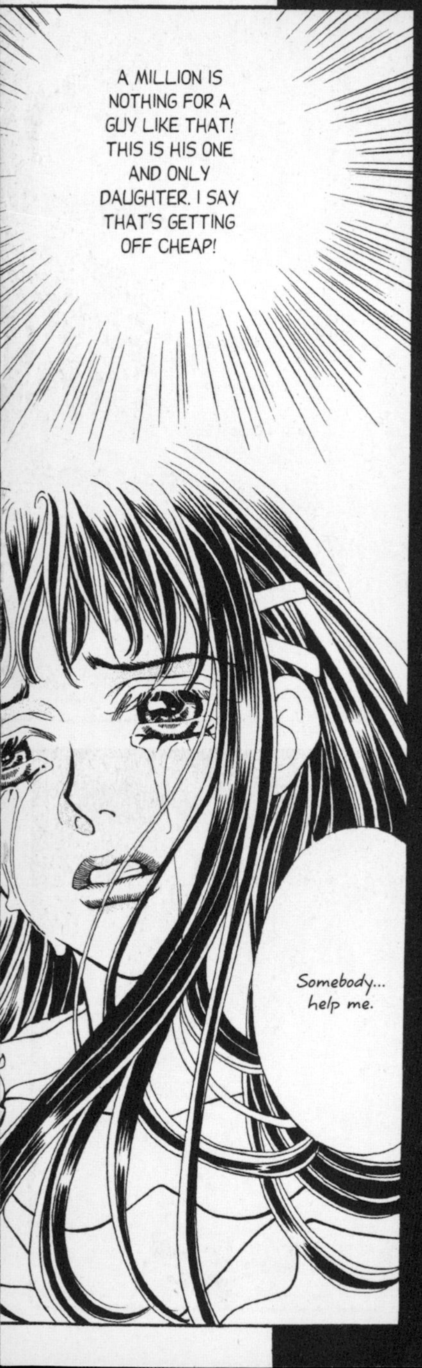
A MILLION IS NOTHING FOR A GUY LIKE THAT! THIS IS HIS ONE AND ONLY DAUGHTER. I SAY THAT'S GETTING OFF CHEAP!
Somebody... help me.
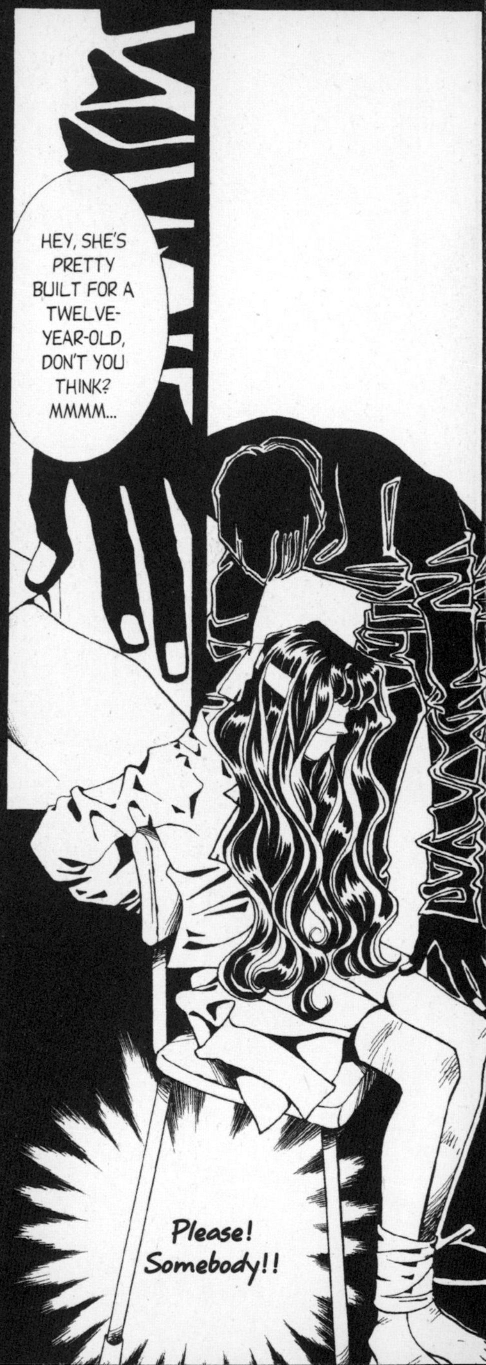
HEY, SHE'S PRETTY BUILT FOR A TWELVE-YEAR-OLD, DON'T YOU THINK? MMMM...
Please! Somebody!!

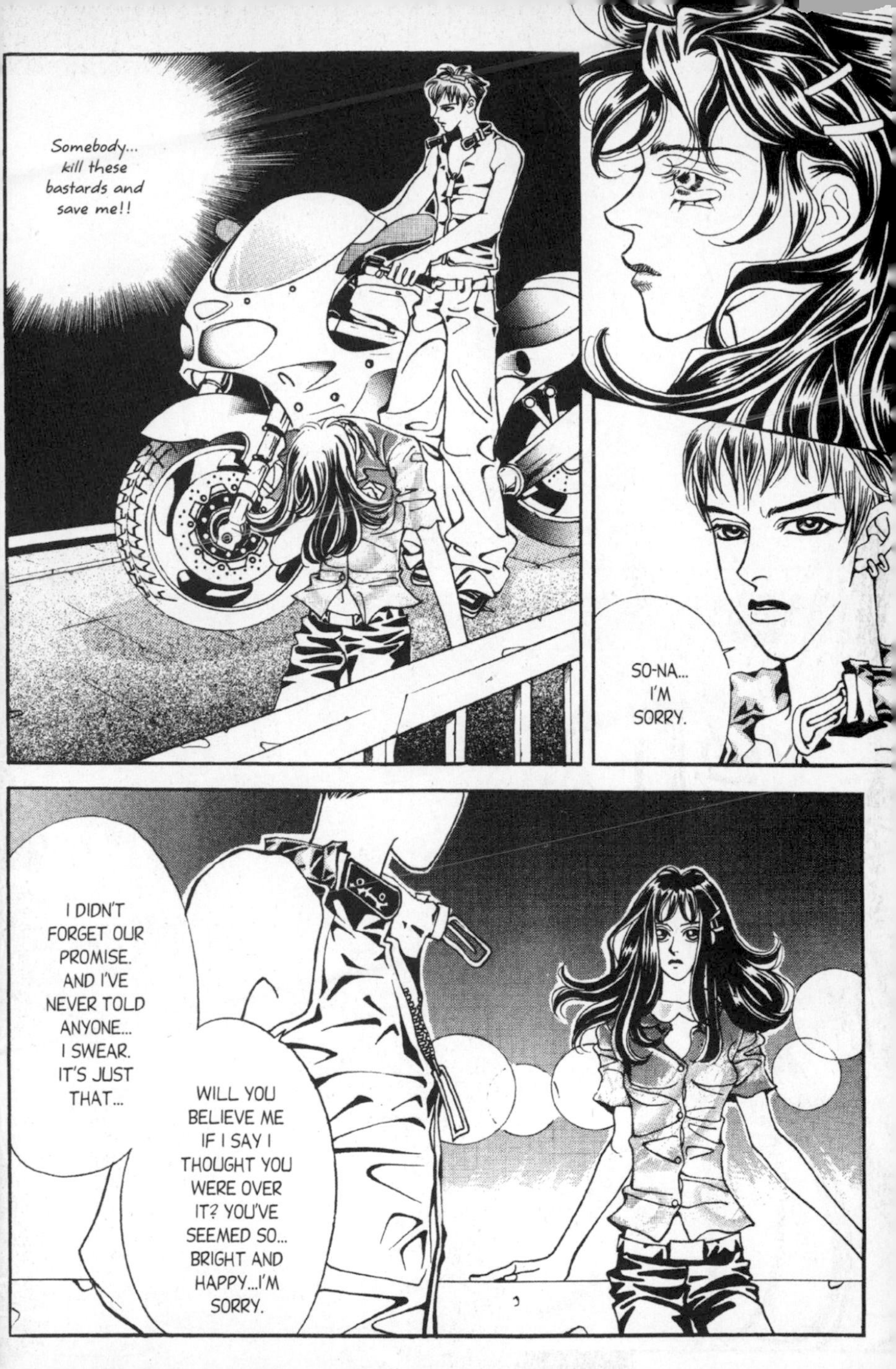
Somebody... kill these bastards and save me!!
SO-NA... I'M SORRY.
I DIDN'T FORGET OUR PROMISE. AND I'VE NEVER TOLD ANYONE... I SWEAR. IT'S JUST THAT...
WILL YOU BELIEVE ME IF I SAY I THOUGHT YOU WERE OVER IT? YOU'VE SEEMED SO... BRIGHT AND HAPPY...I'M SORRY.

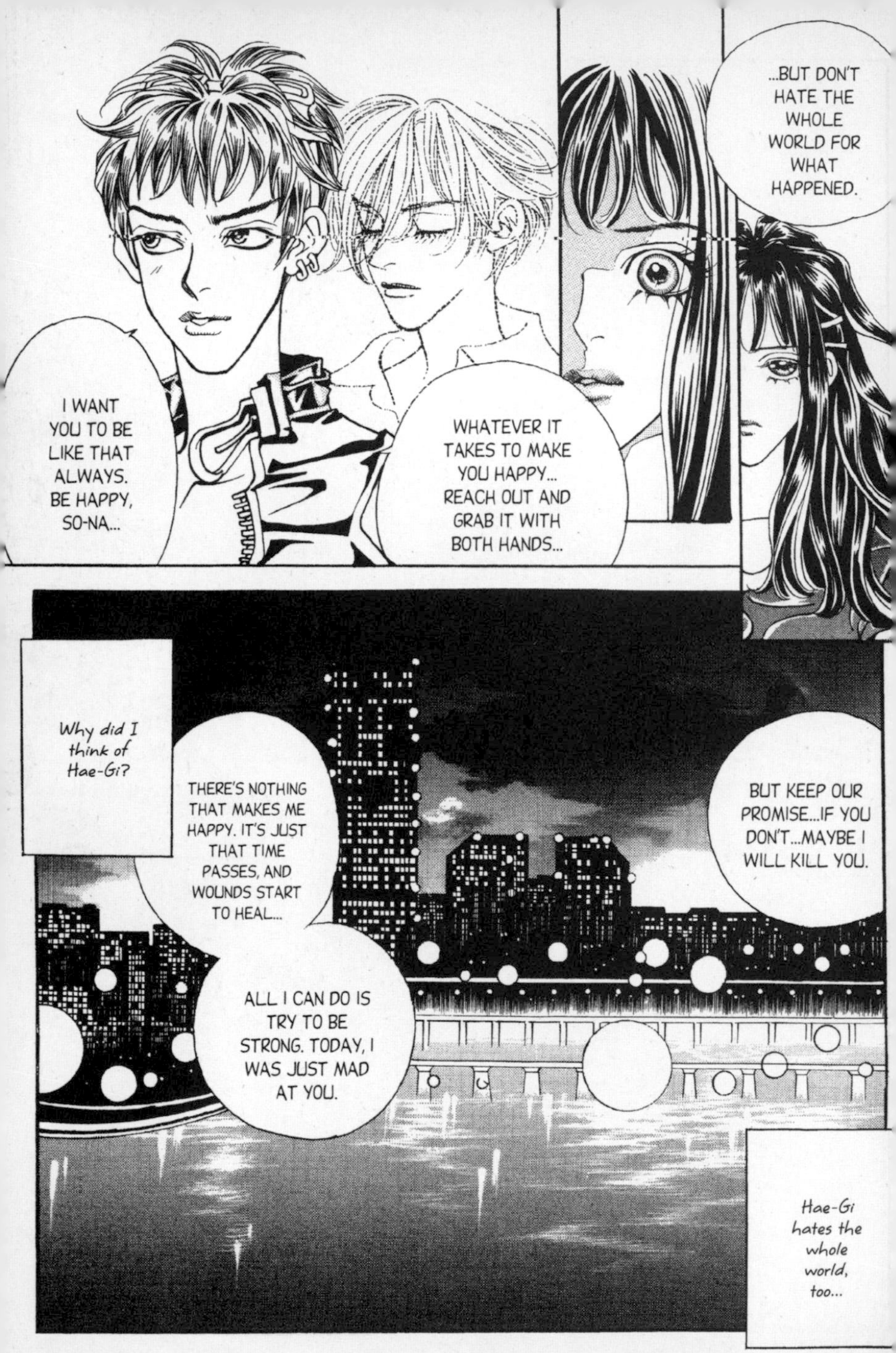
I WANT YOU TO BE LIKE THAT ALWAYS. BE HAPPY, SO-NA...
WHATEVER IT TAKES TO MAKE YOU HAPPY... REACH OUT AND GRAB IT WITH BOTH HANDS...
...BUT DON'T HATE THE WHOLE WORLD FOR WHAT HAPPENED.
Why did I think of Hae-Gi?
THERE'S NOTHING THAT MAKES ME HAPPY. IT'S JUST THAT TIME PASSES, AND WOUNDS START TO HEAL...
ALL I CAN DO IS TRY TO BE STRONG. TODAY, I WAS JUST MAD AT YOU.
BUT KEEP OUR PROMISE...IF YOU DON'T...MAYBE I WILL KILL YOU.
Hae-Gi hates the whole world, too...

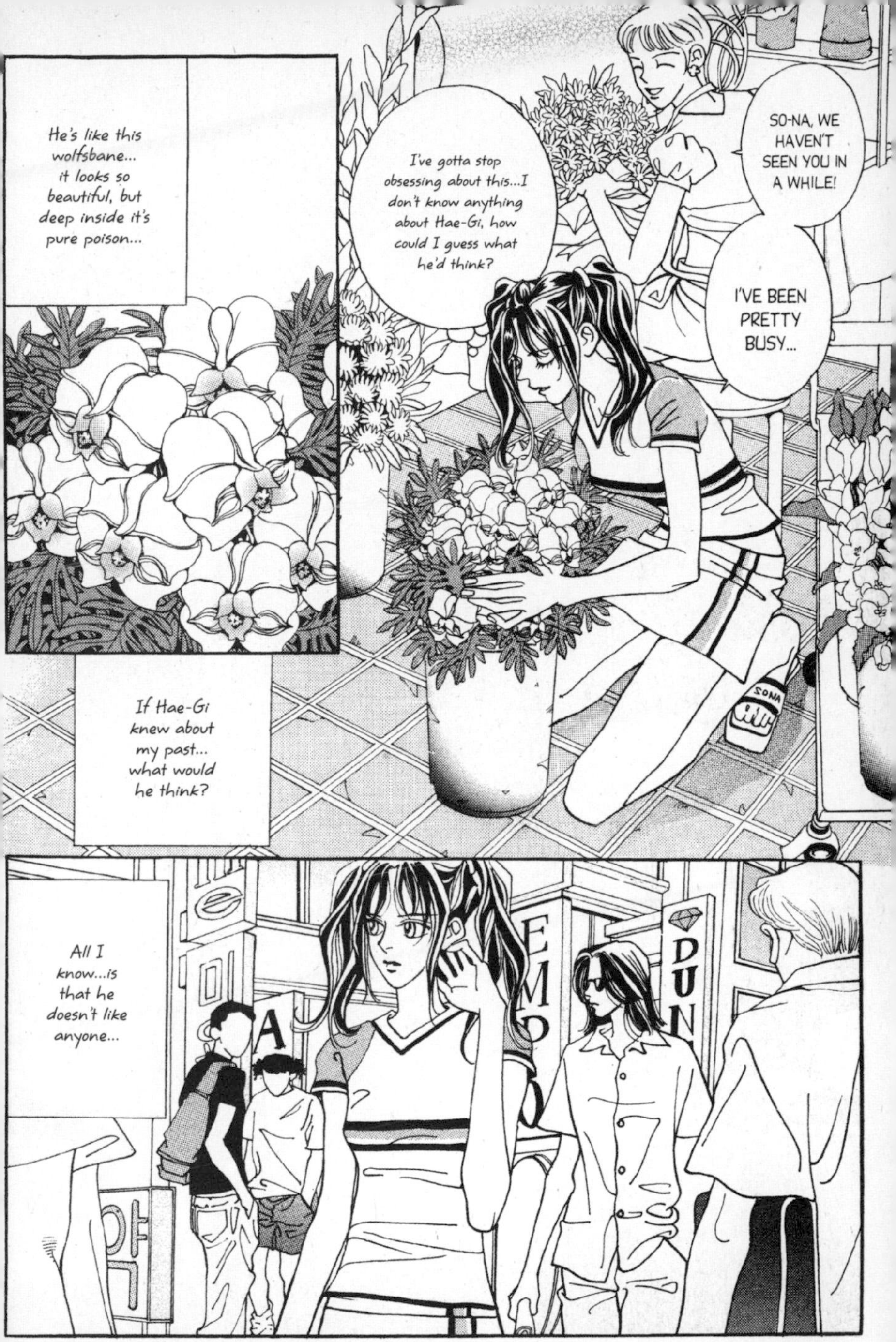
He's like this wolfsbane... it looks so beautiful, but deep inside it's pure poison...
If Hae-Gi knew about my past... what would he think?
I've gotta stop obsessing about this...I don't know anything about Hae-Gi, how could I guess what he'd think?
SO-NA, WE HAVEN'T SEEN YOU IN A WHILE!
I'VE BEEN PRETTY BUSY...
All I know...is that he doesn't like anyone...

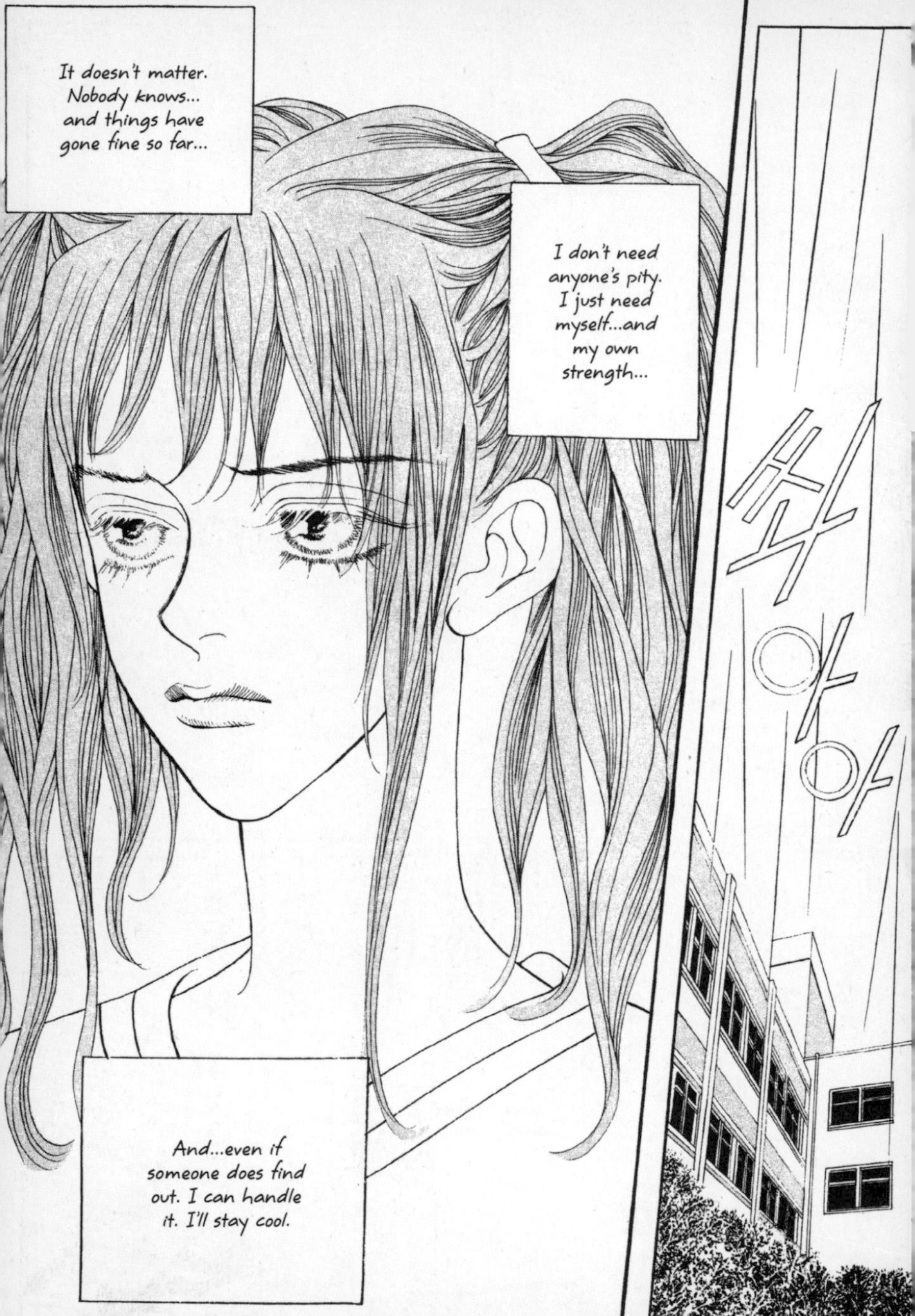
It doesn't matter. Nobody knows... and things have gone fine so far...
I don't need anyone's pity. I just need myself...and my own strength...
And...even if someone does find out. I can handle it. I'll stay cool.

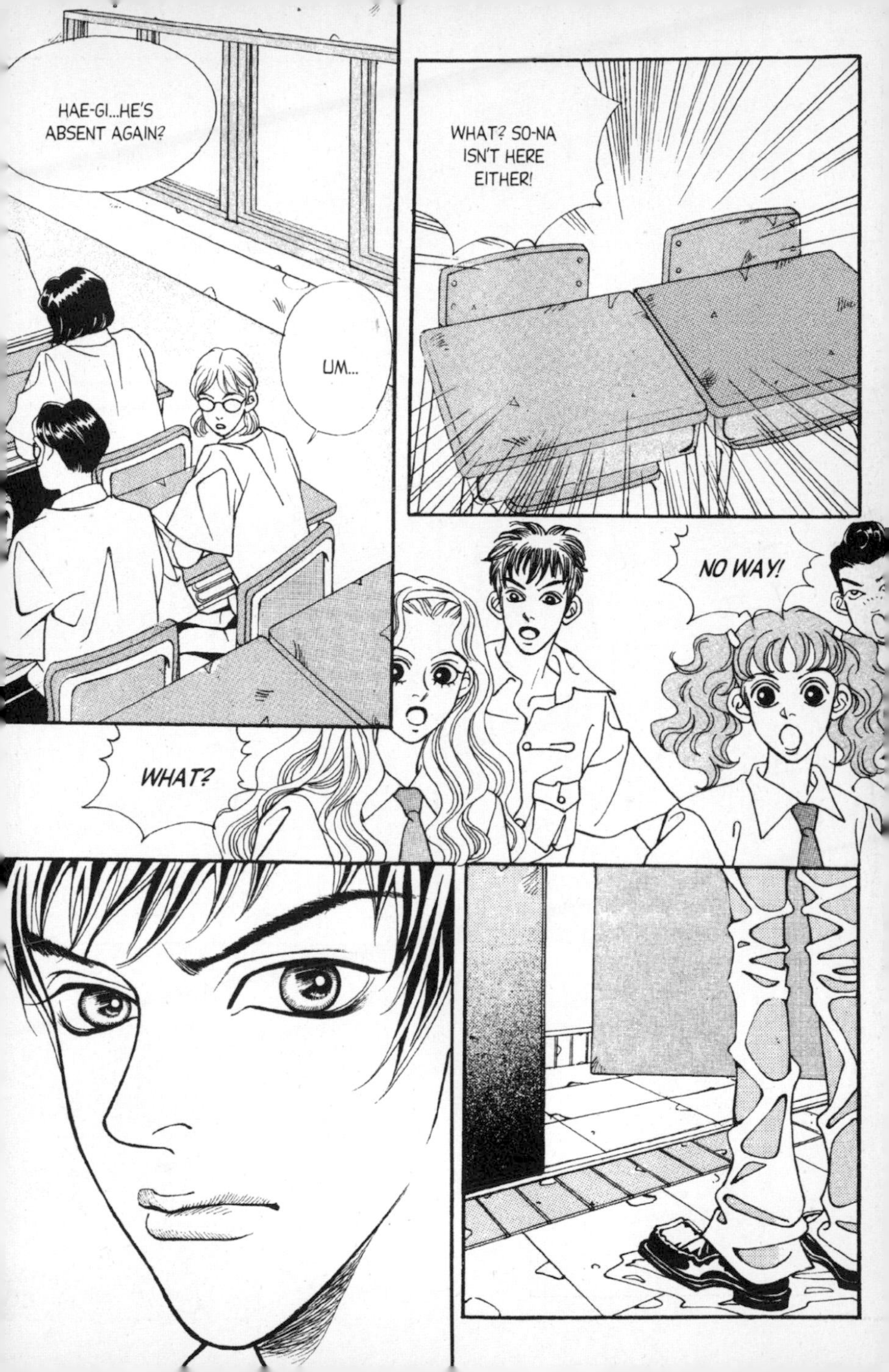
HAE-GI...HE'S ABSENT AGAIN?
UM...
WHAT? SO-NA ISN'T HERE EITHER!
WHAT?
NO WAY!

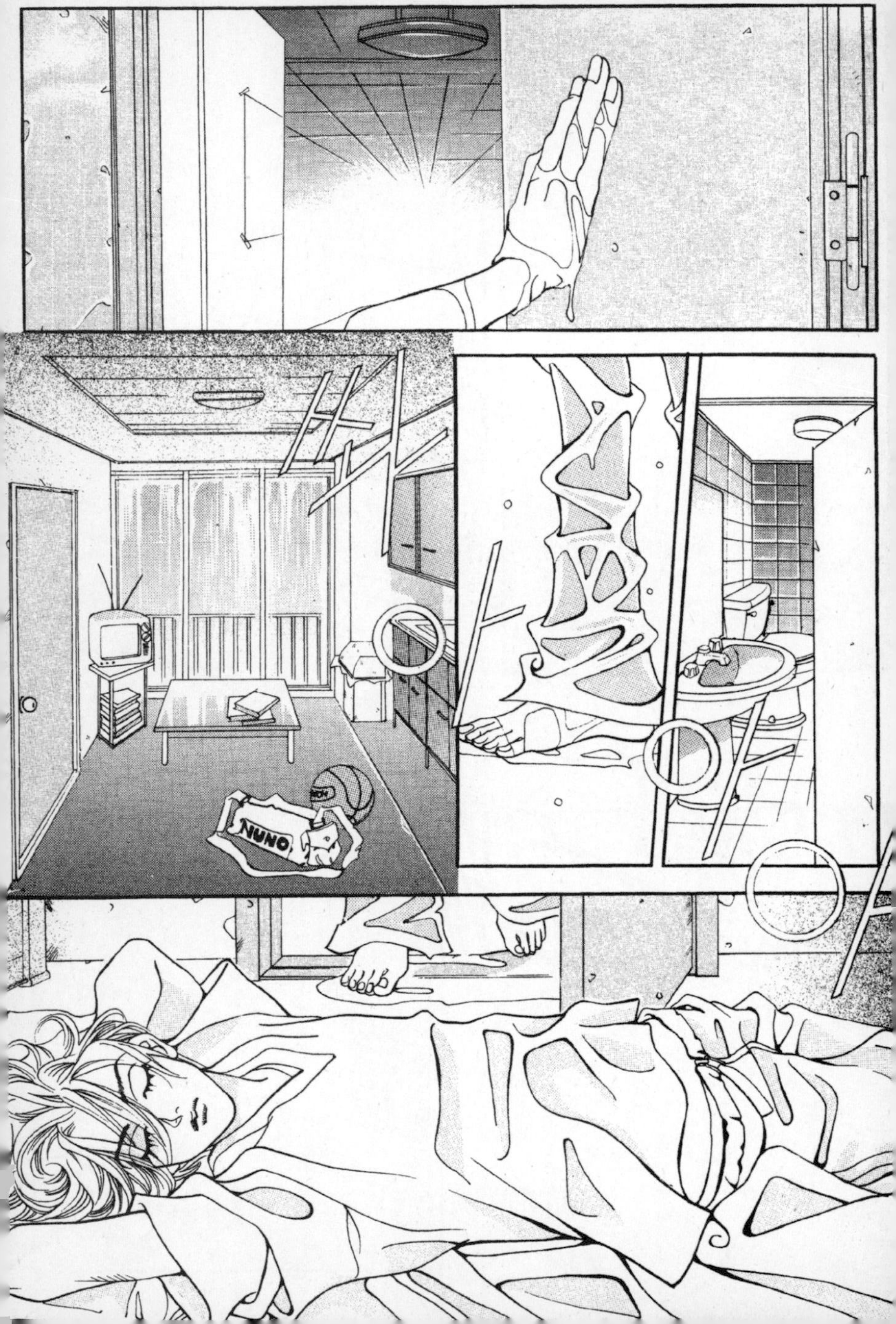
NUNO

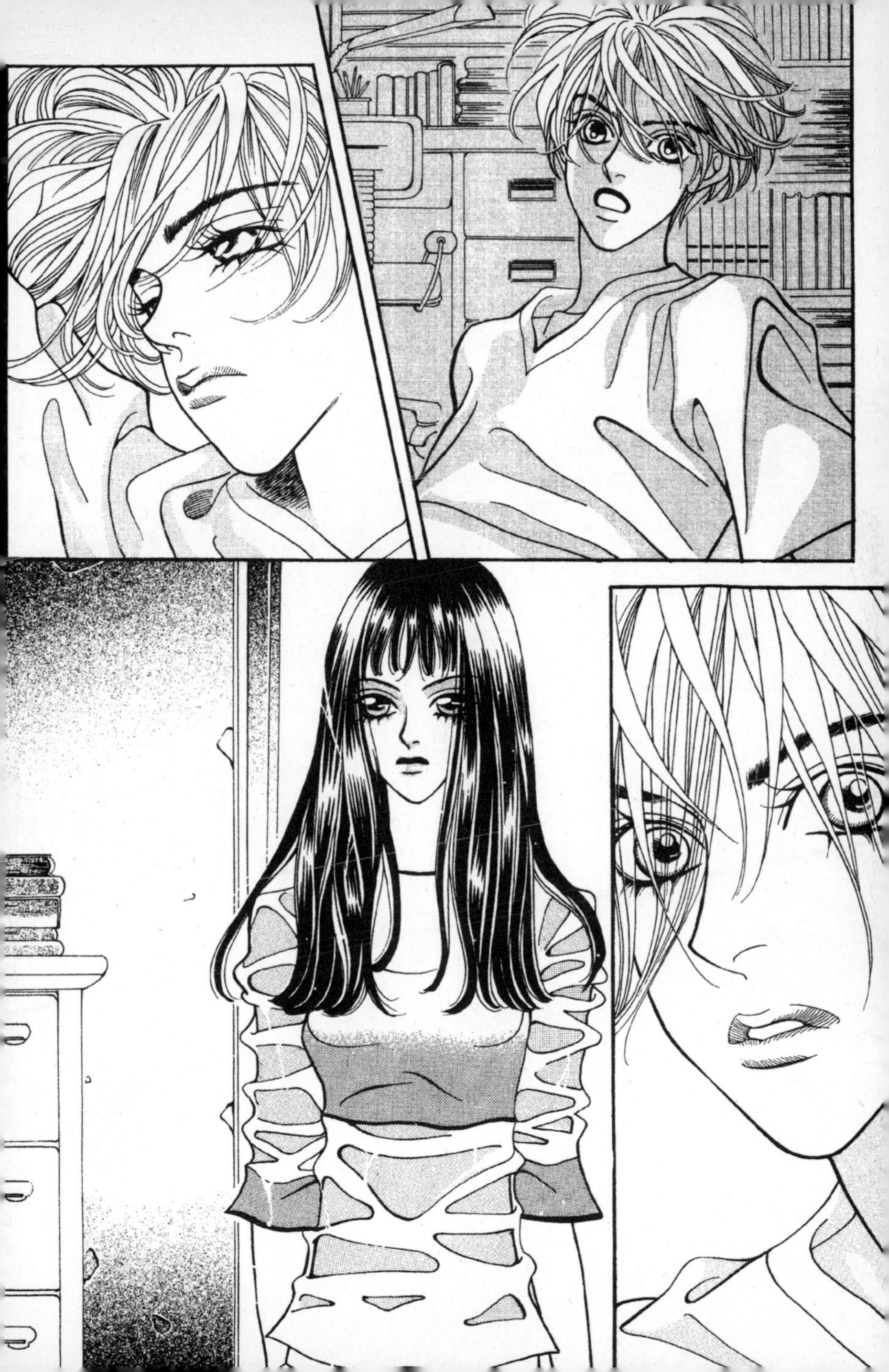

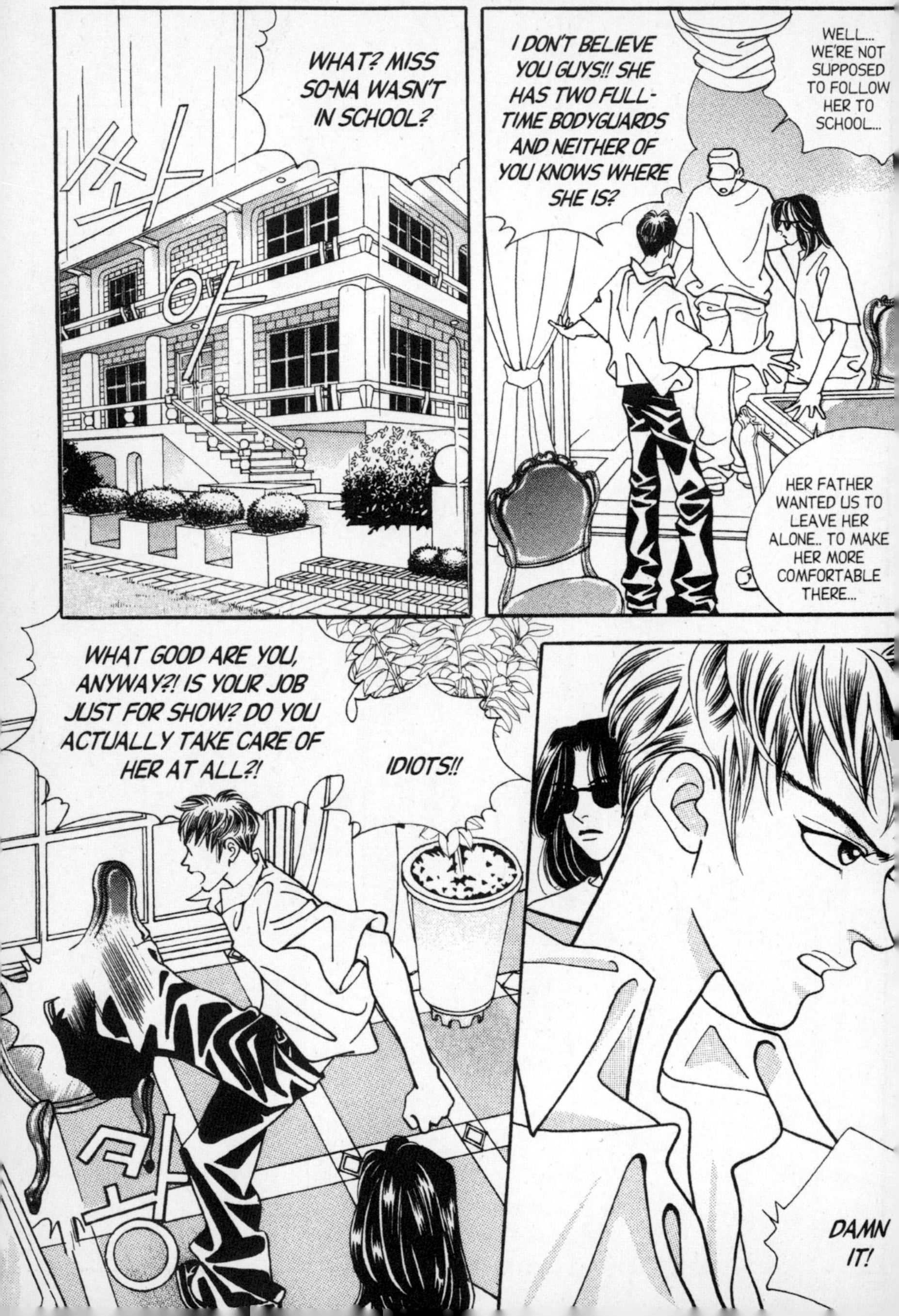
WHAT? MISS SO-NA WASN'T IN SCHOOL?
I DON'T BELIEVE YOU GUYS!! SHE HAS TWO FULL-TIME BODYGUARDS AND NEITHER OF YOU KNOWS WHERE SHE IS?
WELL... WE'RE NOT SUPPOSED TO FOLLOW HER TO SCHOOL...
HER FATHER WANTED US TO LEAVE HER ALONE.. TO MAKE HER MORE COMFORTABLE THERE...
WHAT GOOD ARE YOU, ANYWAY?! IS YOUR JOB JUST FOR SHOW? DO YOU ACTUALLY TAKE CARE OF HER AT ALL?!
IDIOTS!!
DAMN IT!

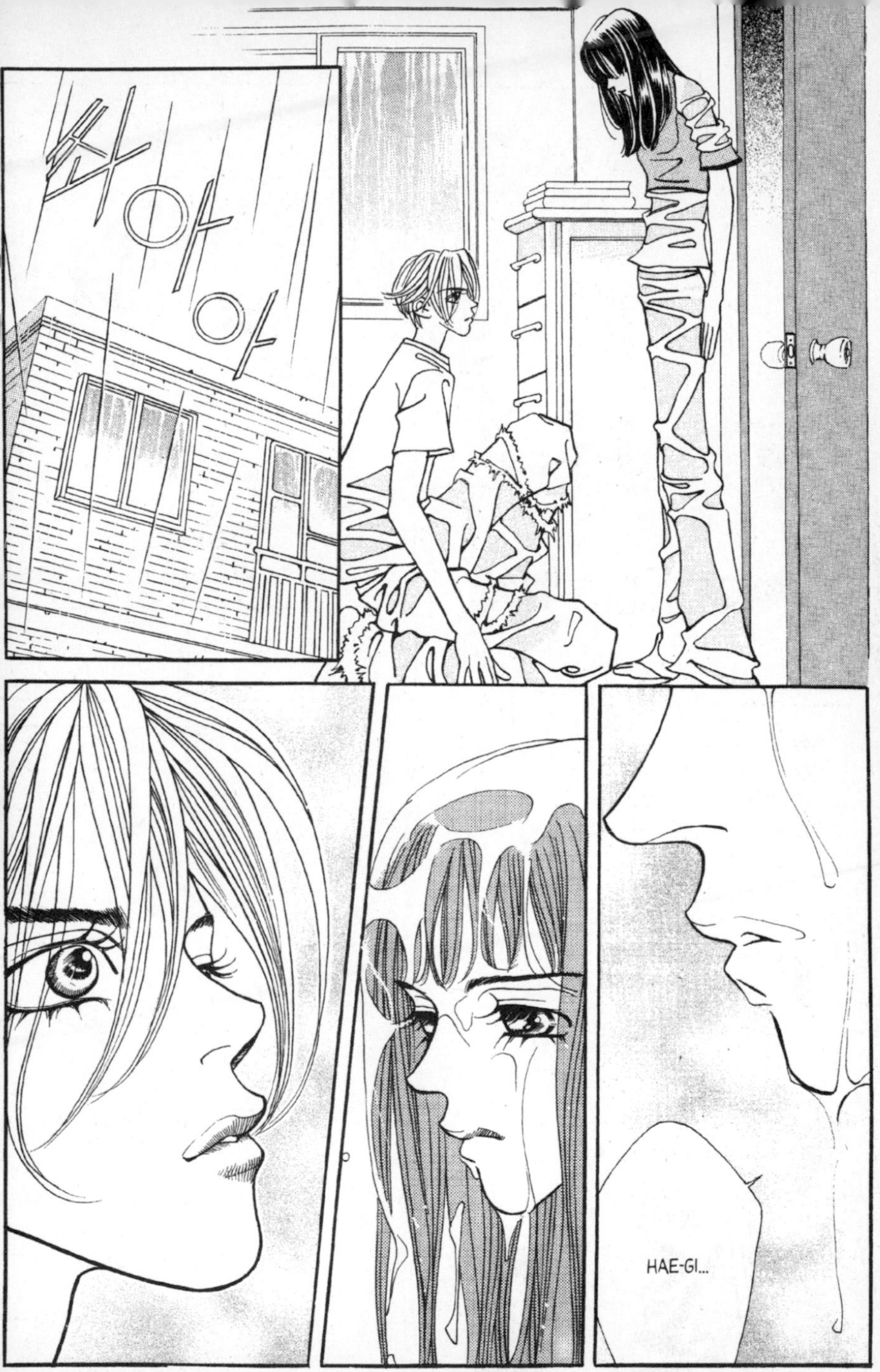
쏴아아
HAE-GI...

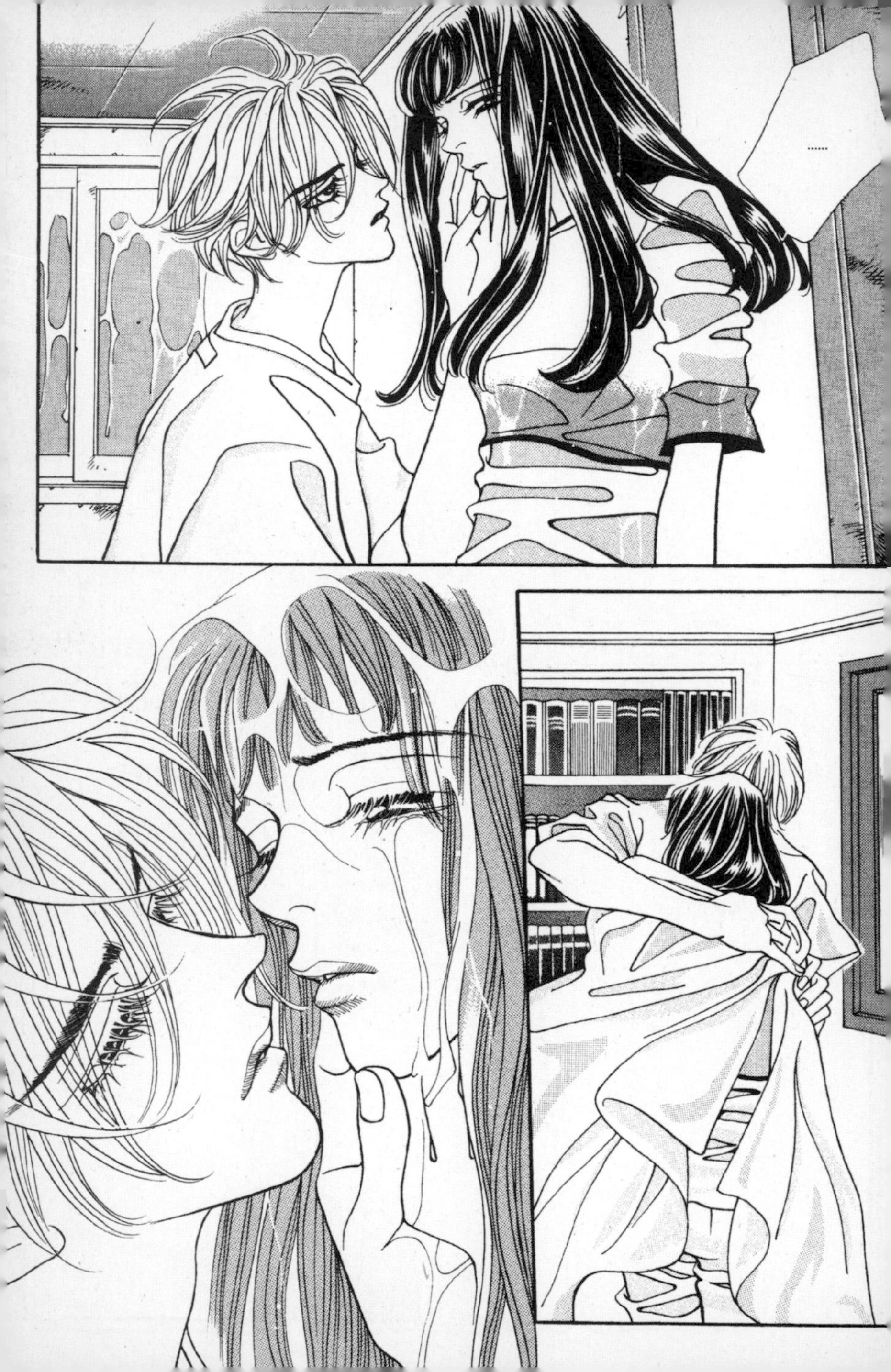
......

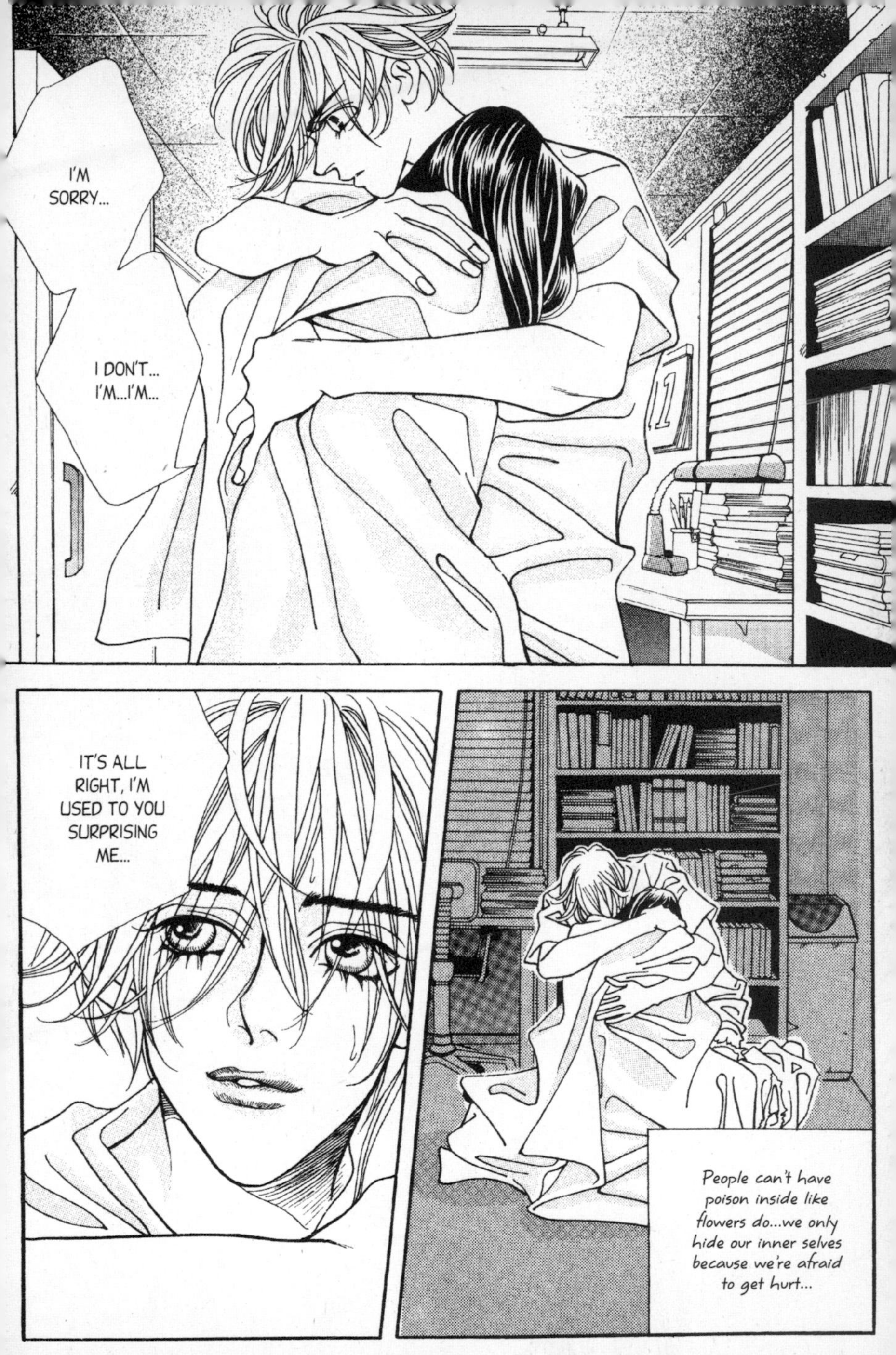
I'M SORRY...
I DON'T... I'M...I'M...
IT'S ALL RIGHT, I'M USED TO YOU SURPRISING ME...
People can't have poison inside like flowers do...we only hide our inner selves because we're afraid to get hurt...

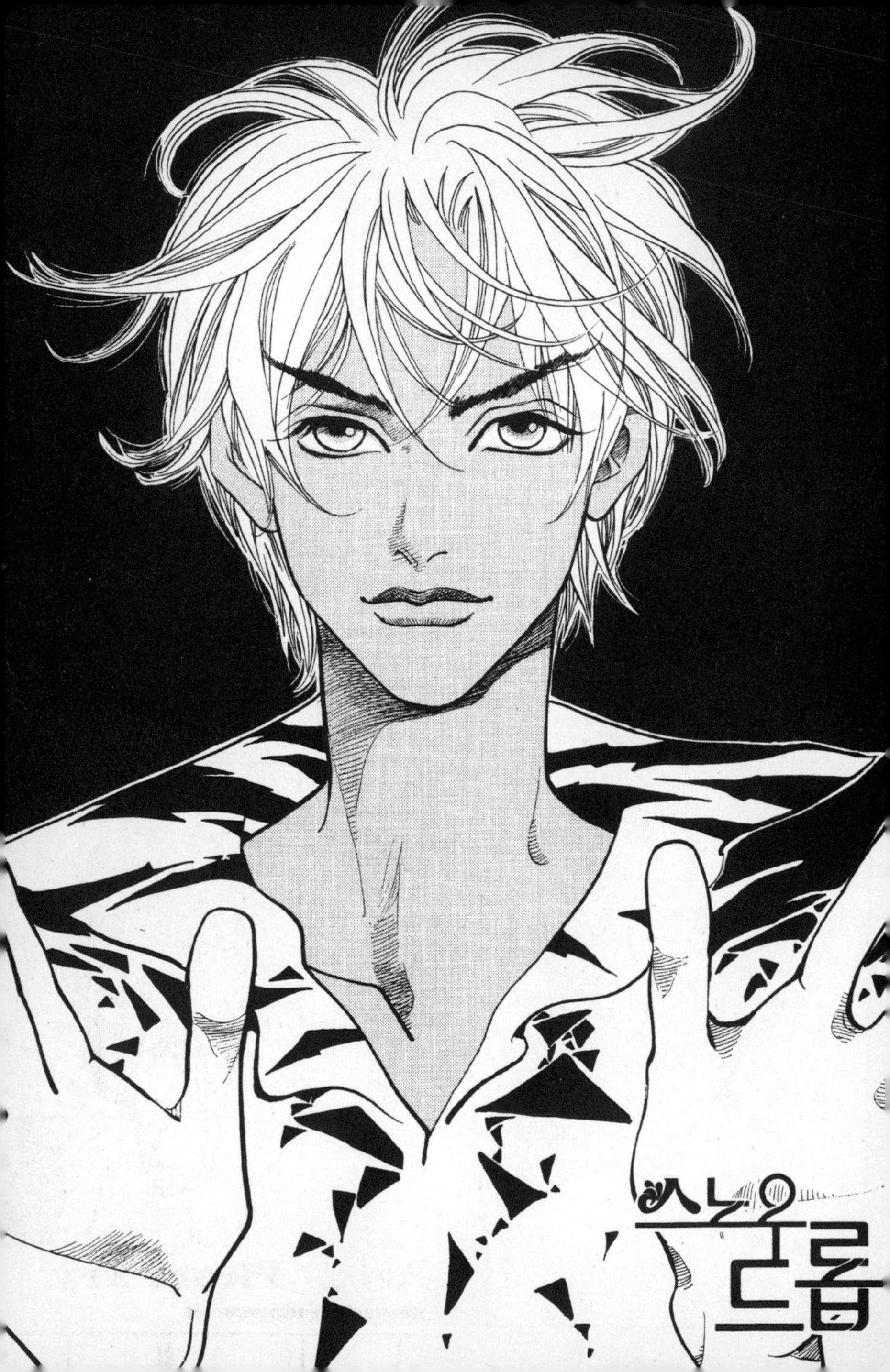
스노우 드롭

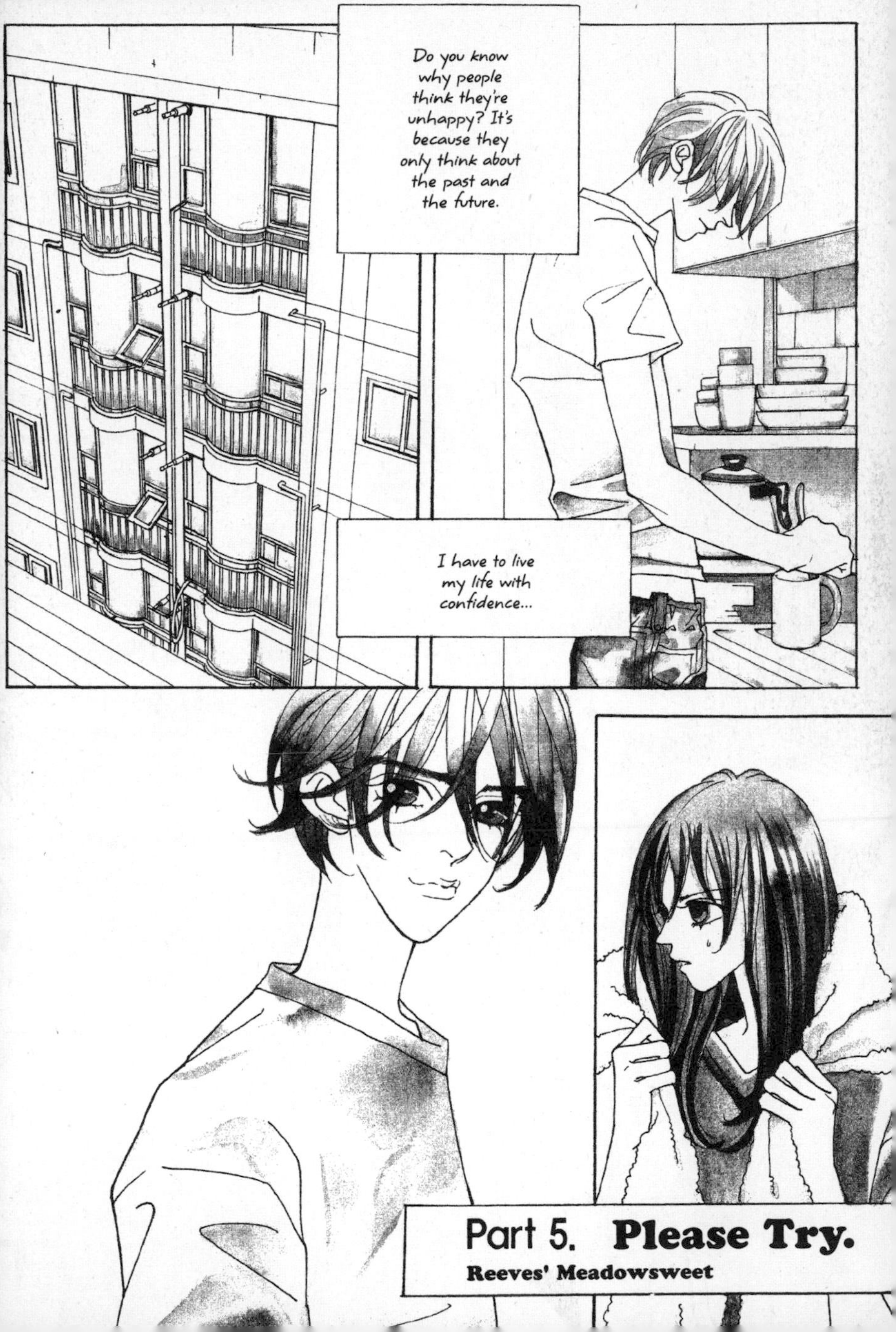
Do you know why people think they're unhappy? It's because they only think about the past and the future.
I have to live my life with confidence...
Part 5. Please Try.
Reeves' Meadowsweet

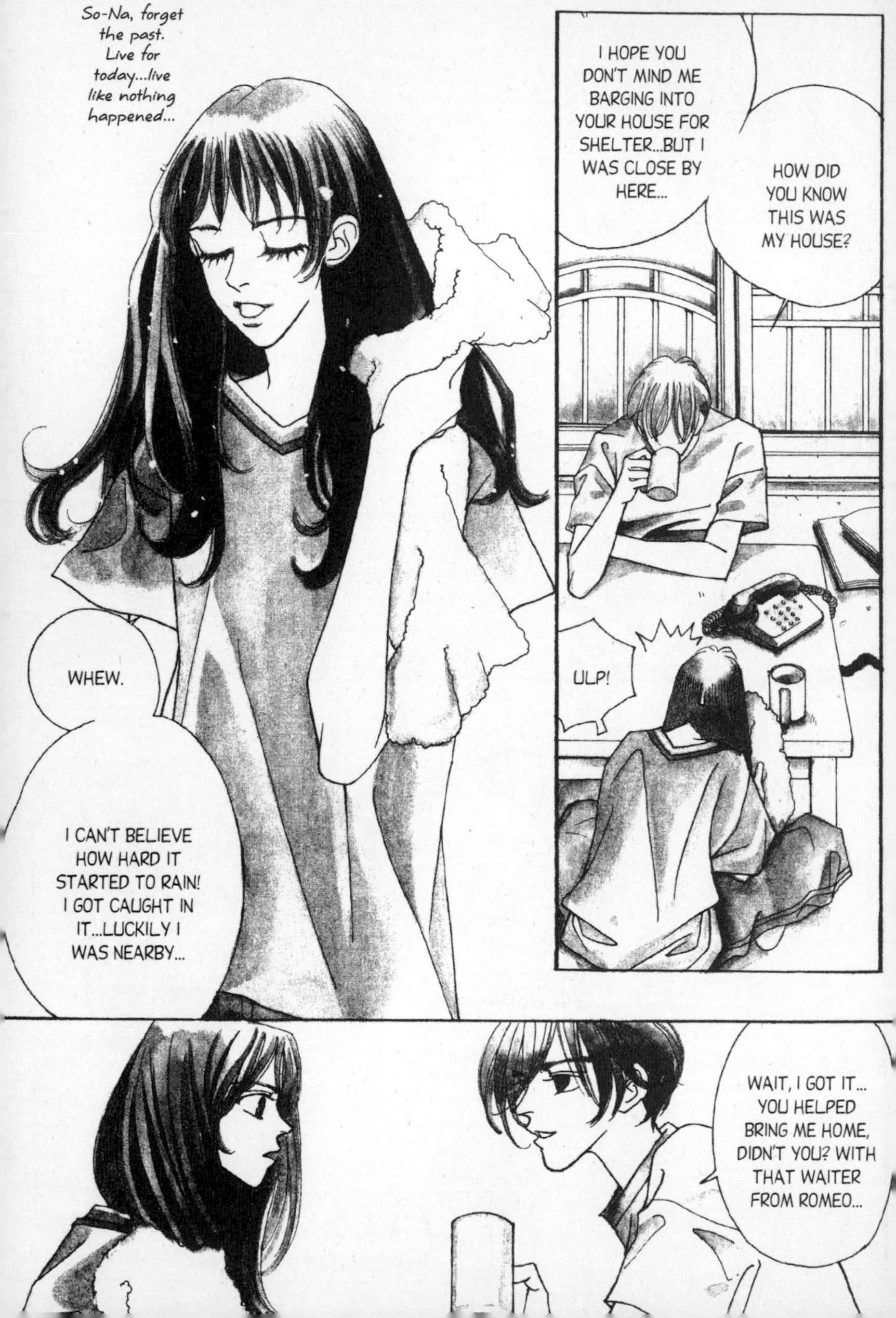

So-Na, forget the past. Live for today...live like nothing happened...
WHEW.
I CAN'T BELIEVE HOW HARD IT STARTED TO RAIN! I GOT CAUGHT IN IT...LUCKILY I WAS NEARBY...
I HOPE YOU DON'T MIND ME BARGING INTO YOUR HOUSE FOR SHELTER...BUT I WAS CLOSE BY HERE...
HOW DID YOU KNOW THIS WAS MY HOUSE?
ULP!
WAIT, I GOT IT... YOU HELPED BRING ME HOME, DIDN'T YOU? WITH THAT WAITER FROM ROMEO...

UM, YEAH, I DID. BUT I DIDN'T COME INSIDE THAT TIME...

He's just being cool, giving me towels and dry clothes...

Thank god he's not asking me why on earth I came here...

If he did ask...I have no idea what I'd say. I don't know what I'm doing.

Argh! I feel totally self-conscious! I don't know where to look or what to do.

SO, HAE-GI, EVERYONE AT SCHOOL SAYS YOU'RE GOING TO TAKE A TEST TO GET YOUR HIGH SCHOOL DIPLOMA...AND THEN BECOME A FAMOUS CELEBRITY KNOWN AS THE "SMART MODEL."

WHAT?

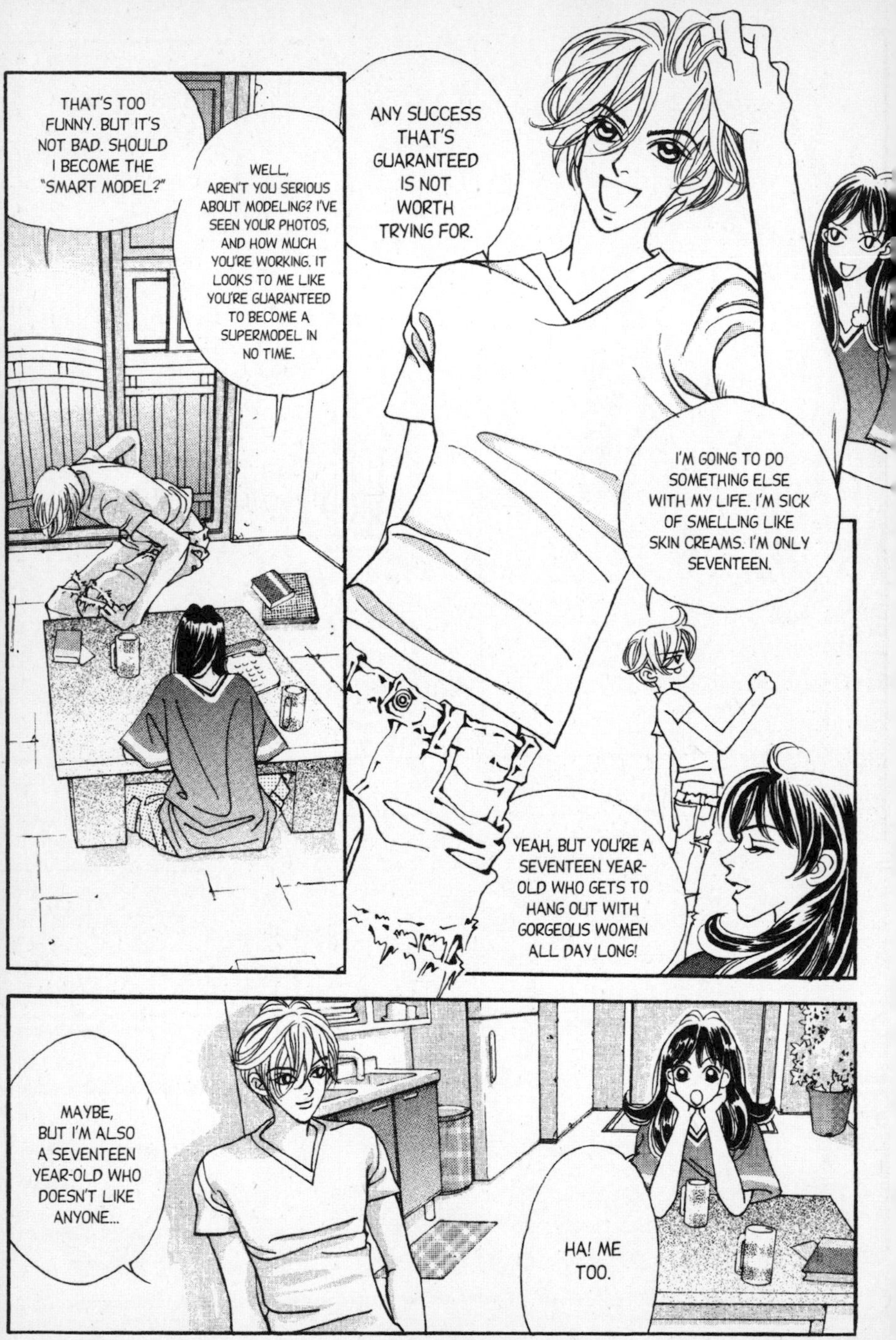

THAT'S TOO FUNNY. BUT IT'S NOT BAD. SHOULD I BECOME THE "SMART MODEL?"
WELL, AREN'T YOU SERIOUS ABOUT MODELING? I'VE SEEN YOUR PHOTOS, AND HOW MUCH YOU'RE WORKING. IT LOOKS TO ME LIKE YOU'RE GUARANTEED TO BECOME A SUPERMODEL IN NO TIME.
ANY SUCCESS THAT'S GUARANTEED IS NOT WORTH TRYING FOR.
I'M GOING TO DO SOMETHING ELSE WITH MY LIFE. I'M SICK OF SMELLING LIKE SKIN CREAMS. I'M ONLY SEVENTEEN.
YEAH, BUT YOU'RE A SEVENTEEN YEAR-OLD WHO GETS TO HANG OUT WITH GORGEOUS WOMEN ALL DAY LONG!
MAYBE, BUT I'M ALSO A SEVENTEEN YEAR-OLD WHO DOESN'T LIKE ANYONE...
HA! ME TOO.

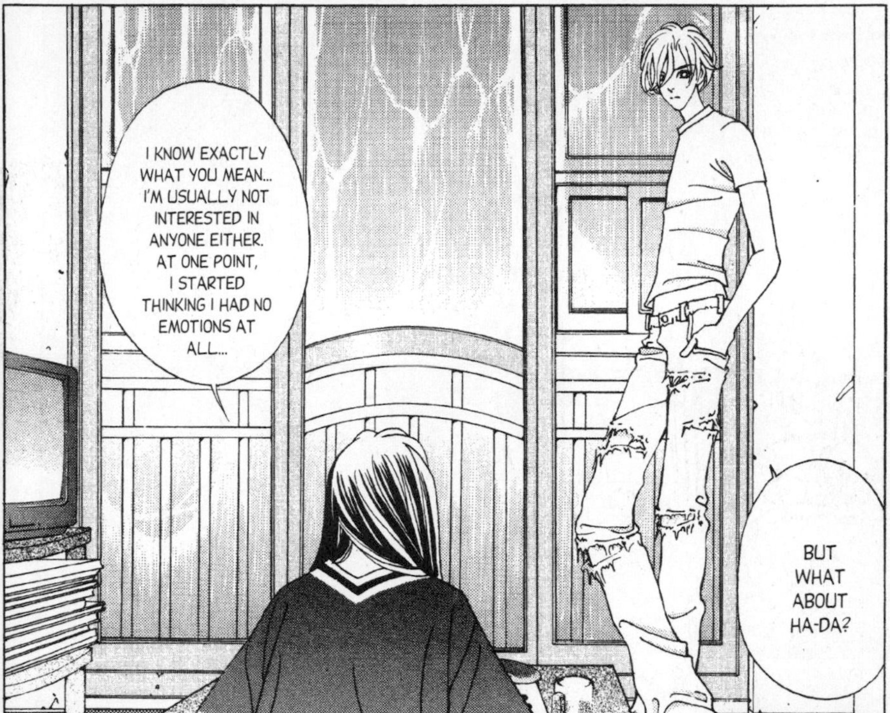
I KNOW EXACTLY WHAT YOU MEAN... I'M USUALLY NOT INTERESTED IN ANYONE EITHER. AT ONE POINT, I STARTED THINKING I HAD NO EMOTIONS AT ALL...
BUT WHAT ABOUT HA-DA?
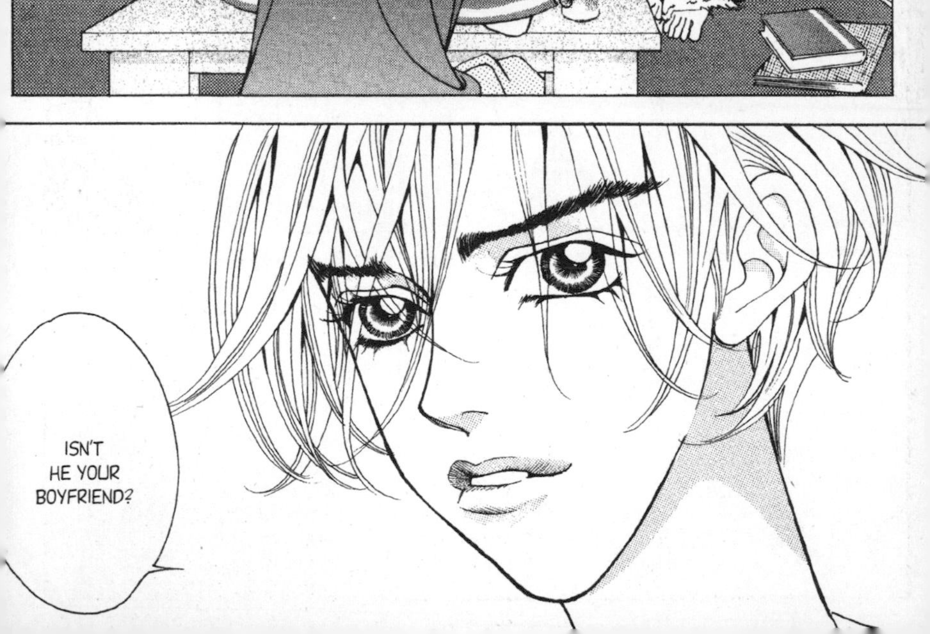
ISN'T HE YOUR BOYFRIEND?

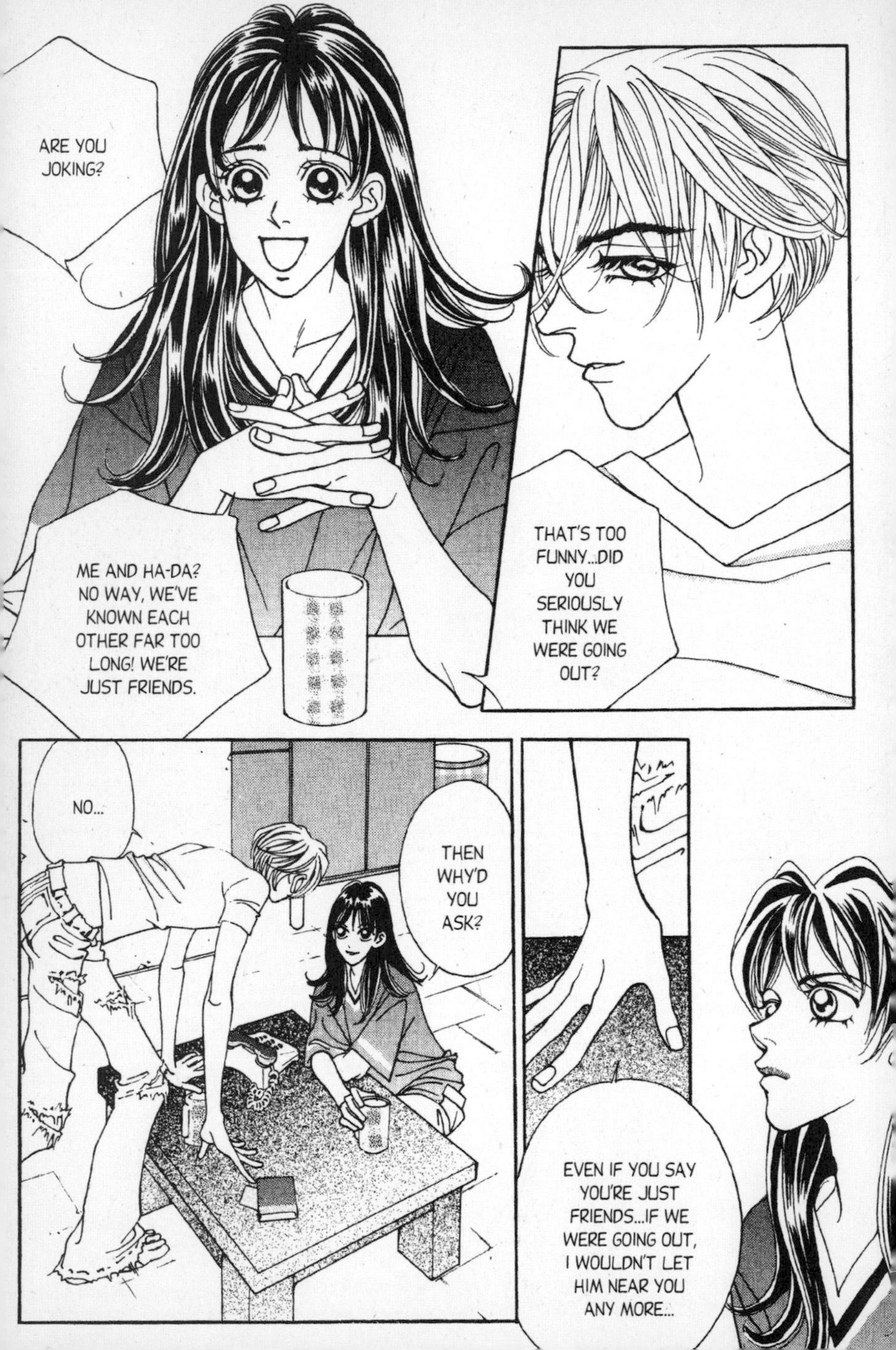
ARE YOU JOKING?
ME AND HA-DA? NO WAY, WE'VE KNOWN EACH OTHER FAR TOO LONG! WE'RE JUST FRIENDS.
THAT'S TOO FUNNY...DID YOU SERIOUSLY THINK WE WERE GOING OUT?
NO...
THEN WHY'D YOU ASK?
EVEN IF YOU SAY YOU'RE JUST FRIENDS...IF WE WERE GOING OUT, I WOULDN'T LET HIM NEAR YOU ANY MORE...

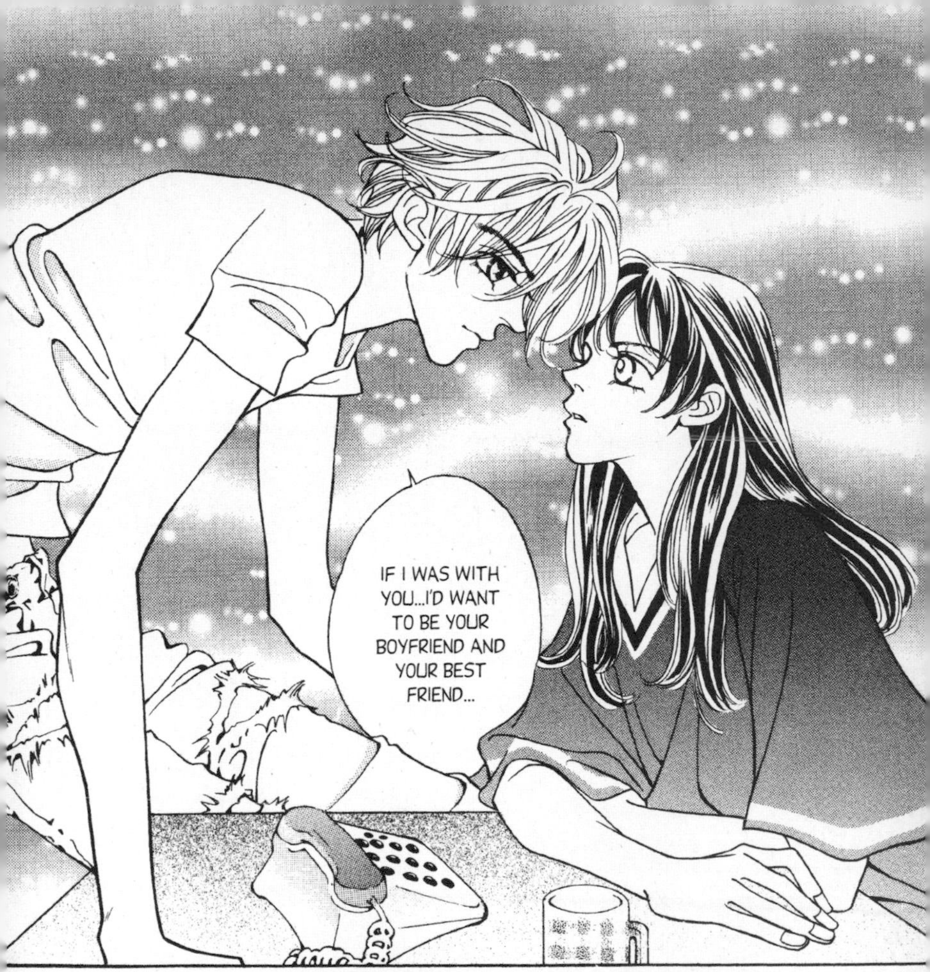
IF I WAS WITH YOU...I'D WANT TO BE YOUR BOYFRIEND AND YOUR BEST FRIEND...

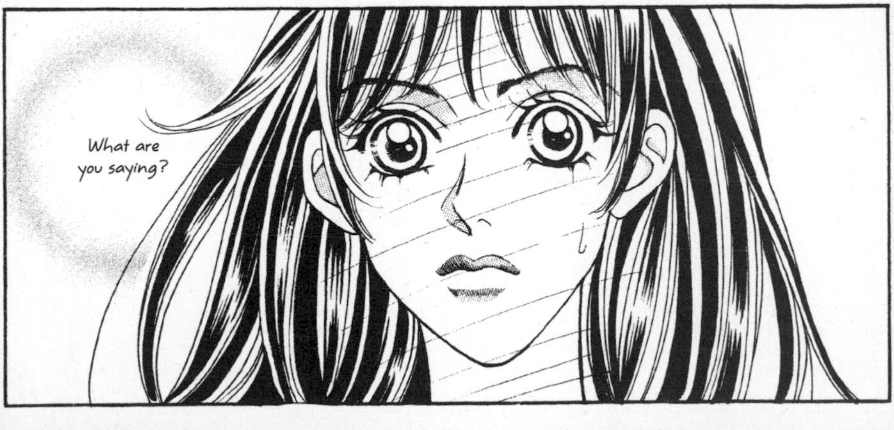
What are you saying?

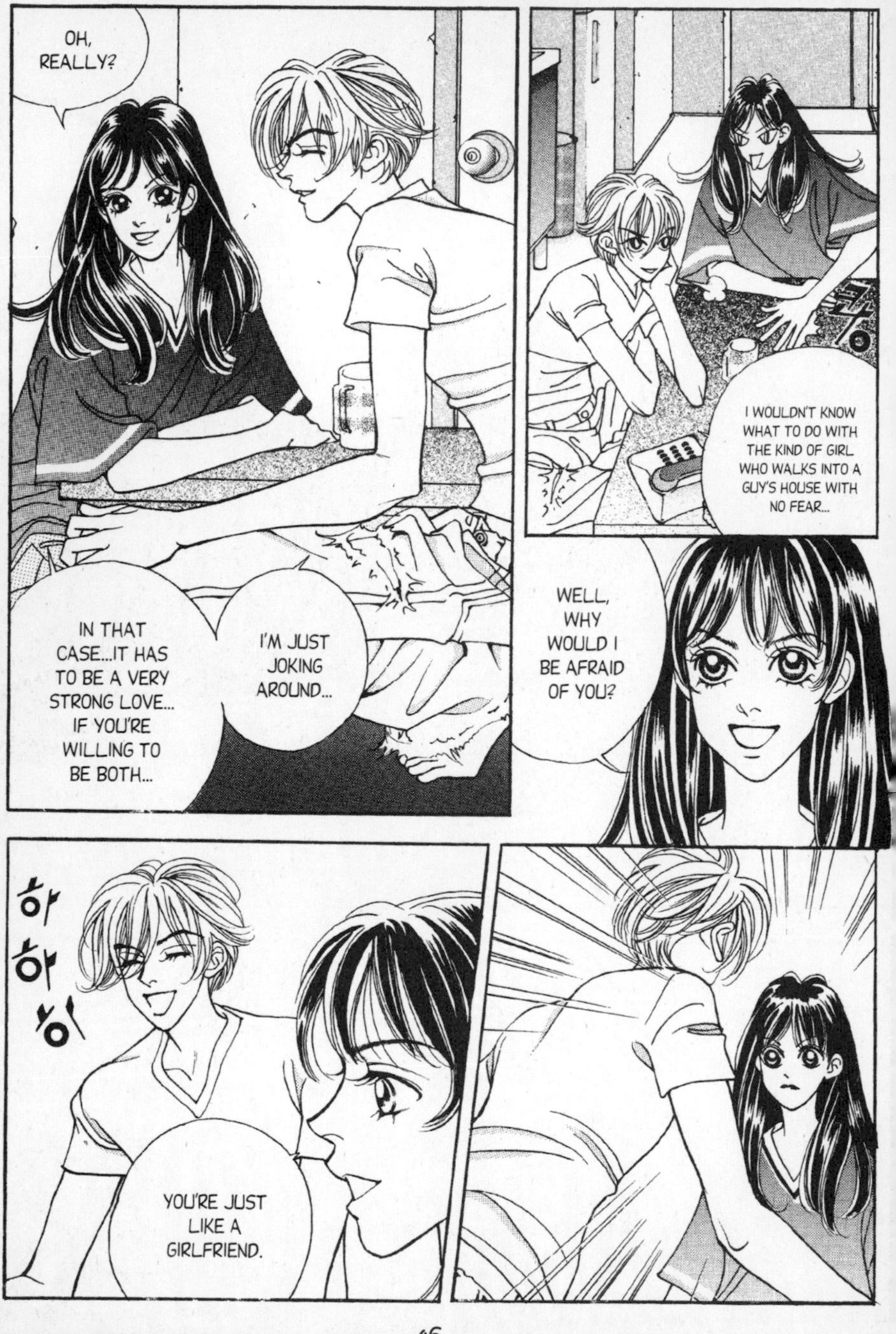
OH, REALLY?
IN THAT CASE...IT HAS TO BE A VERY STRONG LOVE... IF YOU'RE WILLING TO BE BOTH...
I'M JUST JOKING AROUND...
I WOULDN'T KNOW WHAT TO DO WITH THE KIND OF GIRL WHO WALKS INTO A GUY'S HOUSE WITH NO FEAR...
WELL, WHY WOULD I BE AFRAID OF YOU?
하하히
YOU'RE JUST LIKE A GIRLFRIEND.

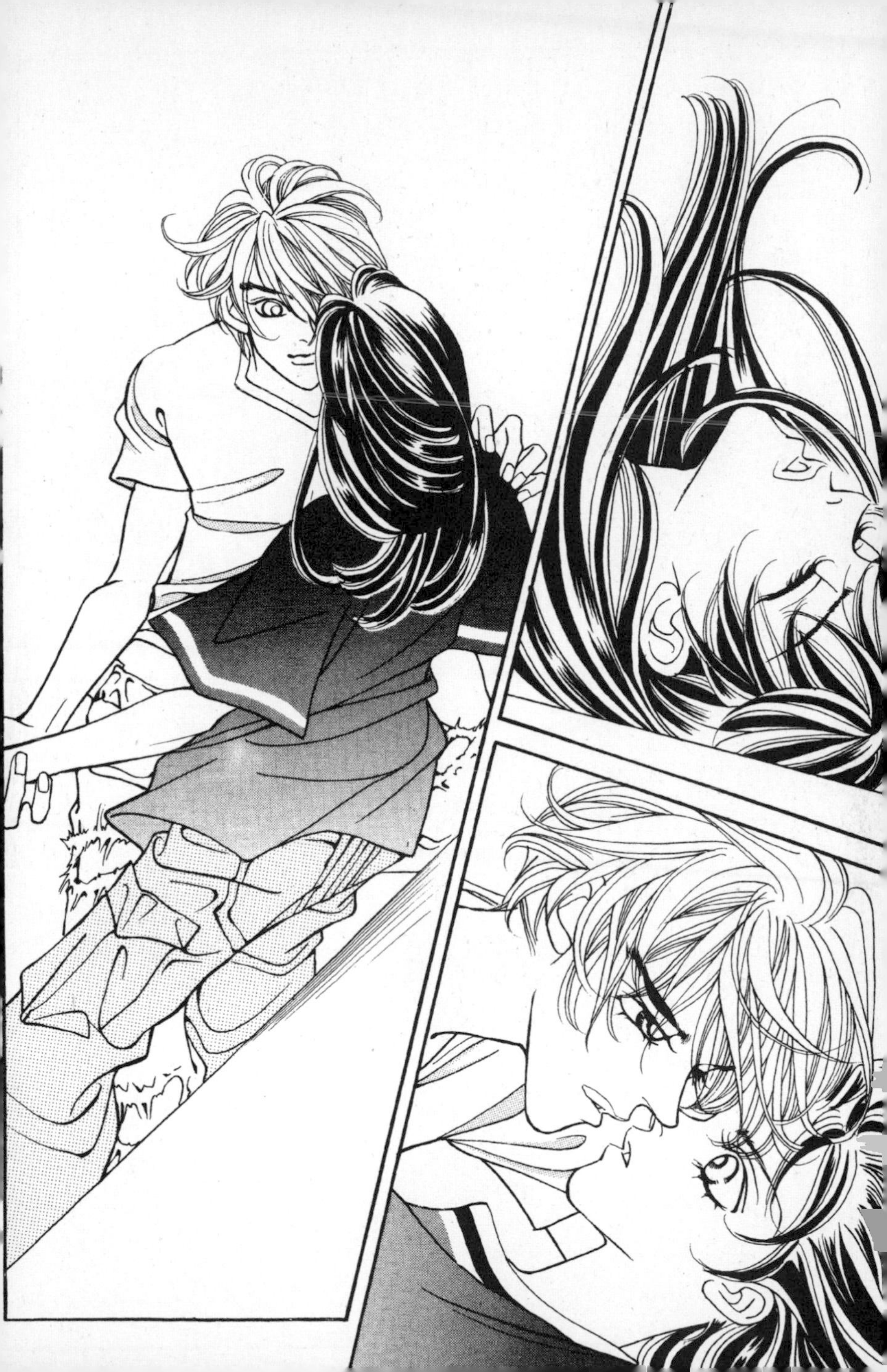

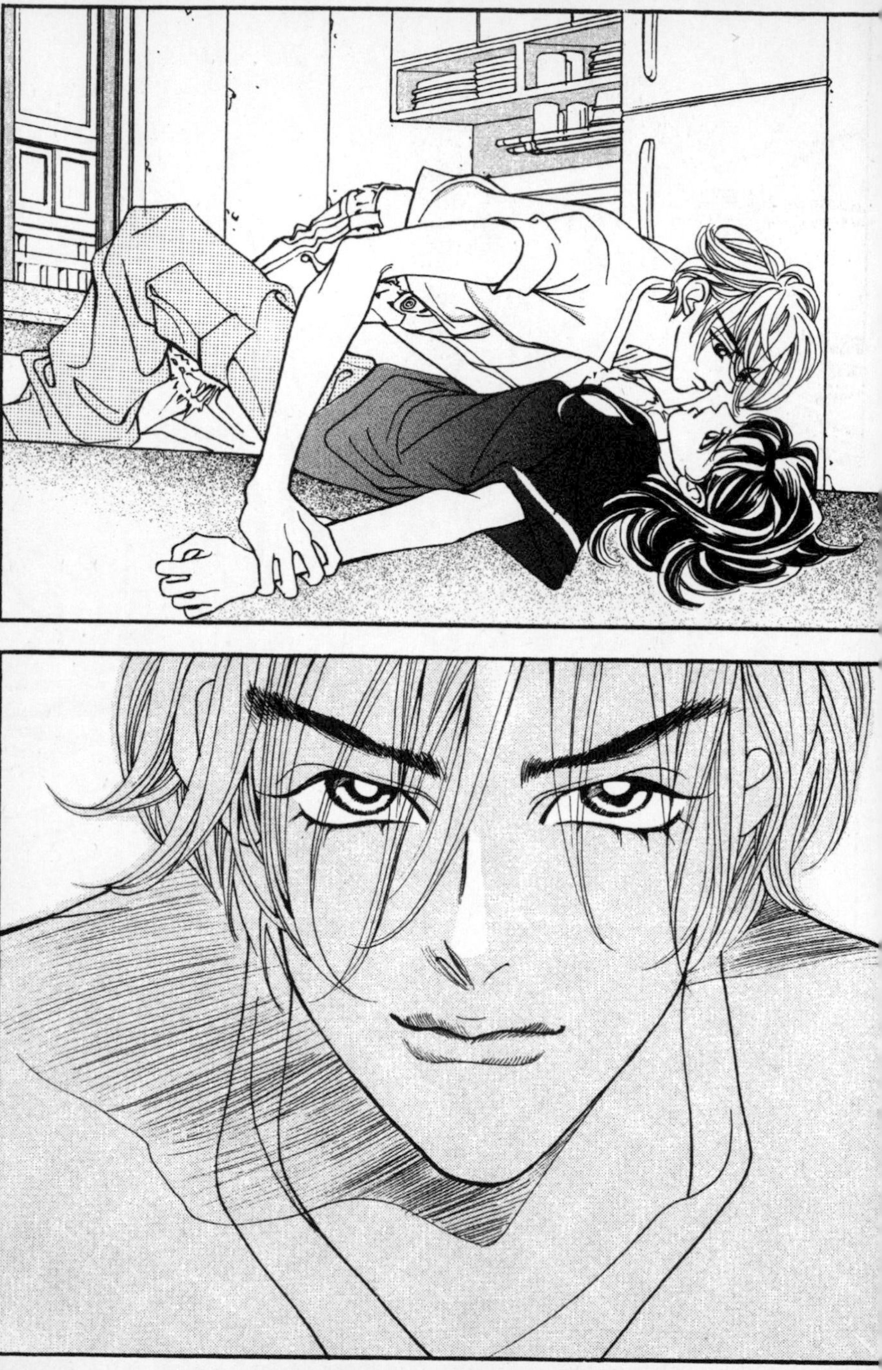

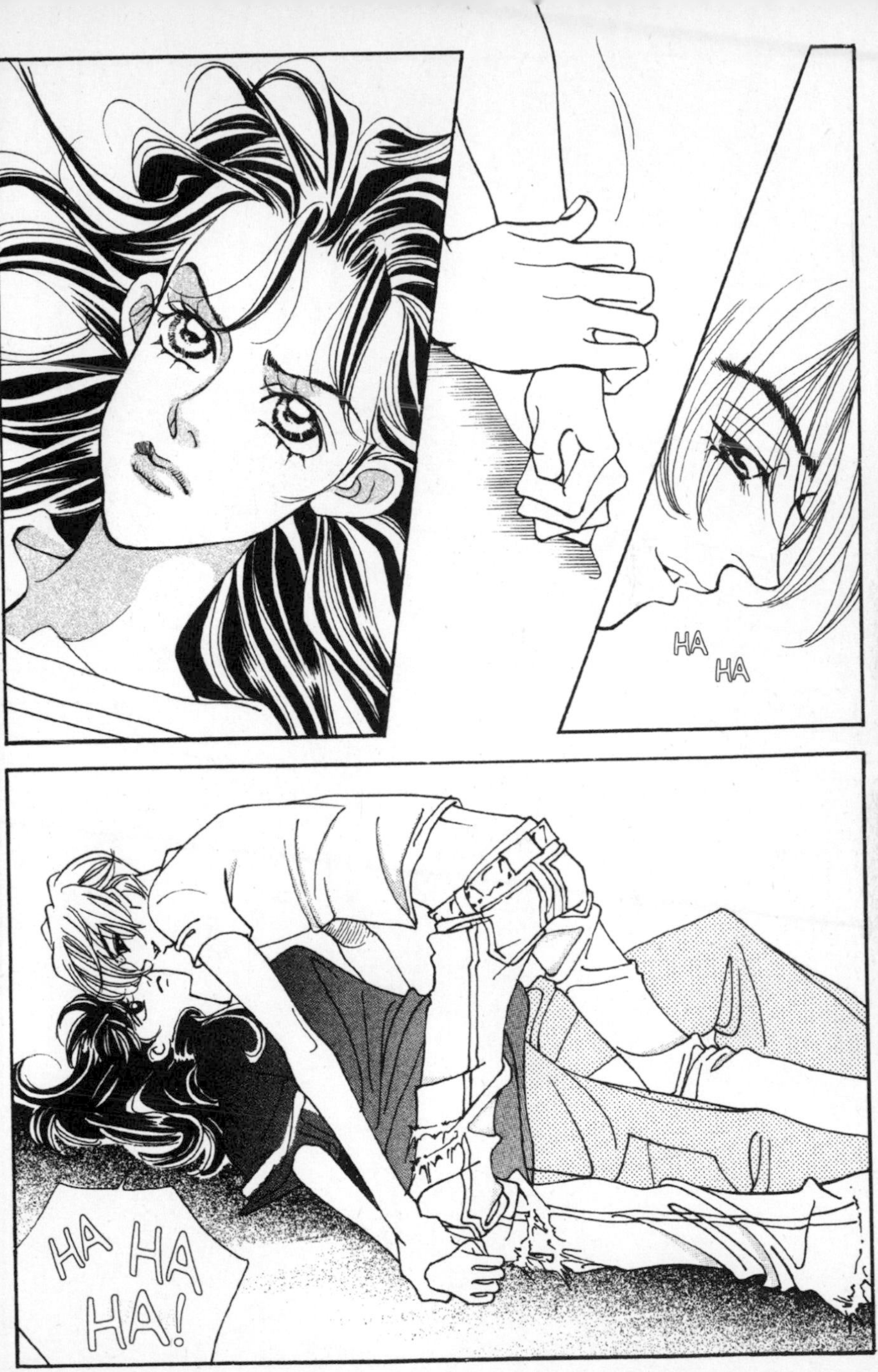
HA
HA
HA HA
HA!

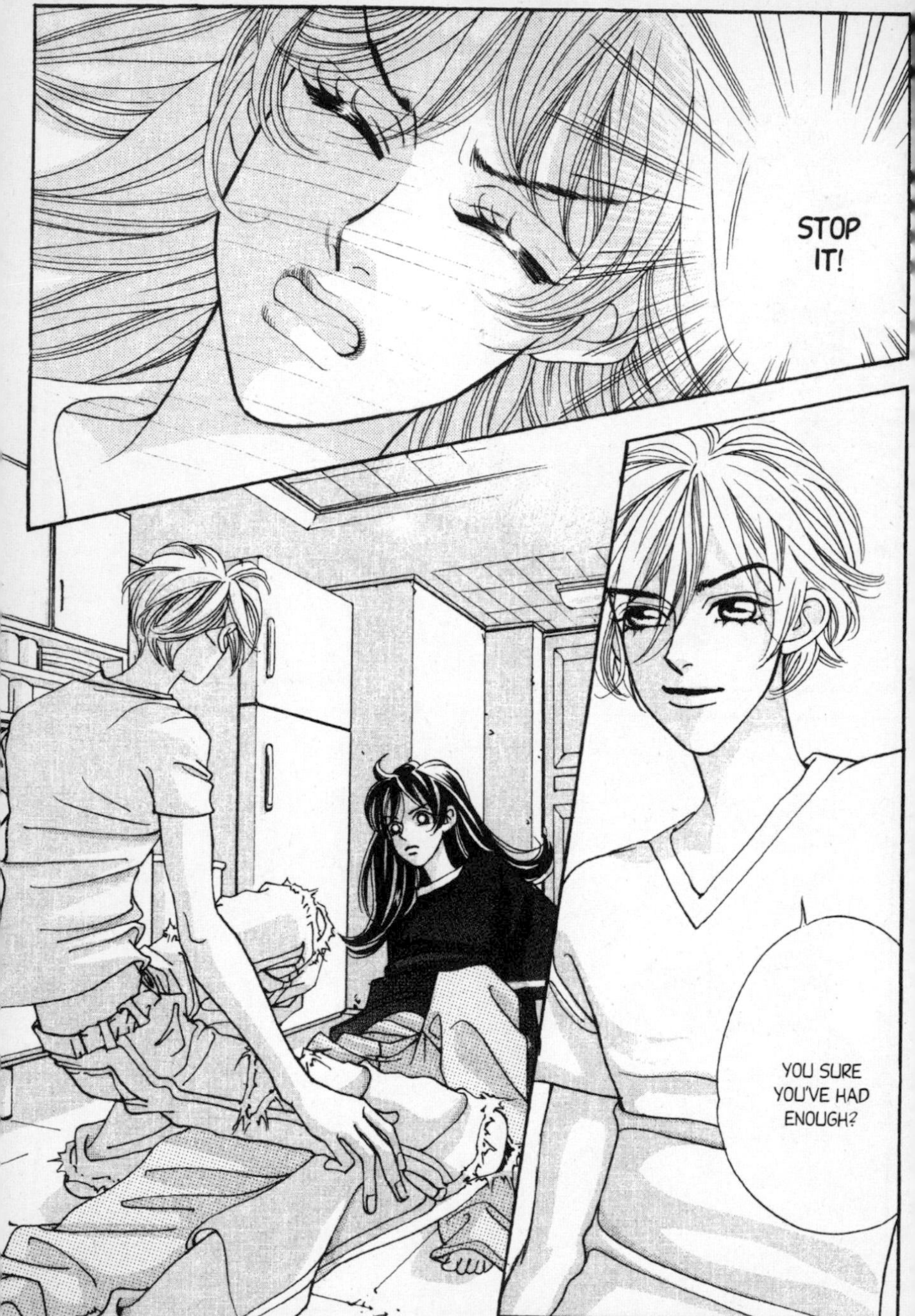
STOP IT!
YOU SURE YOU'VE HAD ENOUGH?

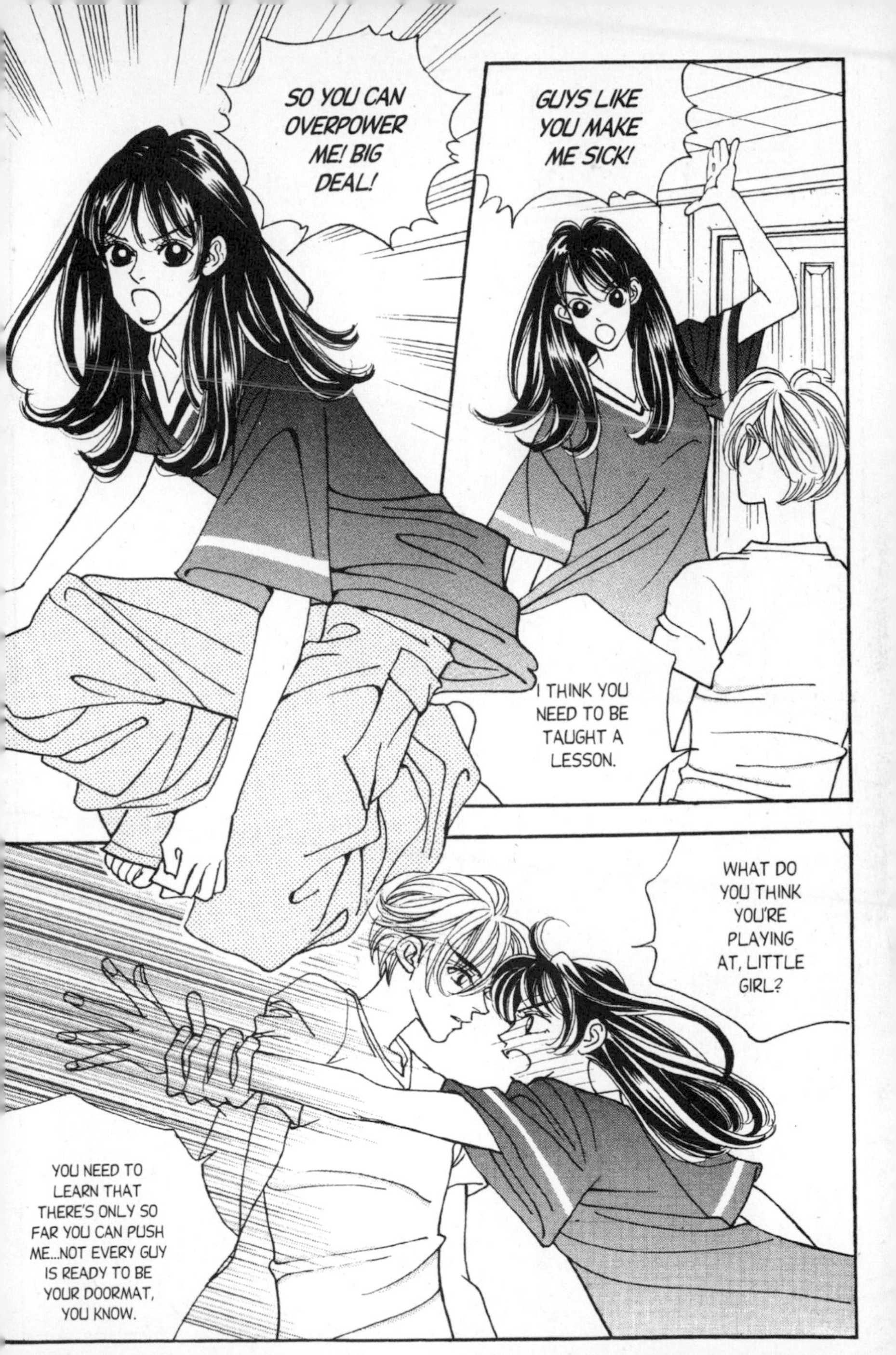
SO YOU CAN OVERPOWER ME! BIG DEAL!
GUYS LIKE YOU MAKE ME SICK!
I THINK YOU NEED TO BE TAUGHT A LESSON.
WHAT DO YOU THINK YOU'RE PLAYING AT, LITTLE GIRL?
YOU NEED TO LEARN THAT THERE'S ONLY SO FAR YOU CAN PUSH ME...NOT EVERY GUY IS READY TO BE YOUR DOORMAT, YOU KNOW.

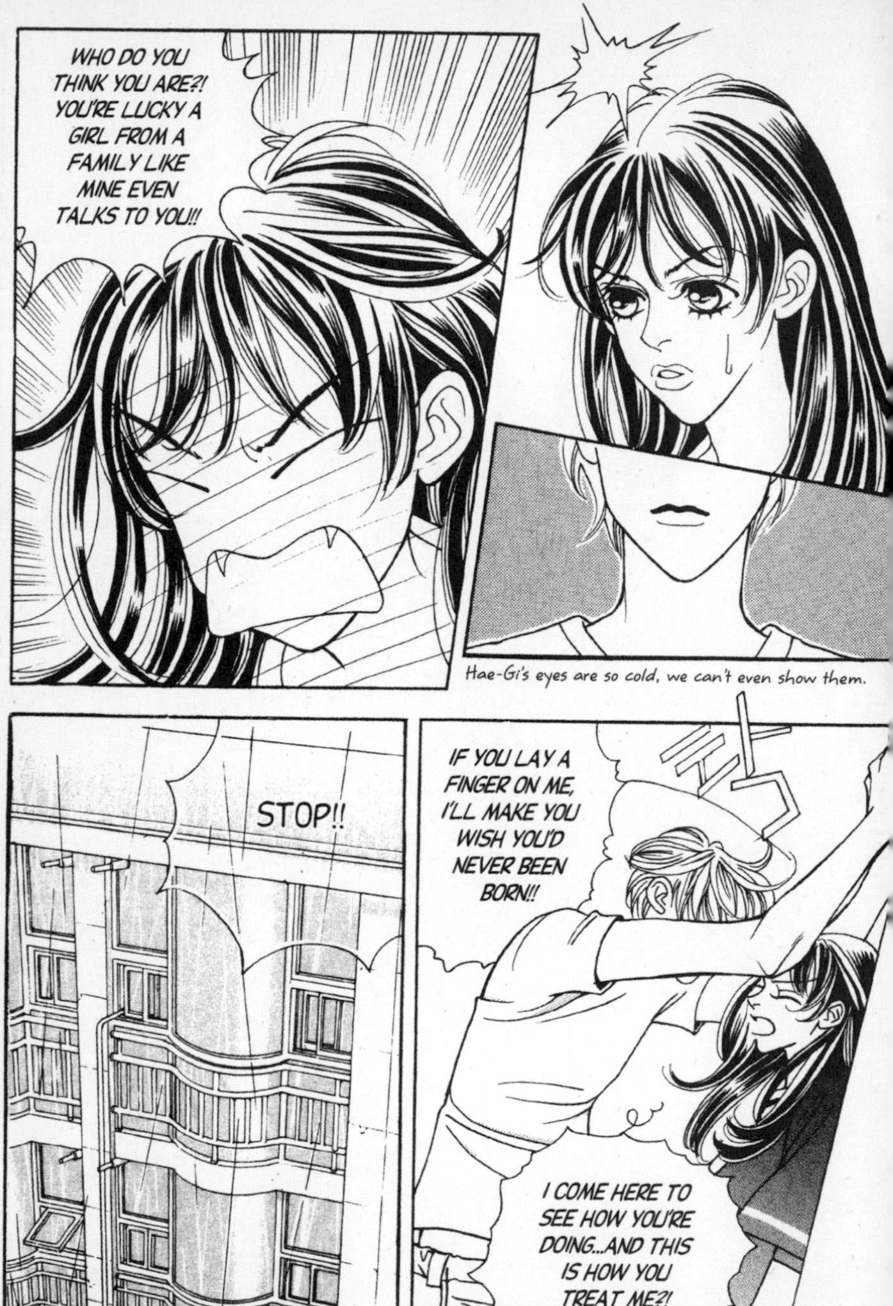
WHO DO YOU THINK YOU ARE?! YOU'RE LUCKY A GIRL FROM A FAMILY LIKE MINE EVEN TALKS TO YOU!!
Hae-Gi's eyes are so cold, we can't even show them.
STOP!!
IF YOU LAY A FINGER ON ME, I'LL MAKE YOU WISH YOU'D NEVER BEEN BORN!!
I COME HERE TO SEE HOW YOU'RE DOING...AND THIS IS HOW YOU TREAT ME?!

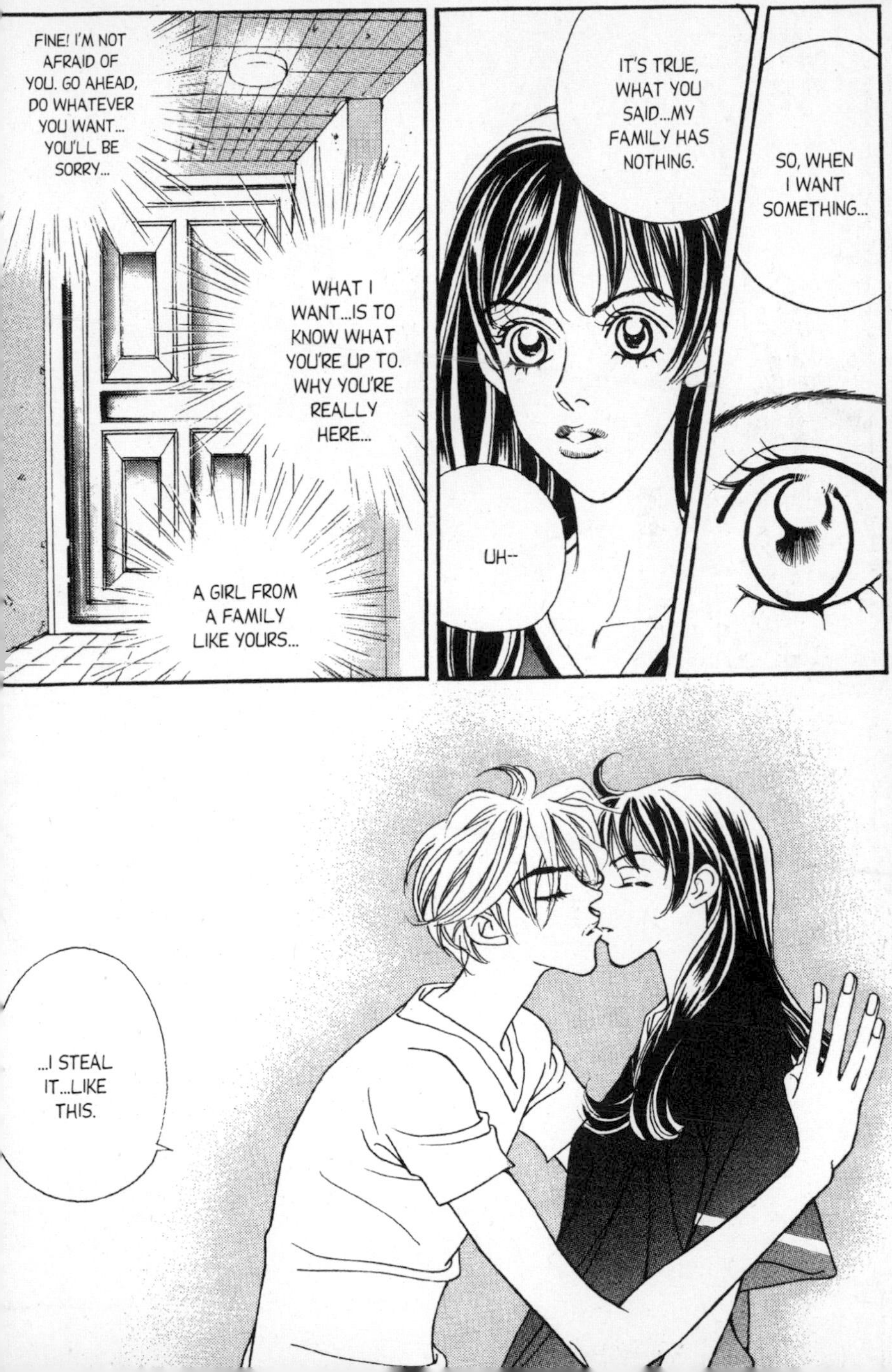
FINE! I'M NOT AFRAID OF YOU. GO AHEAD, DO WHATEVER YOU WANT... YOU'LL BE SORRY...
WHAT I WANT...IS TO KNOW WHAT YOU'RE UP TO. WHY YOU'RE REALLY HERE...
A GIRL FROM A FAMILY LIKE YOURS...
IT'S TRUE, WHAT YOU SAID...MY FAMILY HAS NOTHING.
UH--
SO, WHEN I WANT SOMETHING...
...I STEAL IT...LIKE THIS.

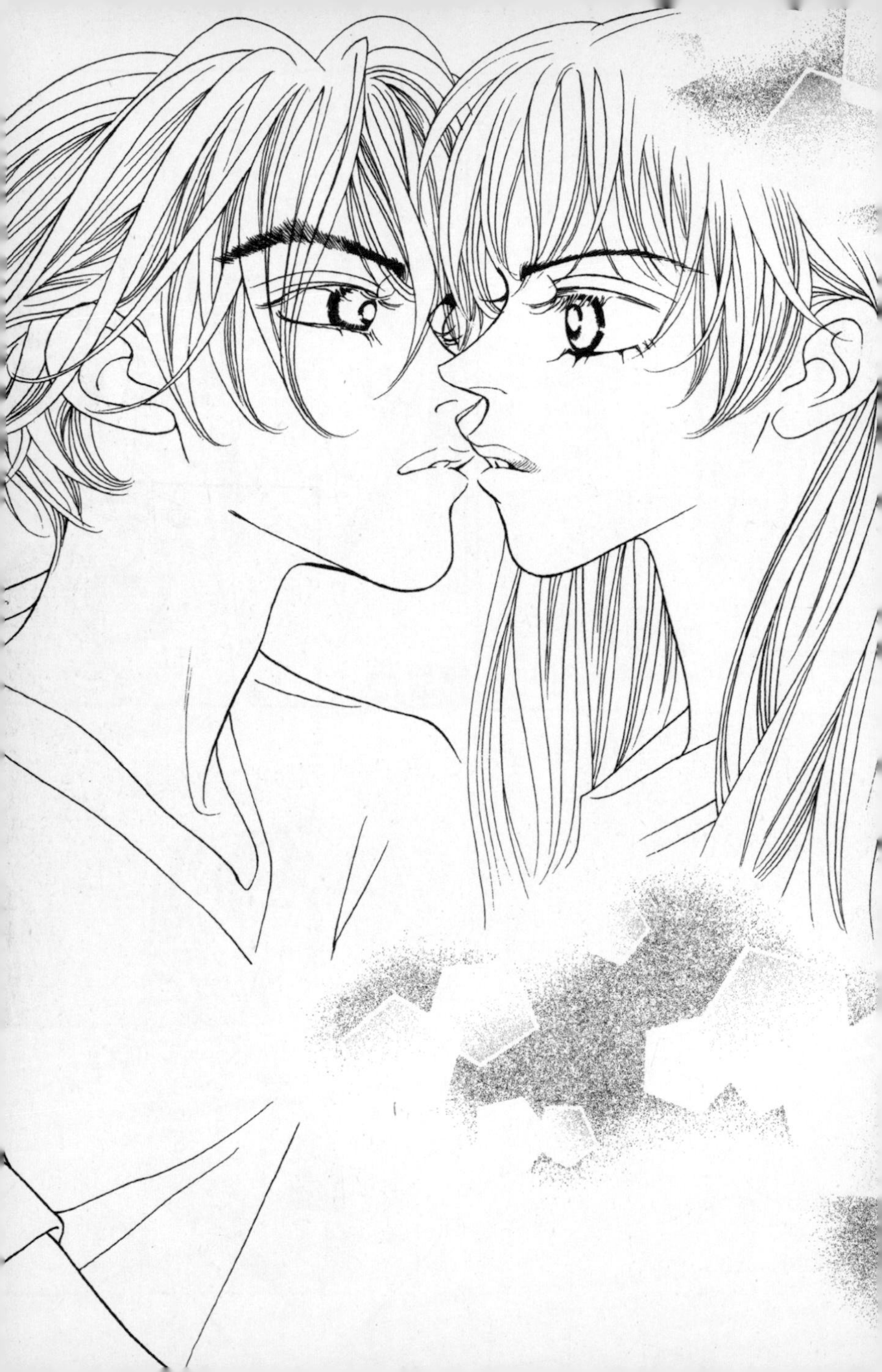

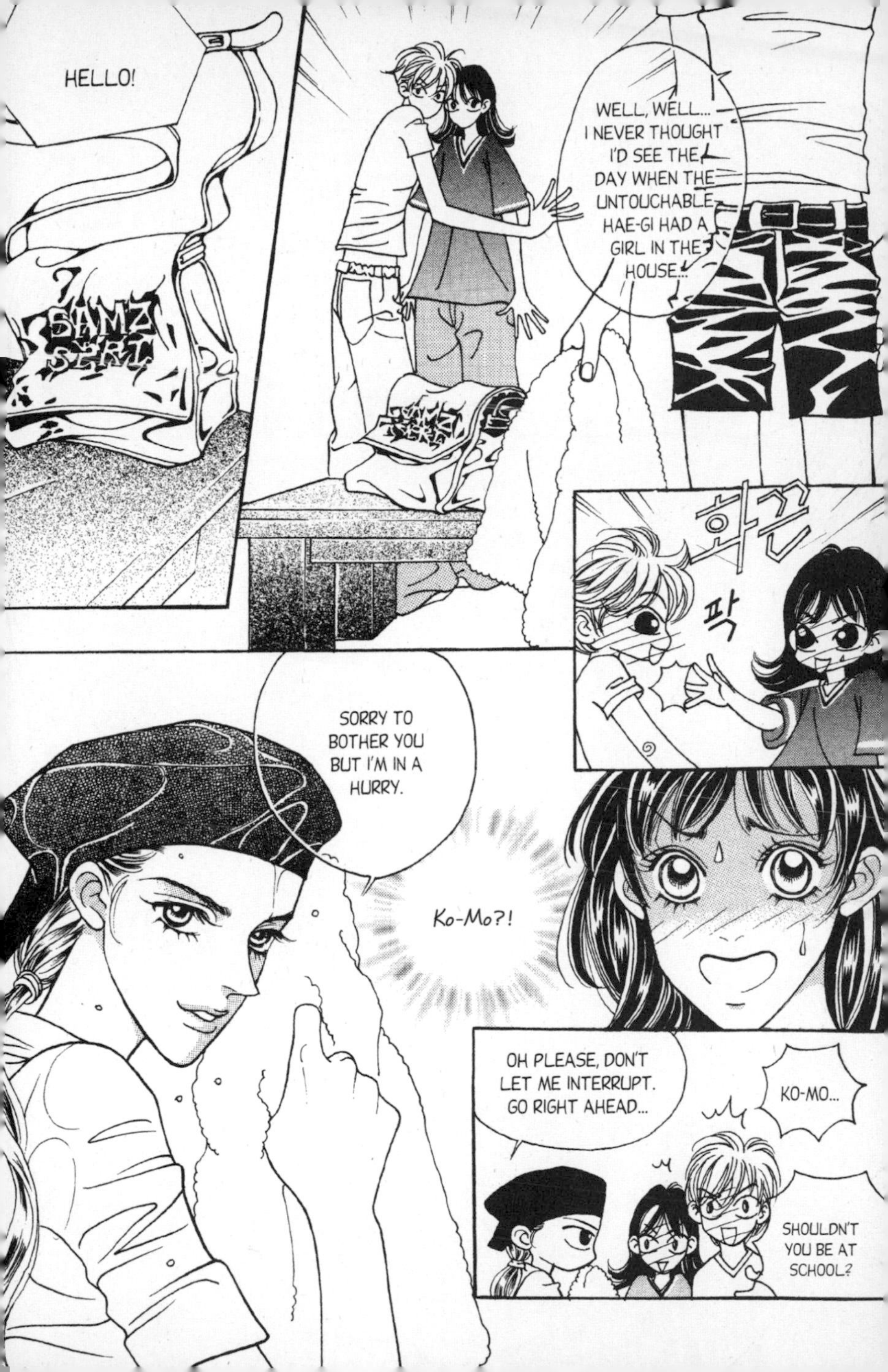
HELLO!
WELL, WELL... I NEVER THOUGHT I'D SEE THE DAY WHEN THE UNTOUCHABLE HAE-GI HAD A GIRL IN THE HOUSE...
화끈
팍
SORRY TO BOTHER YOU BUT I'M IN A HURRY.
Ko-Mo?!
OH PLEASE, DON'T LET ME INTERRUPT. GO RIGHT AHEAD...
KO-MO...
SHOULDN'T YOU BE AT SCHOOL?

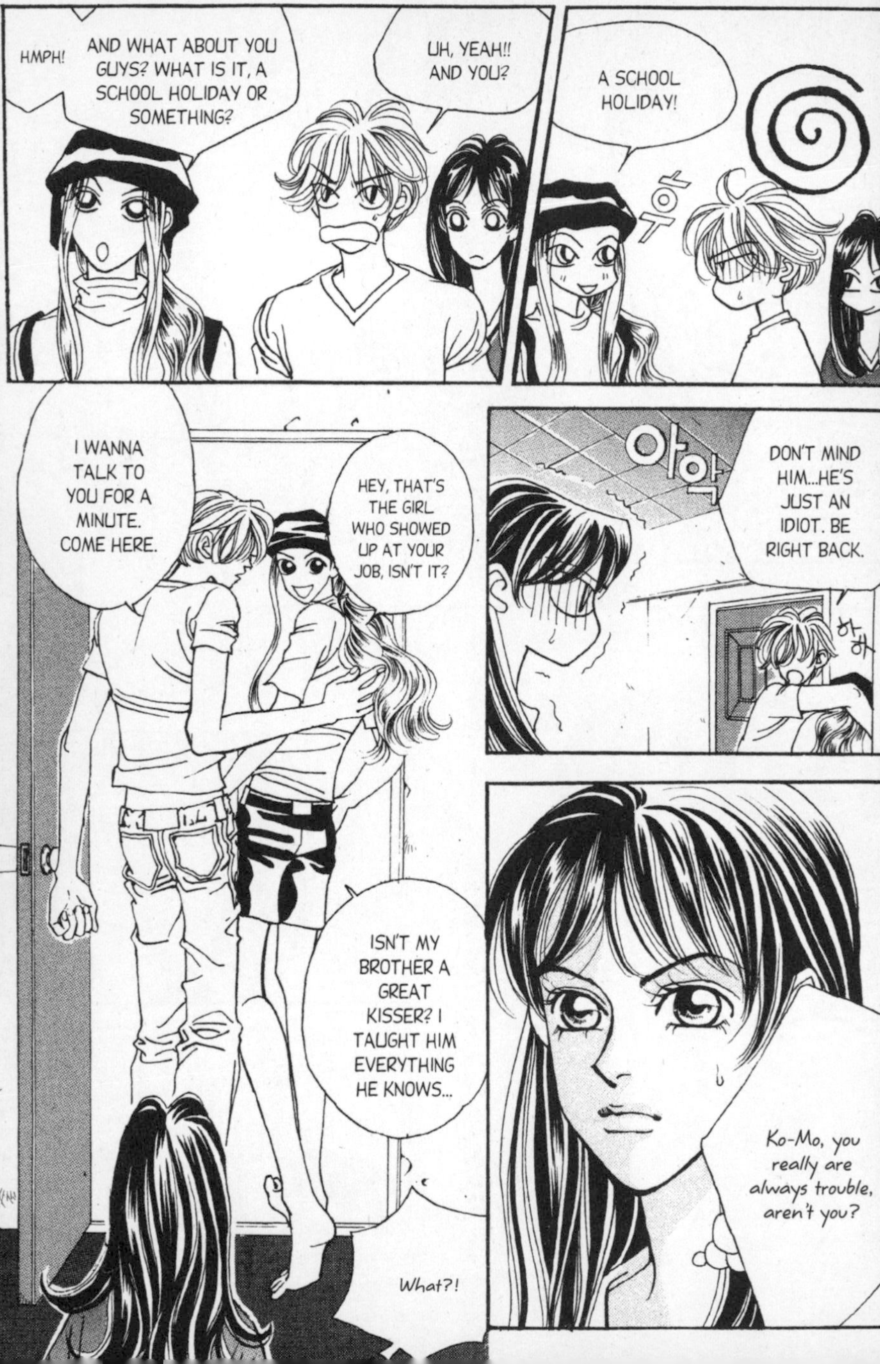
HMPH!
AND WHAT ABOUT YOU GUYS? WHAT IS IT, A SCHOOL HOLIDAY OR SOMETHING?
UH, YEAH!! AND YOU?
A SCHOOL HOLIDAY!
훗
I WANNA TALK TO YOU FOR A MINUTE. COME HERE.
HEY, THAT'S THE GIRL WHO SHOWED UP AT YOUR JOB, ISN'T IT?
ISN'T MY BROTHER A GREAT KISSER? I TAUGHT HIM EVERYTHING HE KNOWS...
What?!
아악
DON'T MIND HIM...HE'S JUST AN IDIOT. BE RIGHT BACK.
하하
Ko-Mo, you really are always trouble, aren't you?

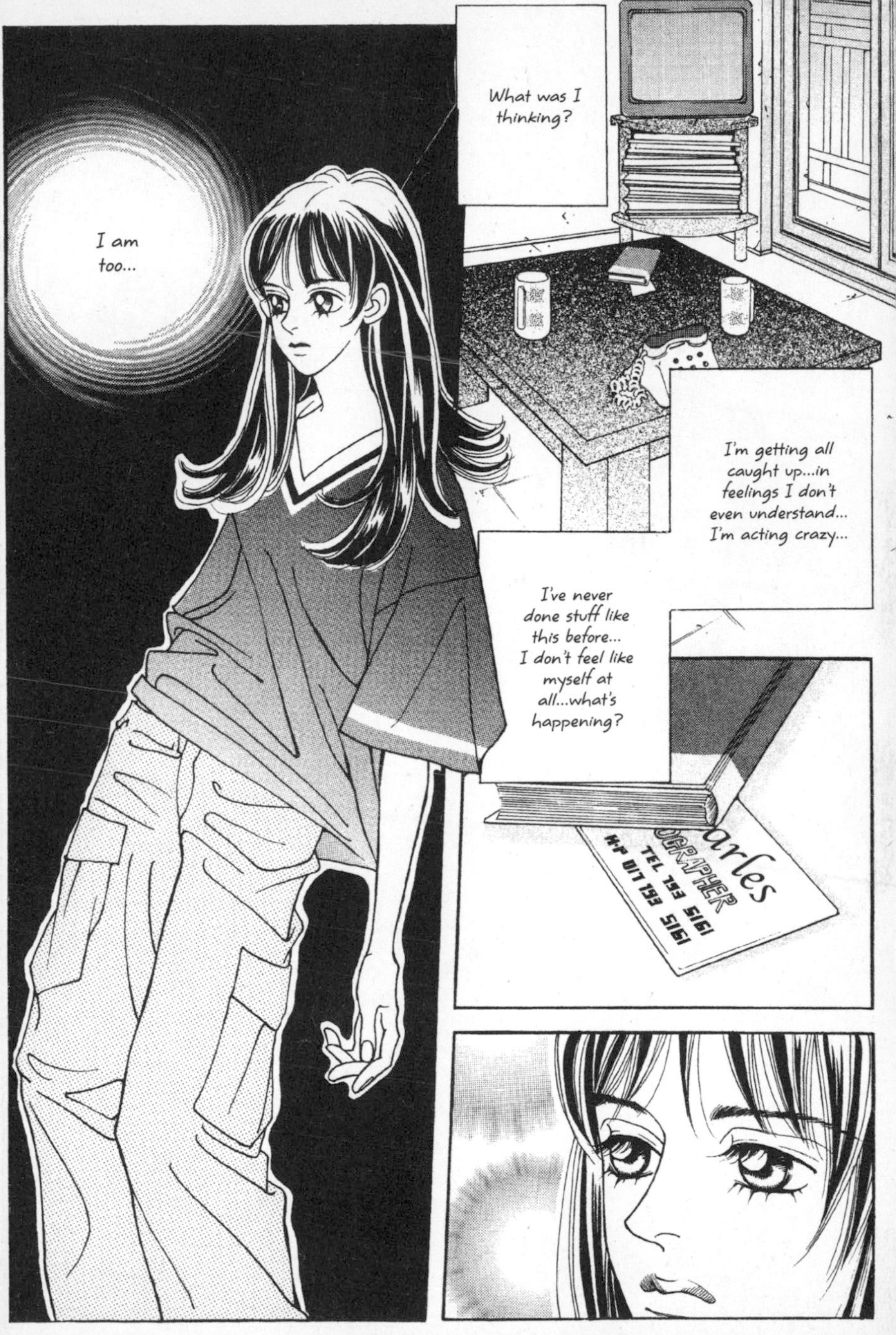
I am too...
What was I thinking?
I'm getting all caught up...in feelings I don't even understand... I'm acting crazy...
I've never done stuff like this before... I don't feel like myself at all...what's happening?
arles
OGRAPHER
TEL 793 5161
H-P 017 793 5161

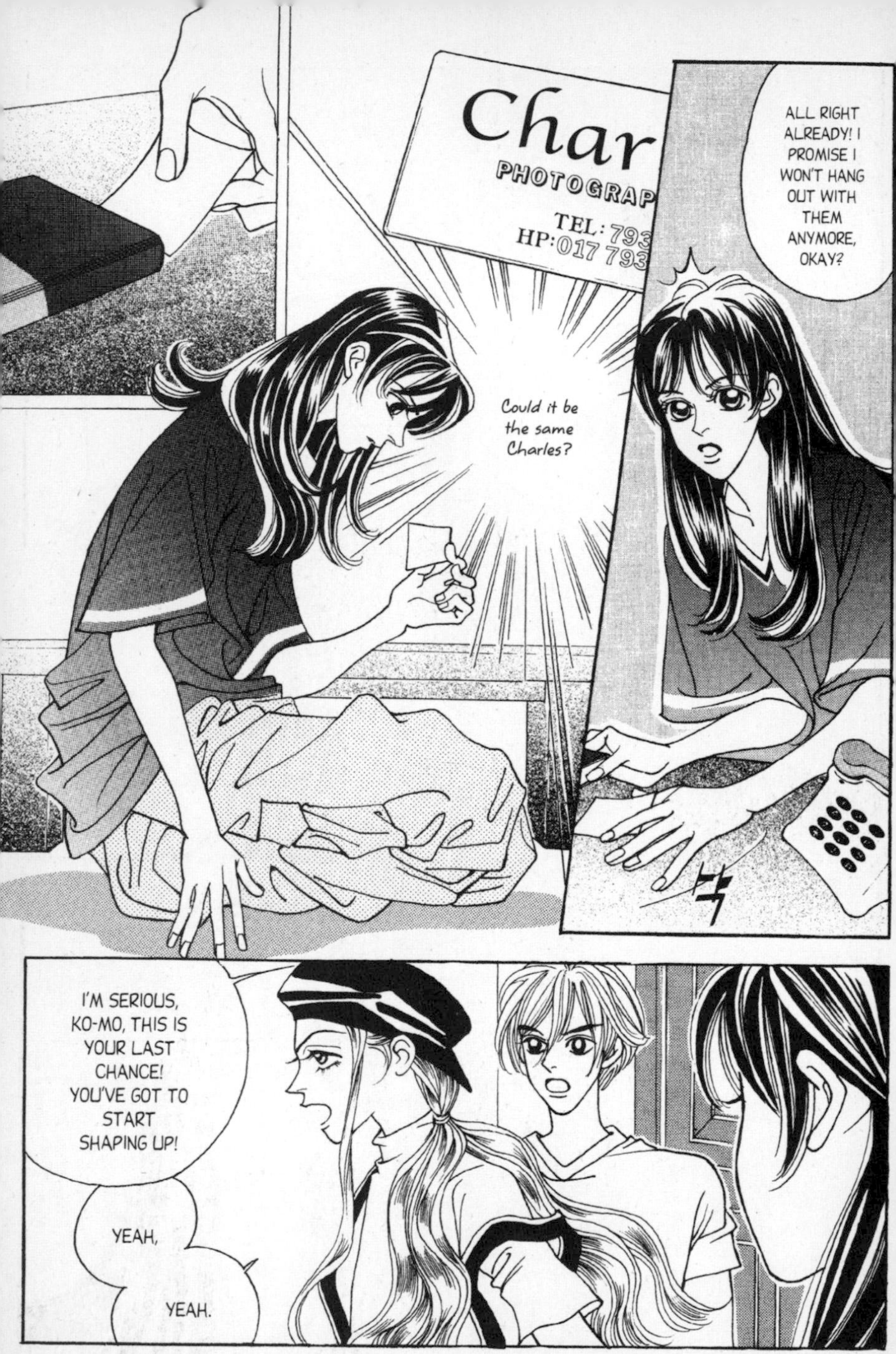

Char
PHOTOGRAP
TEL: 793
HP: 017 793
Could it be the same Charles?
ALL RIGHT ALREADY! I PROMISE I WON'T HANG OUT WITH THEM ANYMORE, OKAY?
I'M SERIOUS, KO-MO, THIS IS YOUR LAST CHANCE! YOU'VE GOT TO START SHAPING UP!
YEAH,
YEAH.

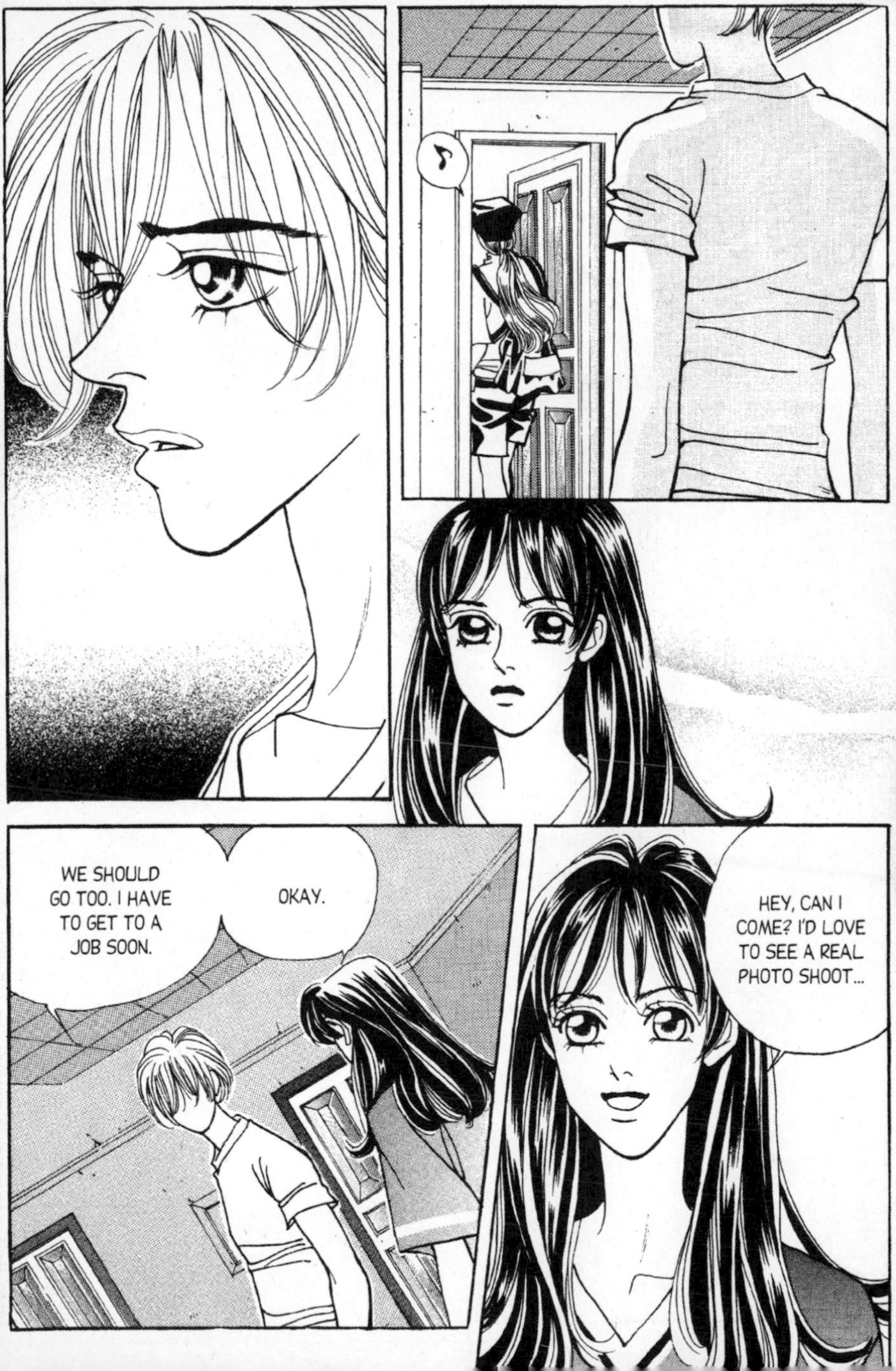
♪
WE SHOULD GO TOO. I HAVE TO GET TO A JOB SOON.
OKAY.
HEY, CAN I COME? I'D LOVE TO SEE A REAL PHOTO SHOOT...

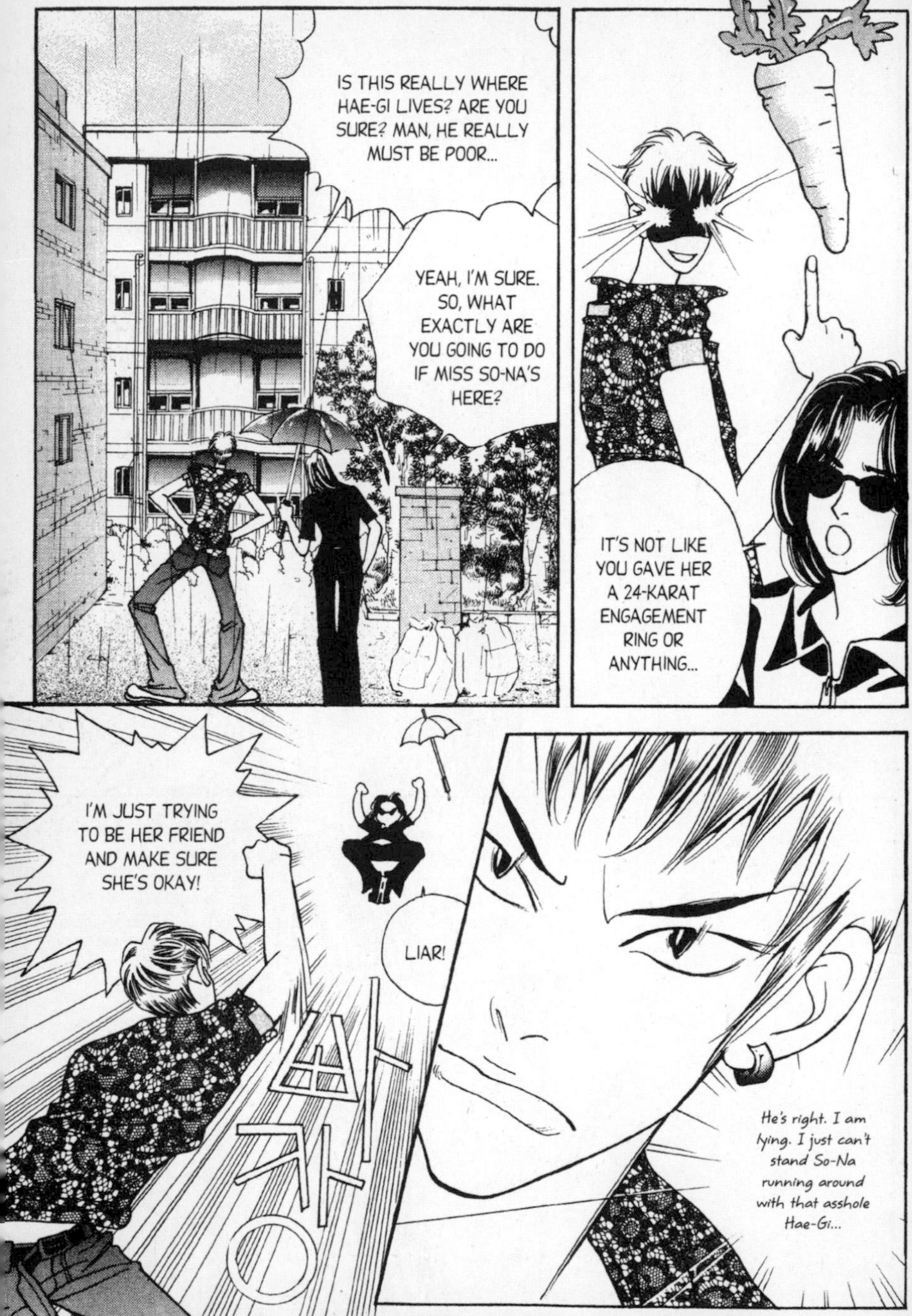
IS THIS REALLY WHERE HAE-GI LIVES? ARE YOU SURE? MAN, HE REALLY MUST BE POOR...
YEAH, I'M SURE. SO, WHAT EXACTLY ARE YOU GOING TO DO IF MISS SO-NA'S HERE?
IT'S NOT LIKE YOU GAVE HER A 24-KARAT ENGAGEMENT RING OR ANYTHING...
I'M JUST TRYING TO BE HER FRIEND AND MAKE SURE SHE'S OKAY!
LIAR!
He's right. I am lying. I just can't stand So-Na running around with that asshole Hae-Gi...

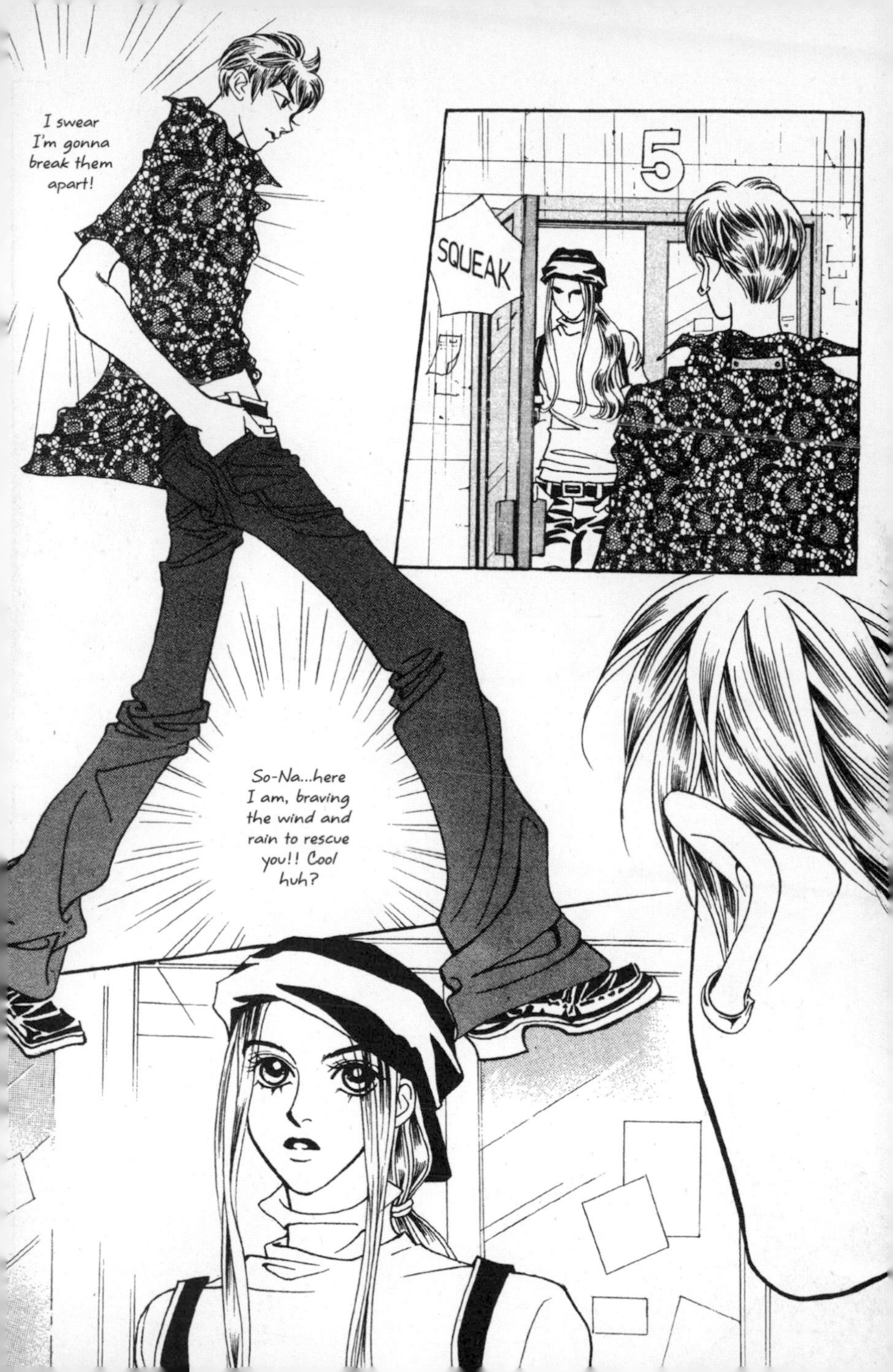

I swear I'm gonna break them apart!
5
SQUEAK
So-Na...here I am, braving the wind and rain to rescue you!! Cool huh?

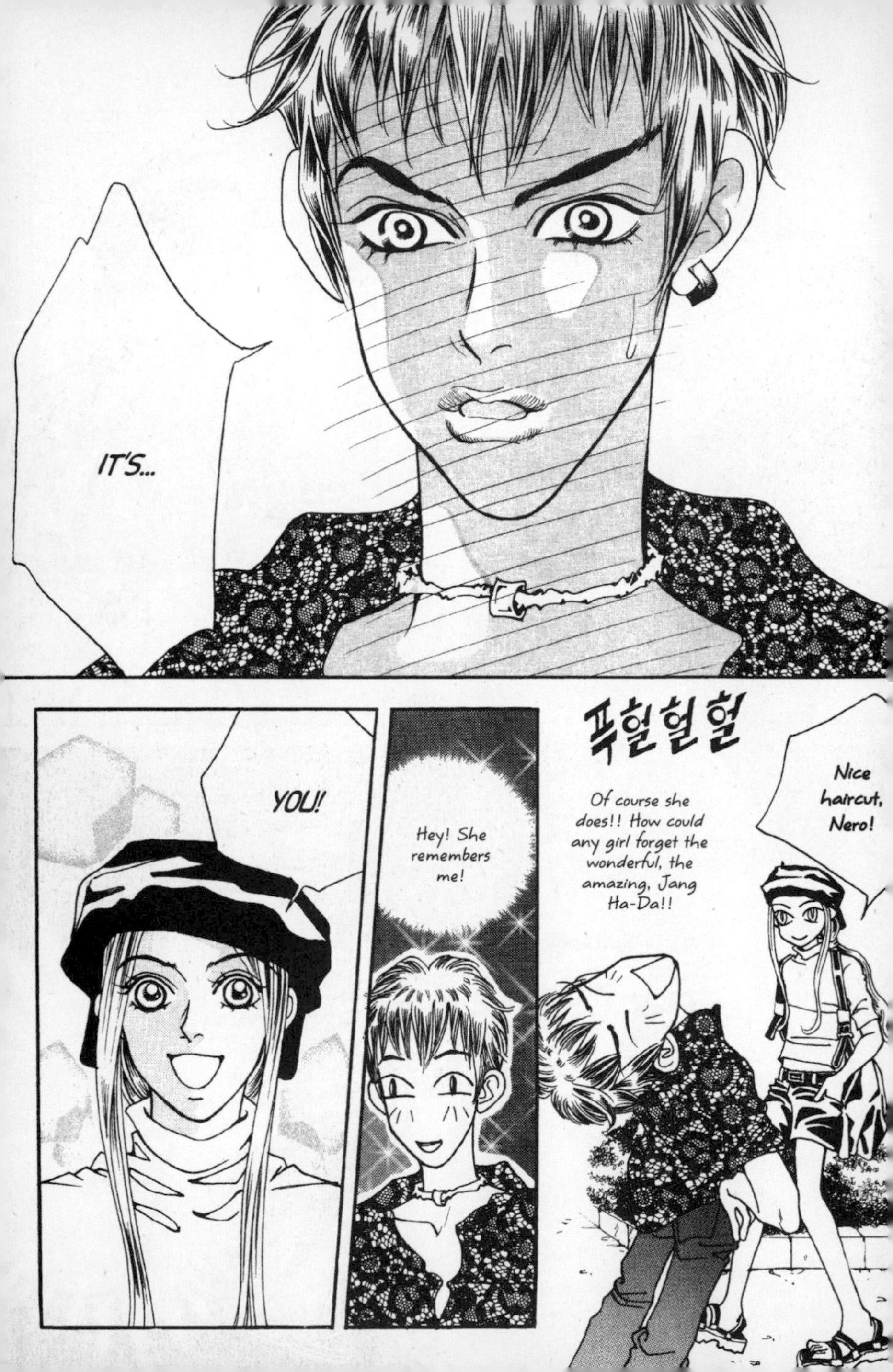
IT'S...
YOU!
Hey! She remembers me!
폭헐헐헐
Of course she does!! How could any girl forget the wonderful, the amazing, Jang Ha-Da!!
Nice haircut, Nero!

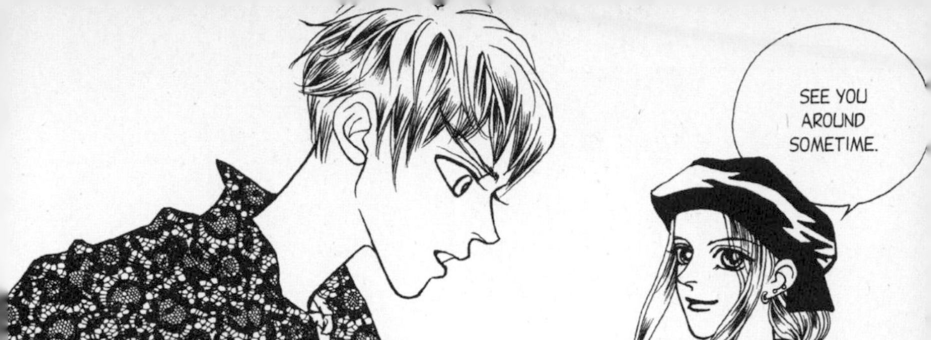
SEE YOU AROUND SOMETIME.
Nero??

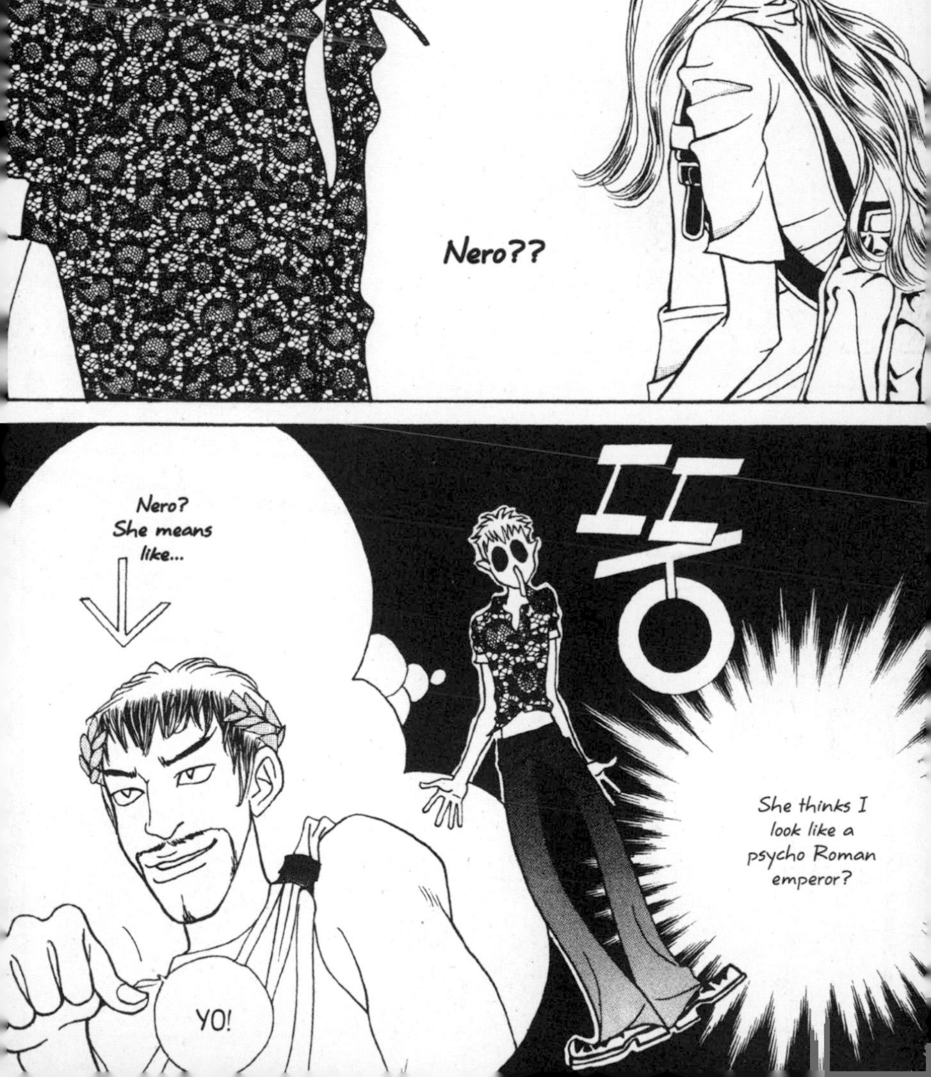
Nero? She means like...
YO!
She thinks I look like a psycho Roman emperor?

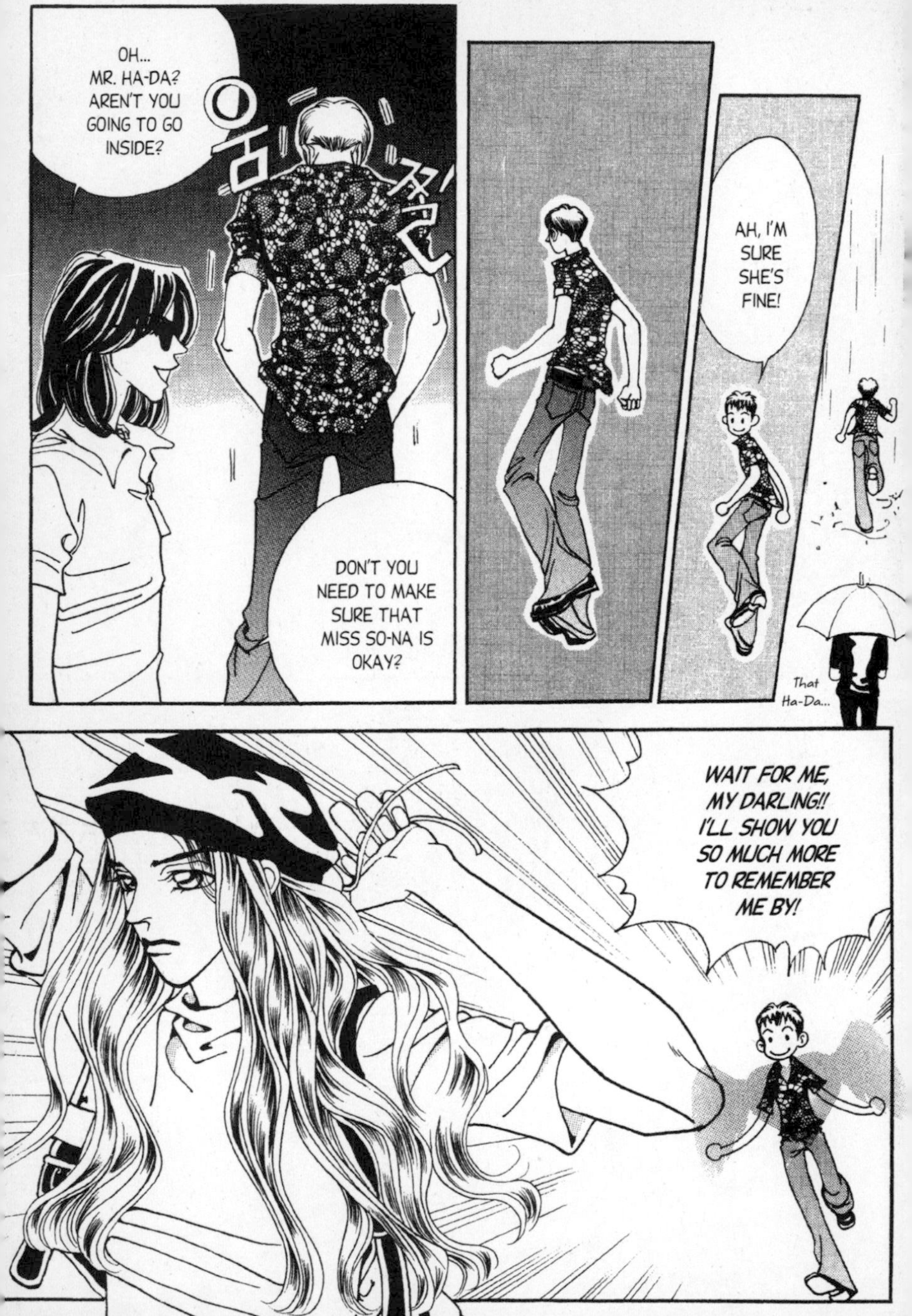
OH... MR. HA-DA? AREN'T YOU GOING TO GO INSIDE?
DON'T YOU NEED TO MAKE SURE THAT MISS SO-NA IS OKAY?
AH, I'M SURE SHE'S FINE!
That Ha-Da...
WAIT FOR ME, MY DARLING!! I'LL SHOW YOU SO MUCH MORE TO REMEMBER ME BY!

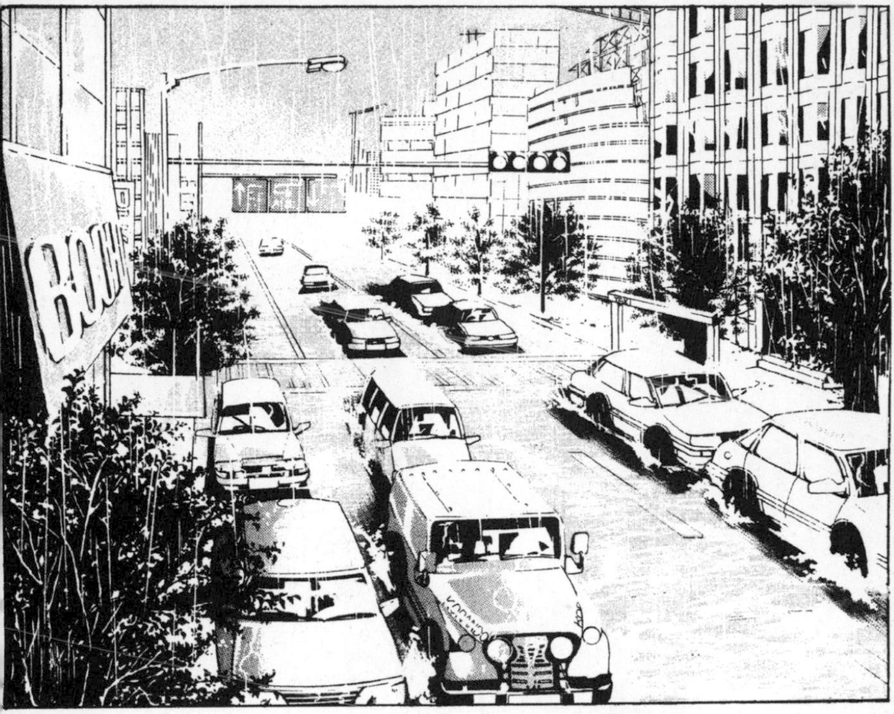

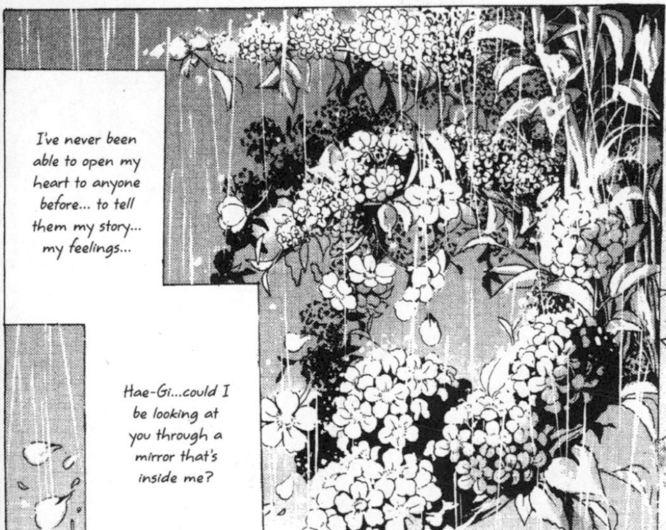
I've never been able to open my heart to anyone before... to tell them my story... my feelings...
Hae-Gi...could I be looking at you through a mirror that's inside me?

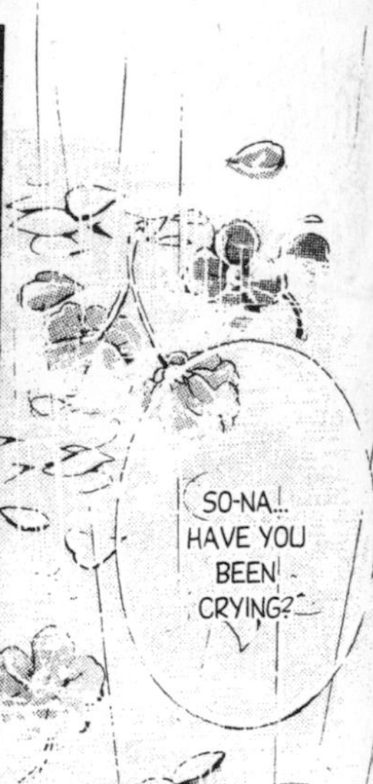
SO-NA... HAVE YOU BEEN CRYING?

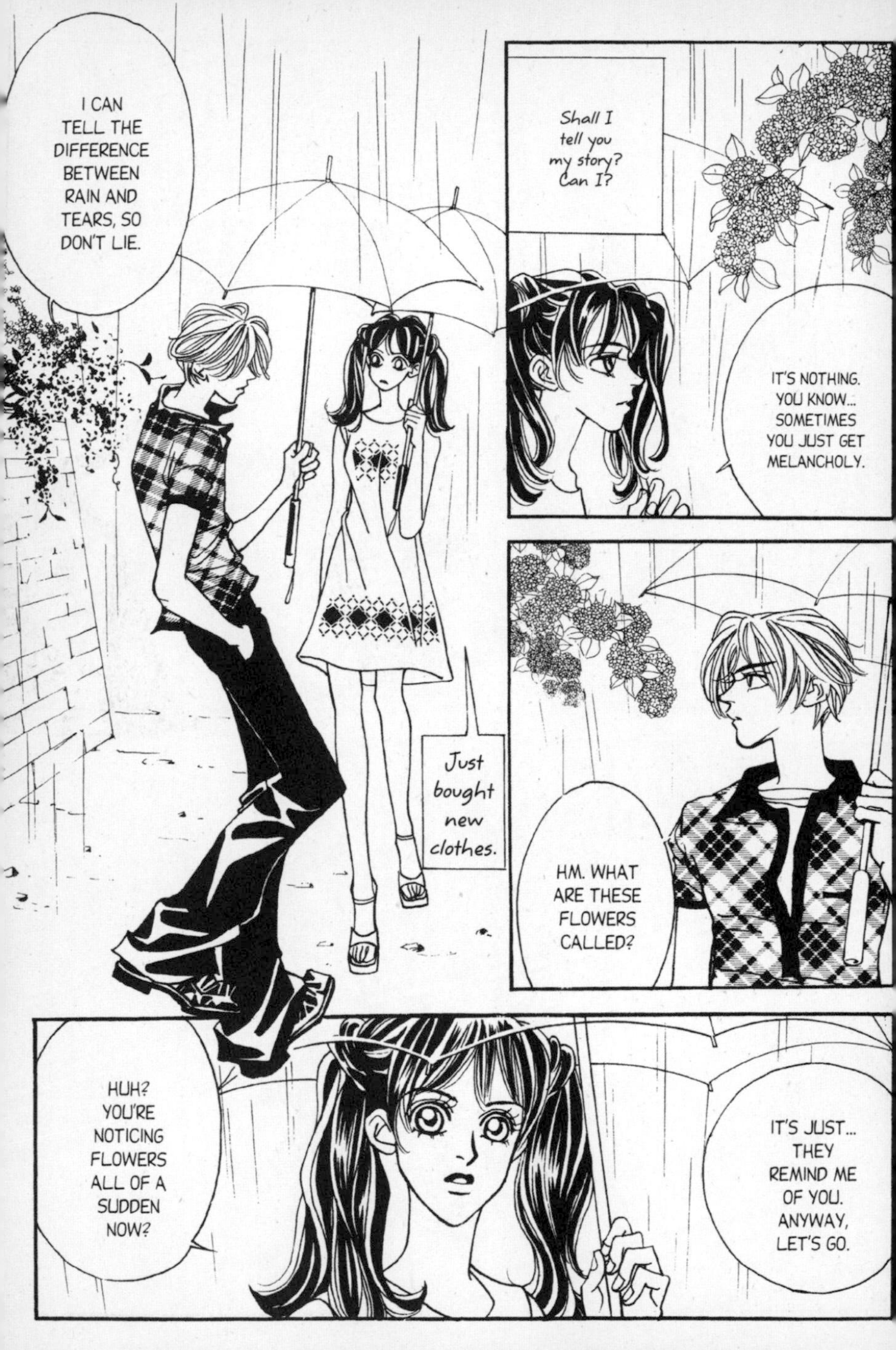
I CAN TELL THE DIFFERENCE BETWEEN RAIN AND TEARS, SO DON'T LIE.
Just bought new clothes.
Shall I tell you my story? Can I?
IT'S NOTHING. YOU KNOW... SOMETIMES YOU JUST GET MELANCHOLY.
HM. WHAT ARE THESE FLOWERS CALLED?
HUH? YOU'RE NOTICING FLOWERS ALL OF A SUDDEN NOW?
IT'S JUST... THEY REMIND ME OF YOU. ANYWAY, LET'S GO.

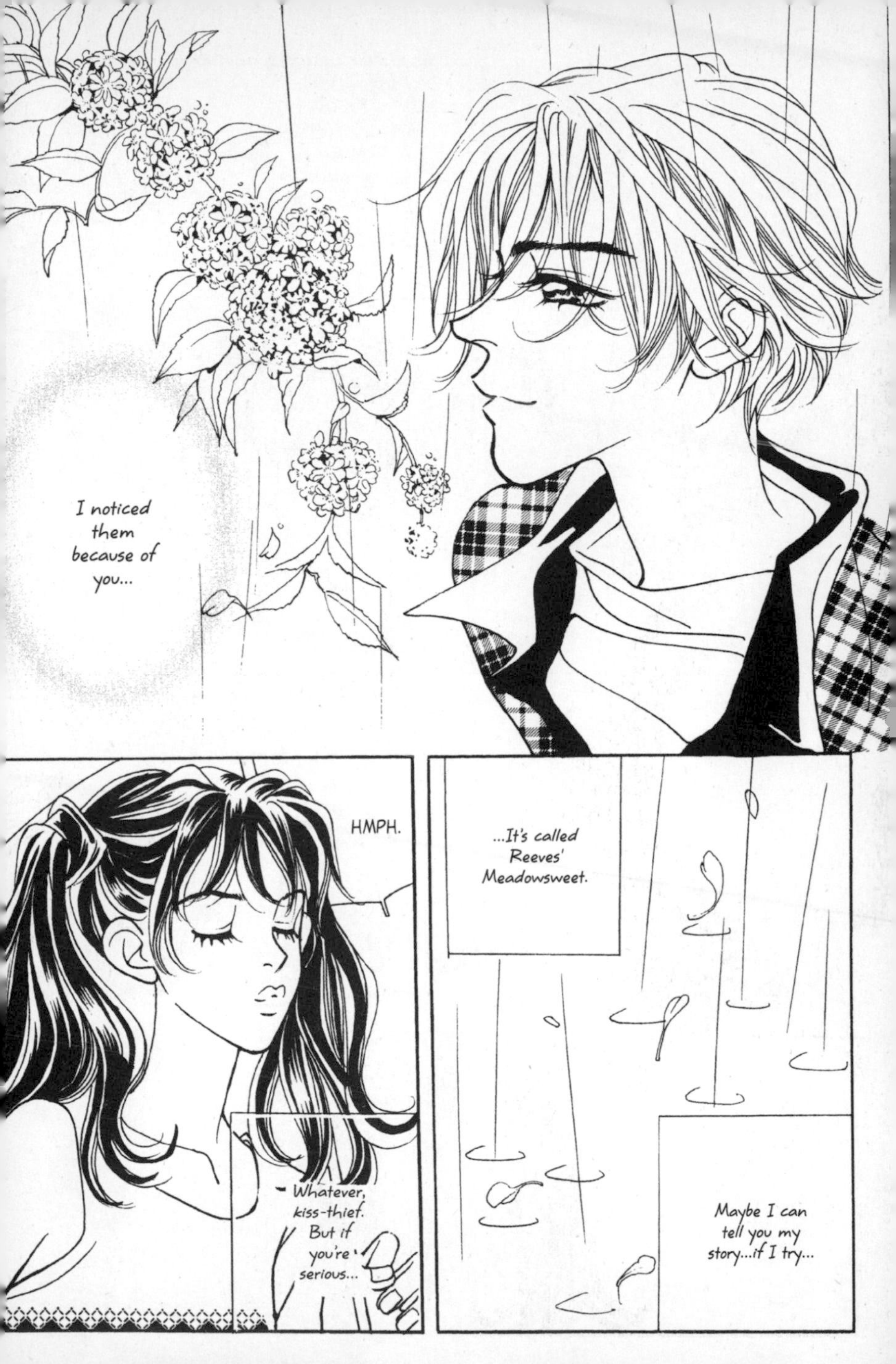
I noticed them because of you...
HMPH.
Whatever, kiss-thief. But if you're serious...
...It's called Reeves' Meadowsweet.
Maybe I can tell you my story...if I try...

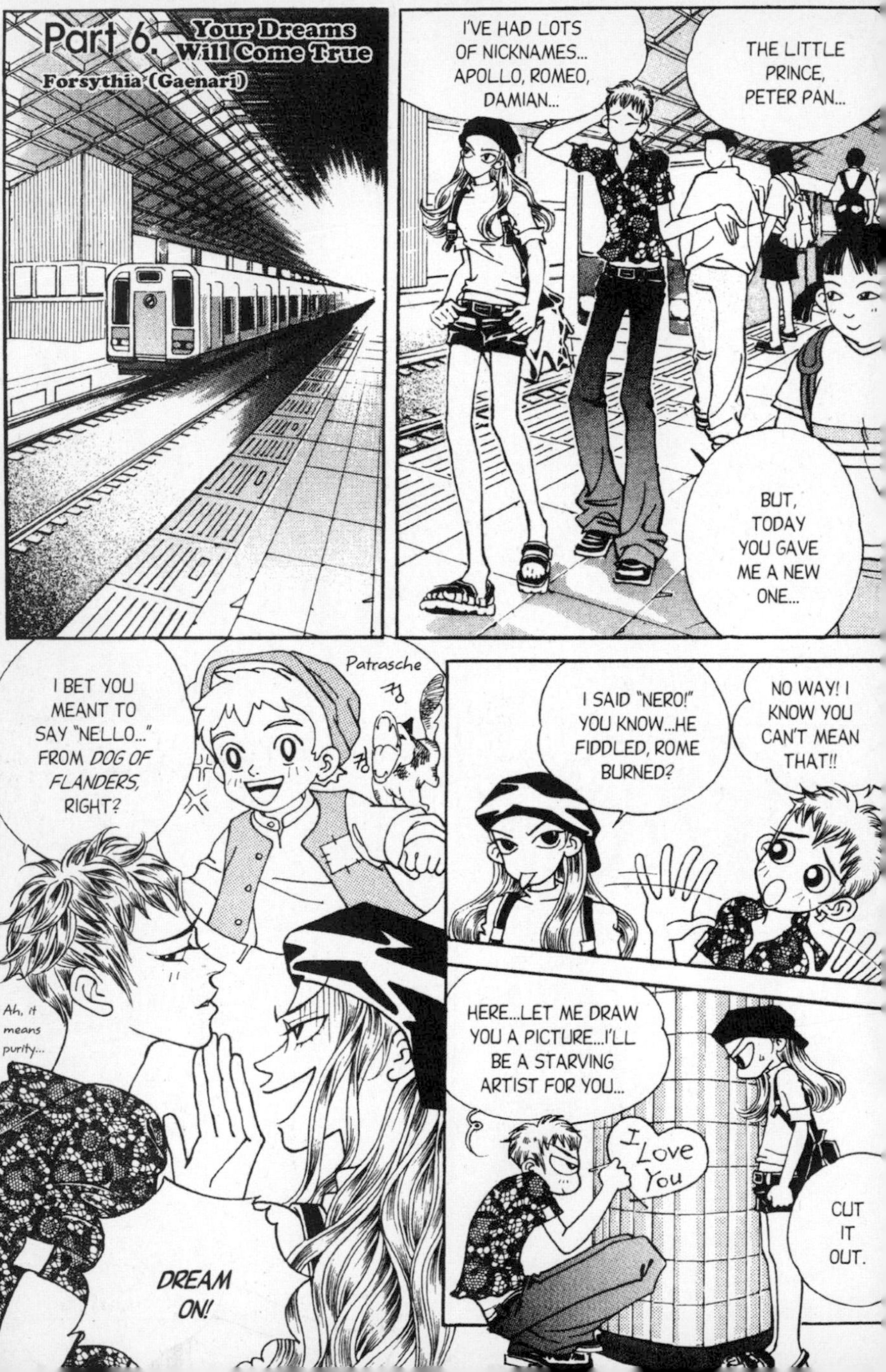
Part 6. Your Dreams Will Come True
Forsythia (Gaenari)
I'VE HAD LOTS OF NICKNAMES... APOLLO, ROMEO, DAMIAN...
THE LITTLE PRINCE, PETER PAN...
BUT, TODAY YOU GAVE ME A NEW ONE...
I BET YOU MEANT TO SAY "NELLO..." FROM *DOG OF FLANDERS,* RIGHT?
Patrasche
Ah, it means purity...
DREAM ON!
I SAID "NERO!" YOU KNOW...HE FIDDLED, ROME BURNED?
NO WAY! I KNOW YOU CAN'T MEAN THAT!!
HERE...LET ME DRAW YOU A PICTURE...I'LL BE A STARVING ARTIST FOR YOU...
I Love You
CUT IT OUT.

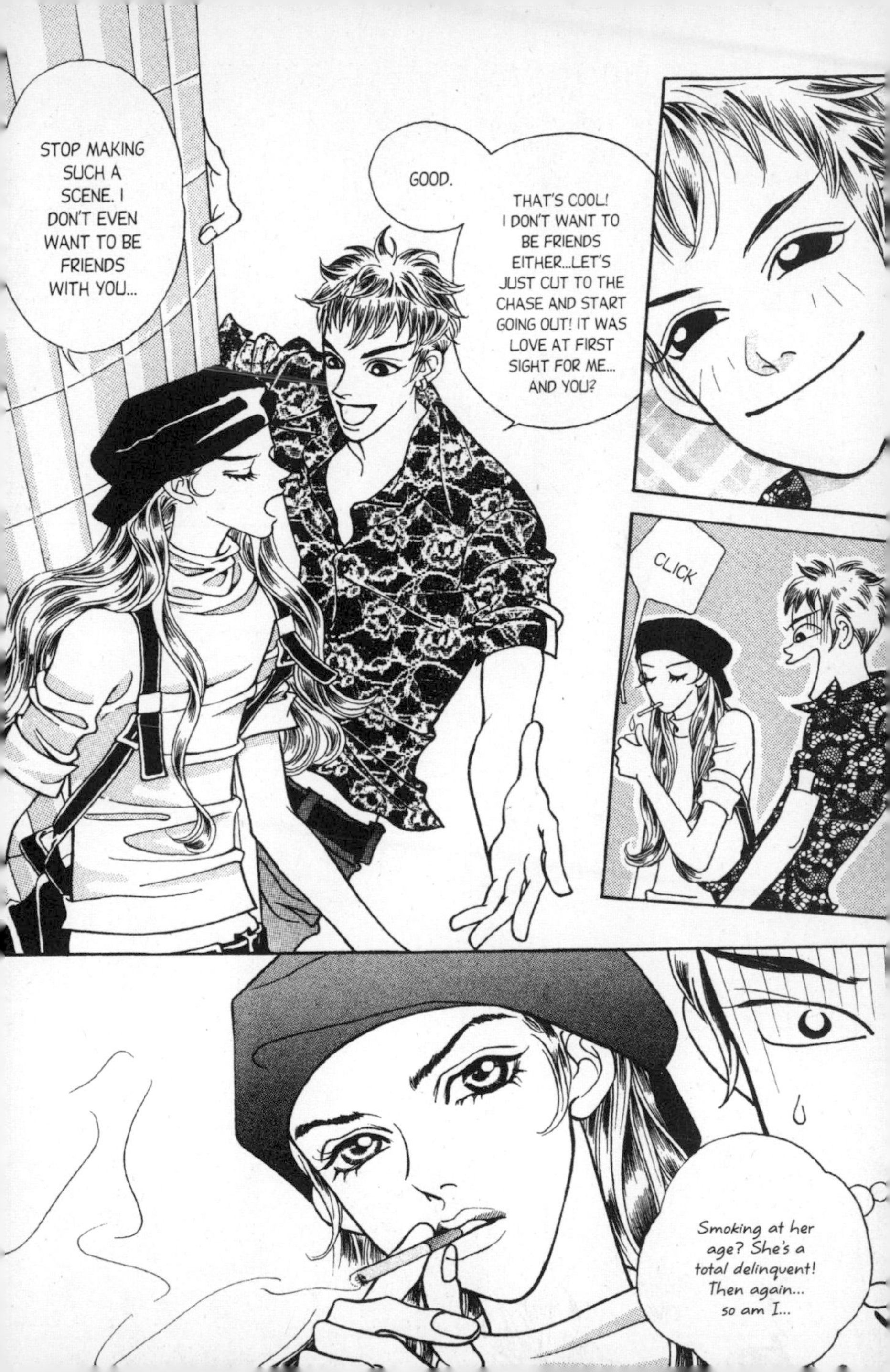
STOP MAKING SUCH A SCENE. I DON'T EVEN WANT TO BE FRIENDS WITH YOU...
GOOD.
THAT'S COOL! I DON'T WANT TO BE FRIENDS EITHER...LET'S JUST CUT TO THE CHASE AND START GOING OUT! IT WAS LOVE AT FIRST SIGHT FOR ME... AND YOU?
CLICK
Smoking at her age? She's a total delinquent! Then again... so am I...

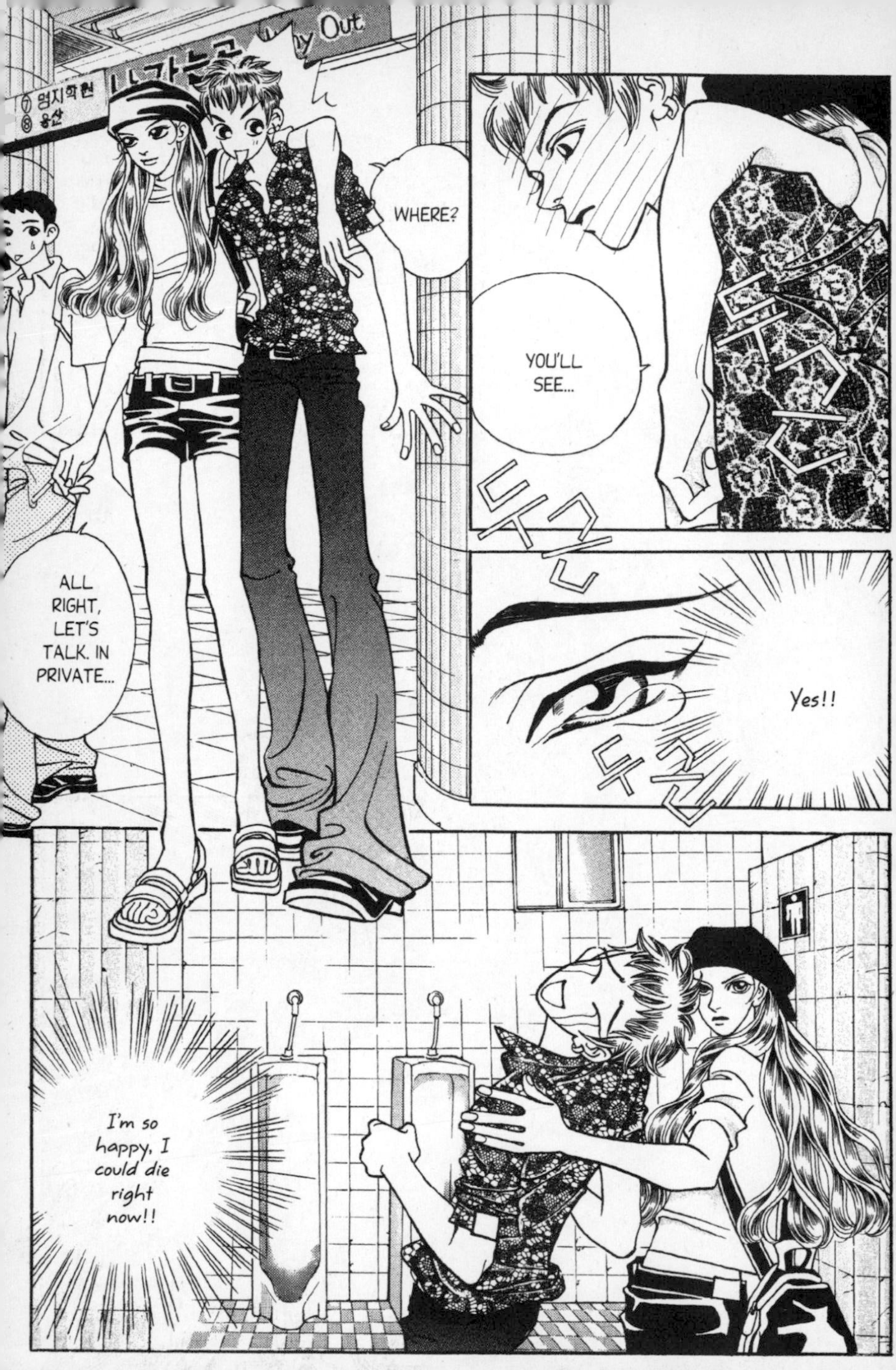
ALL RIGHT, LET'S TALK. IN PRIVATE...
WHERE?
YOU'LL SEE...
두근
두근
Yes!!
두근
I'm so happy, I could die right now!!

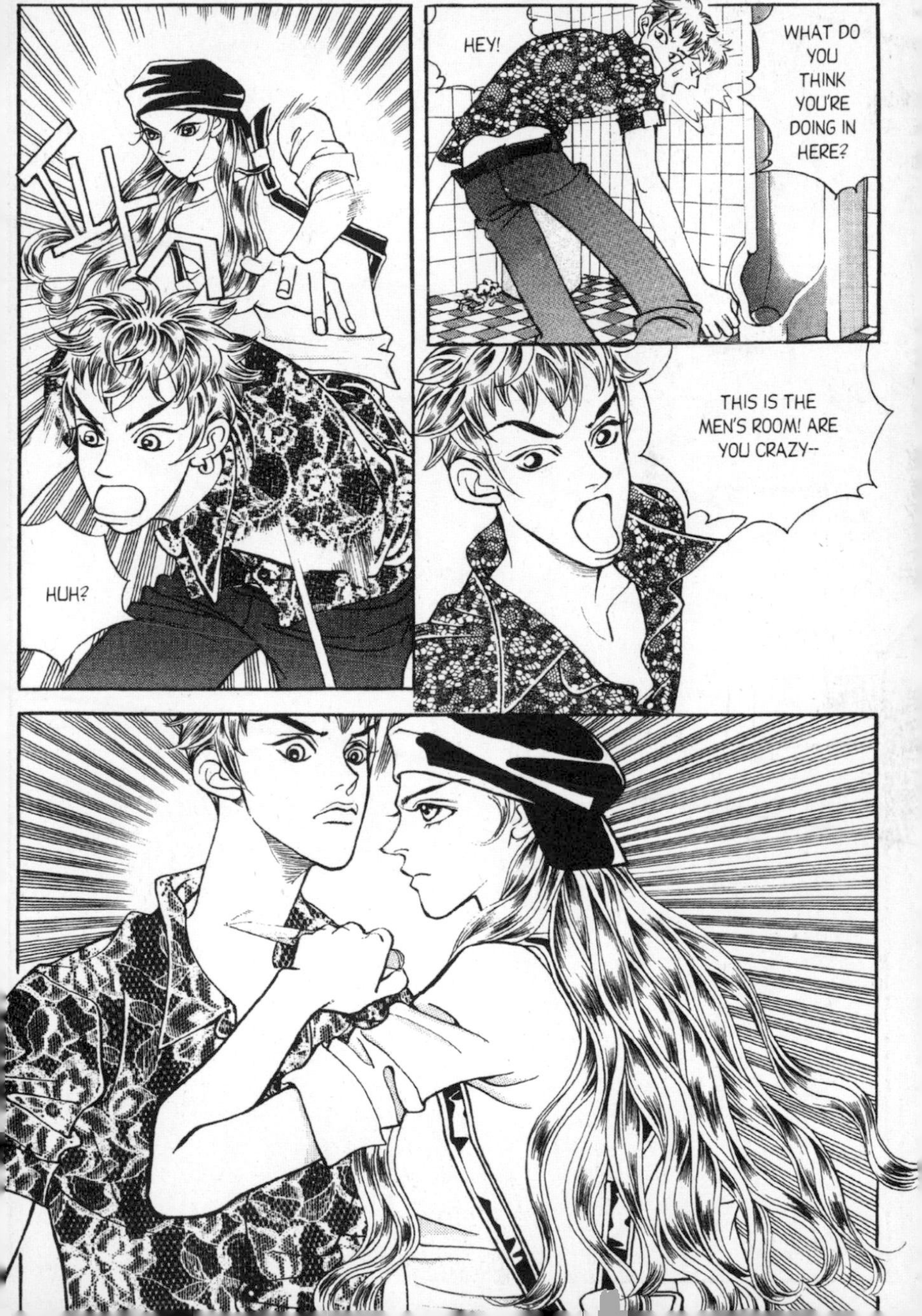
HUH?
HEY!
WHAT DO YOU THINK YOU'RE DOING IN HERE?
THIS IS THE MEN'S ROOM! ARE YOU CRAZY--

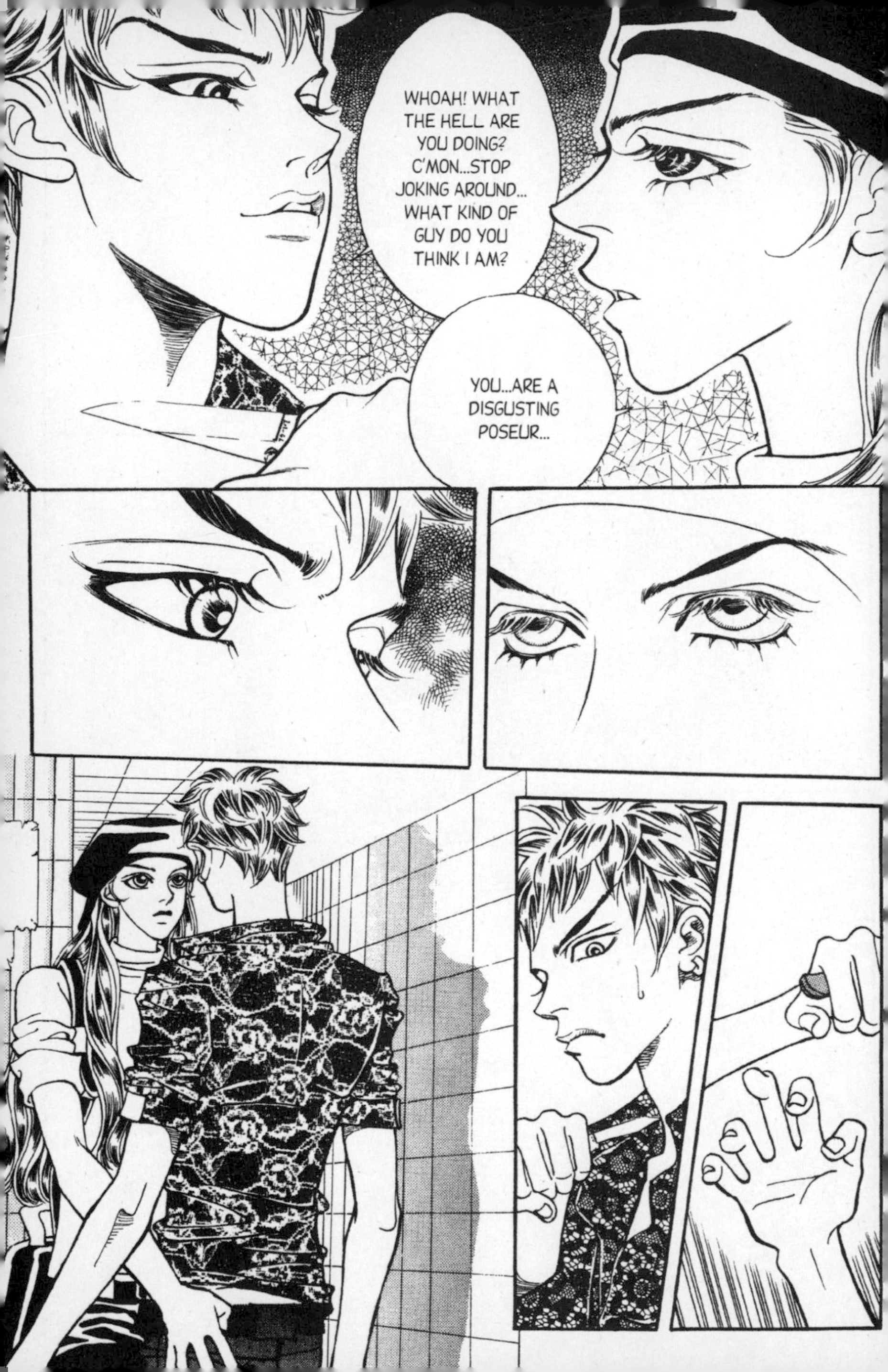
WHOAH! WHAT THE HELL ARE YOU DOING? C'MON...STOP JOKING AROUND... WHAT KIND OF GUY DO YOU THINK I AM?
YOU...ARE A DISGUSTING POSEUR...

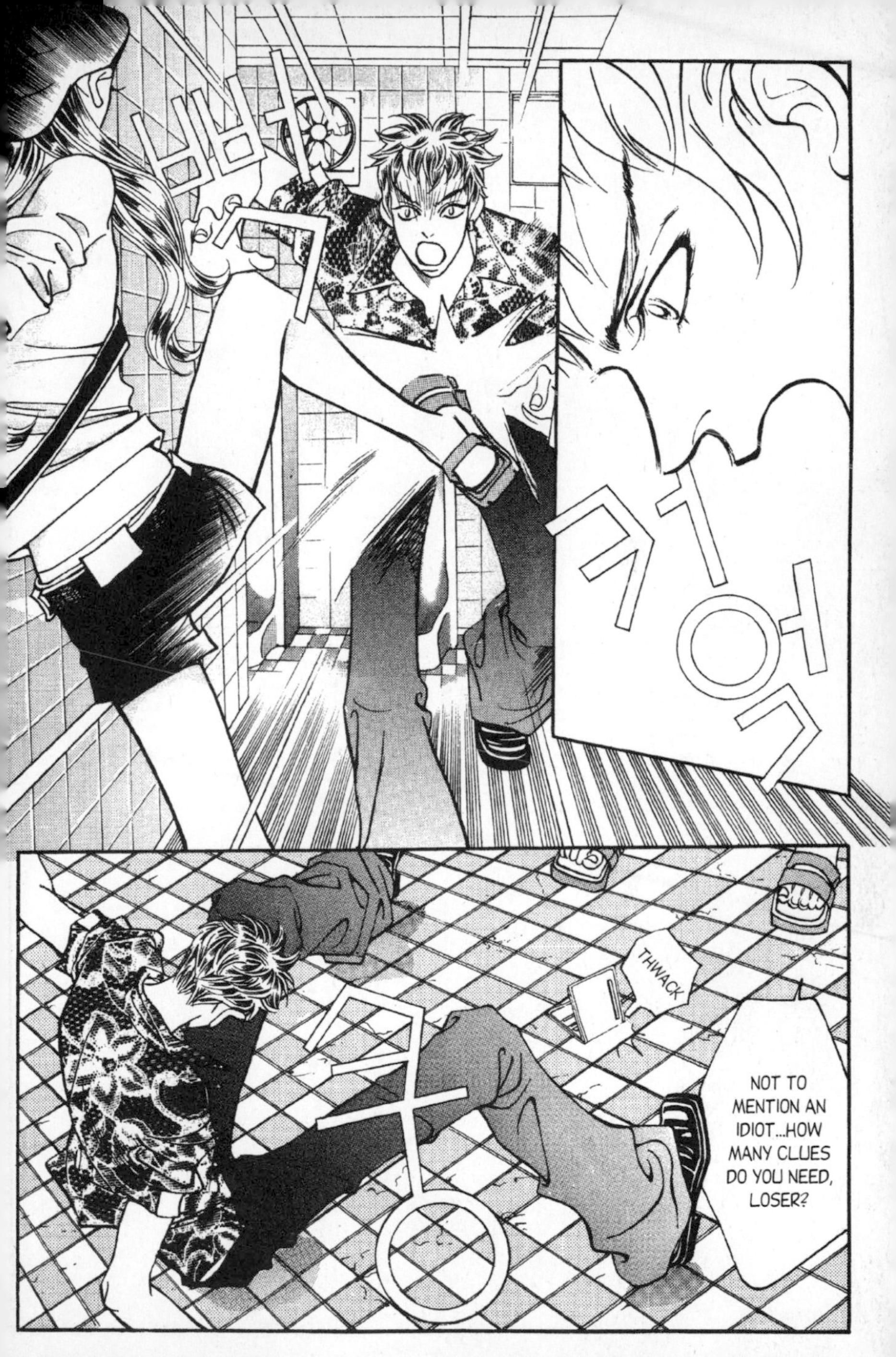
THWACK
NOT TO MENTION AN IDIOT...HOW MANY CLUES DO YOU NEED, LOSER?

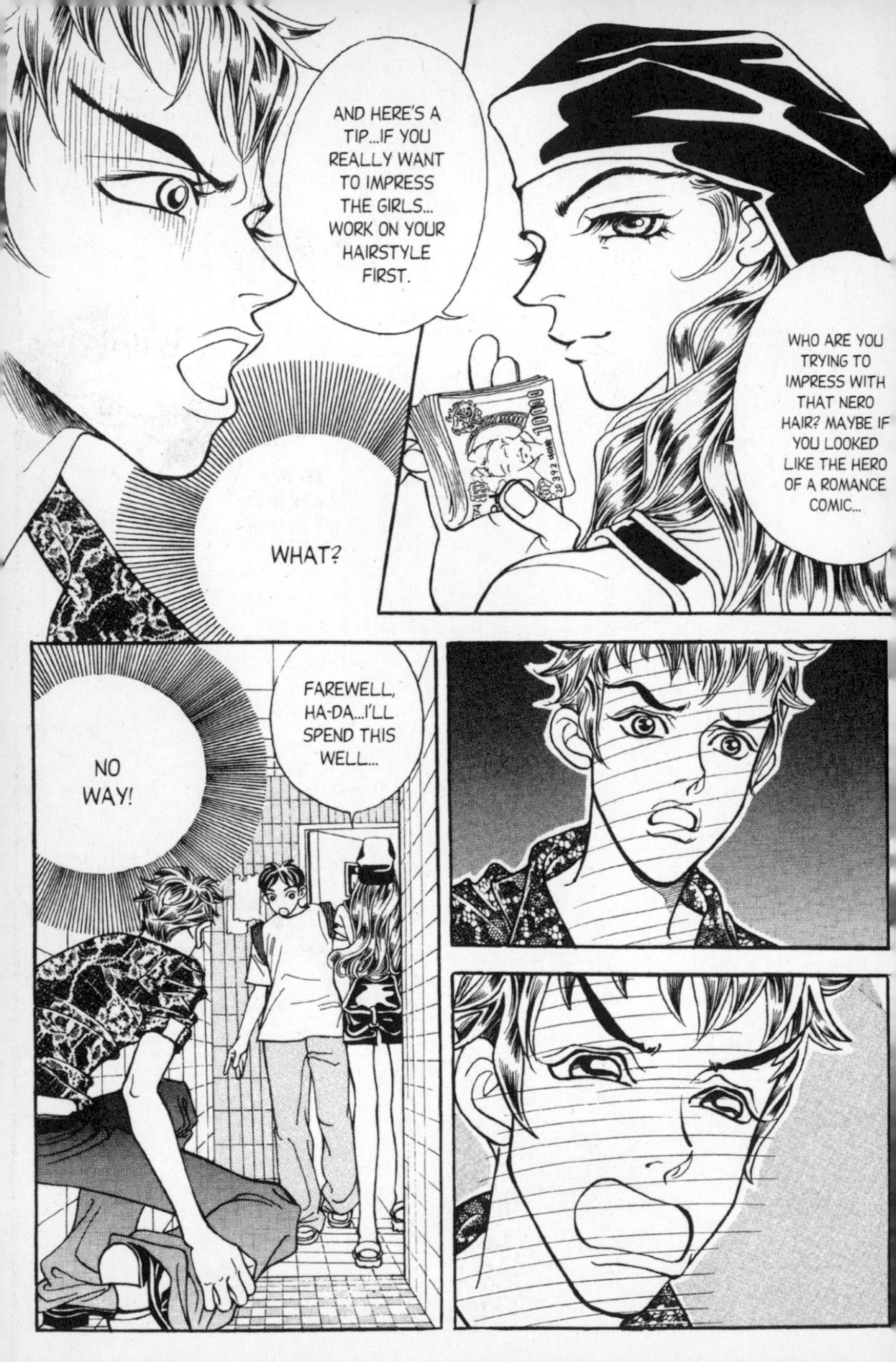
AND HERE'S A TIP...IF YOU REALLY WANT TO IMPRESS THE GIRLS... WORK ON YOUR HAIRSTYLE FIRST.
WHAT?
WHO ARE YOU TRYING TO IMPRESS WITH THAT NERO HAIR? MAYBE IF YOU LOOKED LIKE THE HERO OF A ROMANCE COMIC...
NO WAY!
FAREWELL, HA-DA...I'LL SPEND THIS WELL...

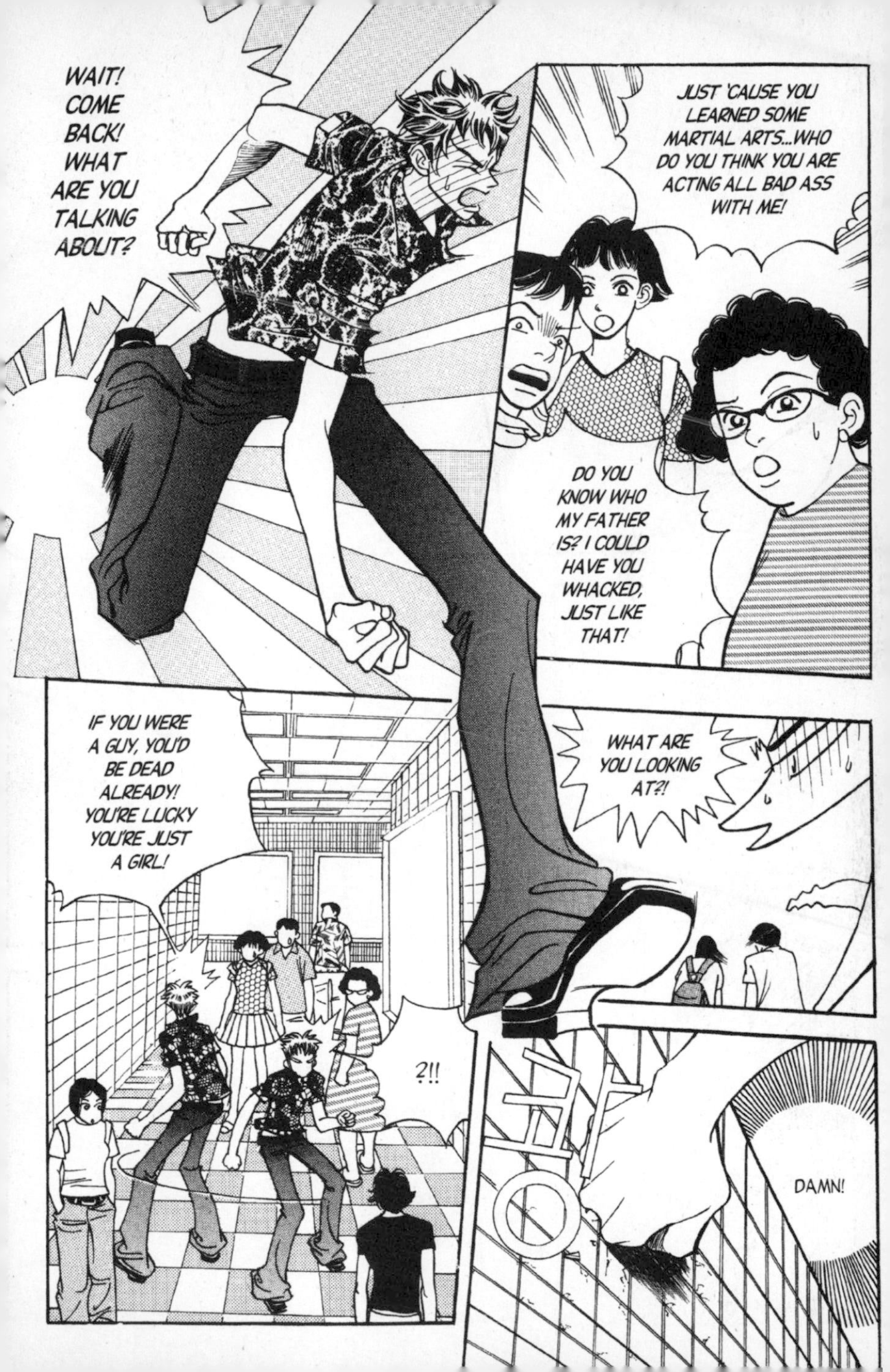
WAIT! COME BACK! WHAT ARE YOU TALKING ABOUT?
JUST 'CAUSE YOU LEARNED SOME MARTIAL ARTS...WHO DO YOU THINK YOU ARE ACTING ALL BAD ASS WITH ME!
DO YOU KNOW WHO MY FATHER IS? I COULD HAVE YOU WHACKED, JUST LIKE THAT!
IF YOU WERE A GUY, YOU'D BE DEAD ALREADY! YOU'RE LUCKY YOU'RE JUST A GIRL!
?!!
WHAT ARE YOU LOOKING AT?!
DAMN!

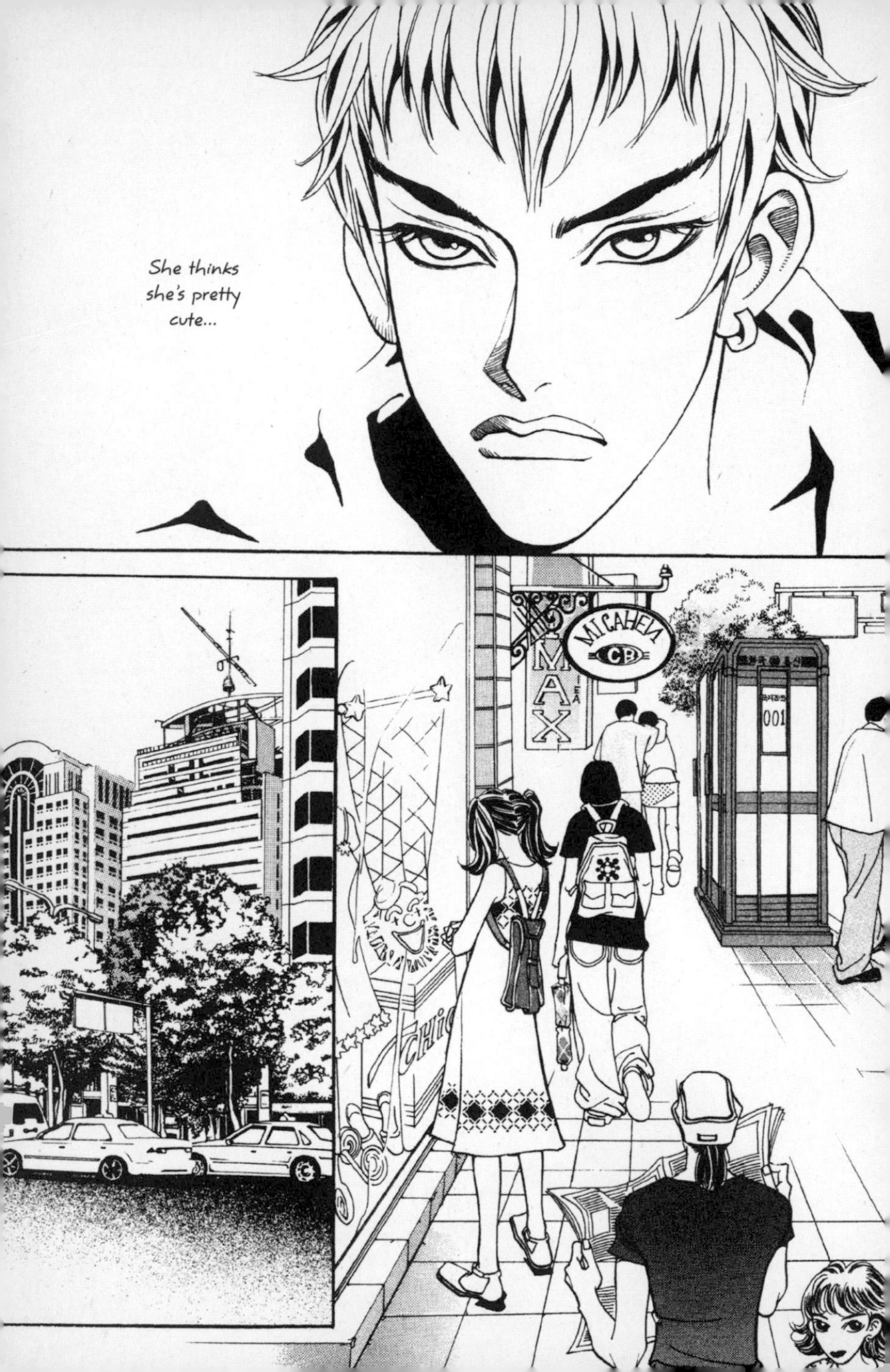
She thinks she's pretty cute...
MAX
001

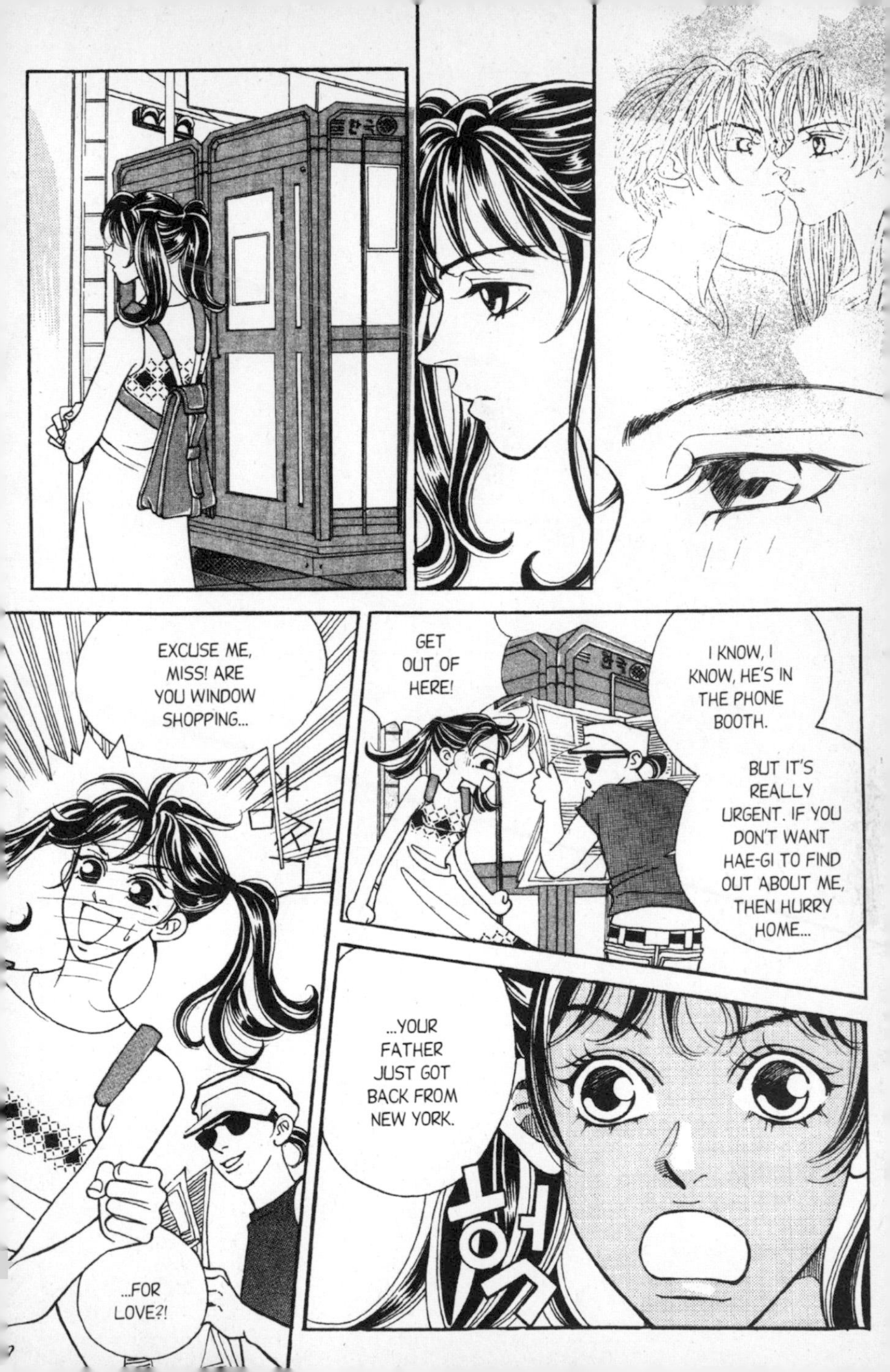
EXCUSE ME, MISS! ARE YOU WINDOW SHOPPING...
...FOR LOVE?!
GET OUT OF HERE!
I KNOW, I KNOW, HE'S IN THE PHONE BOOTH.
BUT IT'S REALLY URGENT. IF YOU DON'T WANT HAE-GI TO FIND OUT ABOUT ME, THEN HURRY HOME...
...YOUR FATHER JUST GOT BACK FROM NEW YORK.

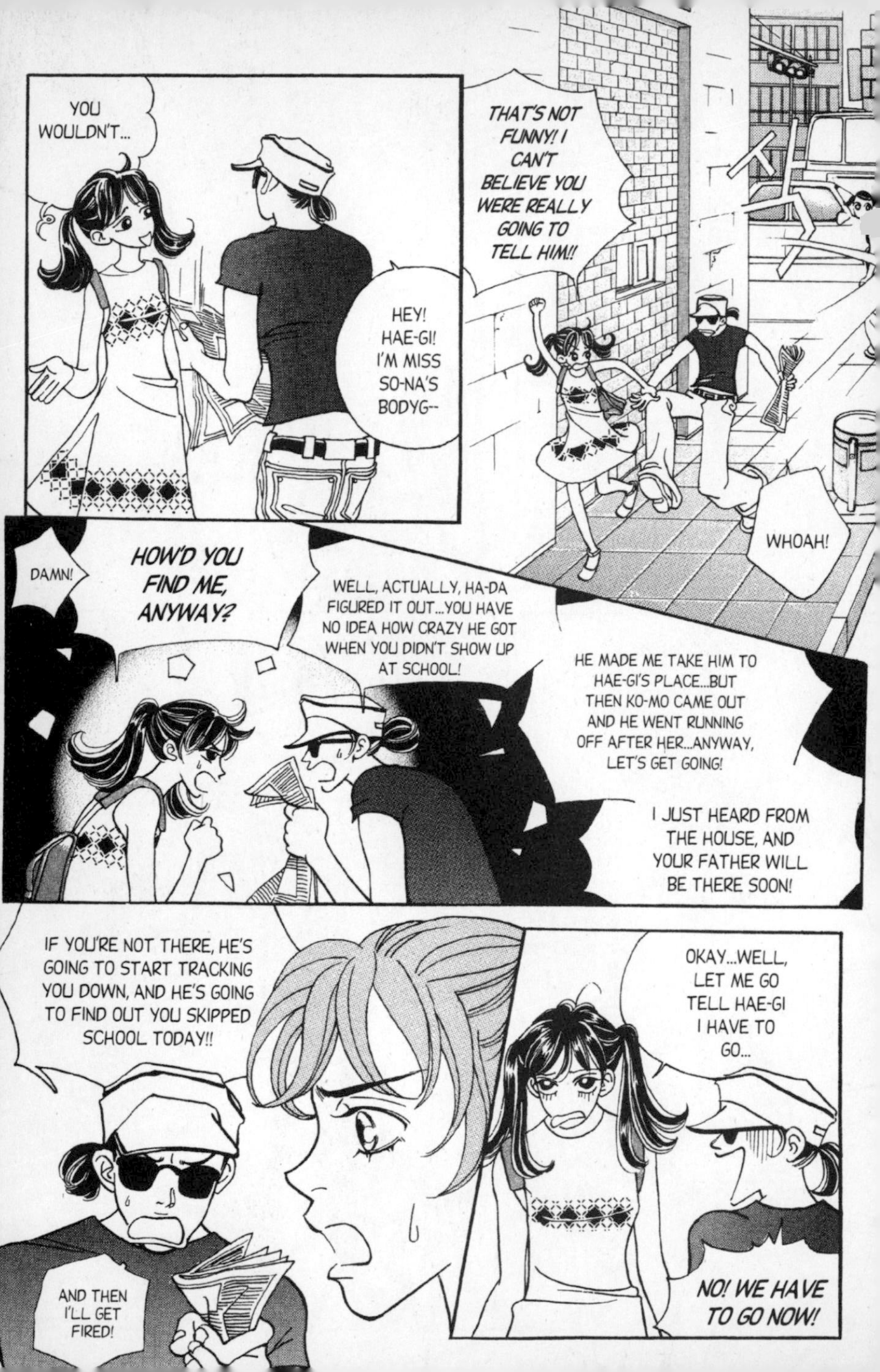
YOU WOULDN'T...
HEY! HAE-GI! I'M MISS SO-NA'S BODYG--
THAT'S NOT FUNNY! I CAN'T BELIEVE YOU WERE REALLY GOING TO TELL HIM!!
WHOAH!
DAMN!
HOW'D YOU FIND ME, ANYWAY?
WELL, ACTUALLY, HA-DA FIGURED IT OUT...YOU HAVE NO IDEA HOW CRAZY HE GOT WHEN YOU DIDN'T SHOW UP AT SCHOOL!
HE MADE ME TAKE HIM TO HAE-GI'S PLACE...BUT THEN KO-MO CAME OUT AND HE WENT RUNNING OFF AFTER HER...ANYWAY, LET'S GET GOING!
I JUST HEARD FROM THE HOUSE, AND YOUR FATHER WILL BE THERE SOON!
IF YOU'RE NOT THERE, HE'S GOING TO START TRACKING YOU DOWN, AND HE'S GOING TO FIND OUT YOU SKIPPED SCHOOL TODAY!!
AND THEN I'LL GET FIRED!
OKAY...WELL, LET ME GO TELL HAE-GI I HAVE TO GO...
NO! WE HAVE TO GO NOW!

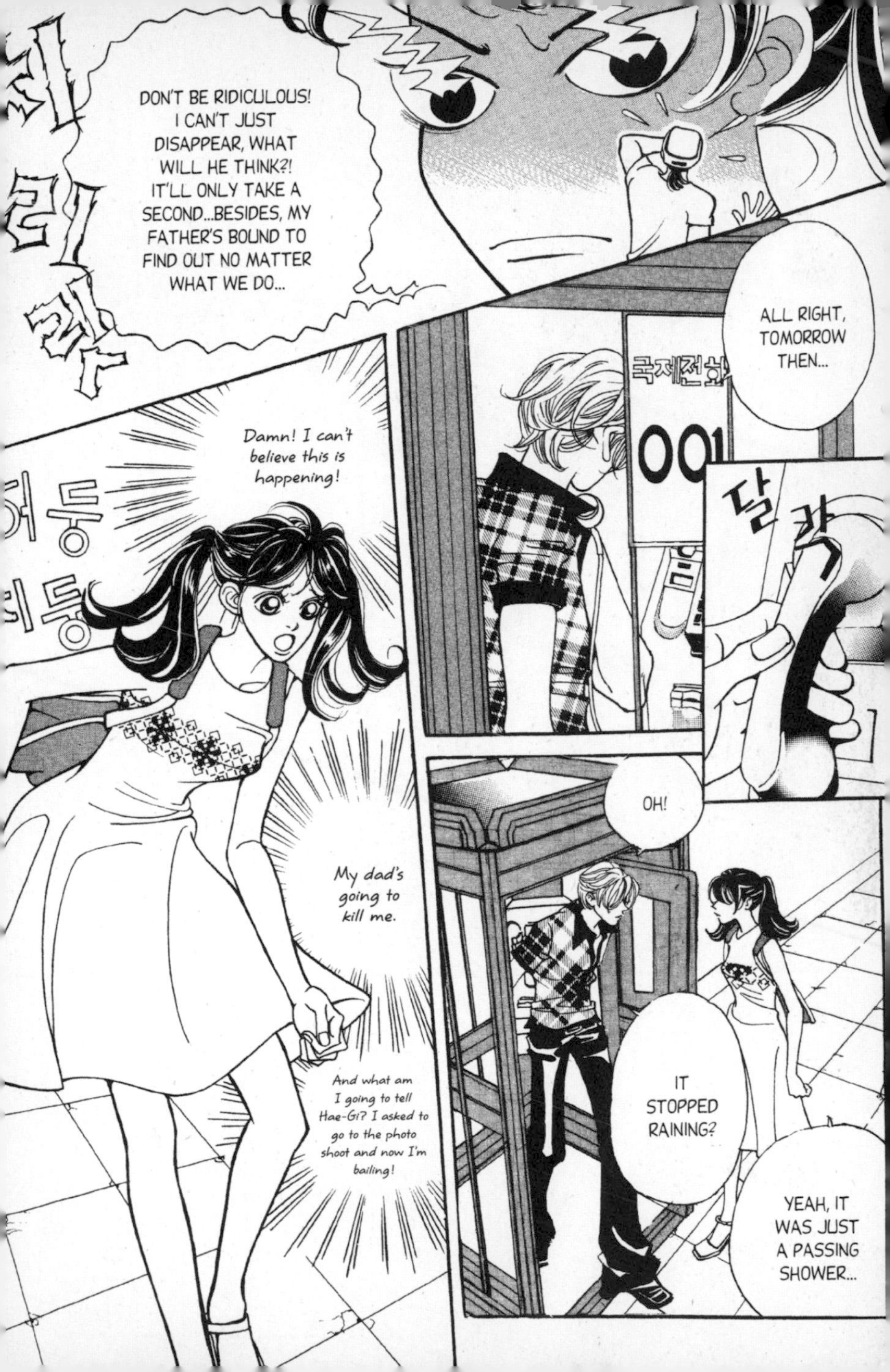
DON'T BE RIDICULOUS! I CAN'T JUST DISAPPEAR, WHAT WILL HE THINK?! IT'LL ONLY TAKE A SECOND...BESIDES, MY FATHER'S BOUND TO FIND OUT NO MATTER WHAT WE DO...
Damn! I can't believe this is happening!
My dad's going to kill me.
And what am I going to tell Hae-Gi? I asked to go to the photo shoot and now I'm bailing!
ALL RIGHT, TOMORROW THEN...
국제전화
001
달칵
OH!
IT STOPPED RAINING?
YEAH, IT WAS JUST A PASSING SHOWER...

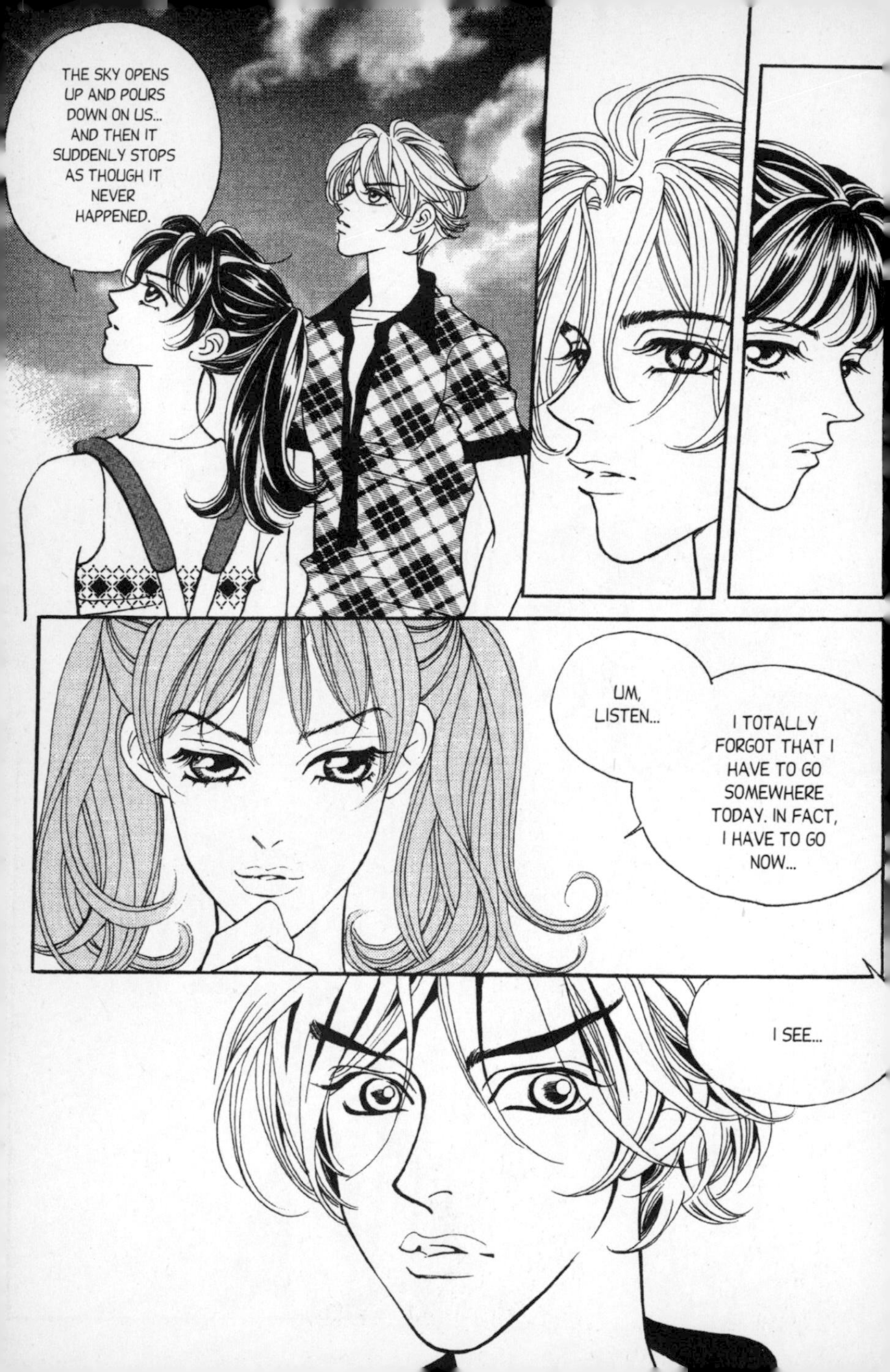
THE SKY OPENS UP AND POURS DOWN ON US... AND THEN IT SUDDENLY STOPS AS THOUGH IT NEVER HAPPENED.
UM, LISTEN...
I TOTALLY FORGOT THAT I HAVE TO GO SOMEWHERE TODAY. IN FACT, I HAVE TO GO NOW...
I SEE...

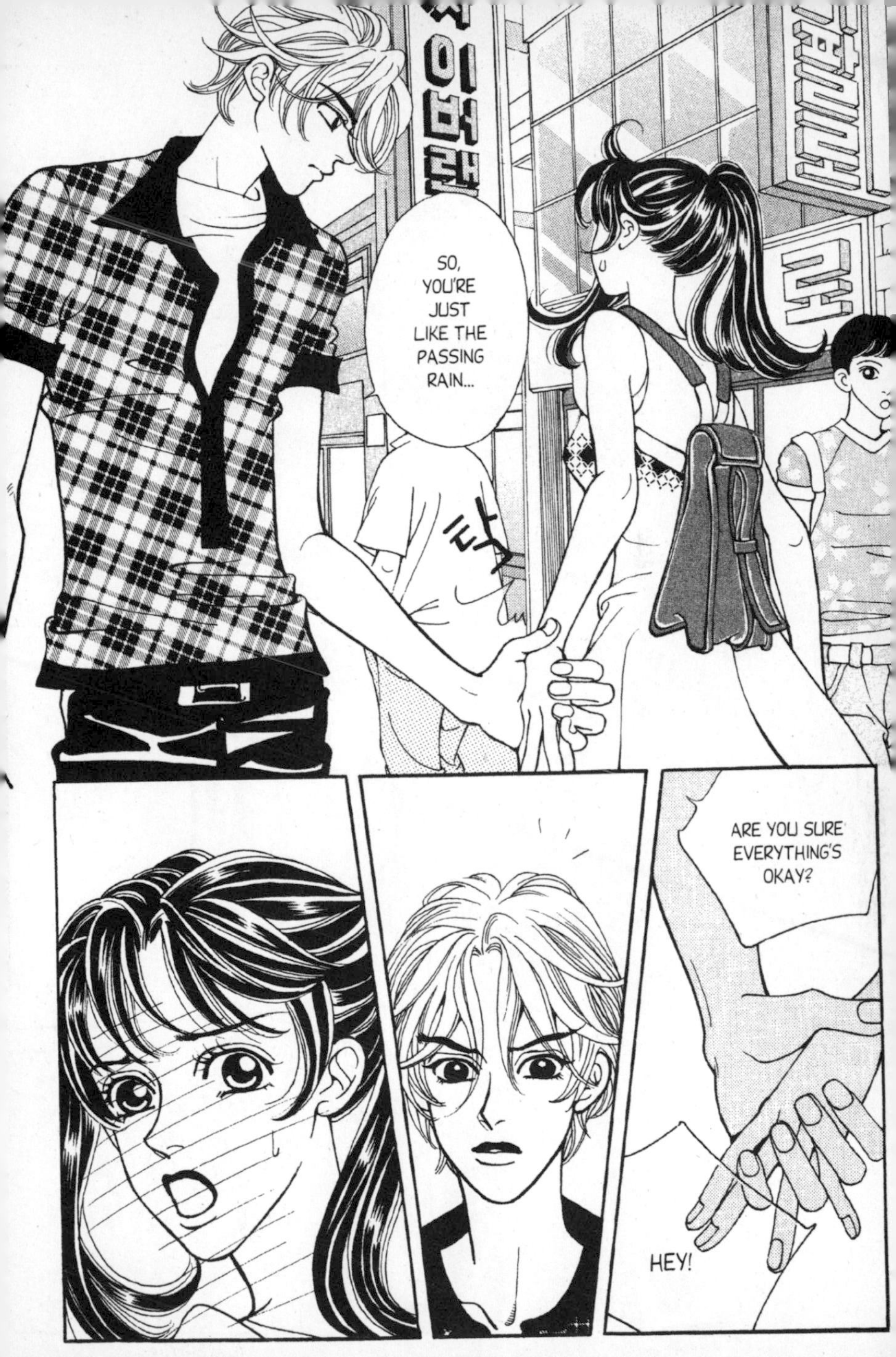
SO, YOU'RE JUST LIKE THE PASSING RAIN...
ARE YOU SURE EVERYTHING'S OKAY?
HEY!

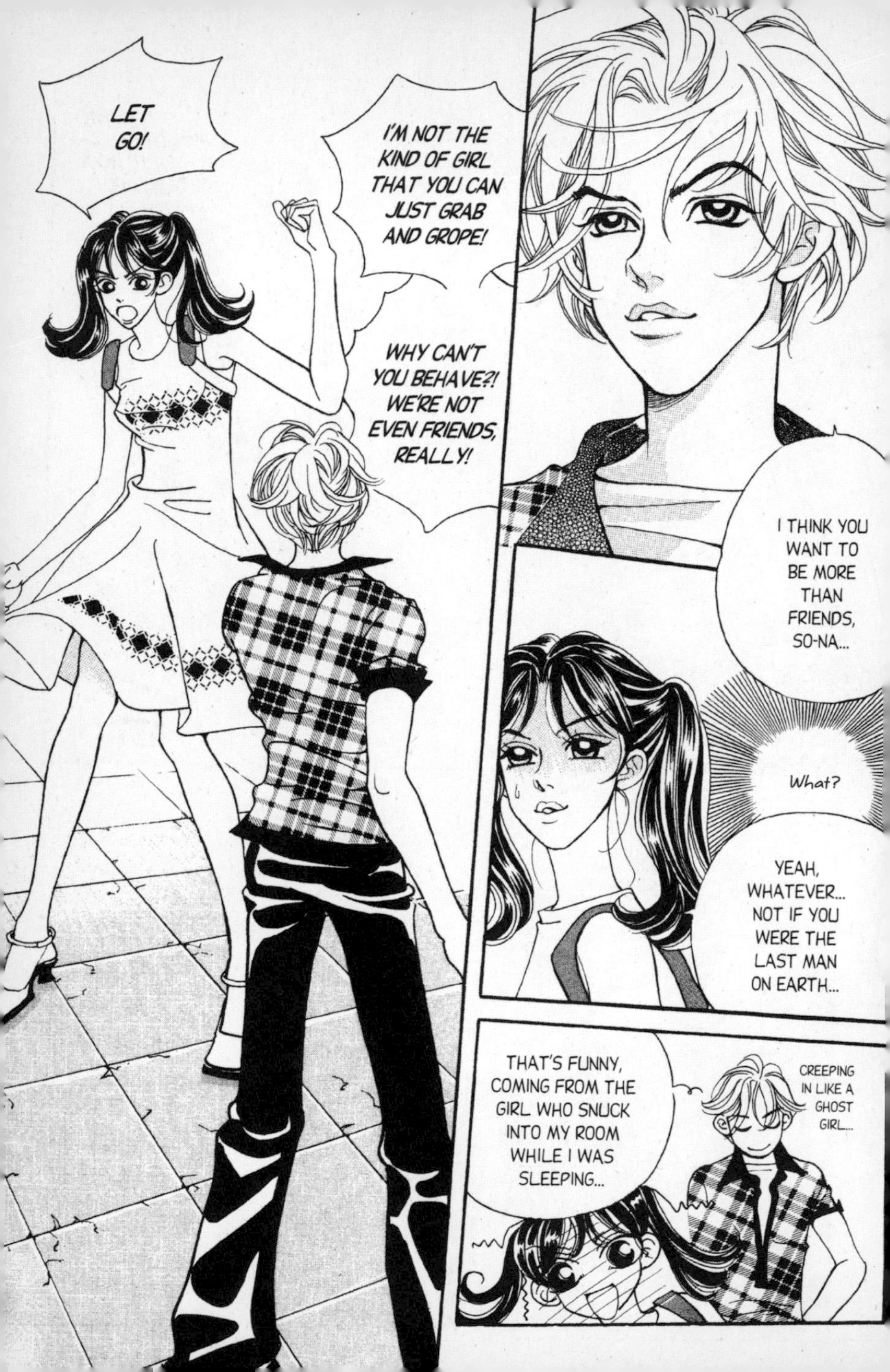
LET GO!
I'M NOT THE KIND OF GIRL THAT YOU CAN JUST GRAB AND GROPE!
WHY CAN'T YOU BEHAVE?! WE'RE NOT EVEN FRIENDS, REALLY!
I THINK YOU WANT TO BE MORE THAN FRIENDS, SO-NA...
What?
YEAH, WHATEVER... NOT IF YOU WERE THE LAST MAN ON EARTH...
THAT'S FUNNY, COMING FROM THE GIRL WHO SNUCK INTO MY ROOM WHILE I WAS SLEEPING...
CREEPING IN LIKE A GHOST GIRL...

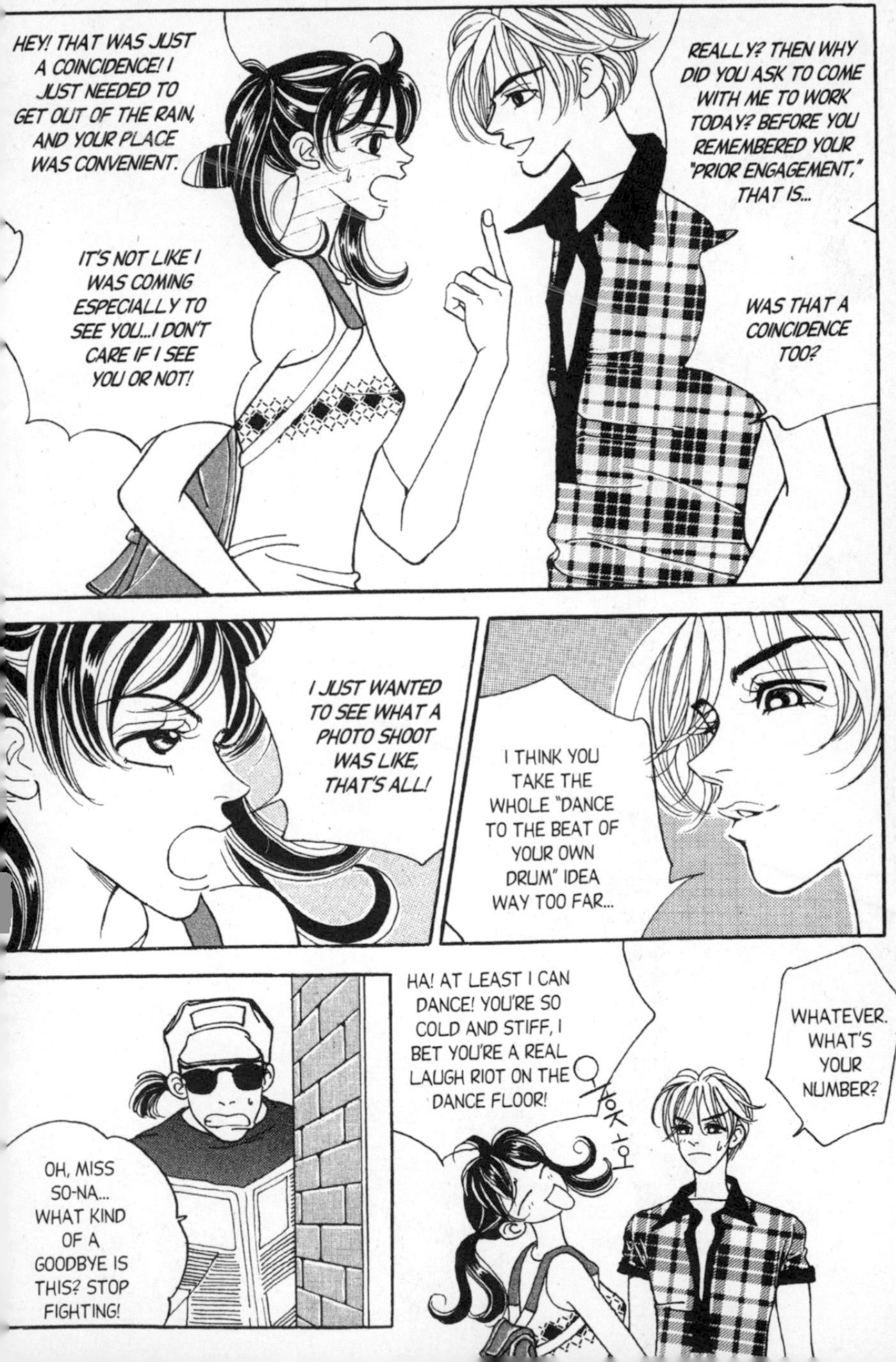
HEY! THAT WAS JUST A COINCIDENCE! I JUST NEEDED TO GET OUT OF THE RAIN, AND YOUR PLACE WAS CONVENIENT.
IT'S NOT LIKE I WAS COMING ESPECIALLY TO SEE YOU...I DON'T CARE IF I SEE YOU OR NOT!
REALLY? THEN WHY DID YOU ASK TO COME WITH ME TO WORK TODAY? BEFORE YOU REMEMBERED YOUR "PRIOR ENGAGEMENT," THAT IS...
WAS THAT A COINCIDENCE TOO?
I JUST WANTED TO SEE WHAT A PHOTO SHOOT WAS LIKE, THAT'S ALL!
I THINK YOU TAKE THE WHOLE "DANCE TO THE BEAT OF YOUR OWN DRUM" IDEA WAY TOO FAR...
OH, MISS SO-NA... WHAT KIND OF A GOODBYE IS THIS? STOP FIGHTING!
HA! AT LEAST I CAN DANCE! YOU'RE SO COLD AND STIFF, I BET YOU'RE A REAL LAUGH RIOT ON THE DANCE FLOOR!
WHATEVER. WHAT'S YOUR NUMBER?

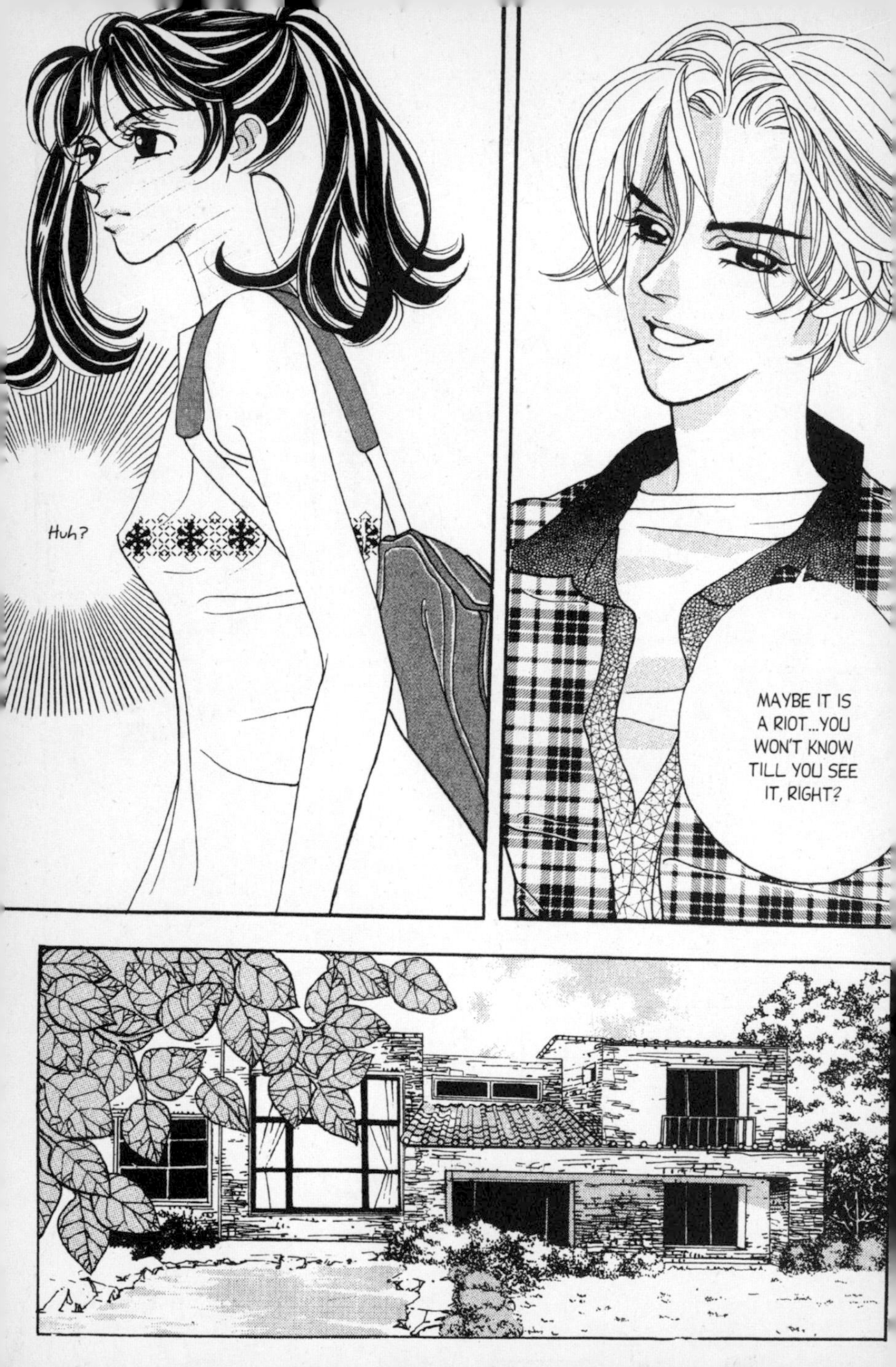
Huh?
MAYBE IT IS A RIOT...YOU WON'T KNOW TILL YOU SEE IT, RIGHT?

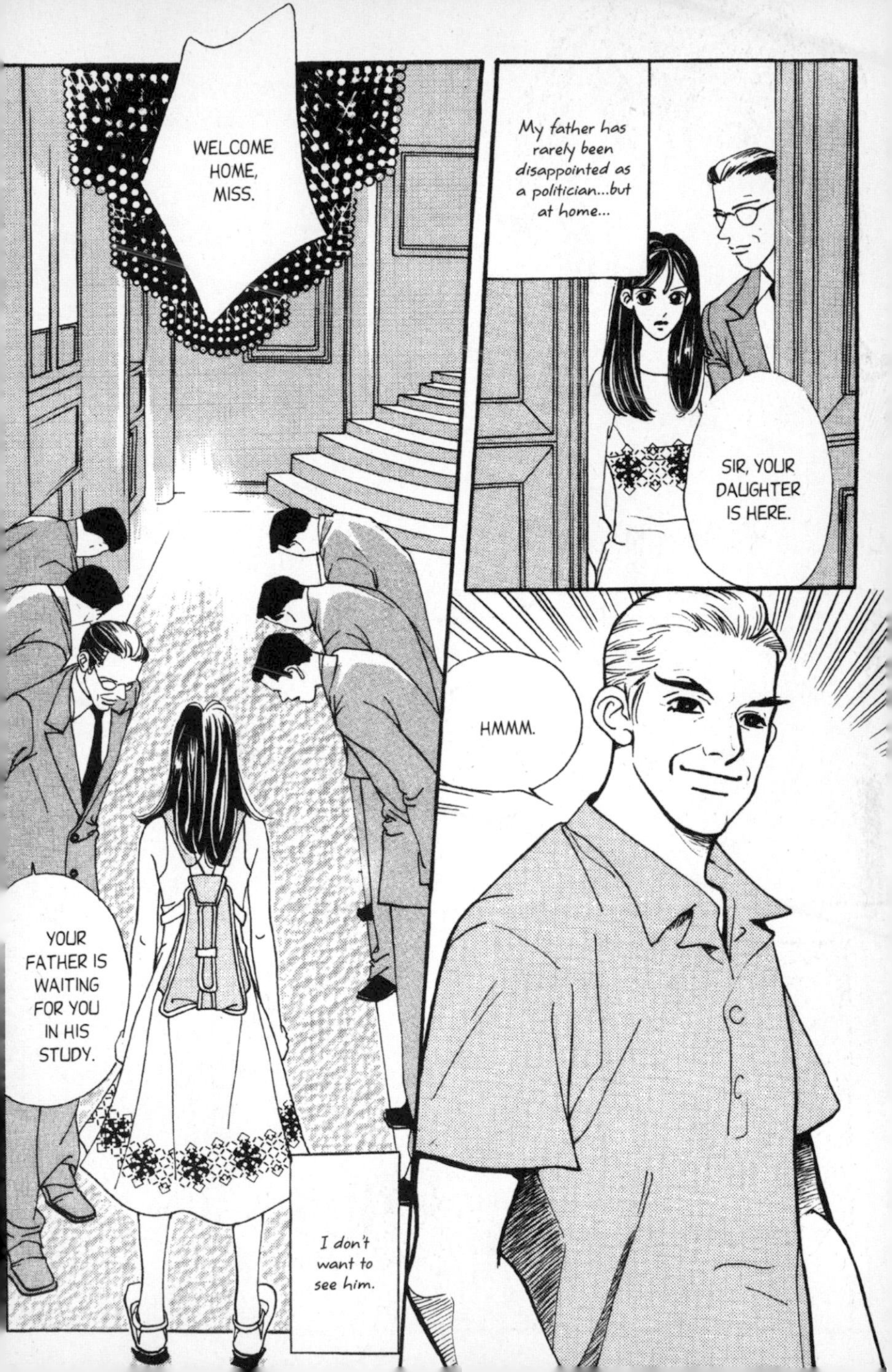
WELCOME HOME, MISS.
YOUR FATHER IS WAITING FOR YOU IN HIS STUDY.
I don't want to see him.
My father has rarely been disappointed as a politician...but at home...
SIR, YOUR DAUGHTER IS HERE.
HMMM.

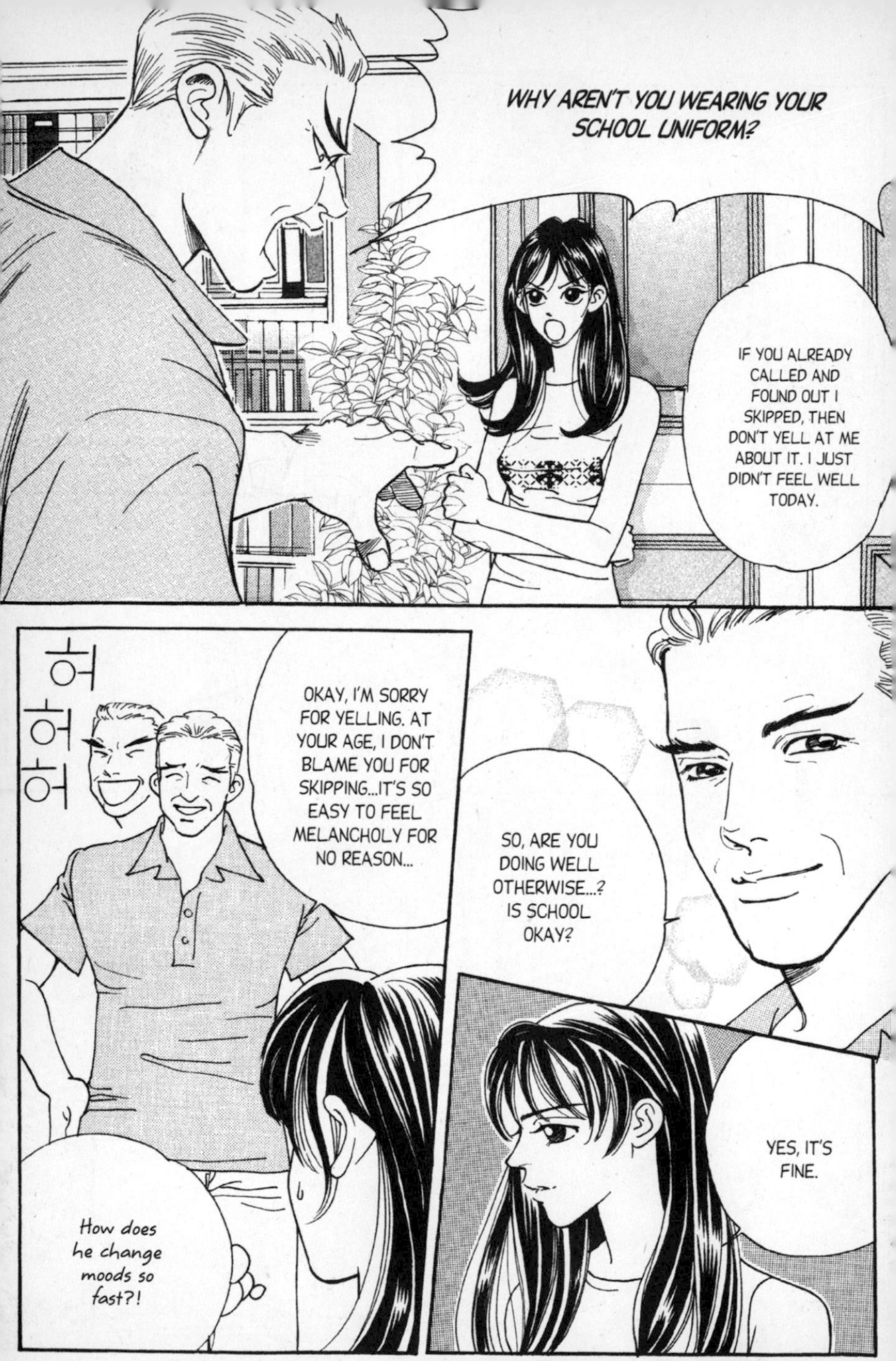
WHY AREN'T YOU WEARING YOUR SCHOOL UNIFORM?
IF YOU ALREADY CALLED AND FOUND OUT I SKIPPED, THEN DON'T YELL AT ME ABOUT IT. I JUST DIDN'T FEEL WELL TODAY.
허허허
OKAY, I'M SORRY FOR YELLING. AT YOUR AGE, I DON'T BLAME YOU FOR SKIPPING...IT'S SO EASY TO FEEL MELANCHOLY FOR NO REASON...
How does he change moods so fast?!
SO, ARE YOU DOING WELL OTHERWISE...? IS SCHOOL OKAY?
YES, IT'S FINE.

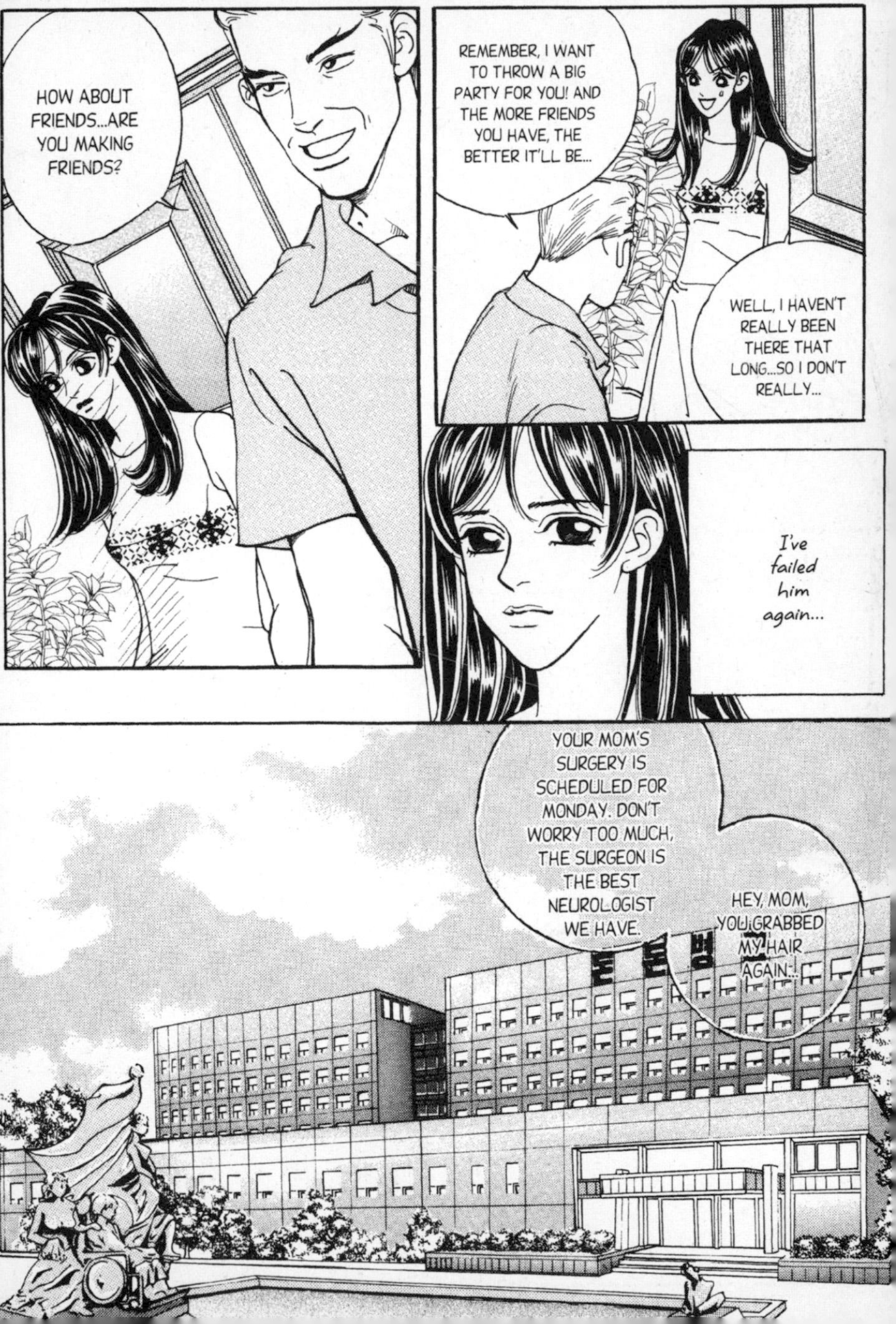
HOW ABOUT FRIENDS...ARE YOU MAKING FRIENDS?
REMEMBER, I WANT TO THROW A BIG PARTY FOR YOU! AND THE MORE FRIENDS YOU HAVE, THE BETTER IT'LL BE...
WELL, I HAVEN'T REALLY BEEN THERE THAT LONG...SO I DON'T REALLY...
I've failed him again...
YOUR MOM'S SURGERY IS SCHEDULED FOR MONDAY. DON'T WORRY TOO MUCH, THE SURGEON IS THE BEST NEUROLOGIST WE HAVE.
HEY, MOM, YOU GRABBED MY HAIR AGAIN...!

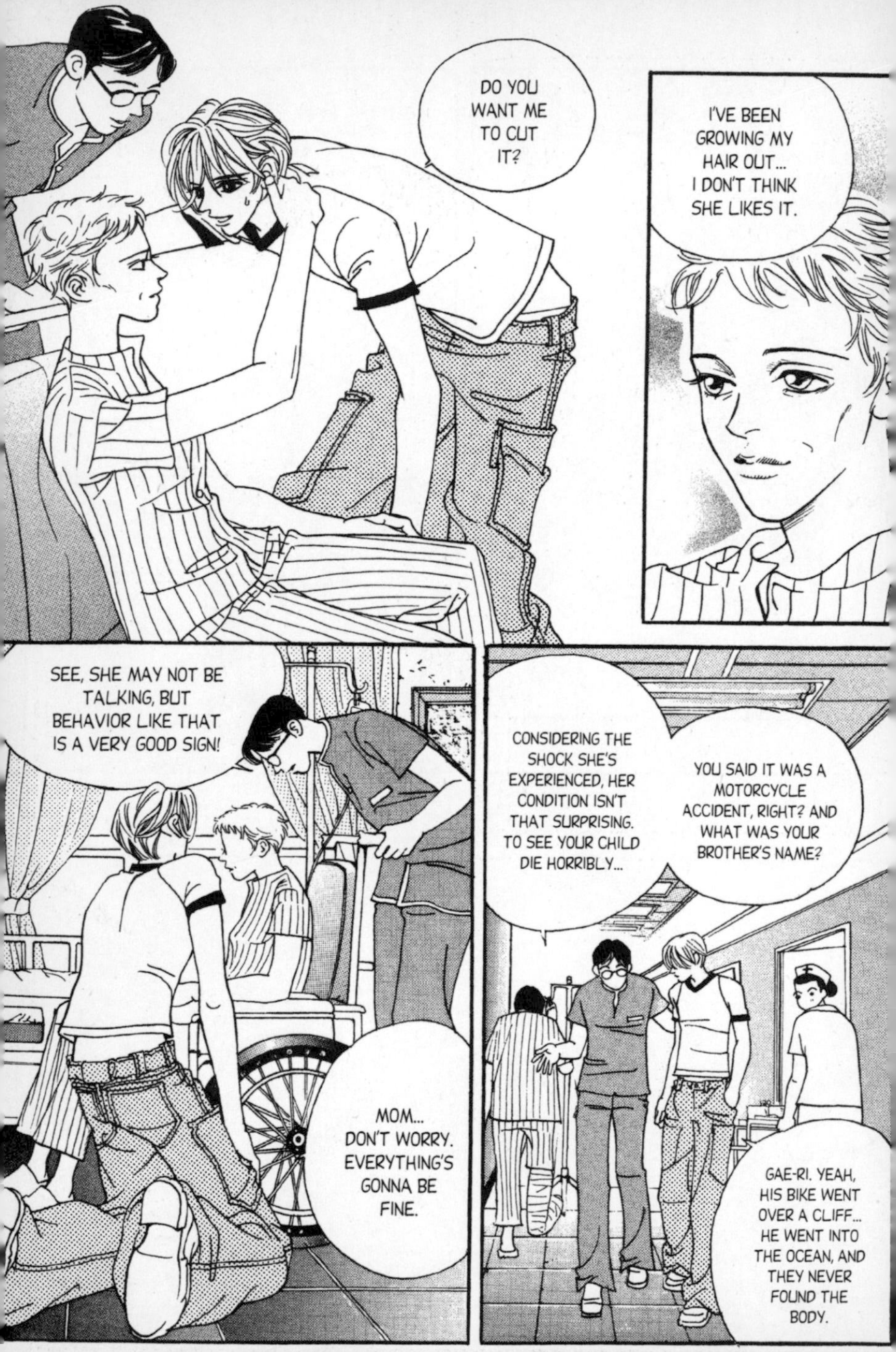
DO YOU WANT ME TO CUT IT?
I'VE BEEN GROWING MY HAIR OUT... I DON'T THINK SHE LIKES IT.
SEE, SHE MAY NOT BE TALKING, BUT BEHAVIOR LIKE THAT IS A VERY GOOD SIGN!
MOM... DON'T WORRY. EVERYTHING'S GONNA BE FINE.
CONSIDERING THE SHOCK SHE'S EXPERIENCED, HER CONDITION ISN'T THAT SURPRISING. TO SEE YOUR CHILD DIE HORRIBLY...
YOU SAID IT WAS A MOTORCYCLE ACCIDENT, RIGHT? AND WHAT WAS YOUR BROTHER'S NAME?
GAE-RI. YEAH, HIS BIKE WENT OVER A CLIFF... HE WENT INTO THE OCEAN, AND THEY NEVER FOUND THE BODY.

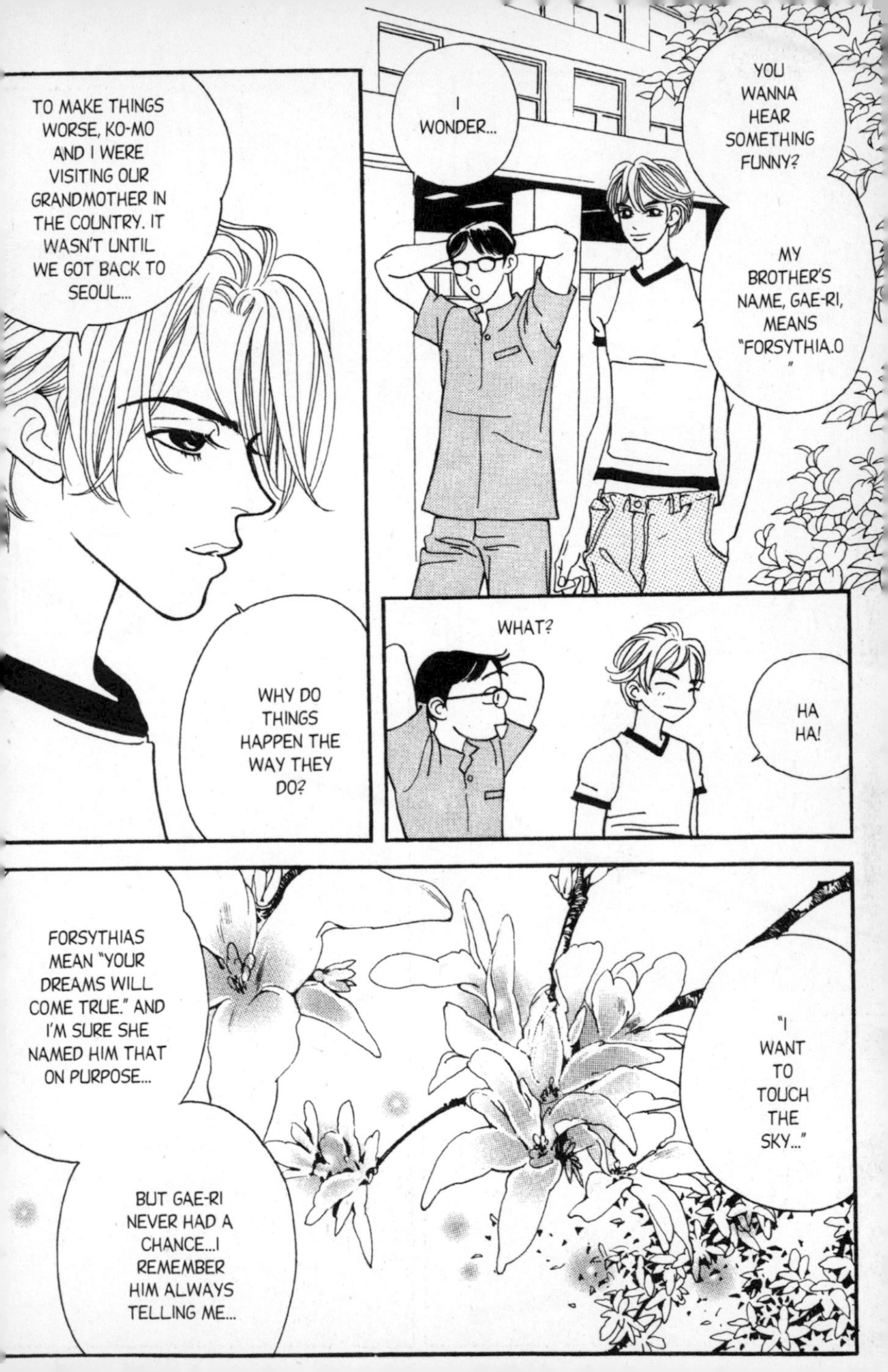
TO MAKE THINGS WORSE, KO-MO AND I WERE VISITING OUR GRANDMOTHER IN THE COUNTRY. IT WASN'T UNTIL WE GOT BACK TO SEOUL...
WHY DO THINGS HAPPEN THE WAY THEY DO?
I WONDER...
YOU WANNA HEAR SOMETHING FUNNY?
MY BROTHER'S NAME, GAE-RI, MEANS "FORSYTHIA.0 "
WHAT?
HA HA!
FORSYTHIAS MEAN "YOUR DREAMS WILL COME TRUE." AND I'M SURE SHE NAMED HIM THAT ON PURPOSE...
BUT GAE-RI NEVER HAD A CHANCE...I REMEMBER HIM ALWAYS TELLING ME...
"I WANT TO TOUCH THE SKY..."

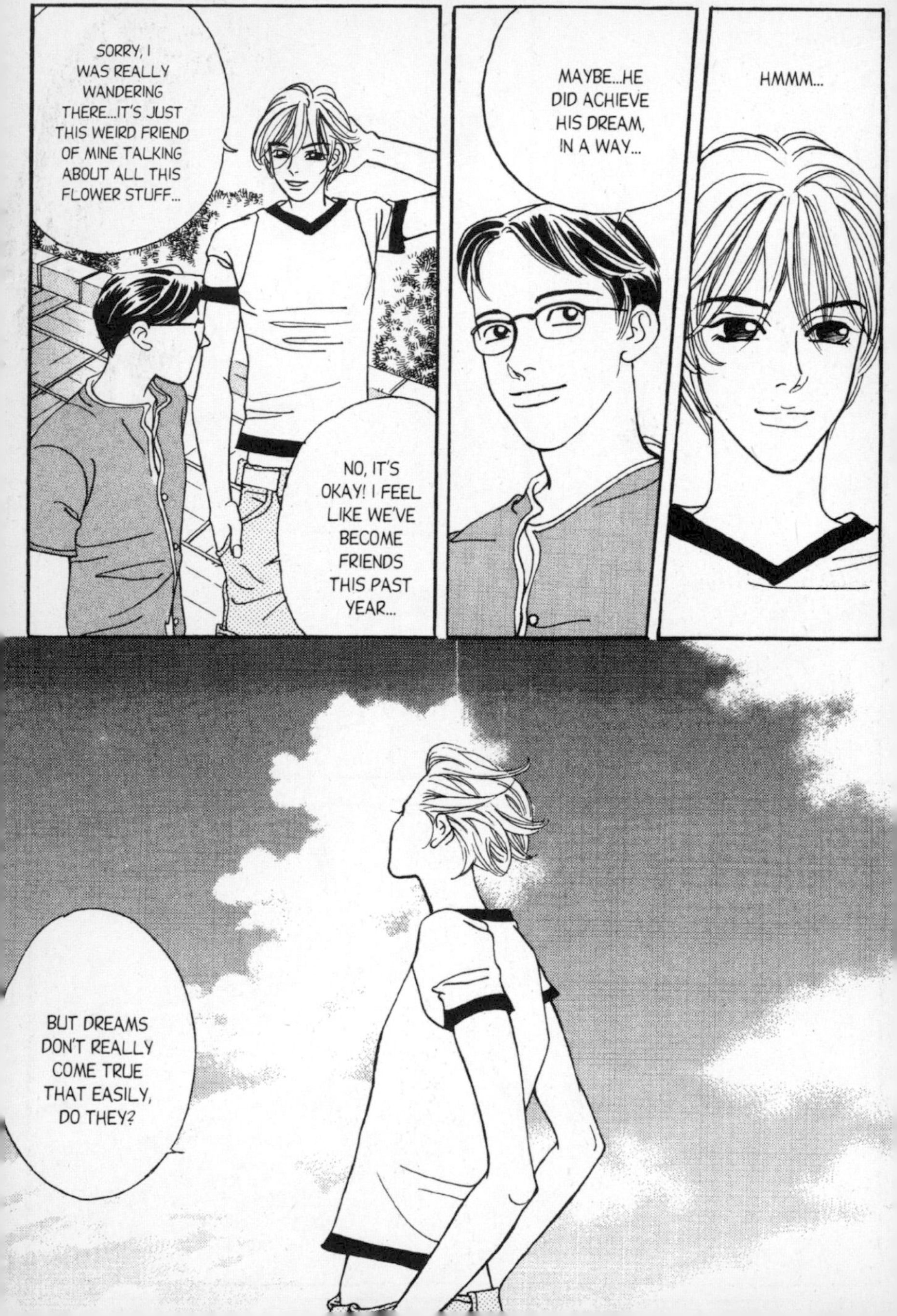
SORRY, I WAS REALLY WANDERING THERE...IT'S JUST THIS WEIRD FRIEND OF MINE TALKING ABOUT ALL THIS FLOWER STUFF...
NO, IT'S OKAY! I FEEL LIKE WE'VE BECOME FRIENDS THIS PAST YEAR...
MAYBE...HE DID ACHIEVE HIS DREAM, IN A WAY...
HMMM...
BUT DREAMS DON'T REALLY COME TRUE THAT EASILY, DO THEY?

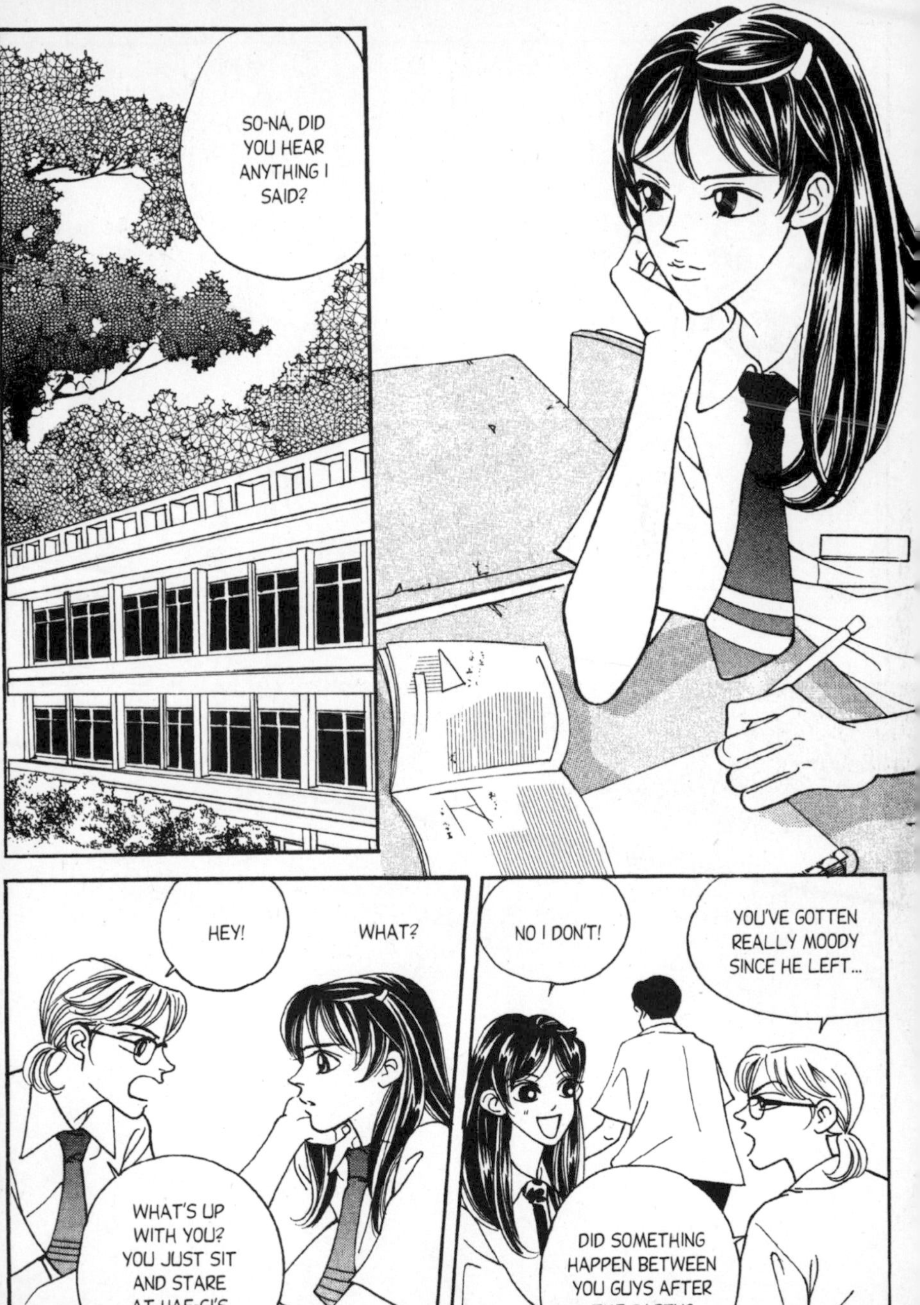
SO-NA, DID YOU HEAR ANYTHING I SAID?
HEY!
WHAT?
WHAT'S UP WITH YOU? YOU JUST SIT AND STARE AT HAE-GI'S SEAT...
NO I DON'T!
YOU'VE GOTTEN REALLY MOODY SINCE HE LEFT...
DID SOMETHING HAPPEN BETWEEN YOU GUYS AFTER THE PARTY?

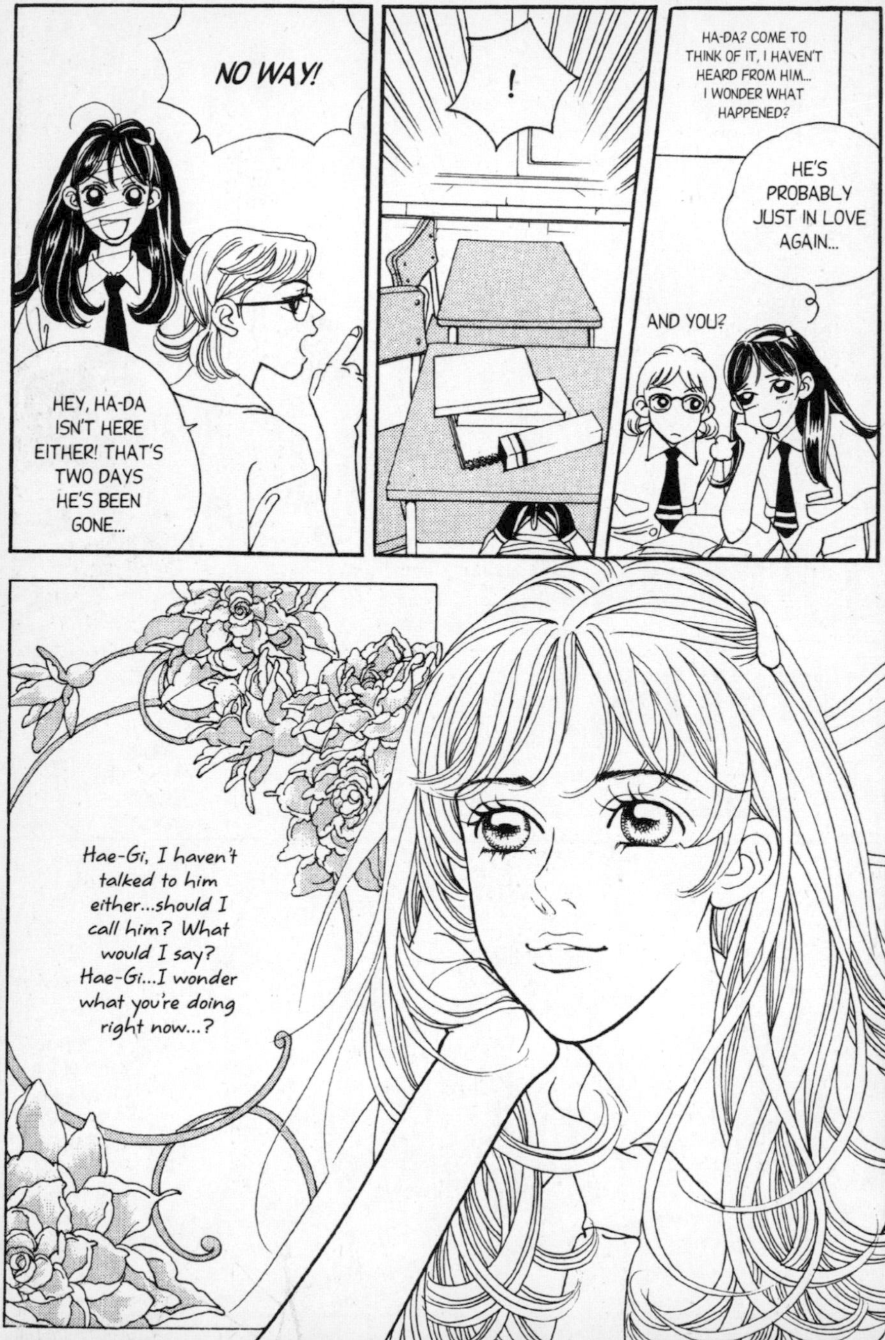
NO WAY!
HEY, HA-DA ISN'T HERE EITHER! THAT'S TWO DAYS HE'S BEEN GONE...
!
HA-DA? COME TO THINK OF IT, I HAVEN'T HEARD FROM HIM... I WONDER WHAT HAPPENED?
HE'S PROBABLY JUST IN LOVE AGAIN...
AND YOU?
Hae-Gi, I haven't talked to him either...should I call him? What would I say? Hae-Gi...I wonder what you're doing right now...?

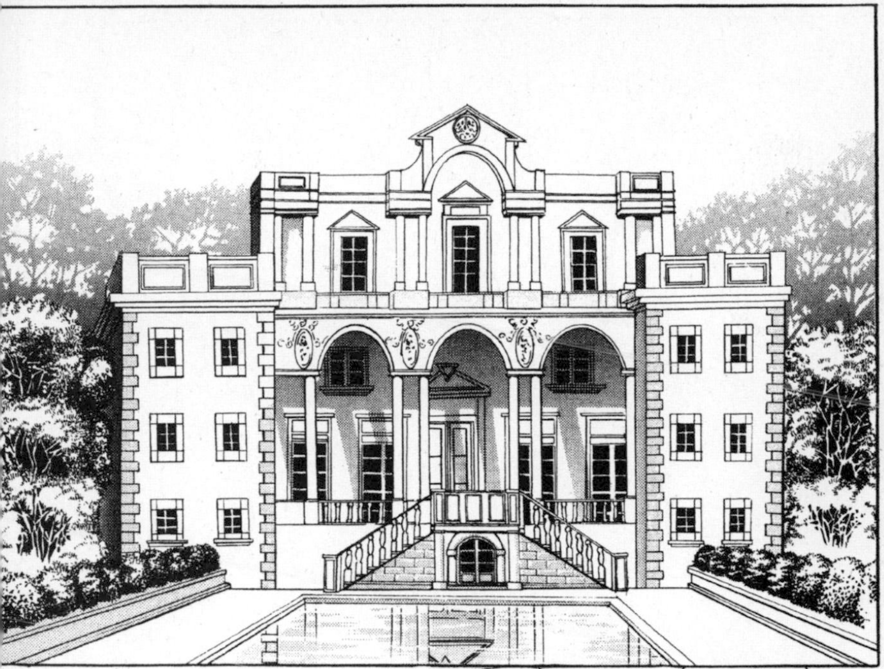

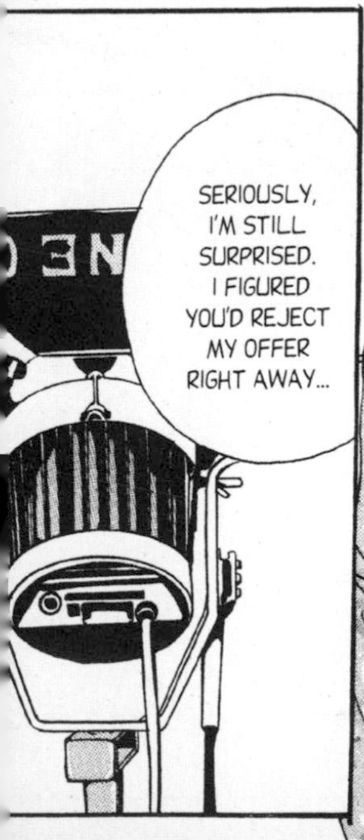
SERIOUSLY, I'M STILL SURPRISED. I FIGURED YOU'D REJECT MY OFFER RIGHT AWAY...

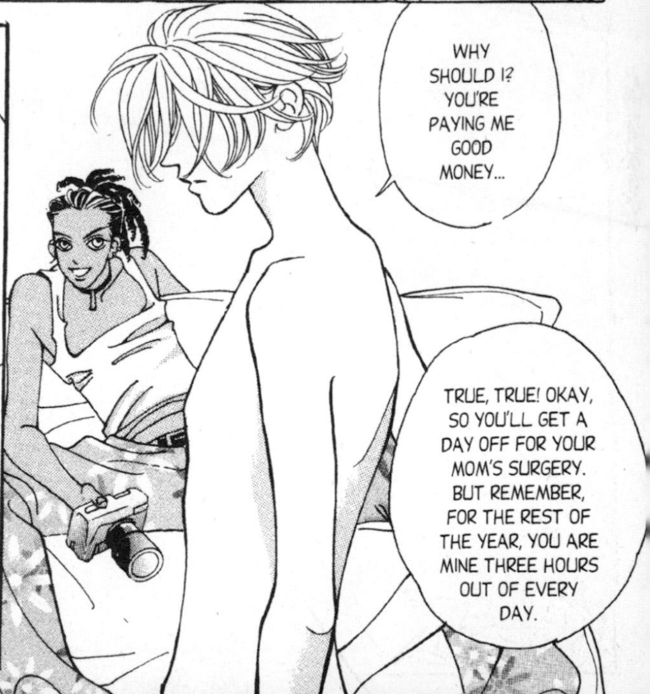
WHY SHOULD I? YOU'RE PAYING ME GOOD MONEY...
TRUE, TRUE! OKAY, SO YOU'LL GET A DAY OFF FOR YOUR MOM'S SURGERY. BUT REMEMBER, FOR THE REST OF THE YEAR, YOU ARE MINE THREE HOURS OUT OF EVERY DAY.

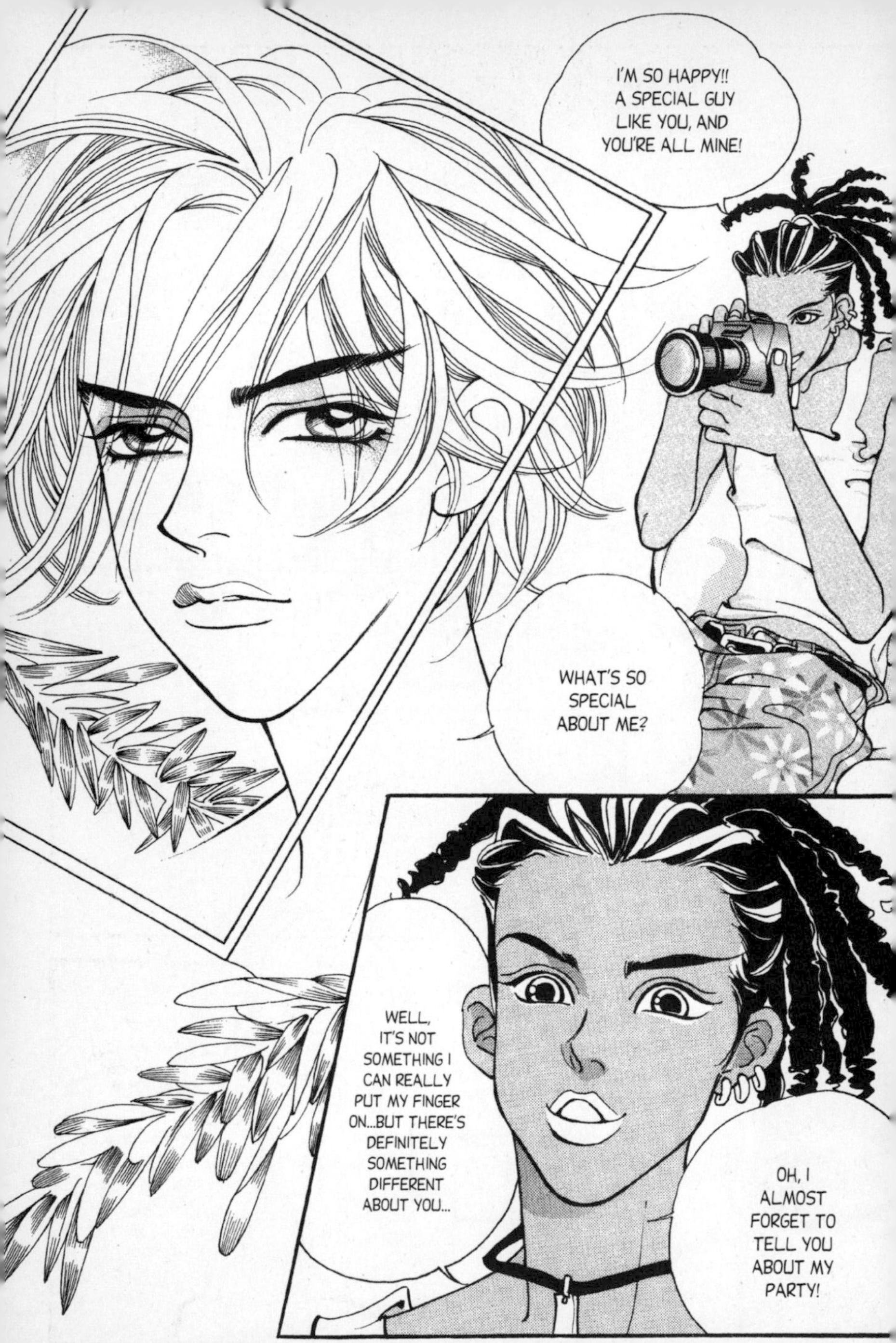
I'M SO HAPPY!! A SPECIAL GUY LIKE YOU, AND YOU'RE ALL MINE!
WHAT'S SO SPECIAL ABOUT ME?
WELL, IT'S NOT SOMETHING I CAN REALLY PUT MY FINGER ON...BUT THERE'S DEFINITELY SOMETHING DIFFERENT ABOUT YOU...
OH, I ALMOST FORGET TO TELL YOU ABOUT MY PARTY!

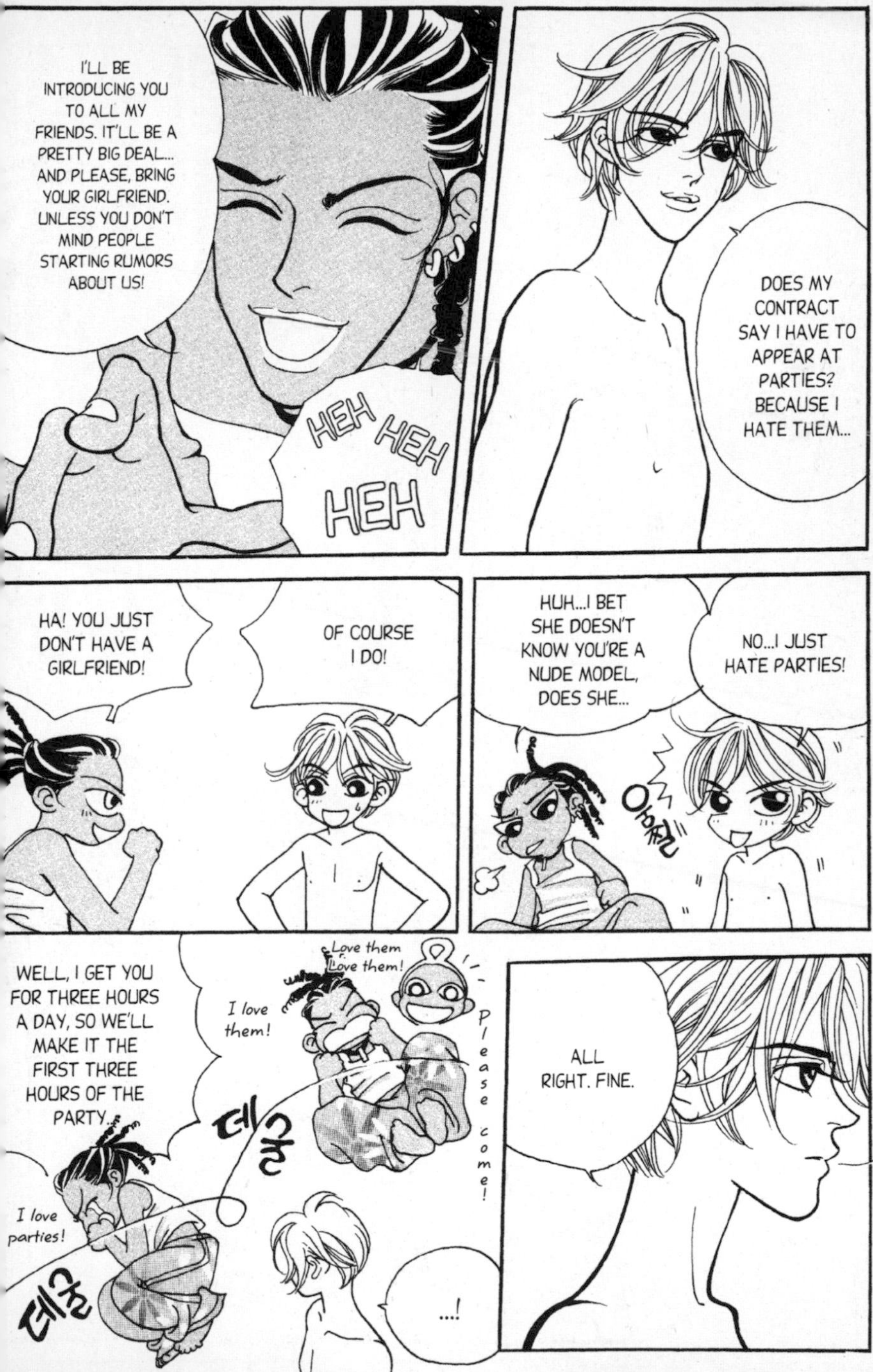
I'LL BE INTRODUCING YOU TO ALL MY FRIENDS. IT'LL BE A PRETTY BIG DEAL... AND PLEASE, BRING YOUR GIRLFRIEND. UNLESS YOU DON'T MIND PEOPLE STARTING RUMORS ABOUT US!
HEH HEH HEH
DOES MY CONTRACT SAY I HAVE TO APPEAR AT PARTIES? BECAUSE I HATE THEM...
HA! YOU JUST DON'T HAVE A GIRLFRIEND!
OF COURSE I DO!
HUH...I BET SHE DOESN'T KNOW YOU'RE A NUDE MODEL, DOES SHE...
NO...I JUST HATE PARTIES!
WELL, I GET YOU FOR THREE HOURS A DAY, SO WE'LL MAKE IT THE FIRST THREE HOURS OF THE PARTY...
I love them!
Love them
Love them!
Please come!
데굴
I love parties!
데굴
...!
ALL RIGHT. FINE.

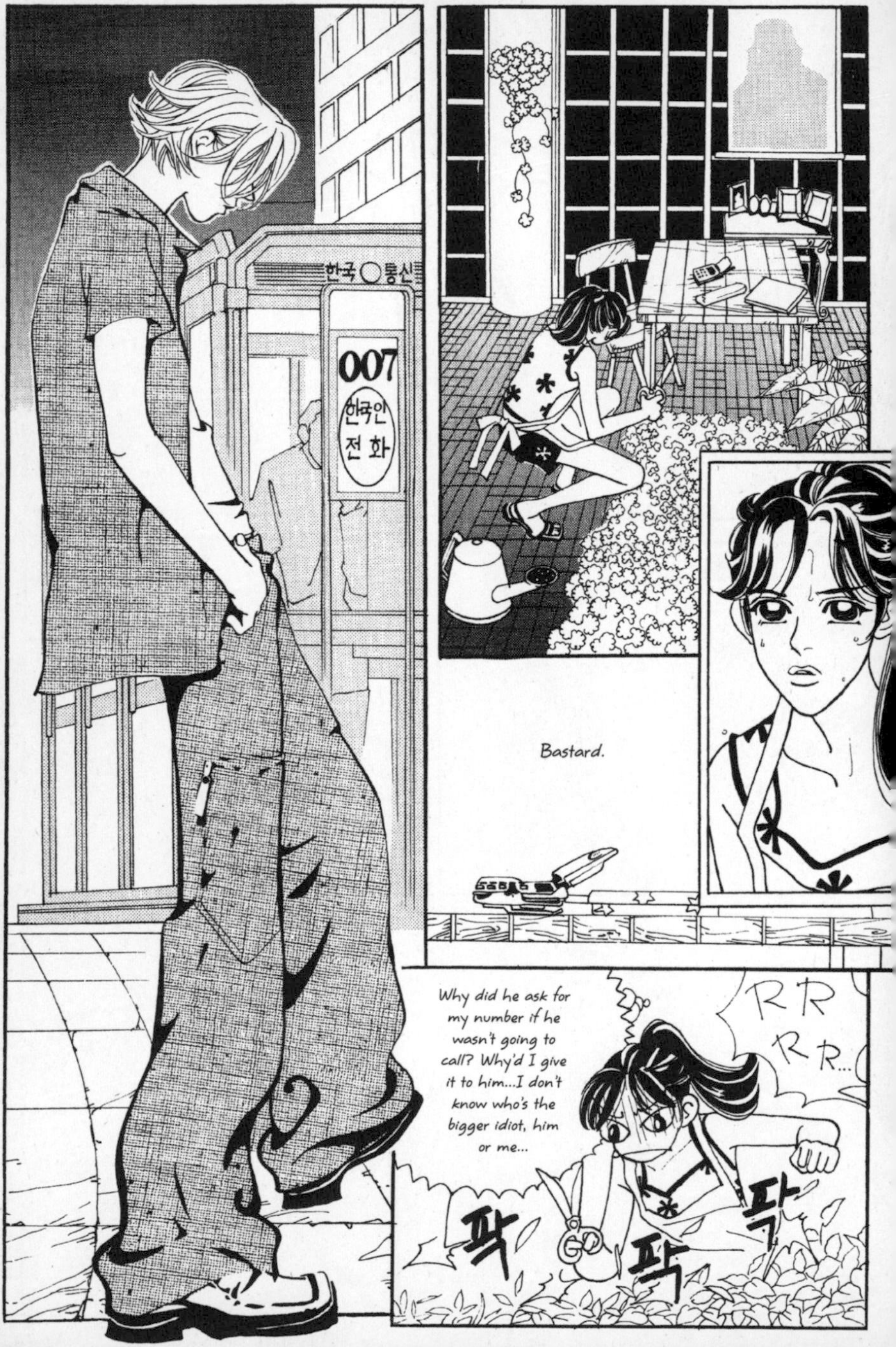
한국◯통신
007
한국인 전화
Bastard.
Why did he ask for my number if he wasn't going to call? Why'd I give it to him...I don't know who's the bigger idiot, him or me...
RR RR...
팍
팍
팍

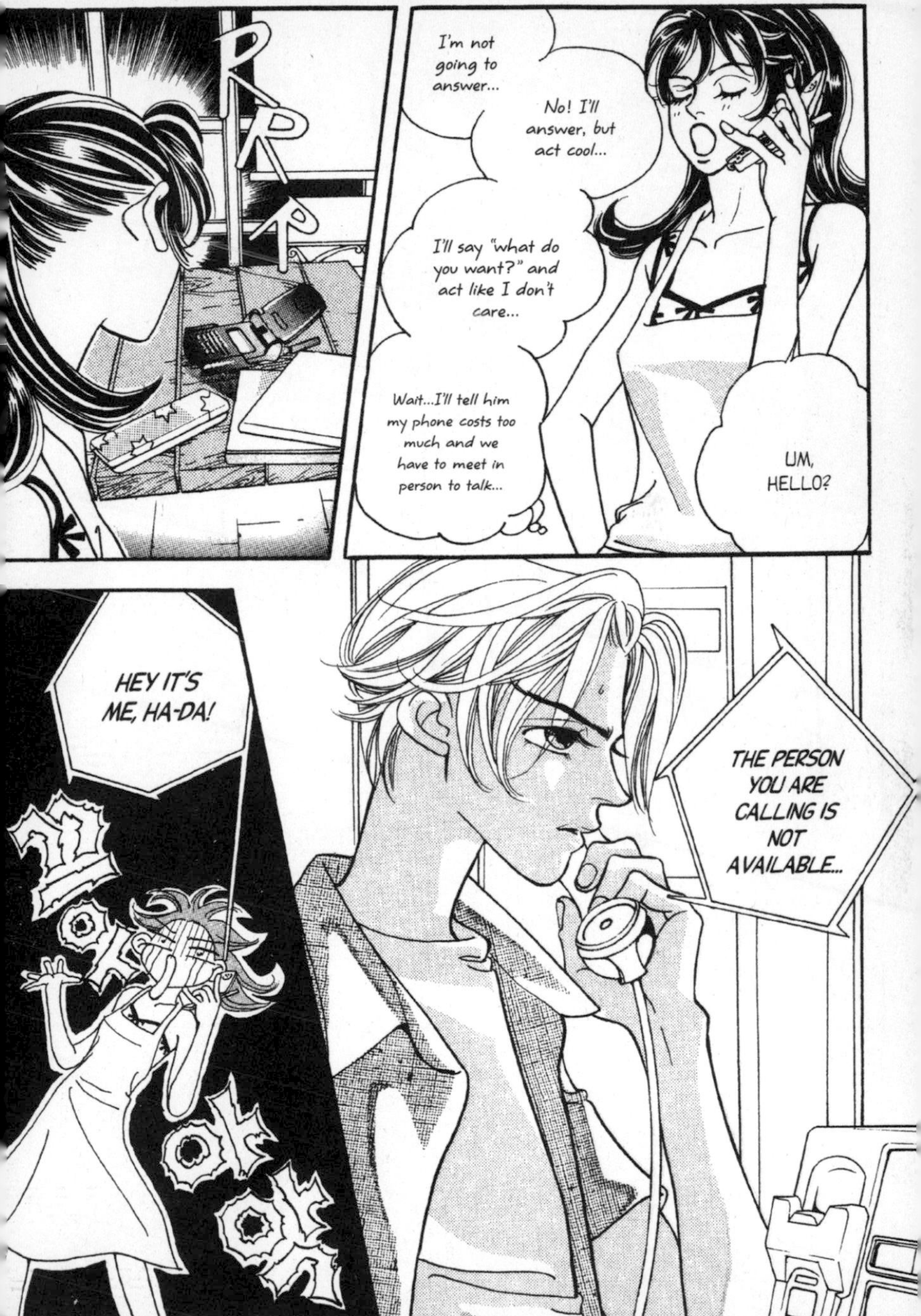

I'm not going to answer...
No! I'll answer, but act cool...
I'll say "what do you want?" and act like I don't care...
Wait...I'll tell him my phone costs too much and we have to meet in person to talk...
UM, HELLO?
HEY IT'S ME, HA-DA!
THE PERSON YOU ARE CALLING IS NOT AVAILABLE...

News From the Studio

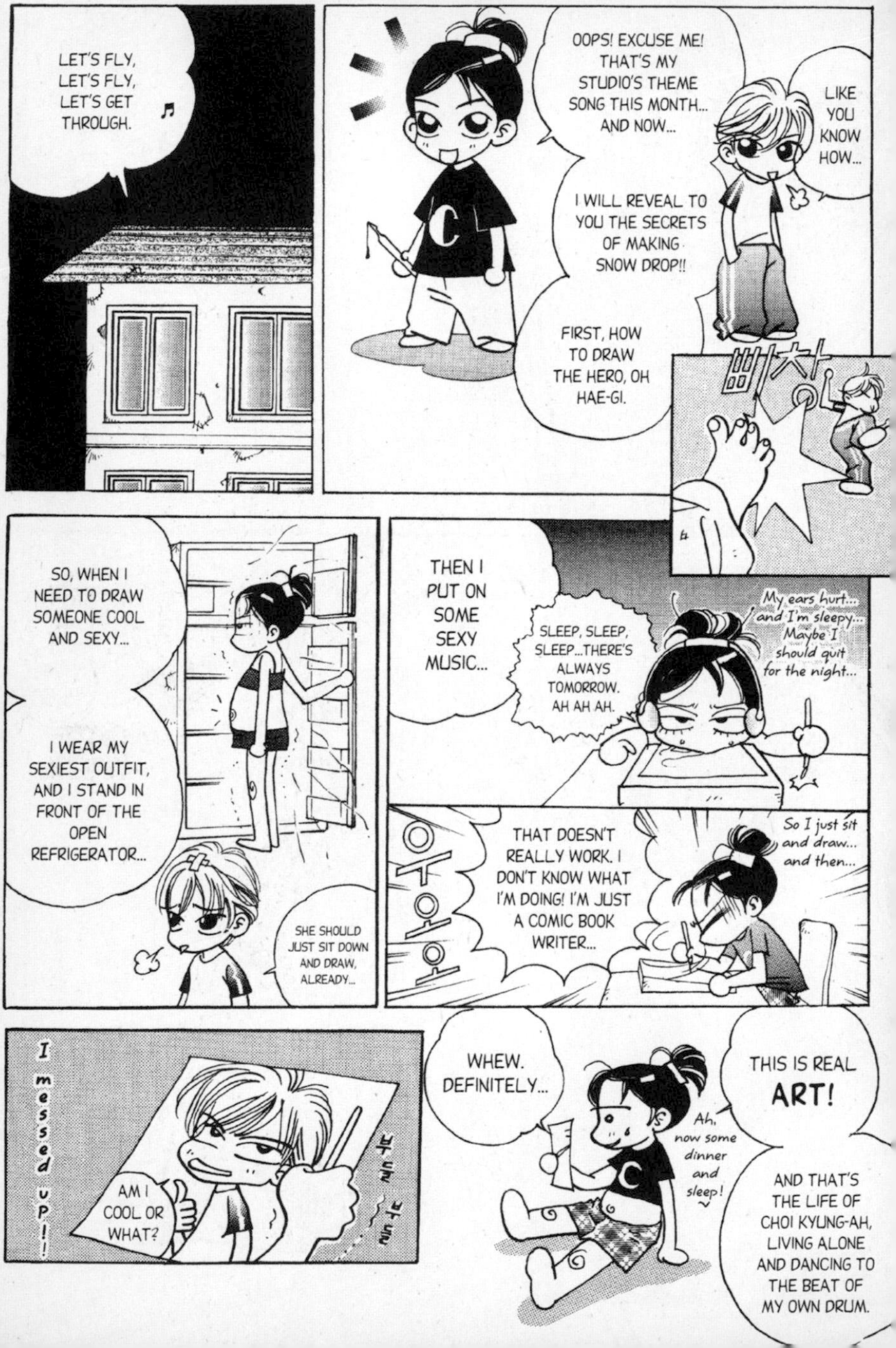
LET'S FLY, LET'S FLY, LET'S GET THROUGH.
OOPS! EXCUSE ME! THAT'S MY STUDIO'S THEME SONG THIS MONTH... AND NOW...
I WILL REVEAL TO YOU THE SECRETS OF MAKING SNOW DROP!!
FIRST, HOW TO DRAW THE HERO, OH HAE-GI.
LIKE YOU KNOW HOW...
SO, WHEN I NEED TO DRAW SOMEONE COOL AND SEXY...
I WEAR MY SEXIEST OUTFIT, AND I STAND IN FRONT OF THE OPEN REFRIGERATOR...
SHE SHOULD JUST SIT DOWN AND DRAW, ALREADY...
THEN I PUT ON SOME SEXY MUSIC...
SLEEP, SLEEP, SLEEP...THERE'S ALWAYS TOMORROW. AH AH AH.
My ears hurt... and I'm sleepy... Maybe I should quit for the night...
THAT DOESN'T REALLY WORK. I DON'T KNOW WHAT I'M DOING! I'M JUST A COMIC BOOK WRITER...
So I just sit and draw... and then...
I messed up!!
AM I COOL OR WHAT?
WHEW. DEFINITELY...
Ah, now some dinner and sleep!
THIS IS REAL ART!
AND THAT'S THE LIFE OF CHOI KYUNG-AH, LIVING ALONE AND DANCING TO THE BEAT OF MY OWN DRUM.

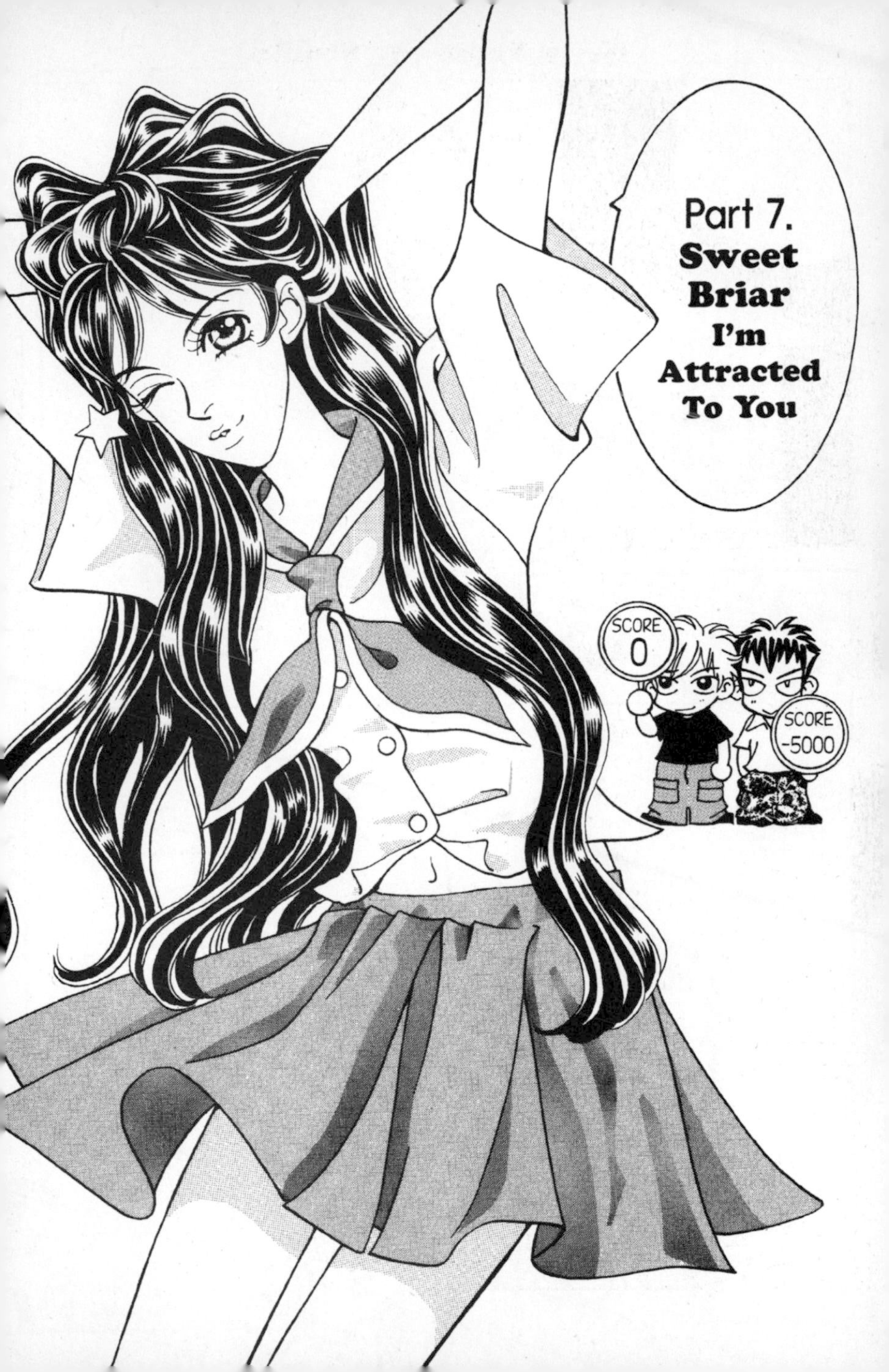
Part 7.
Sweet Briar
I'm Attracted To You
SCORE
0
SCORE
-5000

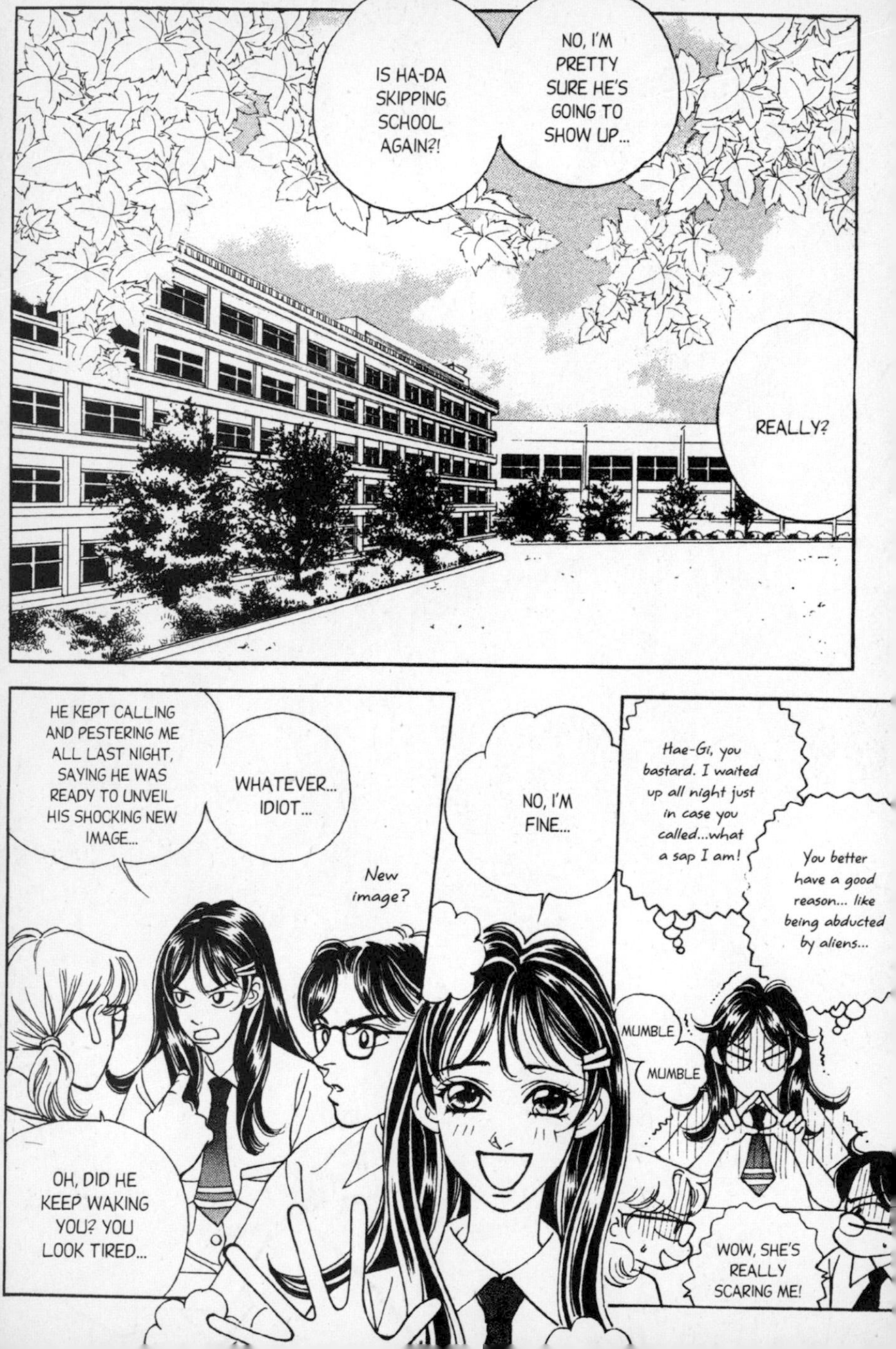
IS HA-DA SKIPPING SCHOOL AGAIN?!
NO, I'M PRETTY SURE HE'S GOING TO SHOW UP...
REALLY?
HE KEPT CALLING AND PESTERING ME ALL LAST NIGHT, SAYING HE WAS READY TO UNVEIL HIS SHOCKING NEW IMAGE...
WHATEVER... IDIOT...
New image?
OH, DID HE KEEP WAKING YOU? YOU LOOK TIRED...
NO, I'M FINE...
Hae-Gi, you bastard. I waited up all night just in case you called...what a sap I am!
You better have a good reason... like being abducted by aliens...
MUMBLE
MUMBLE
WOW, SHE'S REALLY SCARING ME!

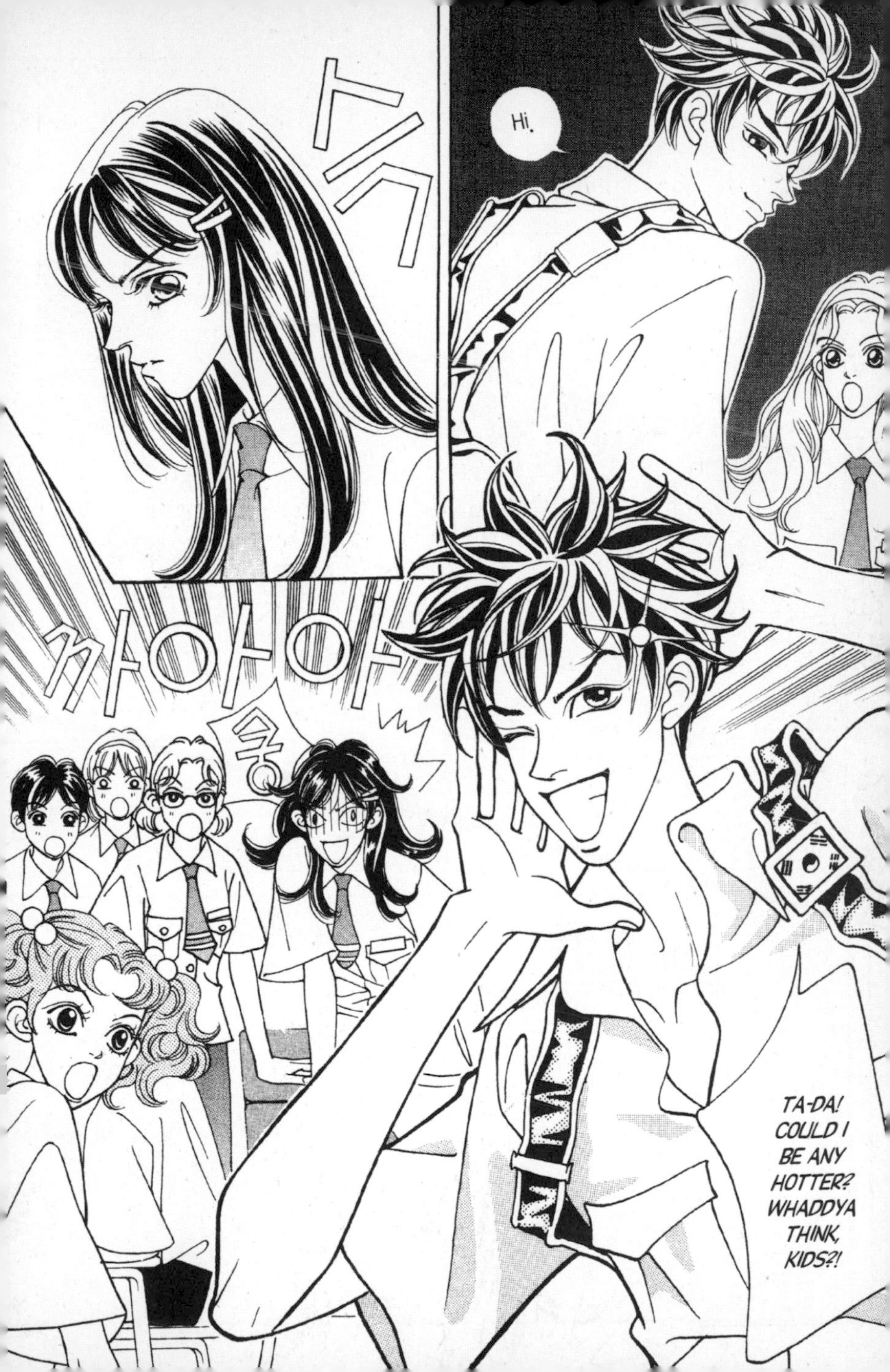
Hi.
까아아아
TA-DA! COULD I BE ANY HOTTER? WHADDYA THINK, KIDS?!

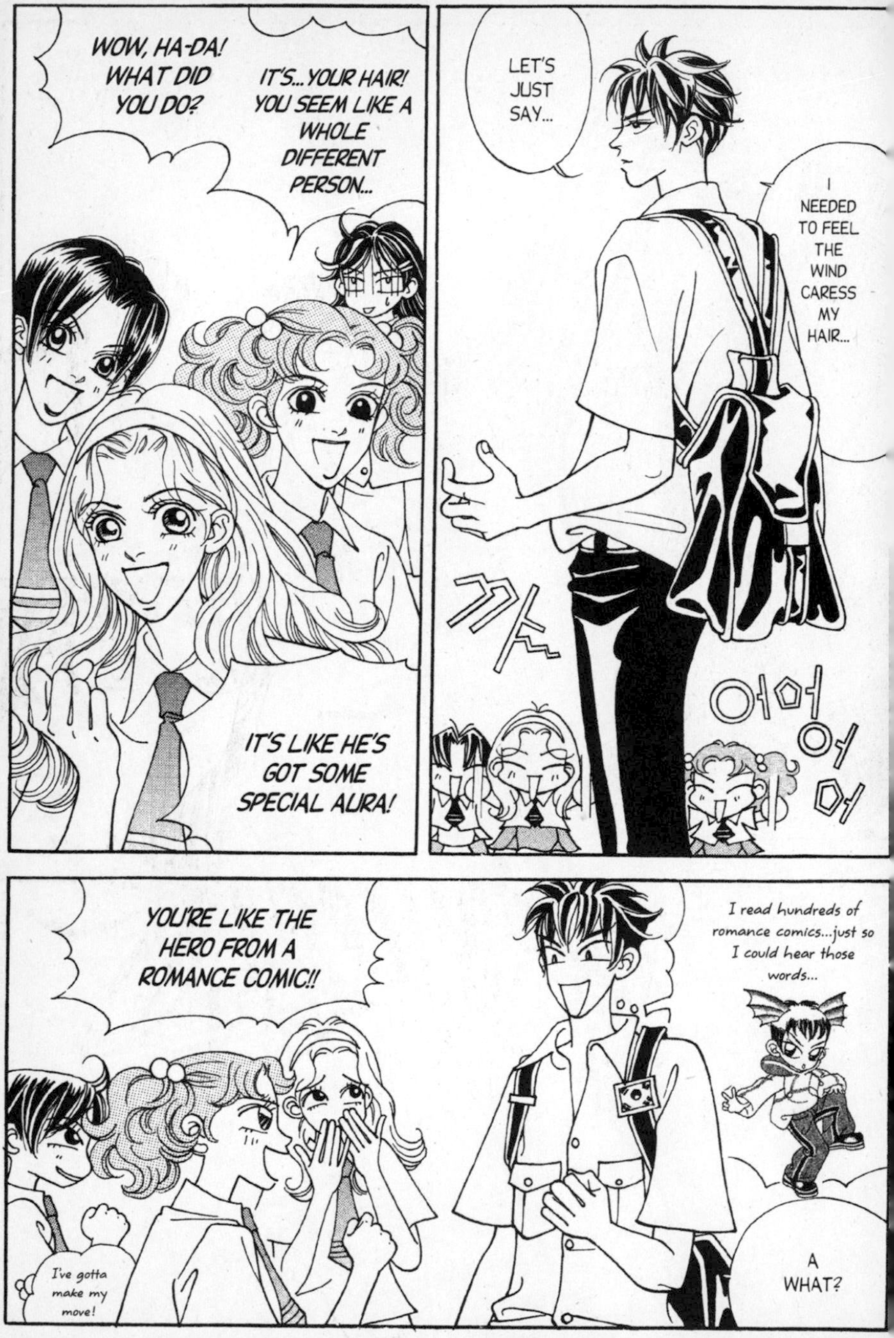
WOW, HA-DA! WHAT DID YOU DO?
IT'S...YOUR HAIR! YOU SEEM LIKE A WHOLE DIFFERENT PERSON...
IT'S LIKE HE'S GOT SOME SPECIAL AURA!
LET'S JUST SAY...
I NEEDED TO FEEL THE WIND CARESS MY HAIR...
YOU'RE LIKE THE HERO FROM A ROMANCE COMIC!!
I've gotta make my move!
I read hundreds of romance comics...just so I could hear those words...
A WHAT?

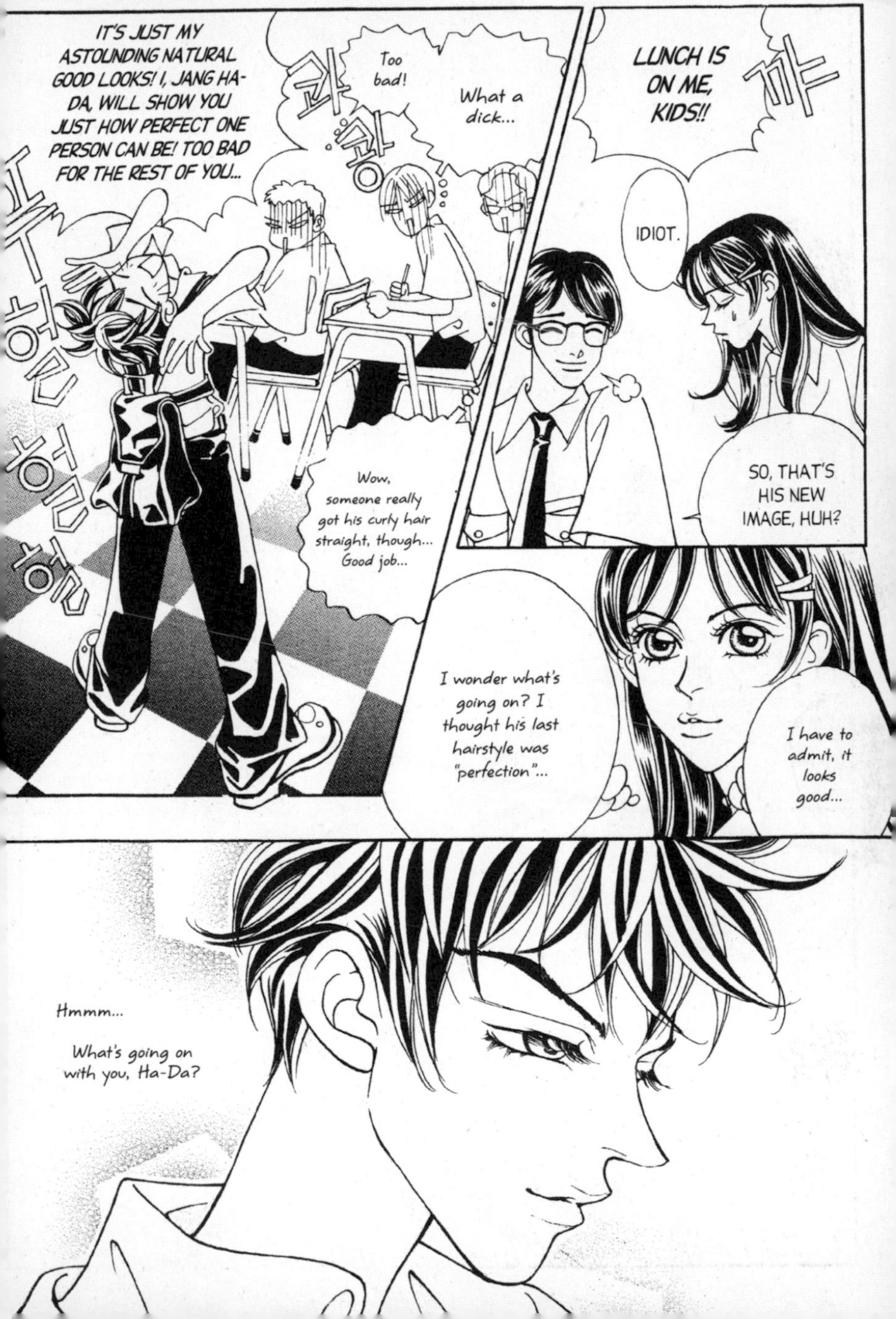
IT'S JUST MY ASTOUNDING NATURAL GOOD LOOKS! I, JANG HA-DA, WILL SHOW YOU JUST HOW PERFECT ONE PERSON CAN BE! TOO BAD FOR THE REST OF YOU...
Too bad!
What a dick...
Wow, someone really got his curly hair straight, though... Good job...
LUNCH IS ON ME, KIDS!!
IDIOT.
SO, THAT'S HIS NEW IMAGE, HUH?
I wonder what's going on? I thought his last hairstyle was "perfection"...
I have to admit, it looks good...
Hmmm...
What's going on with you, Ha-Da?

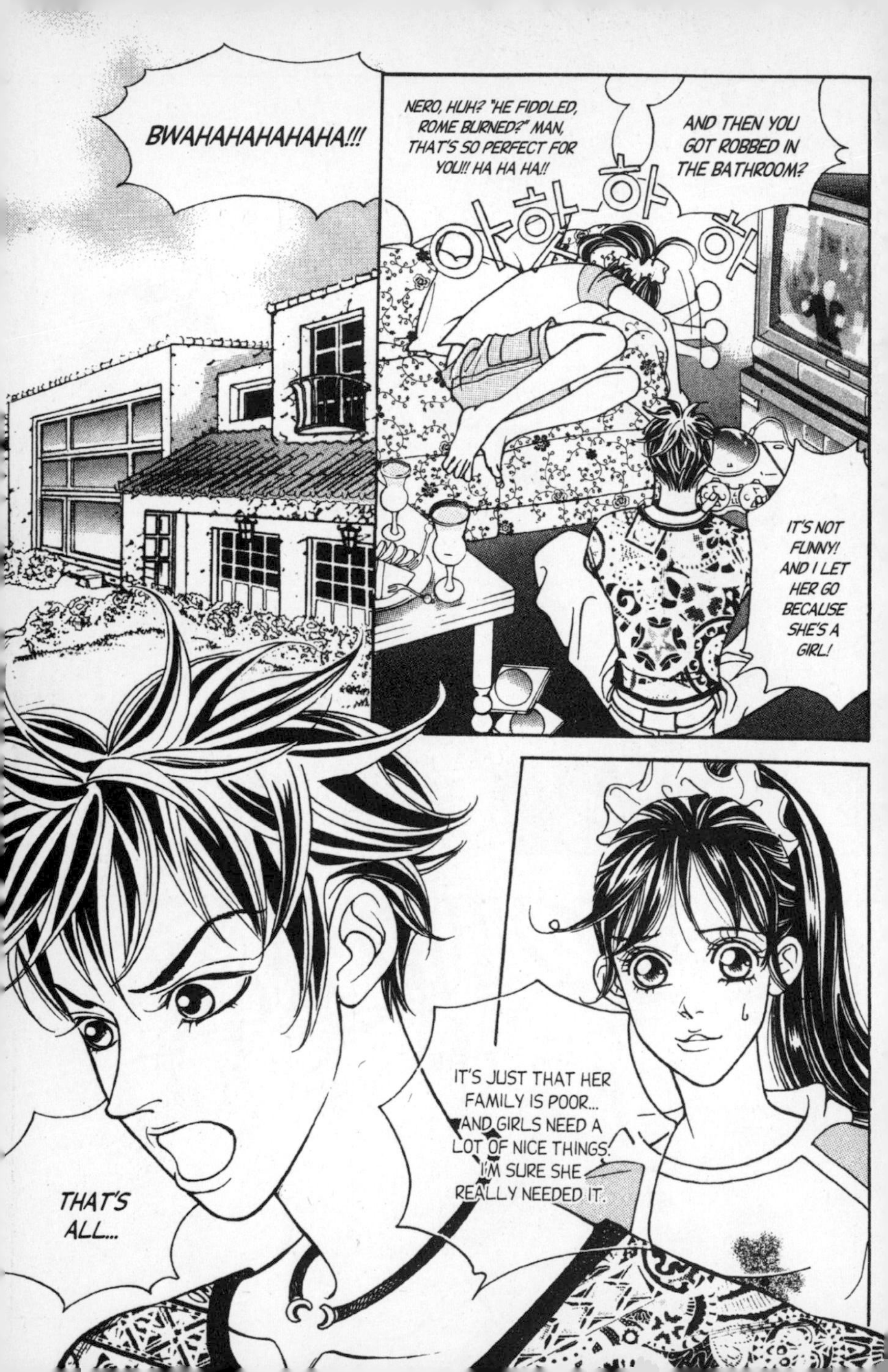
BWAHAHAHAHAHA!!!
NERO, HUH? "HE FIDDLED, ROME BURNED?" MAN, THAT'S SO PERFECT FOR YOU!! HA HA HA!!
AND THEN YOU GOT ROBBED IN THE BATHROOM?
아하하하
IT'S NOT FUNNY! AND I LET HER GO BECAUSE SHE'S A GIRL!
THAT'S ALL...
IT'S JUST THAT HER FAMILY IS POOR... AND GIRLS NEED A LOT OF NICE THINGS. I'M SURE SHE REALLY NEEDED IT.

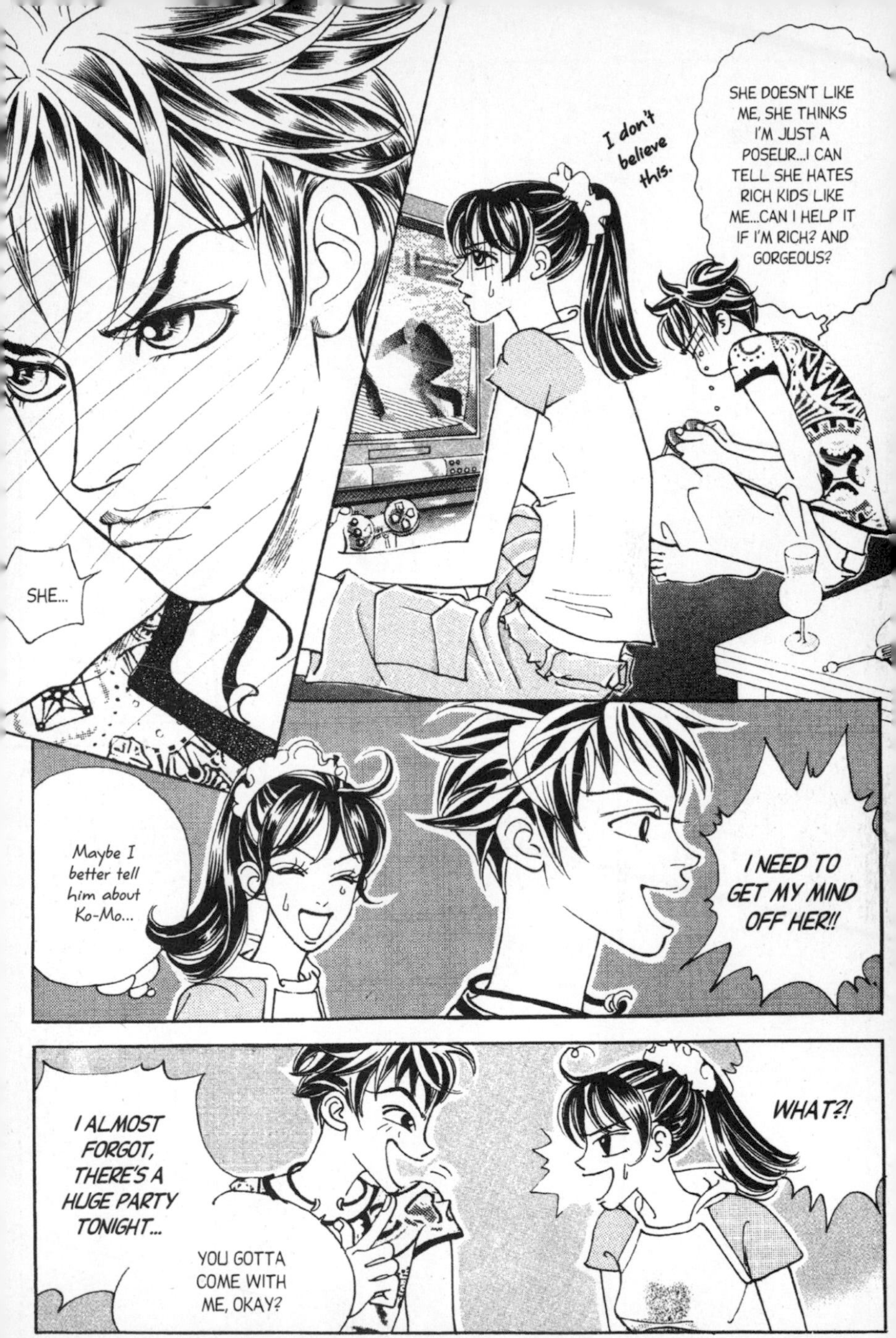
SHE...
I don't believe this.
SHE DOESN'T LIKE ME, SHE THINKS I'M JUST A POSEUR...I CAN TELL SHE HATES RICH KIDS LIKE ME...CAN I HELP IT IF I'M RICH? AND GORGEOUS?
Maybe I better tell him about Ko-Mo...
I NEED TO GET MY MIND OFF HER!!
I ALMOST FORGOT, THERE'S A HUGE PARTY TONIGHT...
YOU GOTTA COME WITH ME, OKAY?
WHAT?!

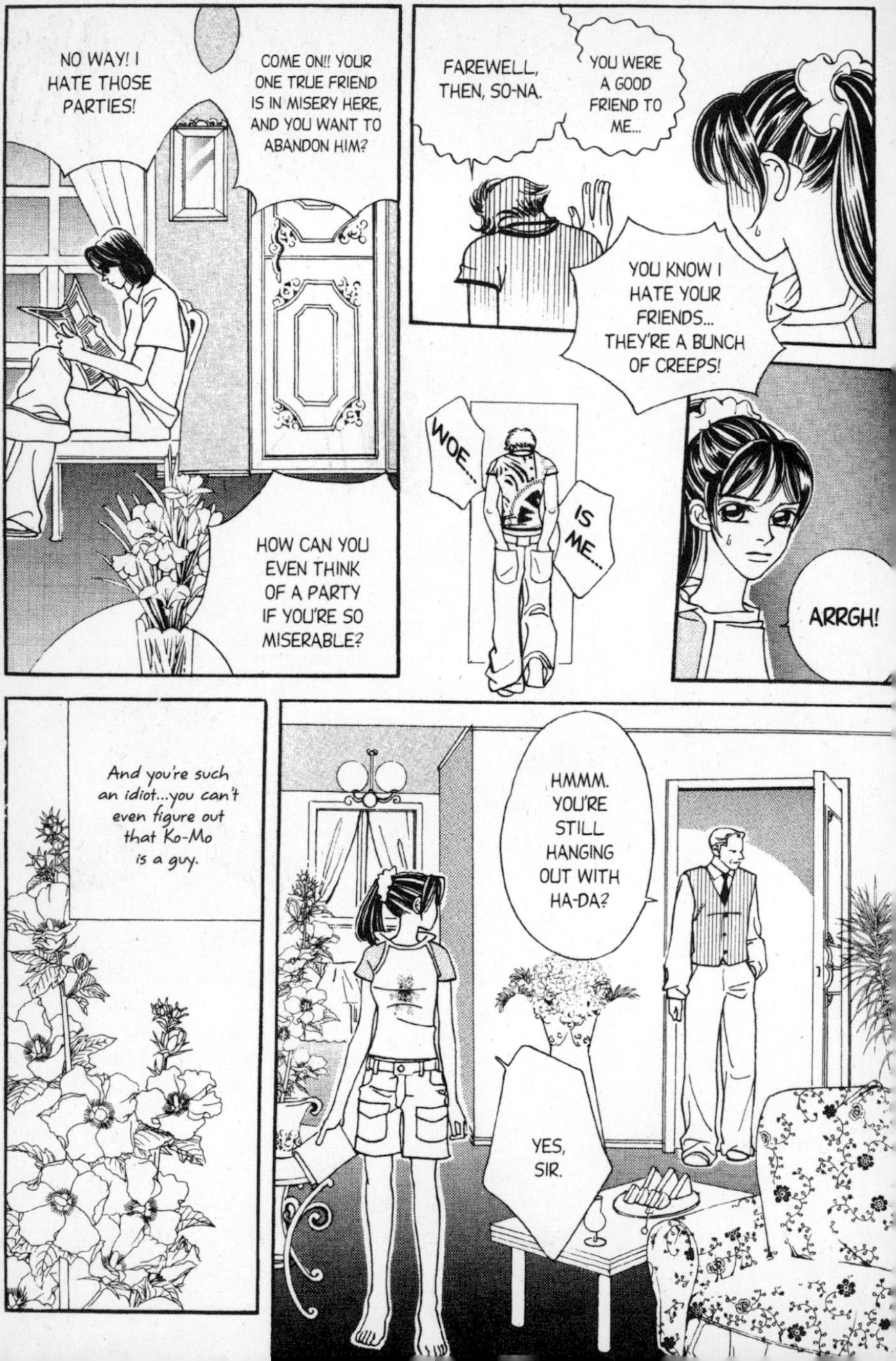
NO WAY! I HATE THOSE PARTIES!
COME ON!! YOUR ONE TRUE FRIEND IS IN MISERY HERE, AND YOU WANT TO ABANDON HIM?
HOW CAN YOU EVEN THINK OF A PARTY IF YOU'RE SO MISERABLE?
FAREWELL, THEN, SO-NA.
YOU WERE A GOOD FRIEND TO ME...
YOU KNOW I HATE YOUR FRIENDS... THEY'RE A BUNCH OF CREEPS!
WOE...
IS ME...
ARRGH!
And you're such an idiot...you can't even figure out that Ko-Mo is a guy.
HMMM. YOU'RE STILL HANGING OUT WITH HA-DA?
YES, SIR.

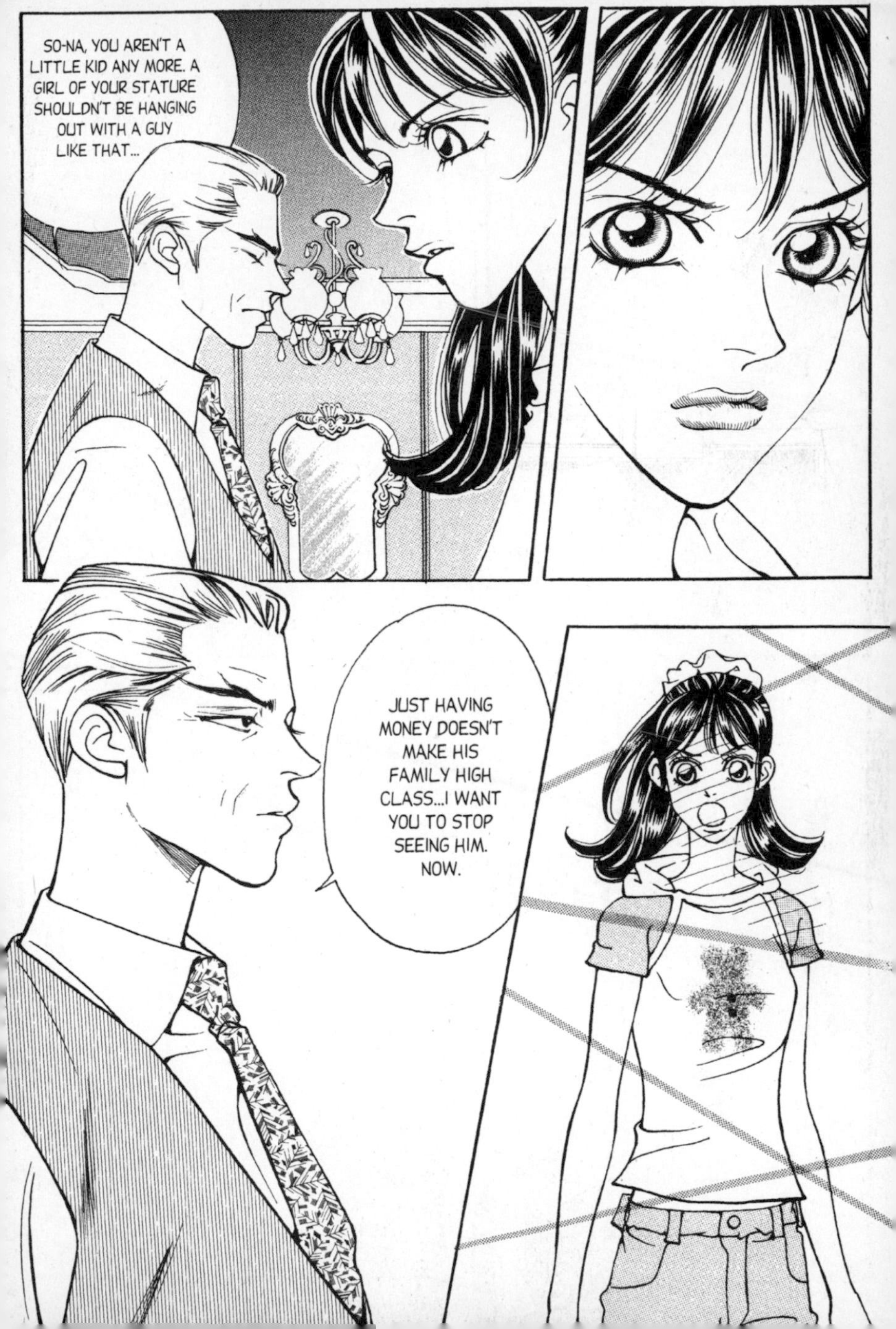
SO-NA, YOU AREN'T A LITTLE KID ANY MORE. A GIRL OF YOUR STATURE SHOULDN'T BE HANGING OUT WITH A GUY LIKE THAT...
JUST HAVING MONEY DOESN'T MAKE HIS FAMILY HIGH CLASS...I WANT YOU TO STOP SEEING HIM. NOW.

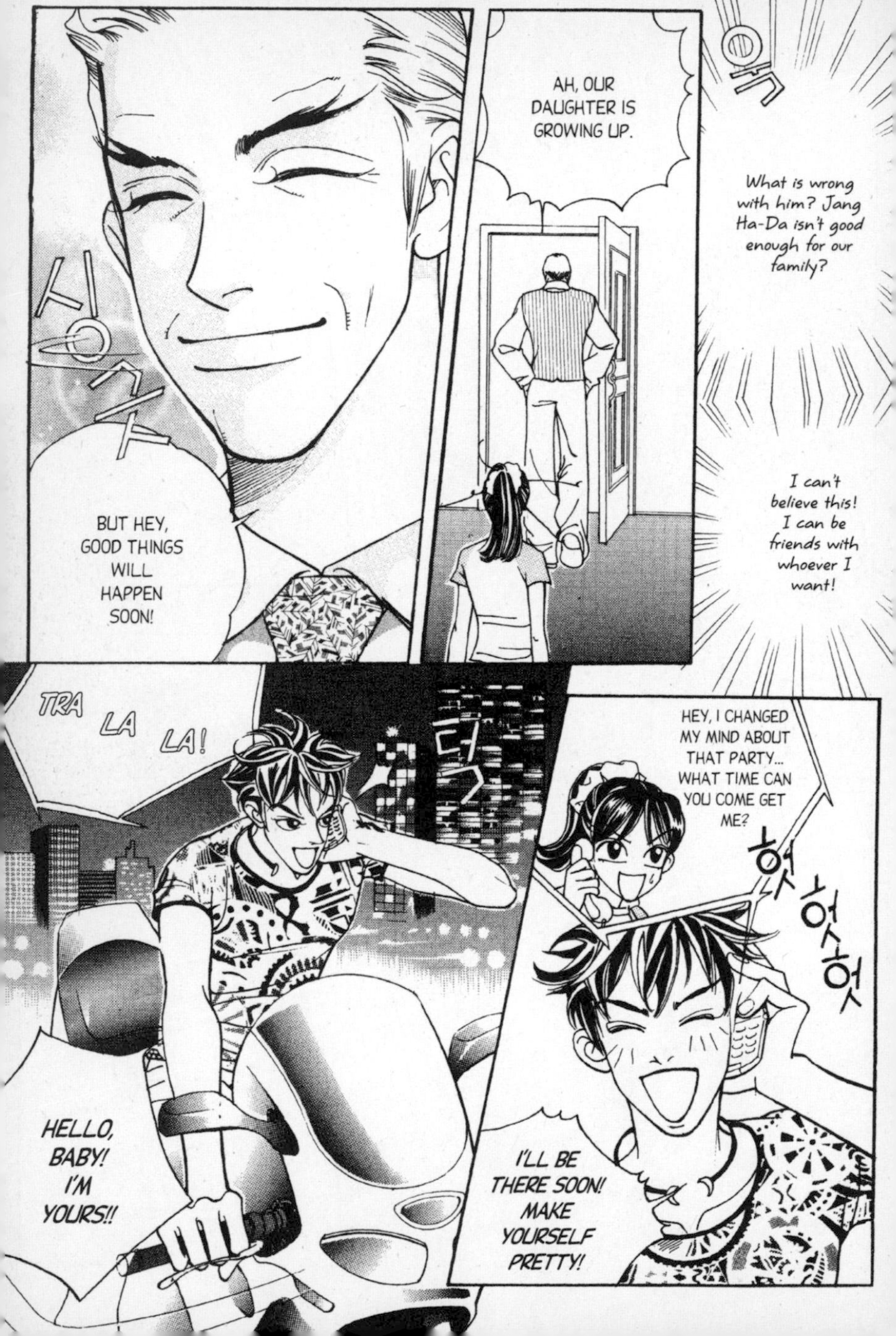
BUT HEY, GOOD THINGS WILL HAPPEN SOON!
AH, OUR DAUGHTER IS GROWING UP.
What is wrong with him? Jang Ha-Da isn't good enough for our family?
I can't believe this! I can be friends with whoever I want!
TRA LA LA!
HELLO, BABY! I'M YOURS!!
HEY, I CHANGED MY MIND ABOUT THAT PARTY... WHAT TIME CAN YOU COME GET ME?
I'LL BE THERE SOON! MAKE YOURSELF PRETTY!

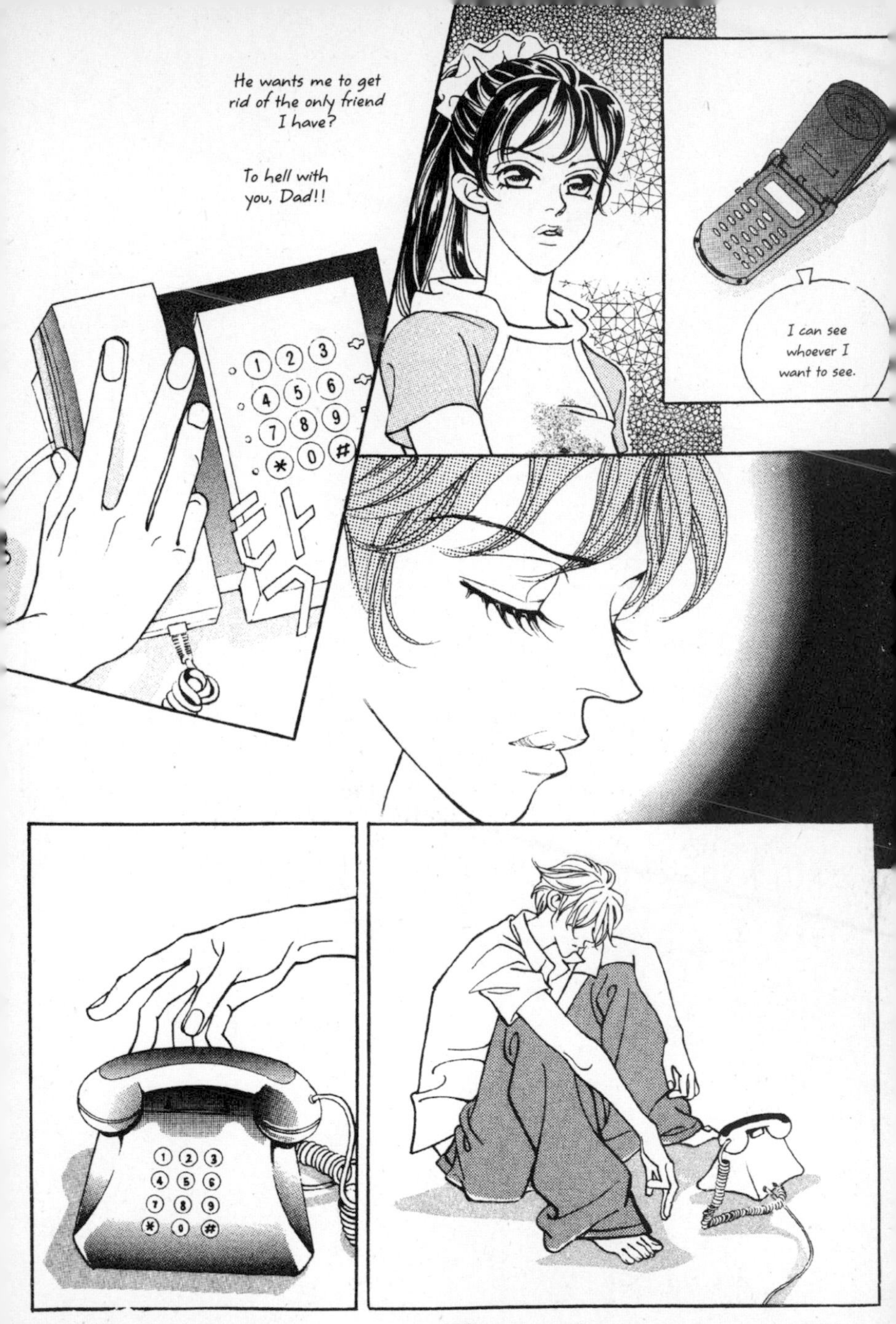
He wants me to get rid of the only friend I have?
To hell with you, Dad!!
I can see whoever I want to see.

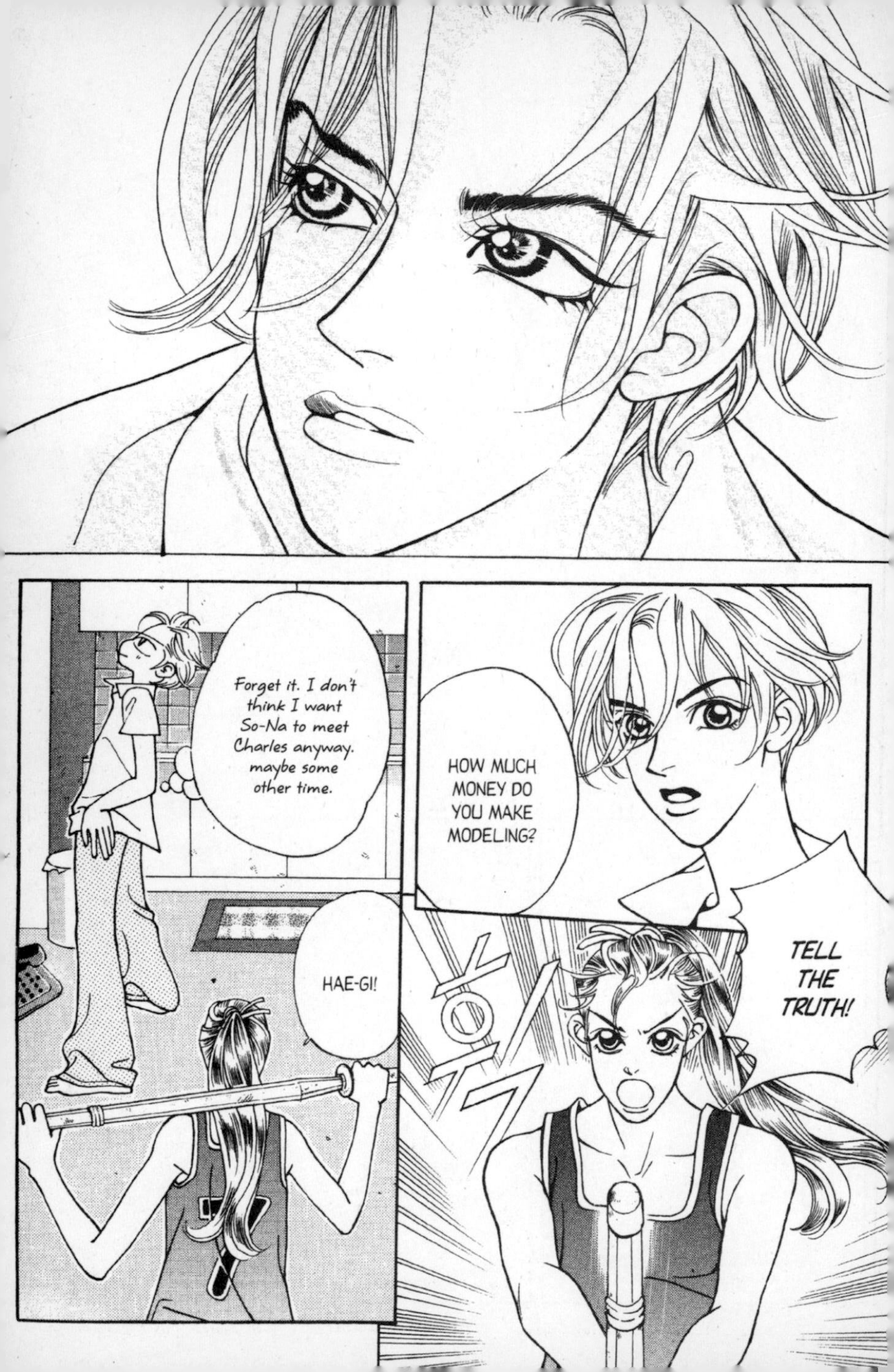

Forget it. I don't think I want So-Na to meet Charles anyway. maybe some other time.
HAE-GI!
HOW MUCH MONEY DO YOU MAKE MODELING?
TELL THE TRUTH!

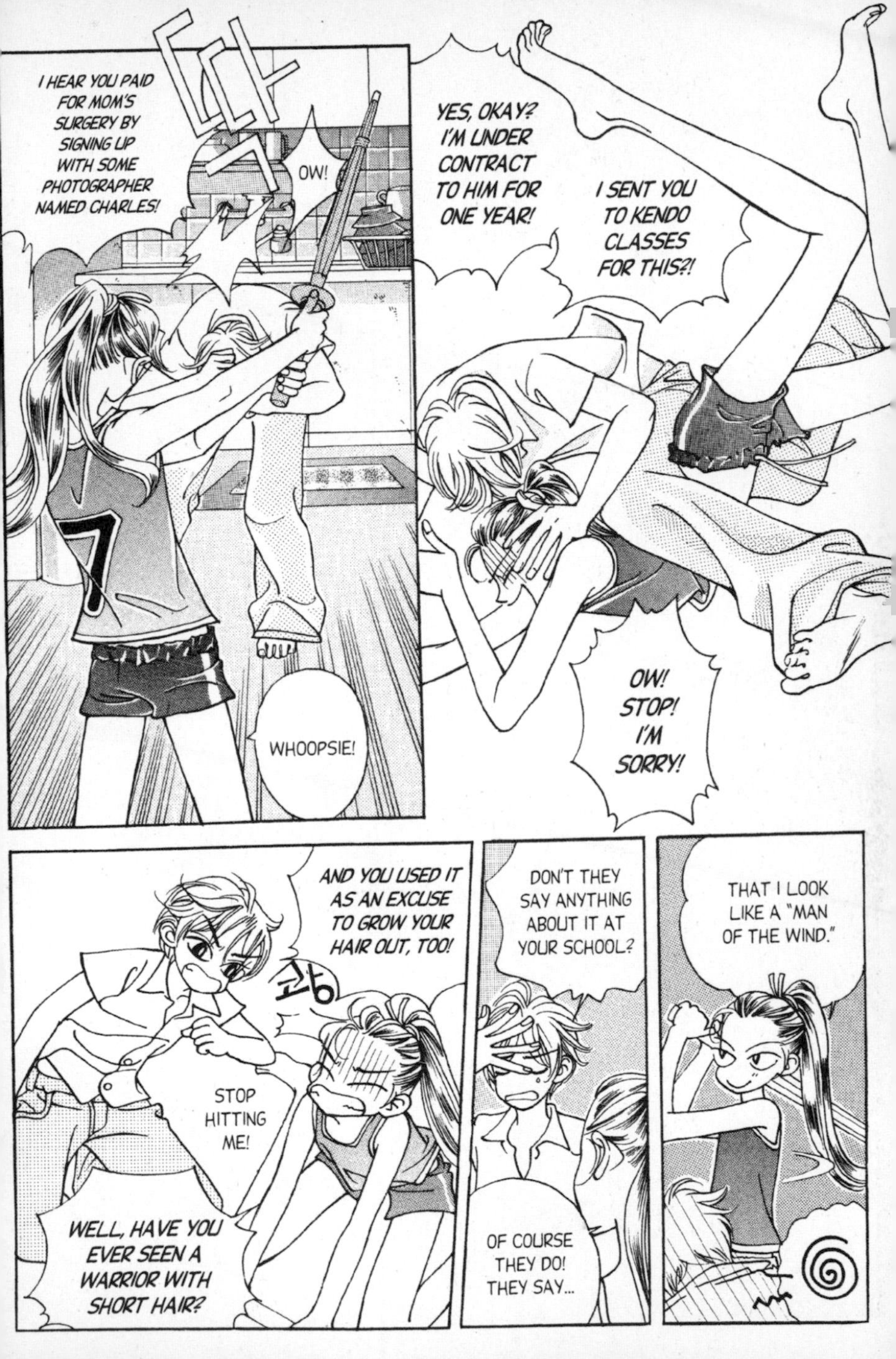
ECK
I HEAR YOU PAID FOR MOM'S SURGERY BY SIGNING UP WITH SOME PHOTOGRAPHER NAMED CHARLES!
OW!
WHOOPSIE!
YES, OKAY? I'M UNDER CONTRACT TO HIM FOR ONE YEAR!
I SENT YOU TO KENDO CLASSES FOR THIS?!
OW! STOP! I'M SORRY!
AND YOU USED IT AS AN EXCUSE TO GROW YOUR HAIR OUT, TOO!
STOP HITTING ME!
WELL, HAVE YOU EVER SEEN A WARRIOR WITH SHORT HAIR?
DON'T THEY SAY ANYTHING ABOUT IT AT YOUR SCHOOL?
OF COURSE THEY DO! THEY SAY...
THAT I LOOK LIKE A "MAN OF THE WIND."

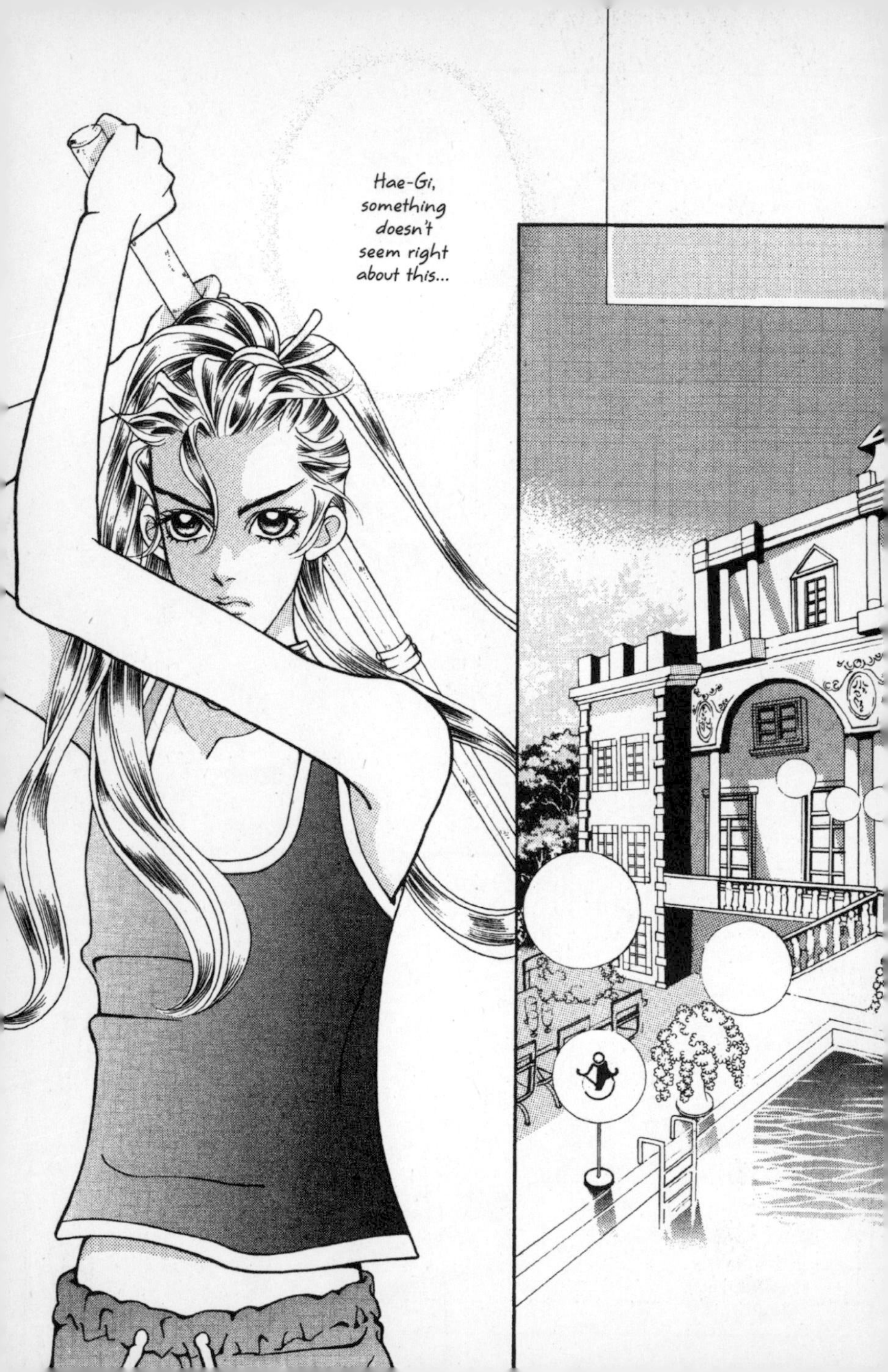
Hae-Gi, something doesn't seem right about this...

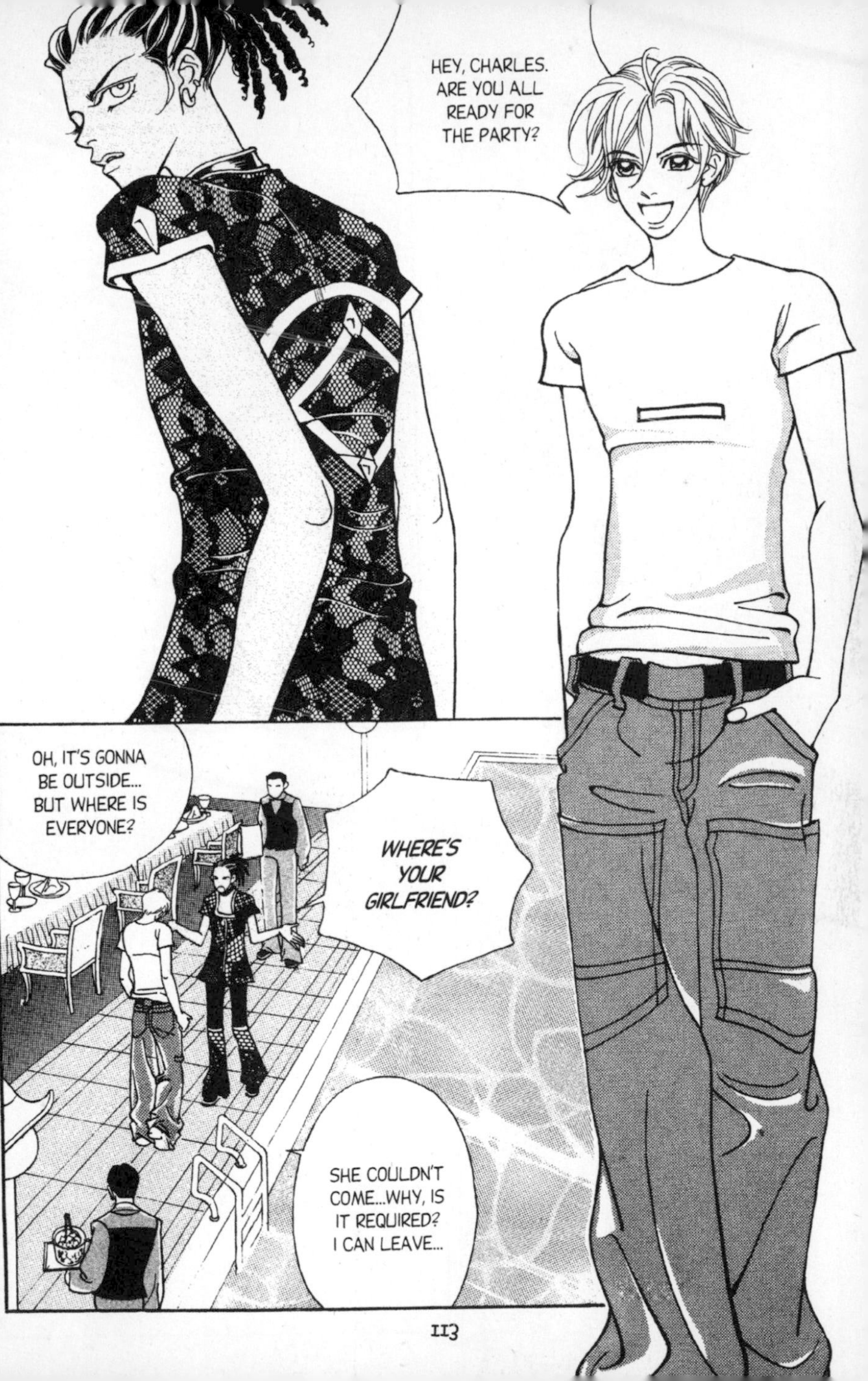
HEY, CHARLES. ARE YOU ALL READY FOR THE PARTY?
OH, IT'S GONNA BE OUTSIDE... BUT WHERE IS EVERYONE?
WHERE'S YOUR GIRLFRIEND?
SHE COULDN'T COME...WHY, IS IT REQUIRED? I CAN LEAVE...

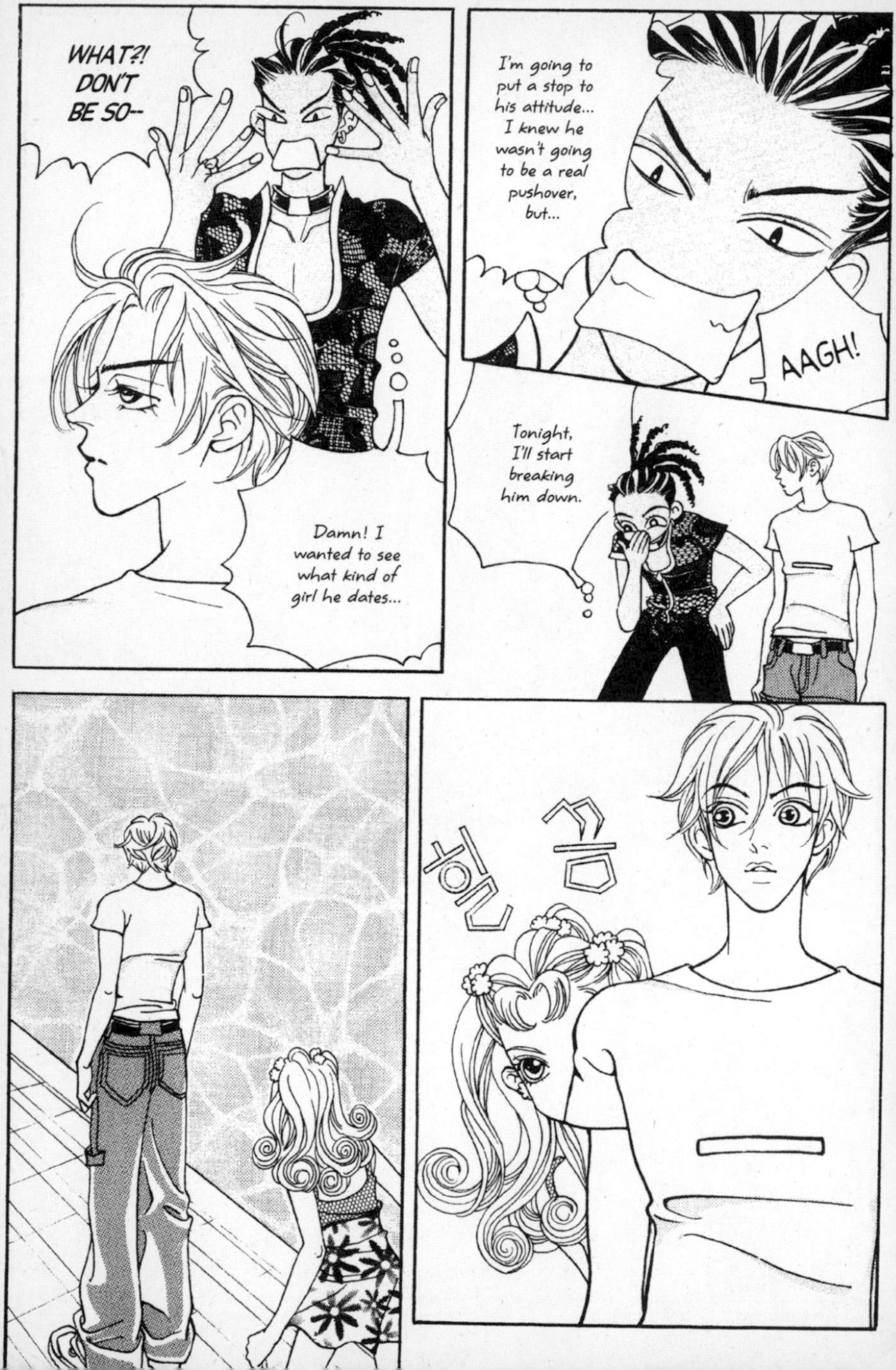
WHAT?! DON'T BE SO--
Damn! I wanted to see what kind of girl he dates...
I'm going to put a stop to his attitude... I knew he wasn't going to be a real pushover, but...
AAGH!
Tonight, I'll start breaking him down.

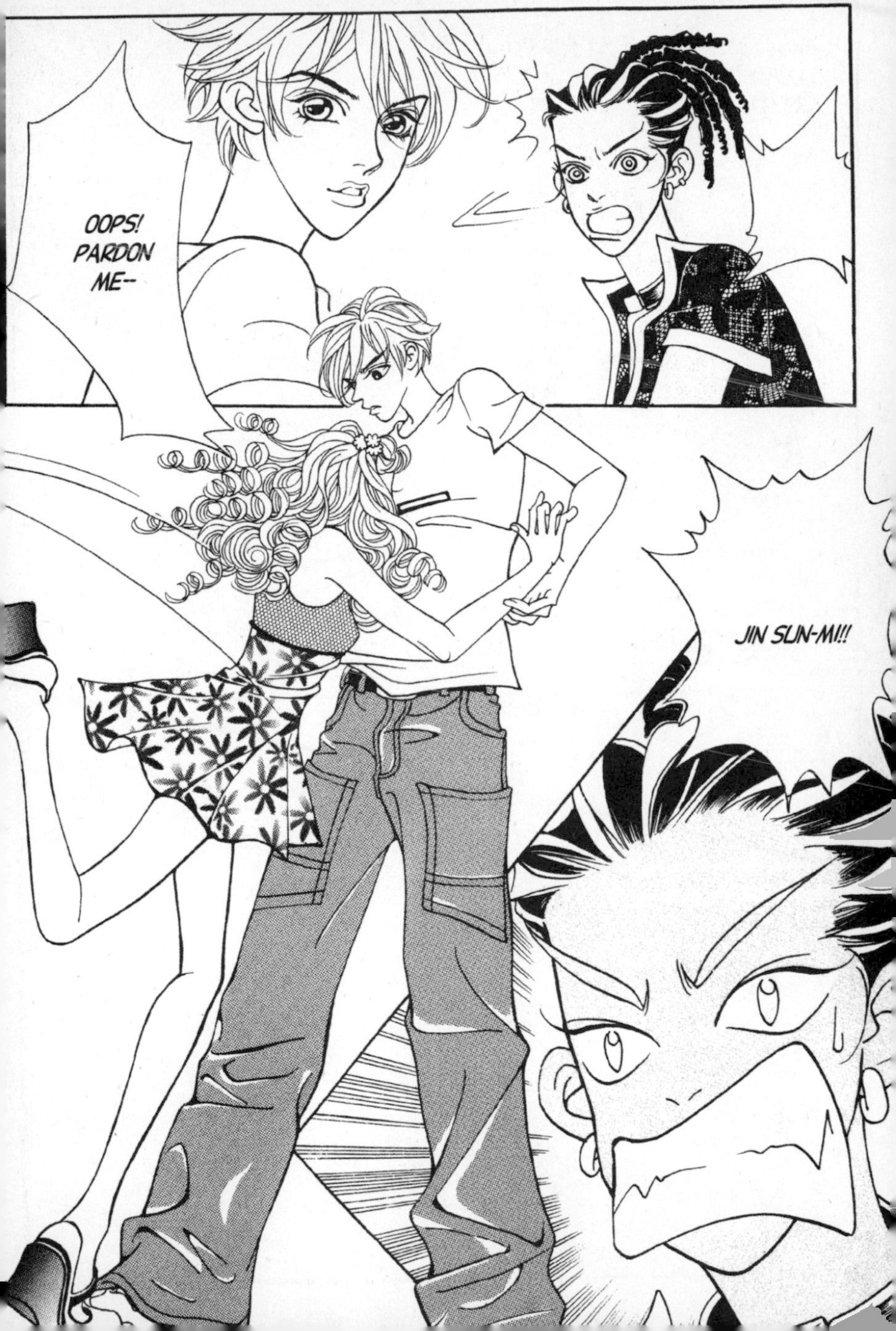
OOPS! PARDON ME--
JIN SUN-MI!!

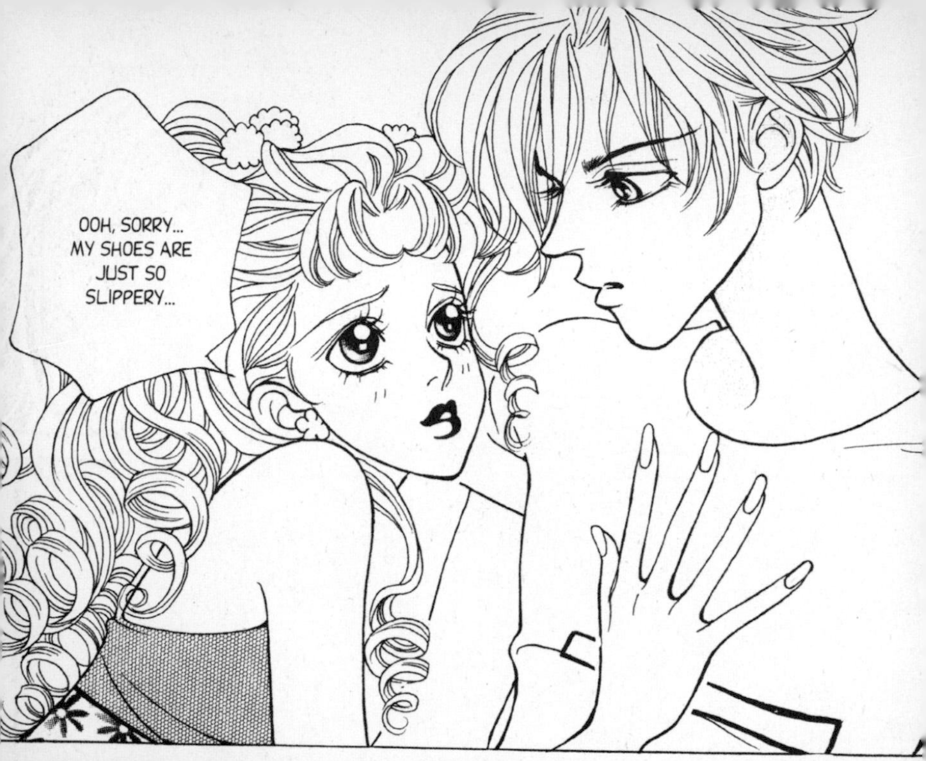
OOH, SORRY... MY SHOES ARE JUST SO SLIPPERY...
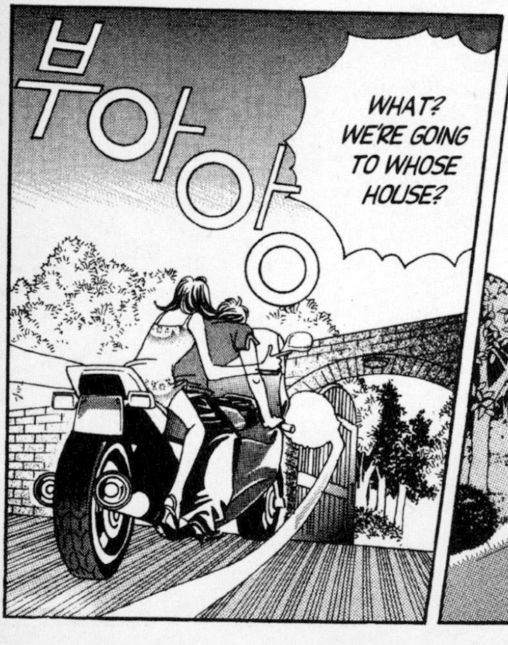
부아아
WHAT? WE'RE GOING TO WHOSE HOUSE?
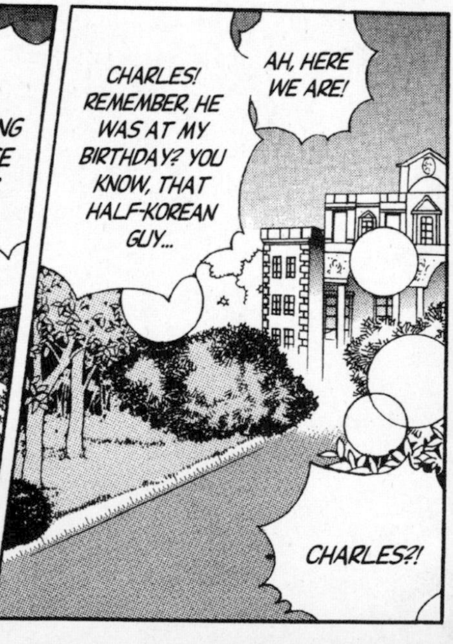
AH, HERE WE ARE!
CHARLES! REMEMBER, HE WAS AT MY BIRTHDAY? YOU KNOW, THAT HALF-KOREAN GUY...
CHARLES?!

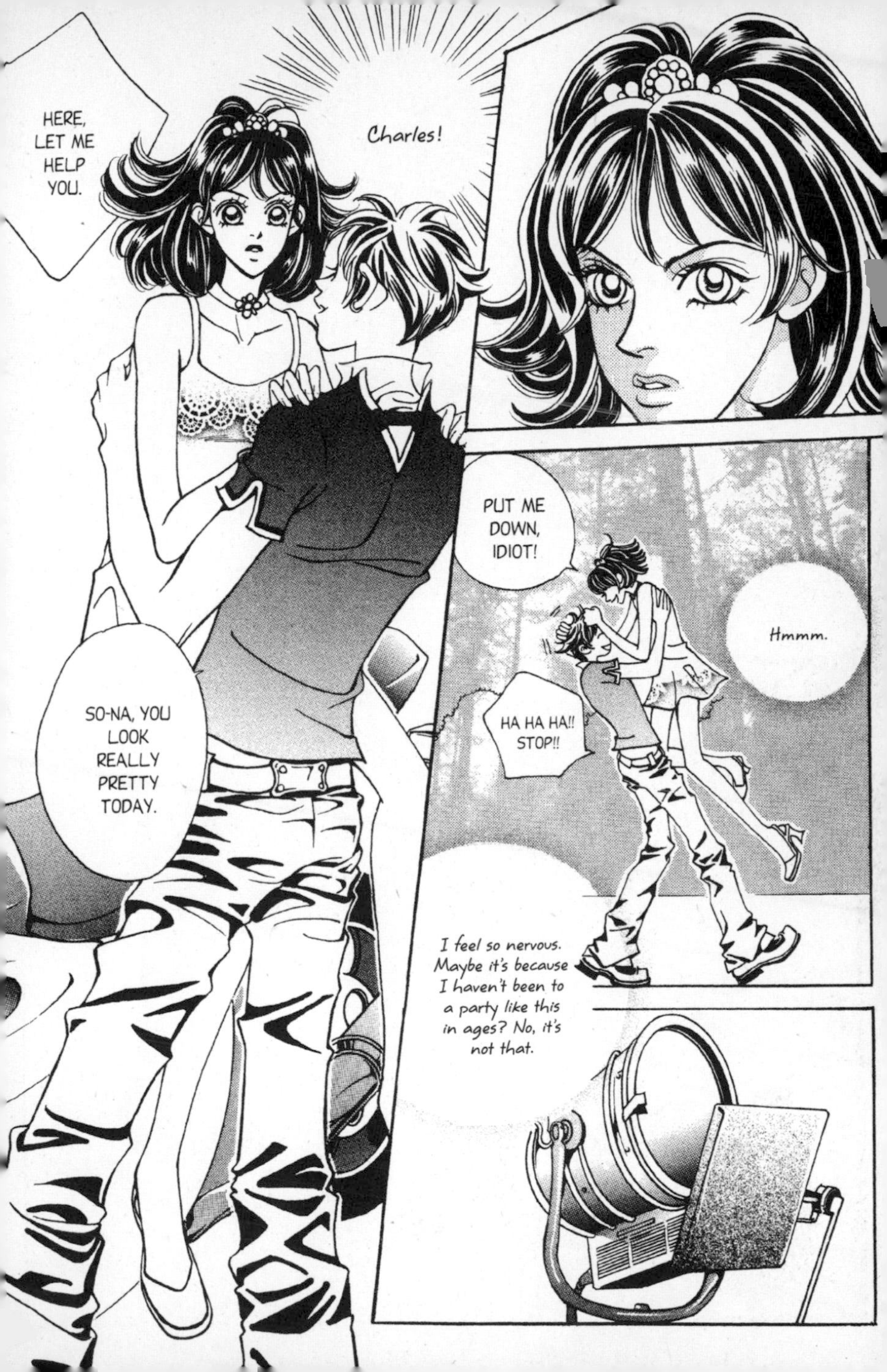
HERE, LET ME HELP YOU.
Charles!
SO-NA, YOU LOOK REALLY PRETTY TODAY.
PUT ME DOWN, IDIOT!
Hmmm.
HA HA HA!! STOP!!
I feel so nervous. Maybe it's because I haven't been to a party like this in ages? No, it's not that.

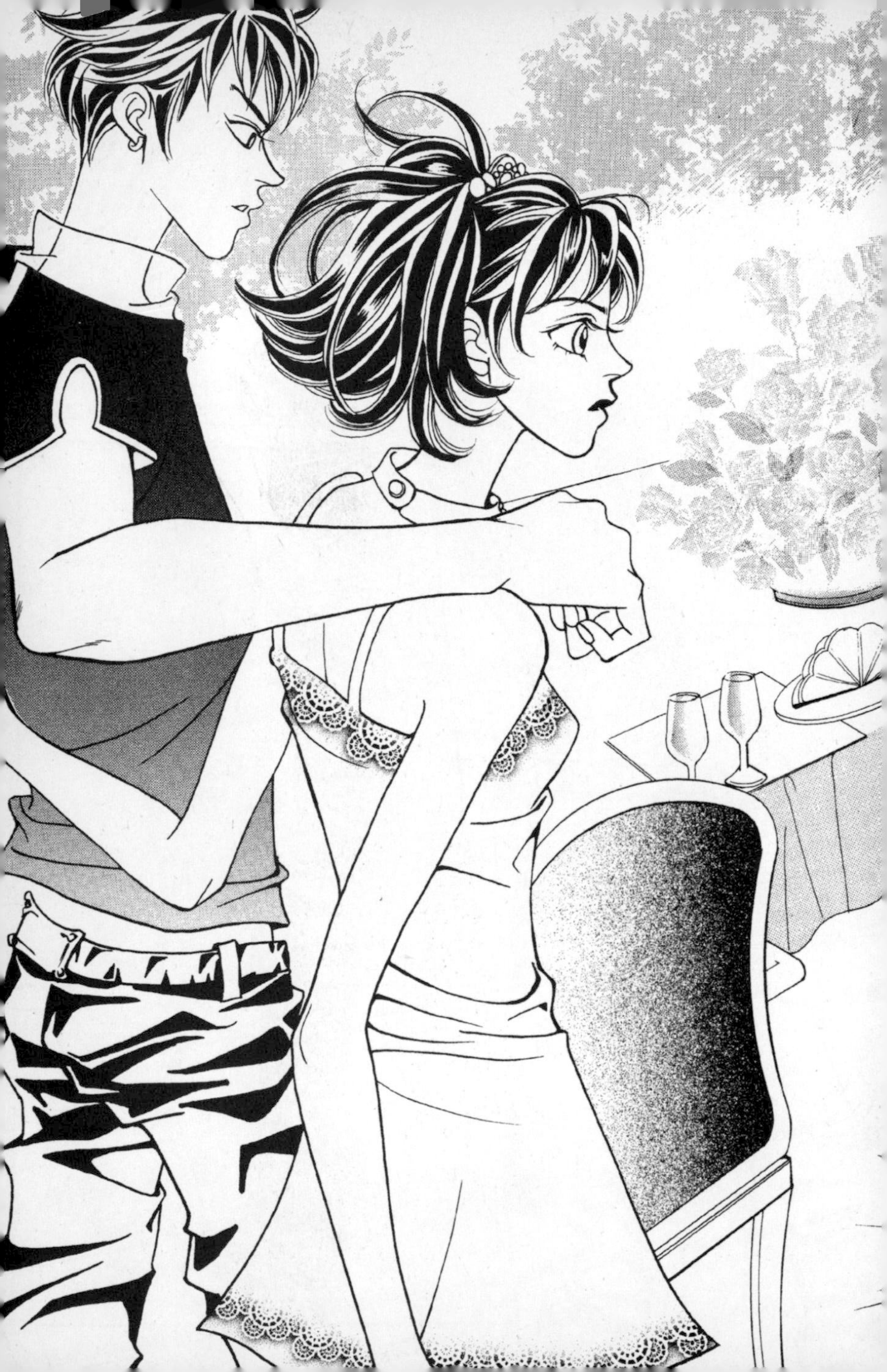

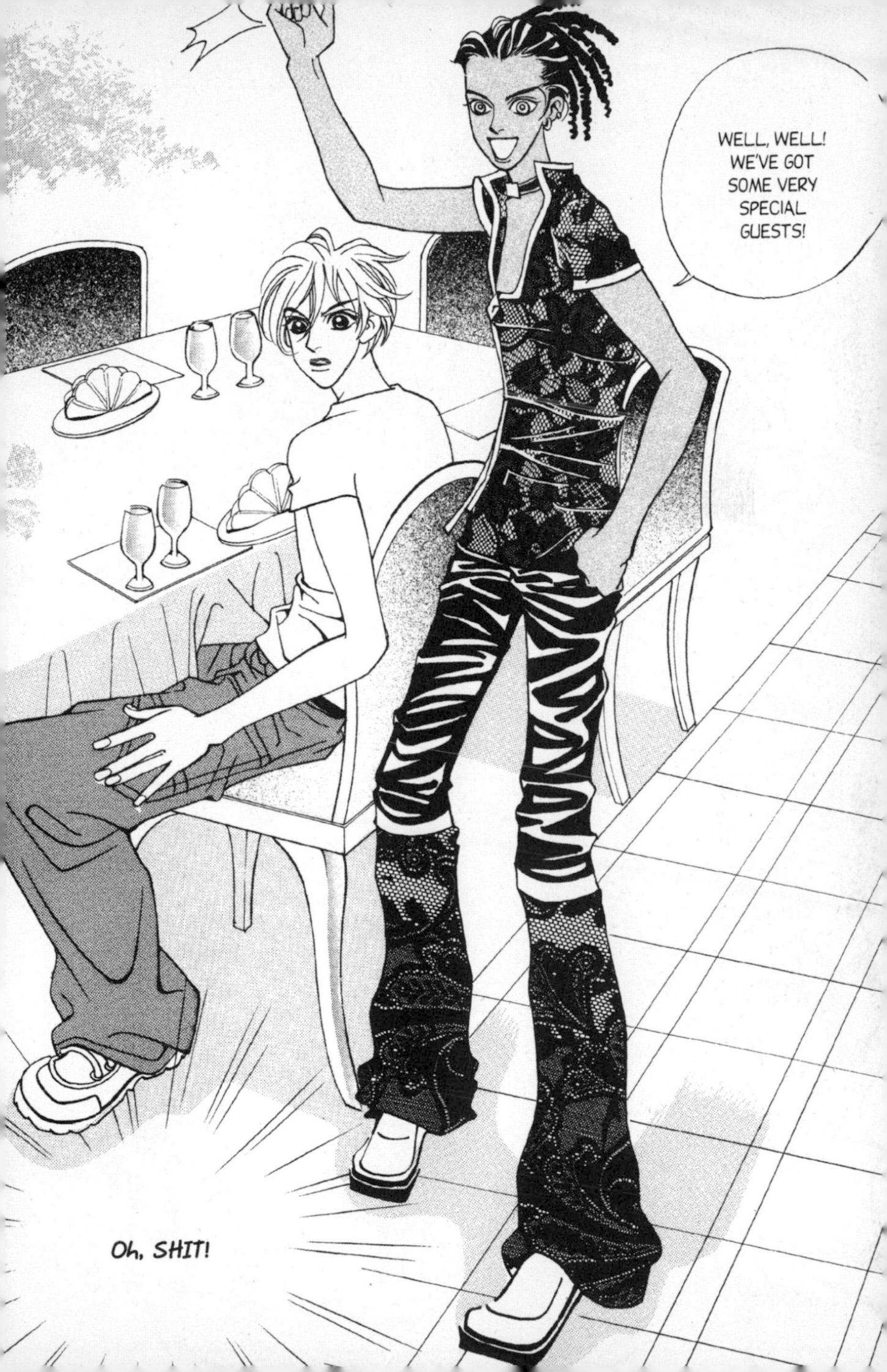
WELL, WELL! WE'VE GOT SOME VERY SPECIAL GUESTS!
Oh, SHIT!

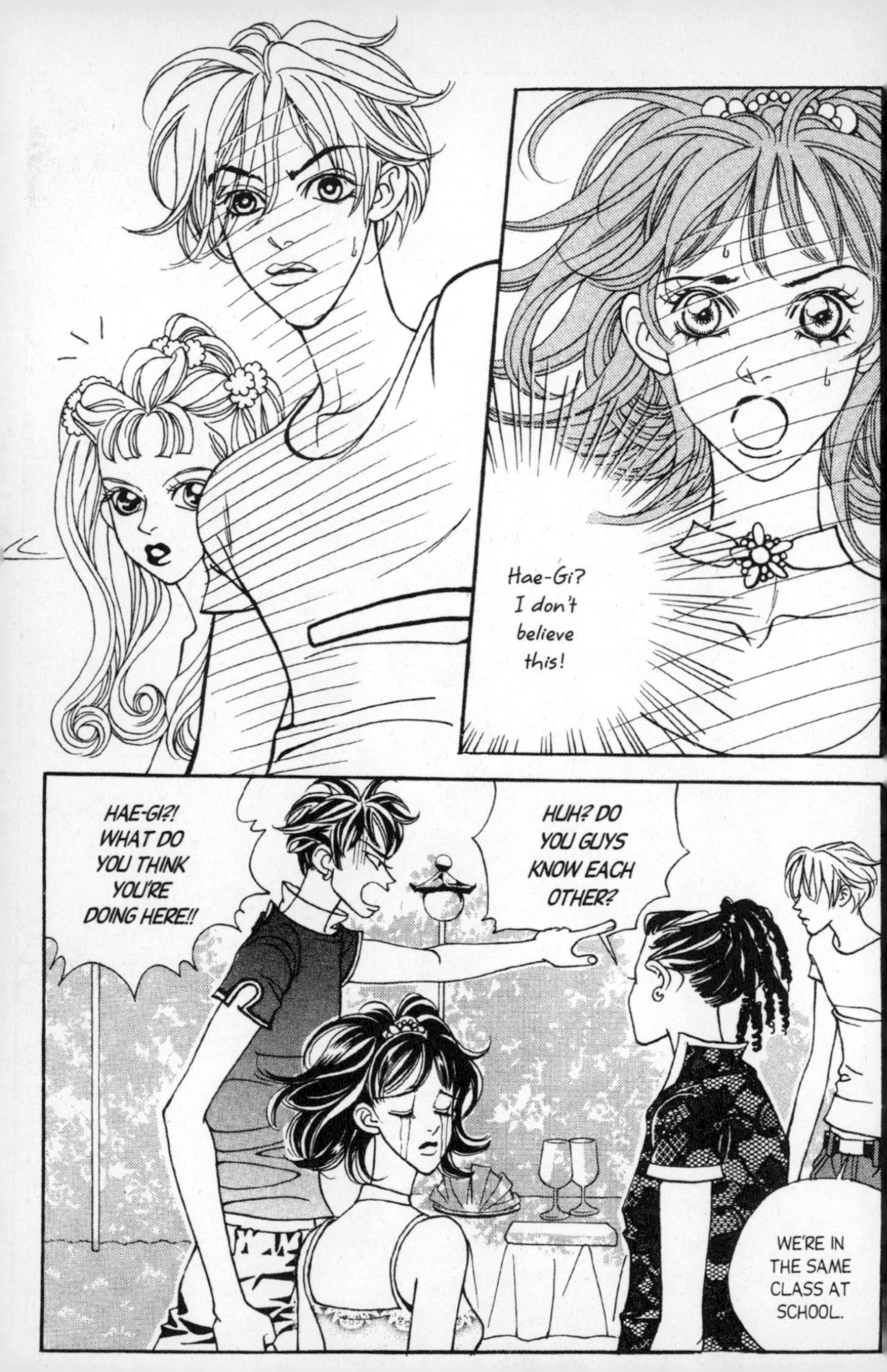
Hae-Gi? I don't believe this!
HAE-GI?! WHAT DO YOU THINK YOU'RE DOING HERE!!
HUH? DO YOU GUYS KNOW EACH OTHER?
WE'RE IN THE SAME CLASS AT SCHOOL.

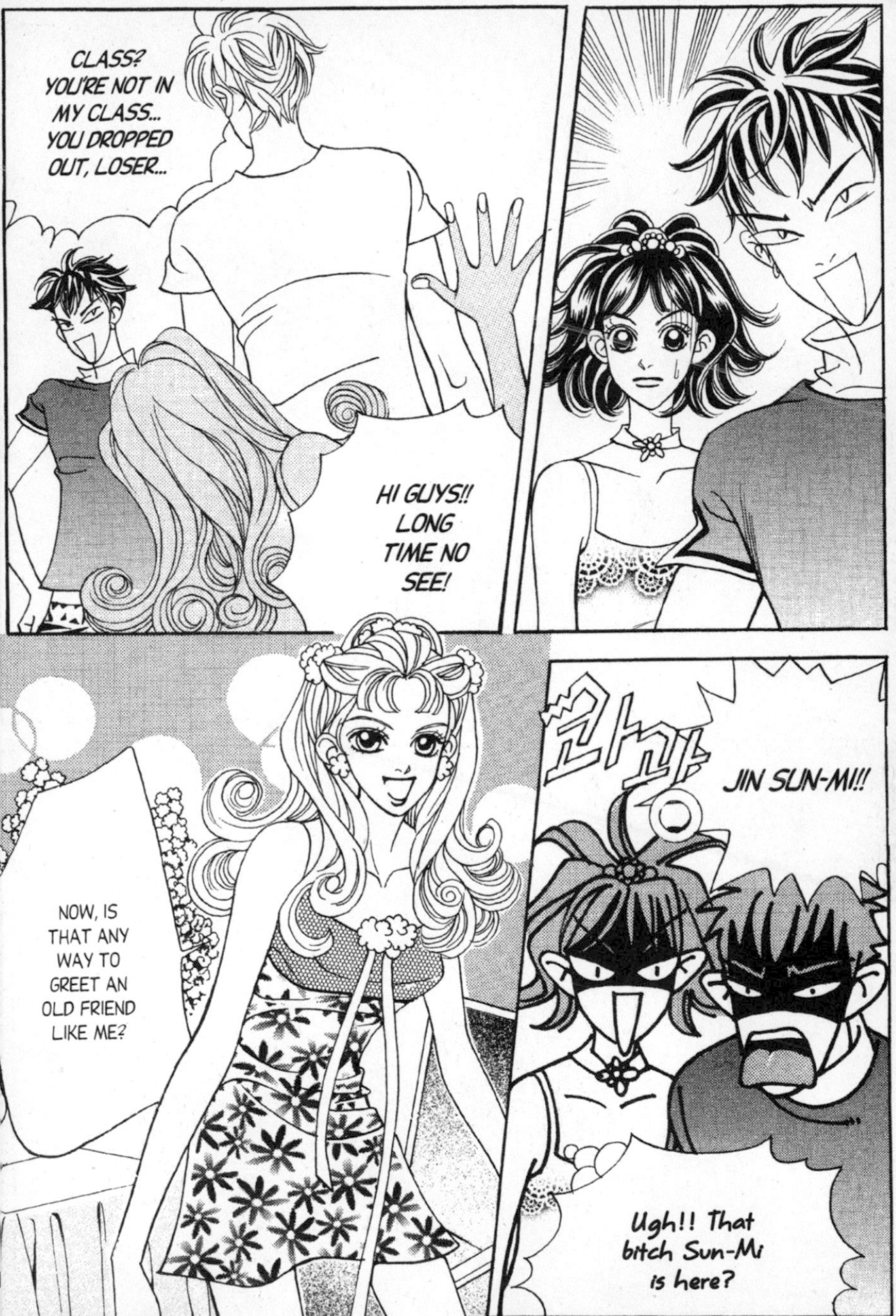
CLASS? YOU'RE NOT IN MY CLASS... YOU DROPPED OUT, LOSER...
HI GUYS!! LONG TIME NO SEE!
NOW, IS THAT ANY WAY TO GREET AN OLD FRIEND LIKE ME?
JIN SUN-MI!!
Ugh!! That bitch Sun-Mi is here?

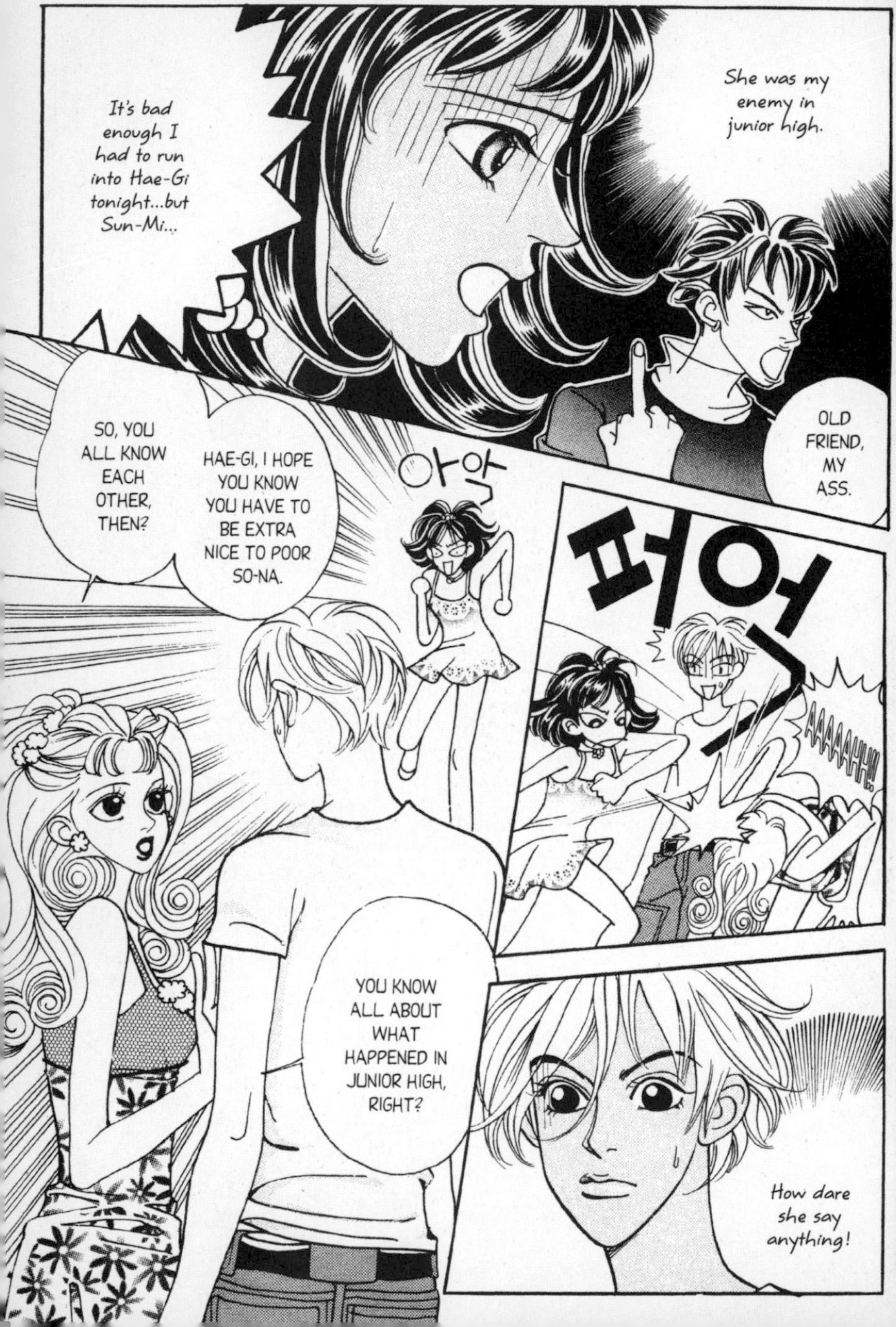

It's bad enough I had to run into Hae-Gi tonight...but Sun-Mi...
She was my enemy in junior high.
OLD FRIEND, MY ASS.
SO, YOU ALL KNOW EACH OTHER, THEN?
HAE-GI, I HOPE YOU KNOW YOU HAVE TO BE EXTRA NICE TO POOR SO-NA.
아얏
YOU KNOW ALL ABOUT WHAT HAPPENED IN JUNIOR HIGH, RIGHT?
퍼억
AAAAAHH!!
How dare she say anything!

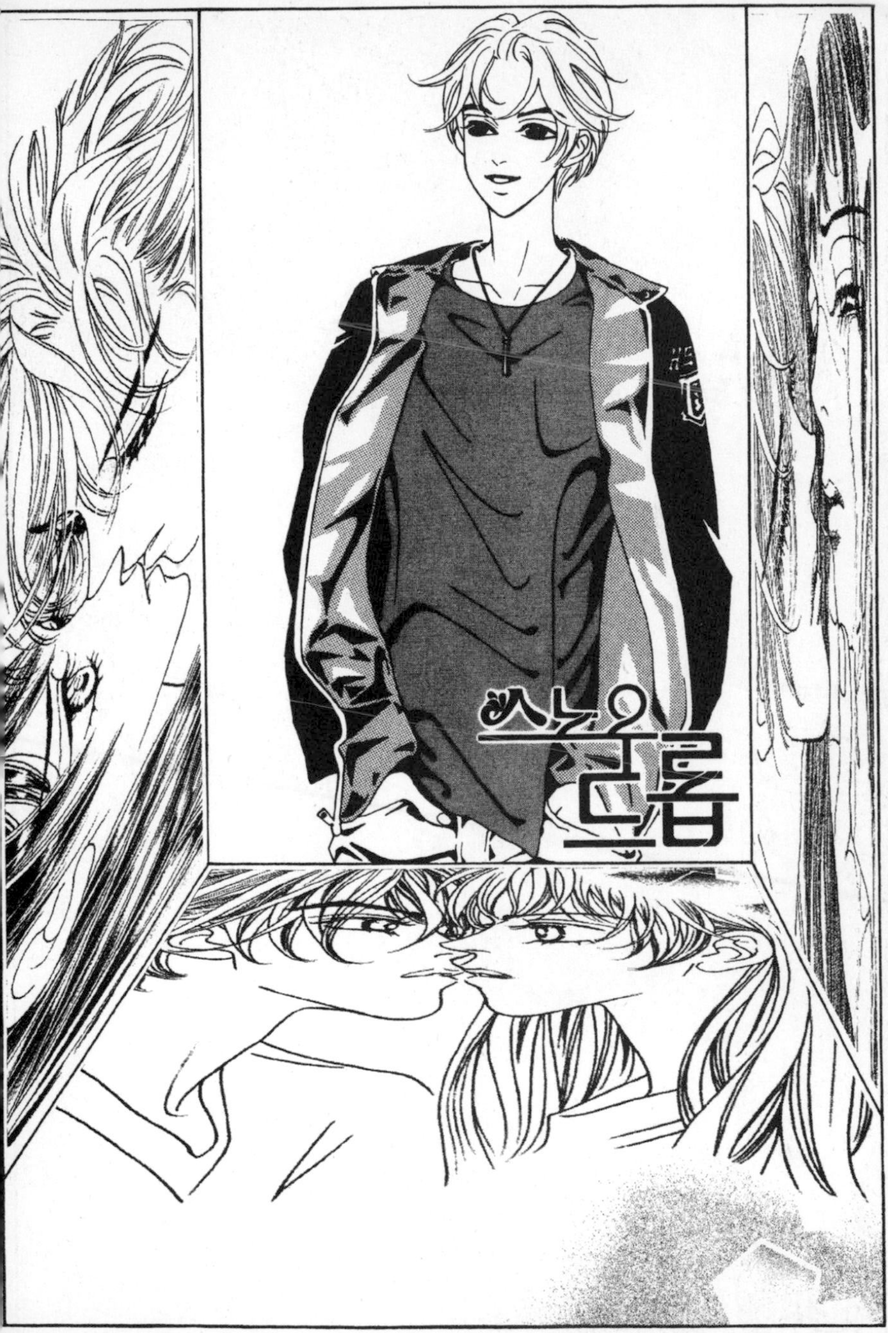
스노우 드롭

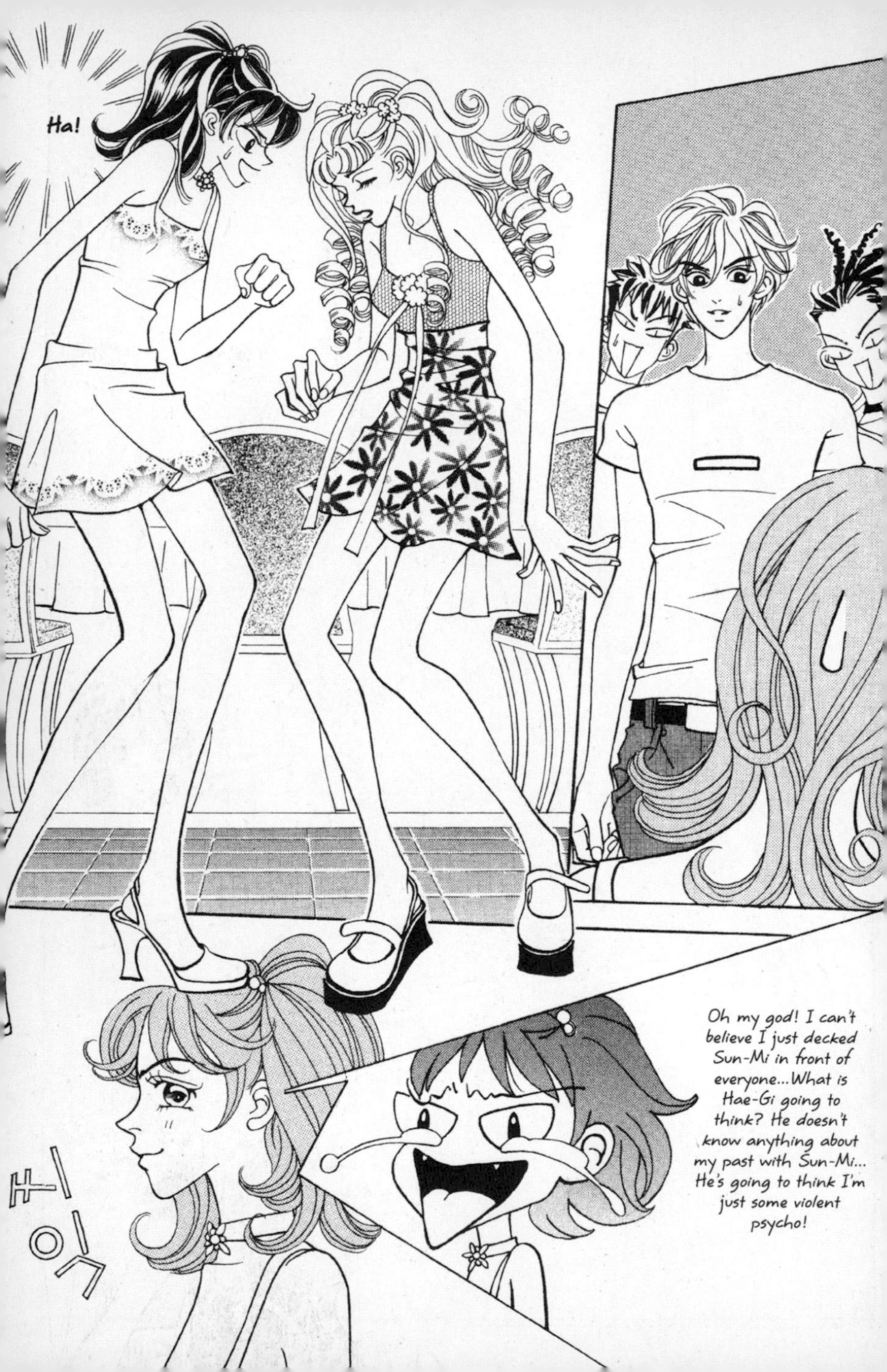
Ha!
Oh my god! I can't believe I just decked Sun-Mi in front of everyone...What is Hae-Gi going to think? He doesn't know anything about my past with Sun-Mi... He's going to think I'm just some violent psycho!

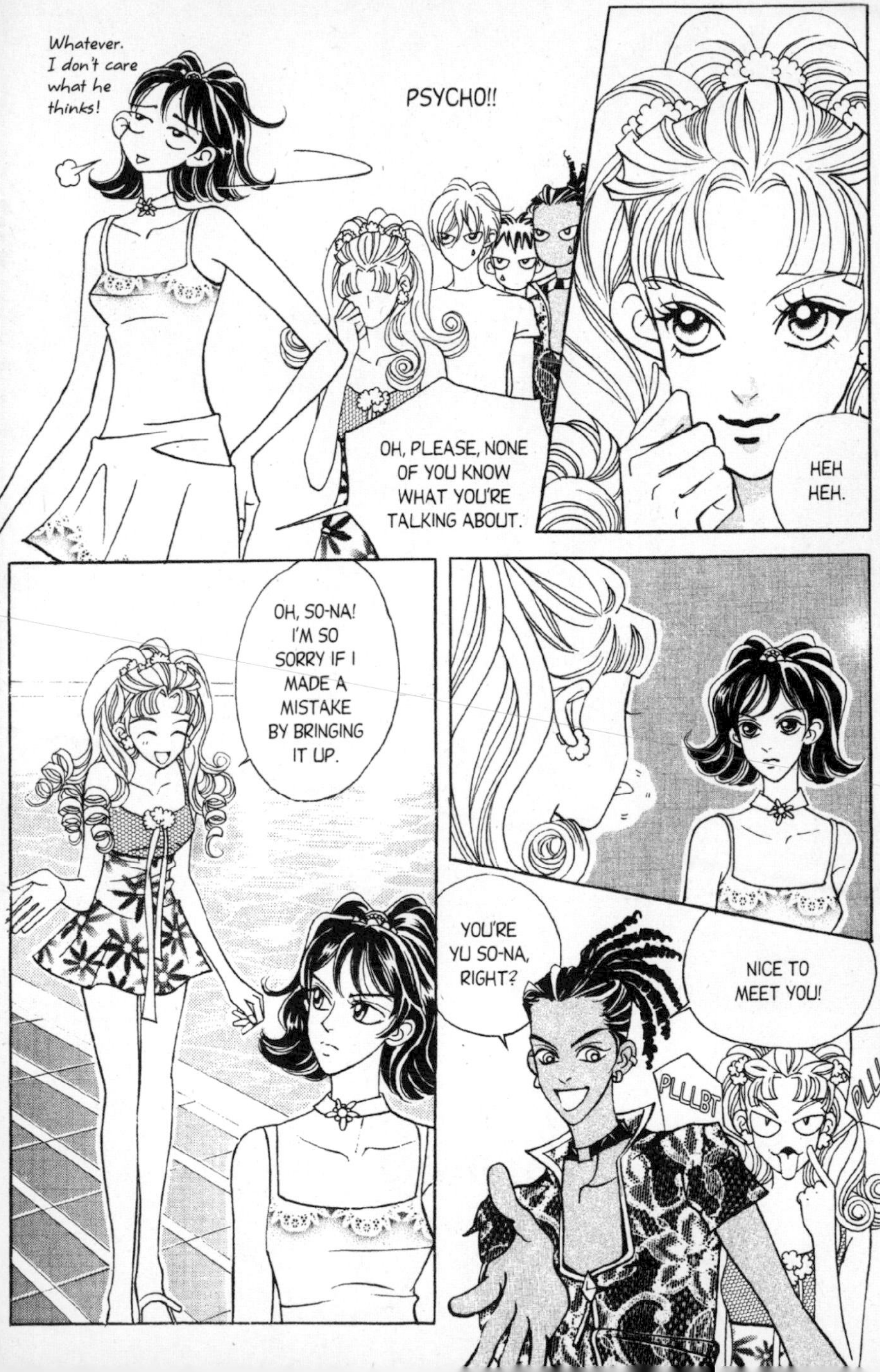
Whatever. I don't care what he thinks!
PSYCHO!!
OH, PLEASE, NONE OF YOU KNOW WHAT YOU'RE TALKING ABOUT.
HEH HEH.
OH, SO-NA! I'M SO SORRY IF I MADE A MISTAKE BY BRINGING IT UP.
YOU'RE YU SO-NA, RIGHT?
NICE TO MEET YOU!
PLLLBT
PLLLBT

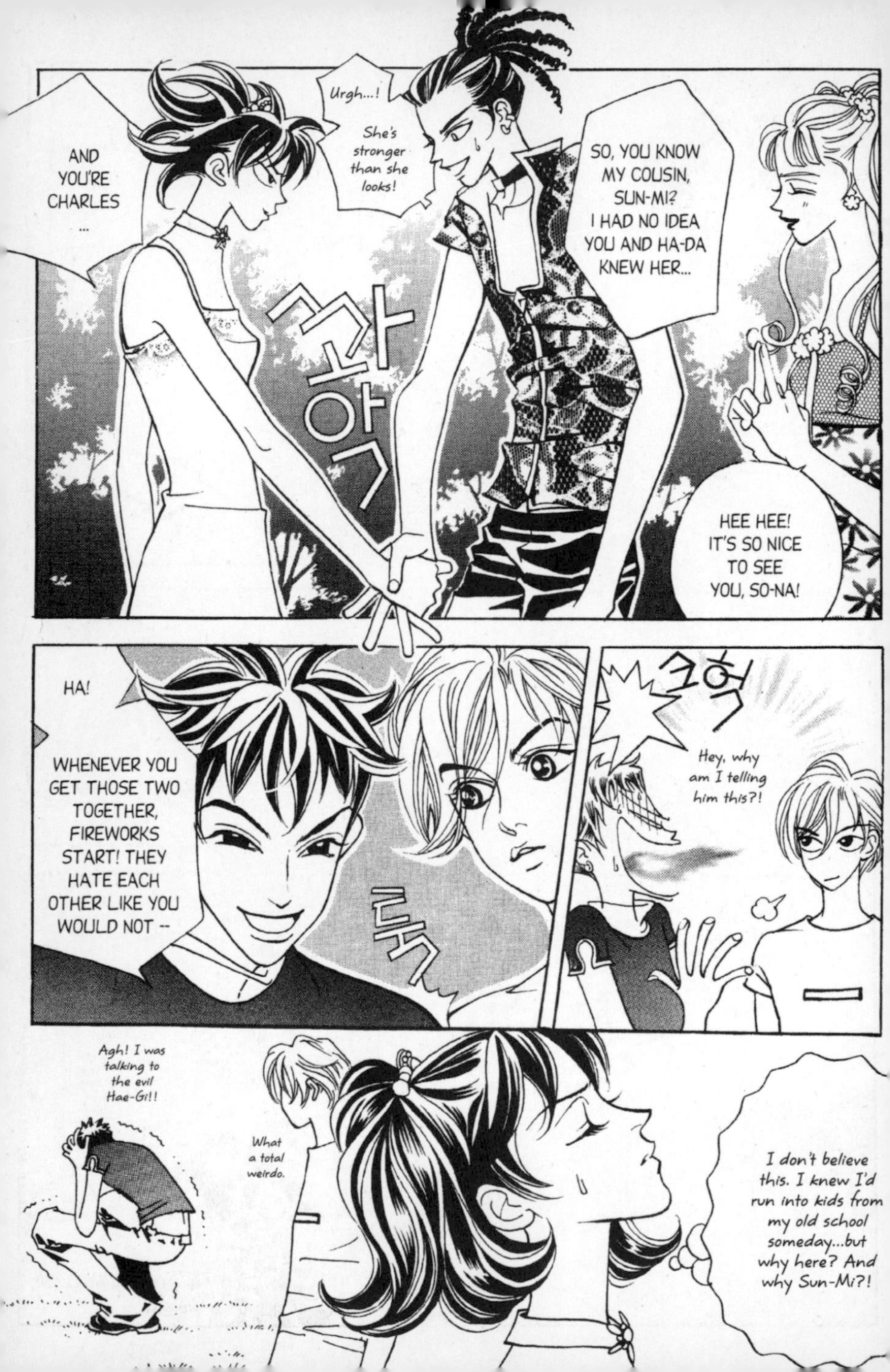
AND YOU'RE CHARLES ...
Urgh...!
She's stronger than she looks!
SO, YOU KNOW MY COUSIN, SUN-MI? I HAD NO IDEA YOU AND HA-DA KNEW HER...
HEE HEE! IT'S SO NICE TO SEE YOU, SO-NA!
HA!
WHENEVER YOU GET THOSE TWO TOGETHER, FIREWORKS START! THEY HATE EACH OTHER LIKE YOU WOULD NOT --
Hey, why am I telling him this?!
Agh! I was talking to the evil Hae-Gi!!
What a total weirdo.
I don't believe this. I knew I'd run into kids from my old school someday...but why here? And why Sun-Mi?!

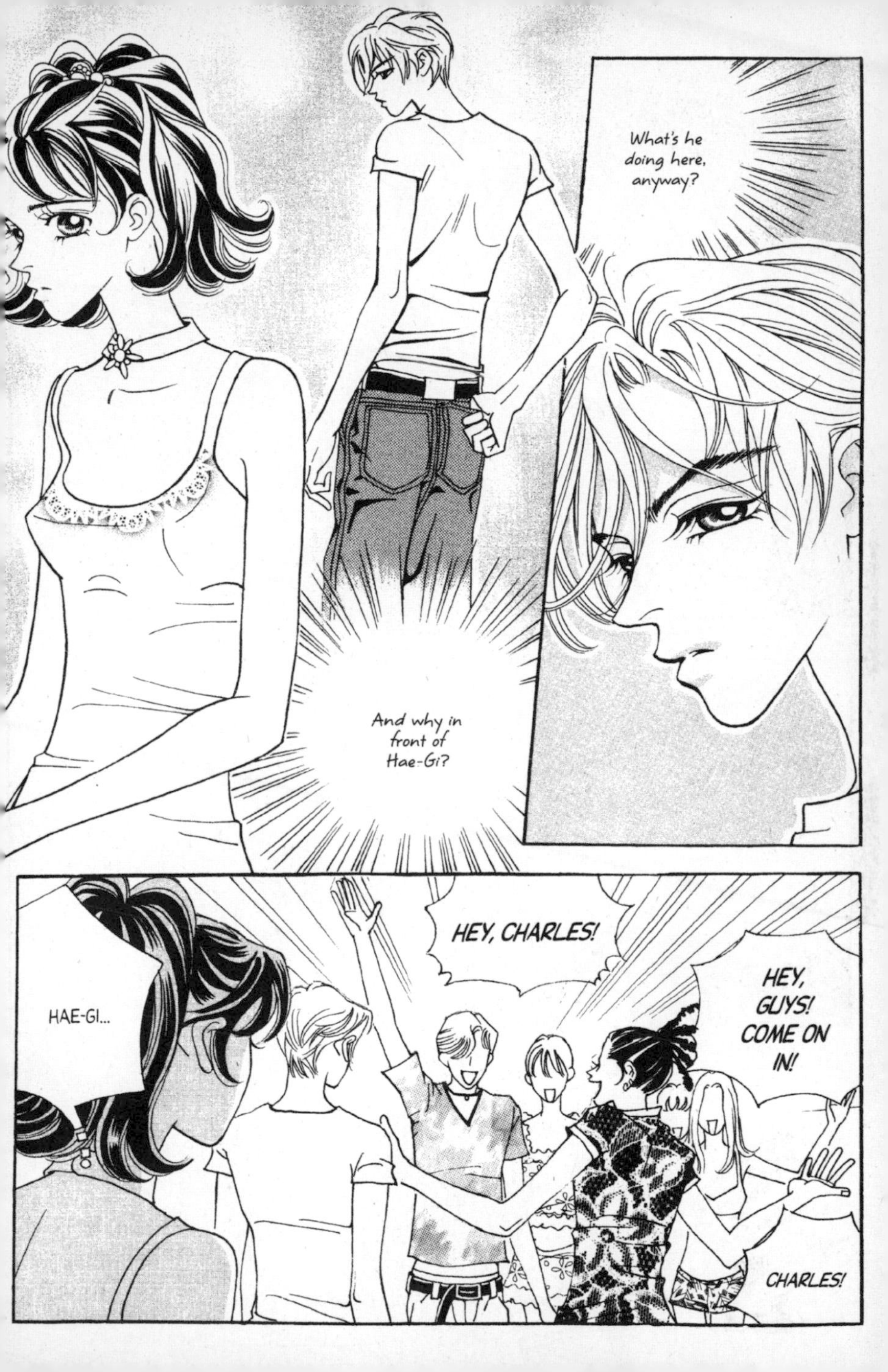
What's he doing here, anyway?
And why in front of Hae-Gi?
HAE-GI...
HEY, CHARLES!
HEY, GUYS! COME ON IN!
CHARLES!

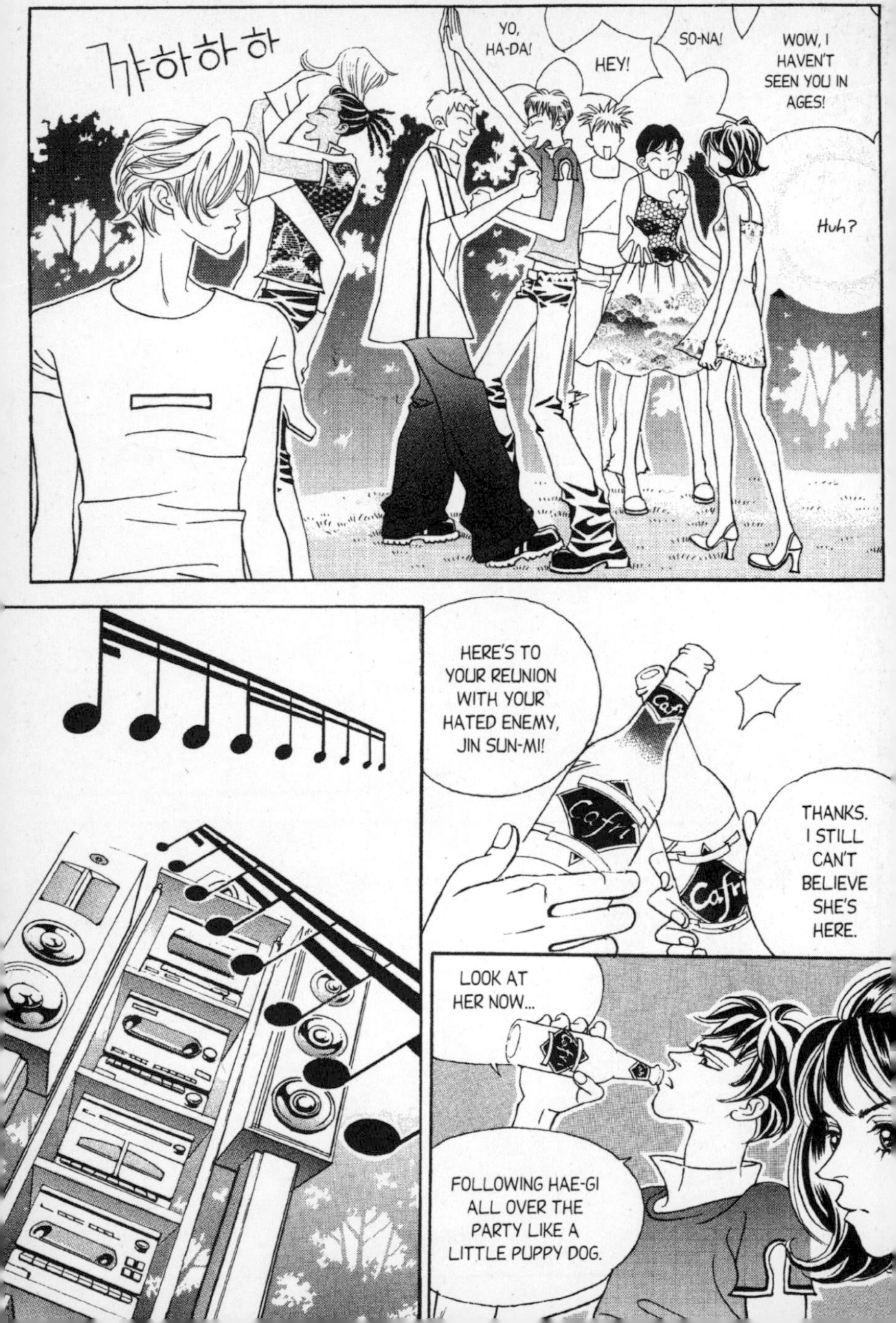
꺄하하 하
YO, HA-DA!
HEY!
SO-NA!
WOW, I HAVEN'T SEEN YOU IN AGES!
Huh?
HERE'S TO YOUR REUNION WITH YOUR HATED ENEMY, JIN SUN-MI!
Cafri
THANKS. I STILL CAN'T BELIEVE SHE'S HERE.
LOOK AT HER NOW...
FOLLOWING HAE-GI ALL OVER THE PARTY LIKE A LITTLE PUPPY DOG.

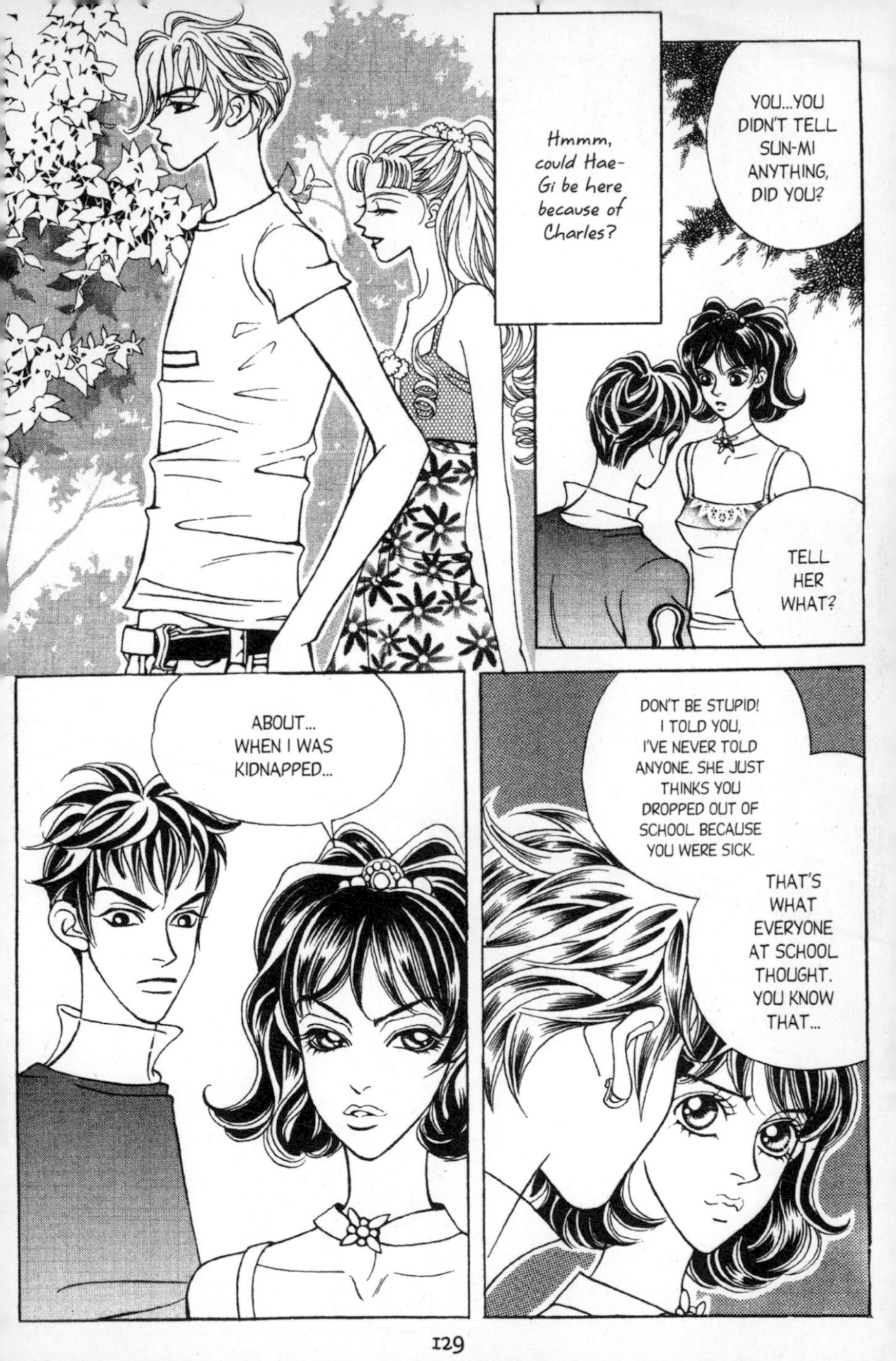

Hmmm, could Hae-Gi be here because of Charles?
YOU...YOU DIDN'T TELL SUN-MI ANYTHING, DID YOU?
TELL HER WHAT?
ABOUT... WHEN I WAS KIDNAPPED...
DON'T BE STUPID! I TOLD YOU, I'VE NEVER TOLD ANYONE. SHE JUST THINKS YOU DROPPED OUT OF SCHOOL BECAUSE YOU WERE SICK.
THAT'S WHAT EVERYONE AT SCHOOL THOUGHT. YOU KNOW THAT...

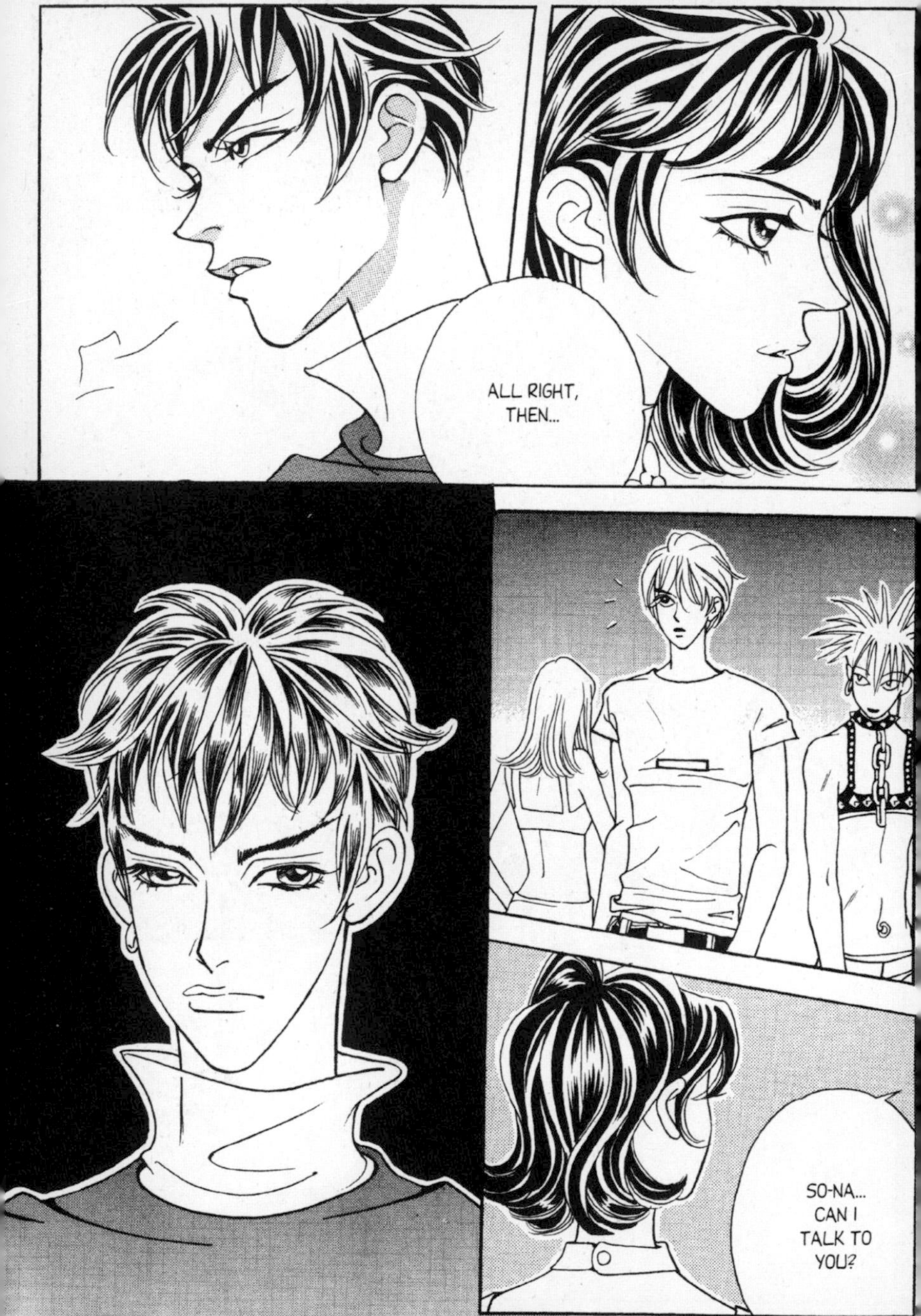
ALL RIGHT, THEN...
SO-NA... CAN I TALK TO YOU?

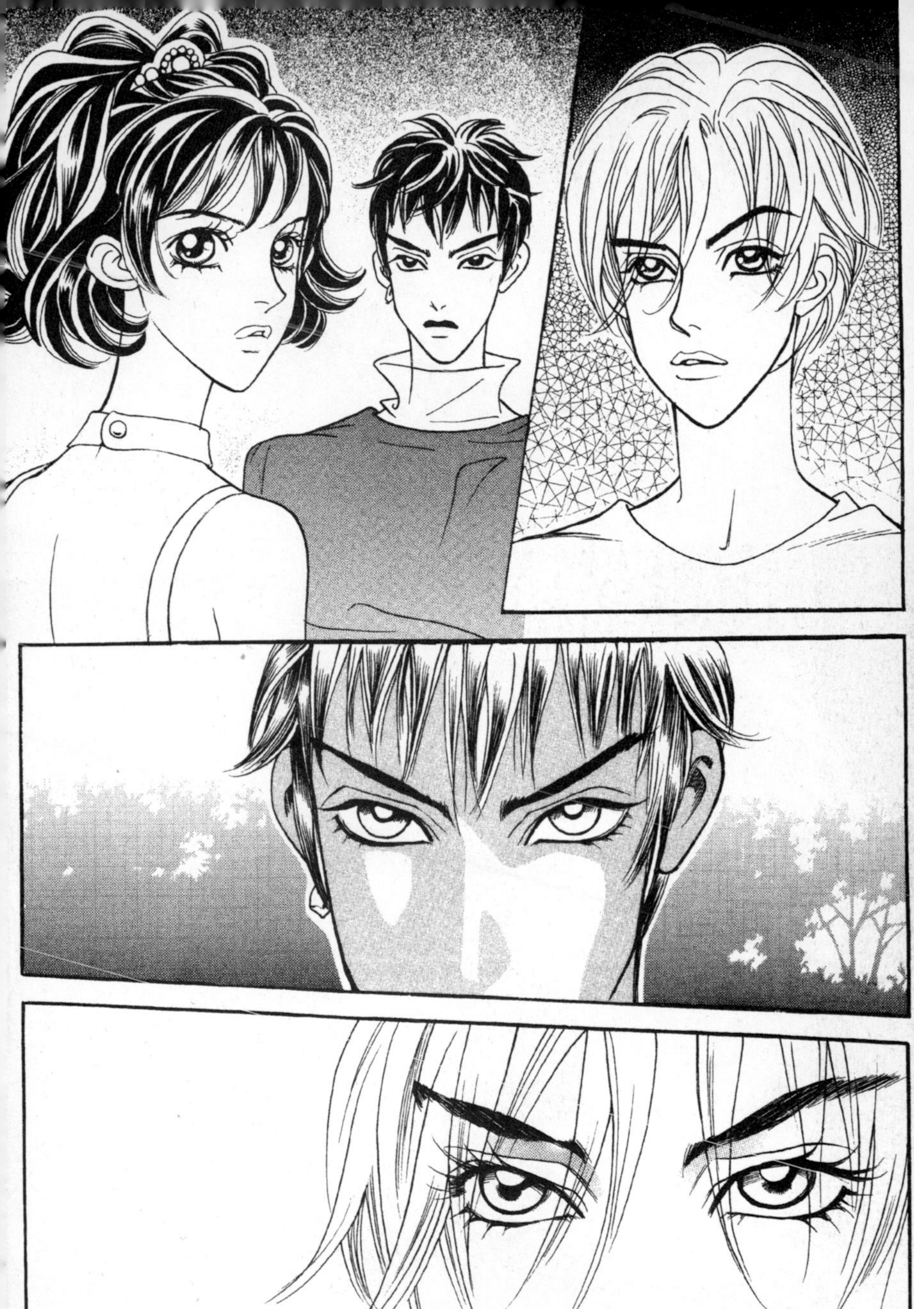

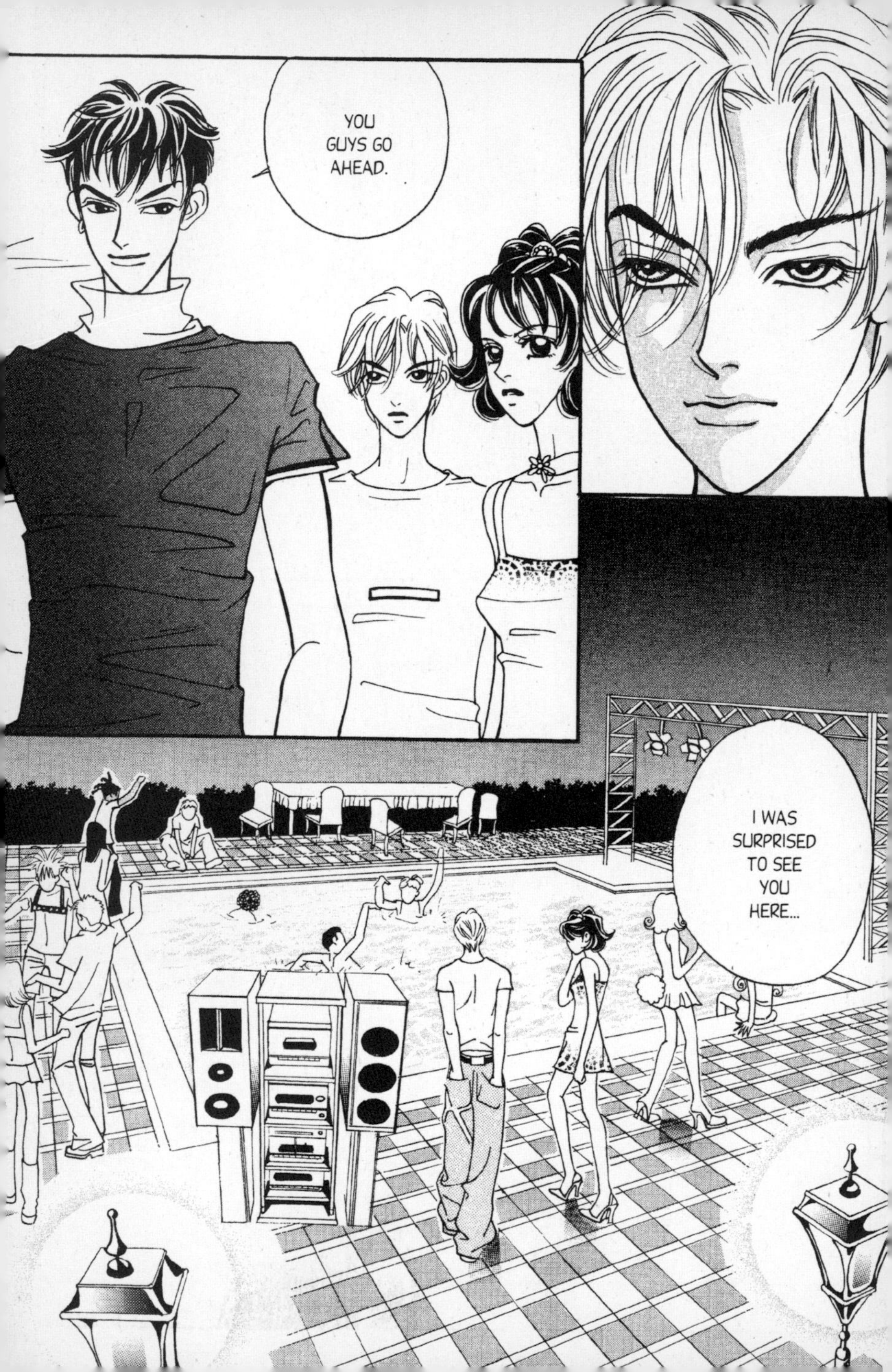
YOU GUYS GO AHEAD.
I WAS SURPRISED TO SEE YOU HERE...

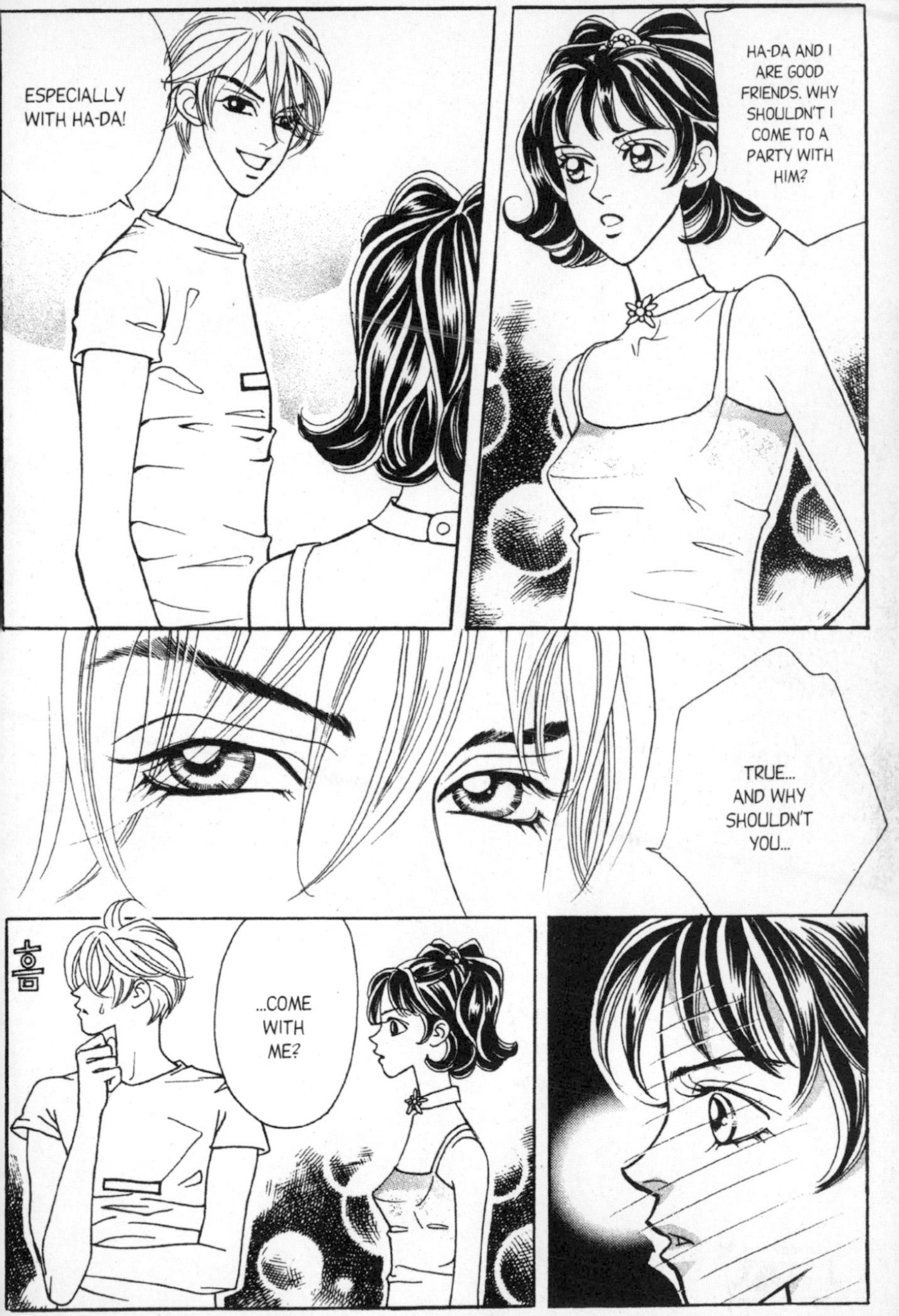
ESPECIALLY WITH HA-DA!
HA-DA AND I ARE GOOD FRIENDS. WHY SHOULDN'T I COME TO A PARTY WITH HIM?
TRUE... AND WHY SHOULDN'T YOU...
흠
...COME WITH ME?

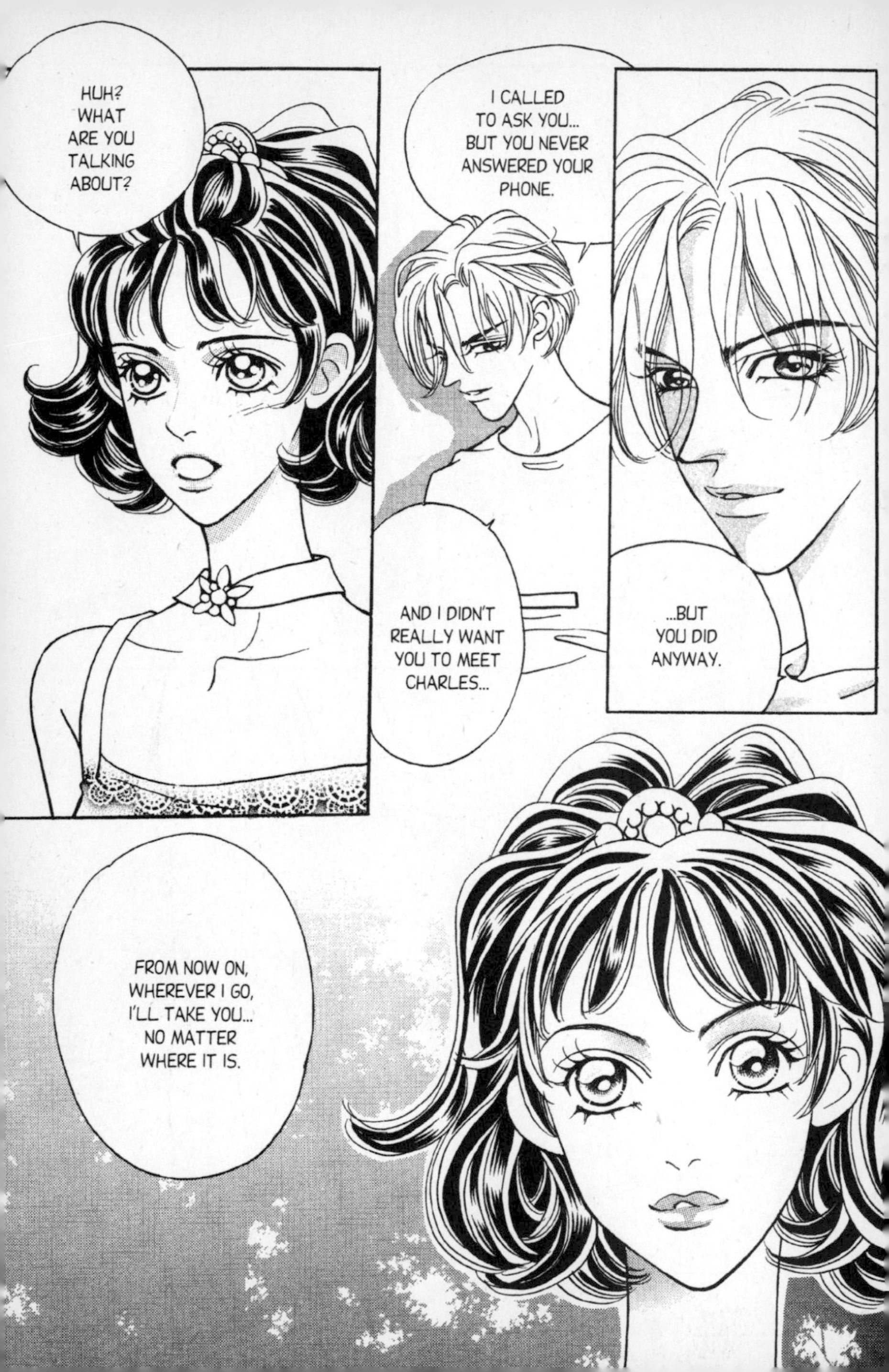
HUH? WHAT ARE YOU TALKING ABOUT?
I CALLED TO ASK YOU... BUT YOU NEVER ANSWERED YOUR PHONE.
AND I DIDN'T REALLY WANT YOU TO MEET CHARLES...
...BUT YOU DID ANYWAY.
FROM NOW ON, WHEREVER I GO, I'LL TAKE YOU... NO MATTER WHERE IT IS.

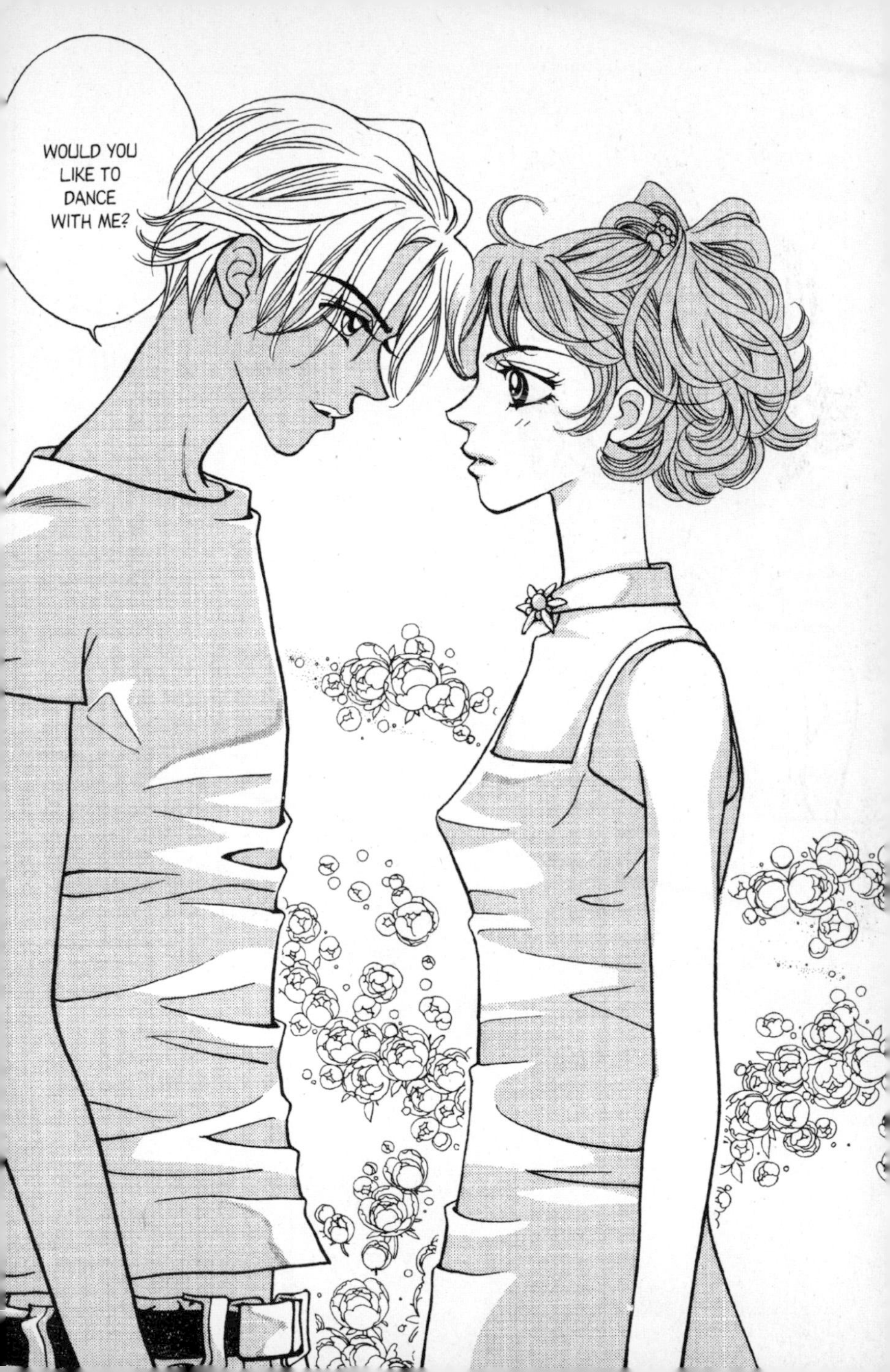
WOULD YOU LIKE TO DANCE WITH ME?

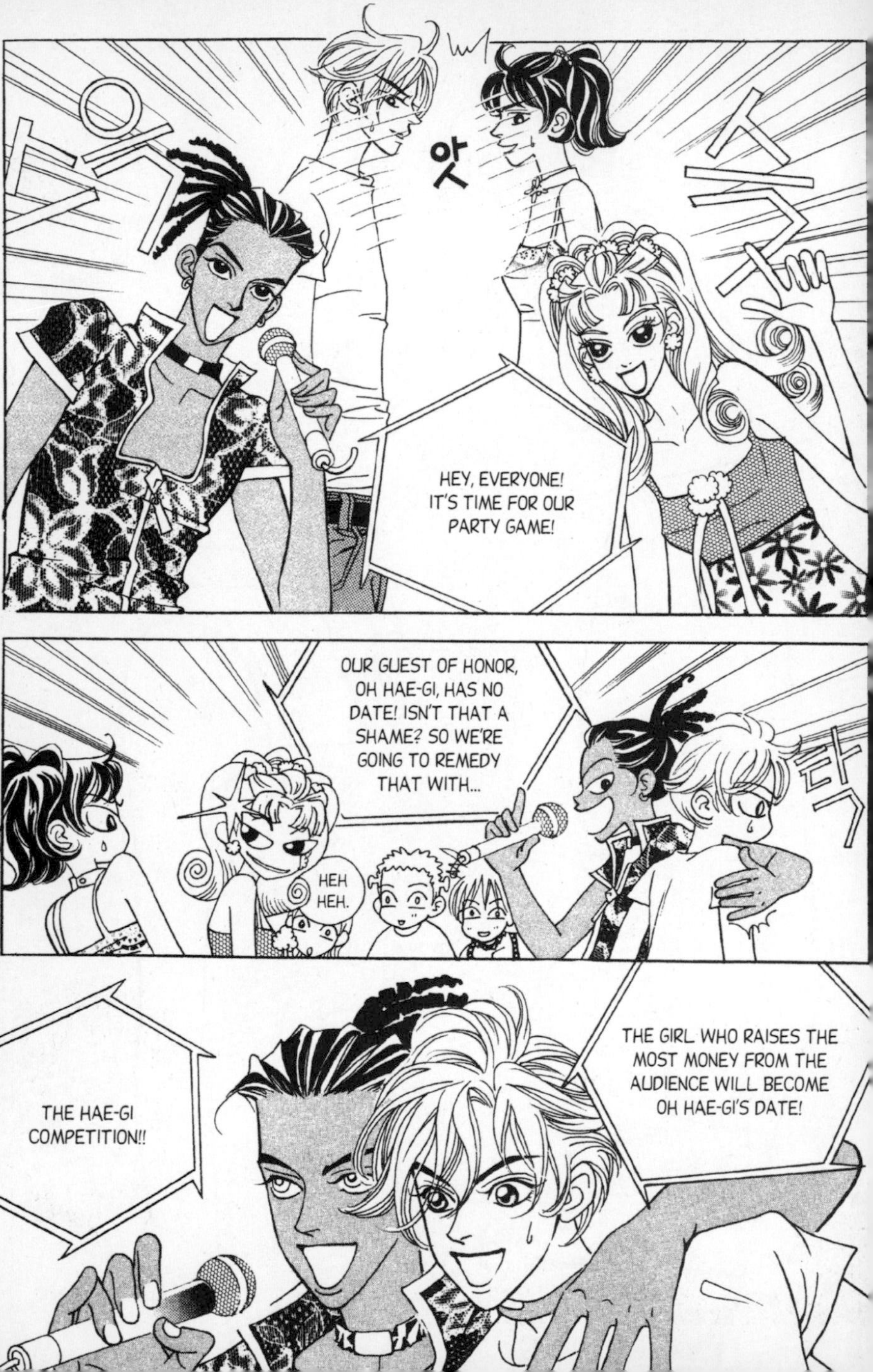
앗
HEY, EVERYONE! IT'S TIME FOR OUR PARTY GAME!
OUR GUEST OF HONOR, OH HAE-GI, HAS NO DATE! ISN'T THAT A SHAME? SO WE'RE GOING TO REMEDY THAT WITH...
HEH HEH.
탁
THE HAE-GI COMPETITION!!
THE GIRL WHO RAISES THE MOST MONEY FROM THE AUDIENCE WILL BECOME OH HAE-GI'S DATE!

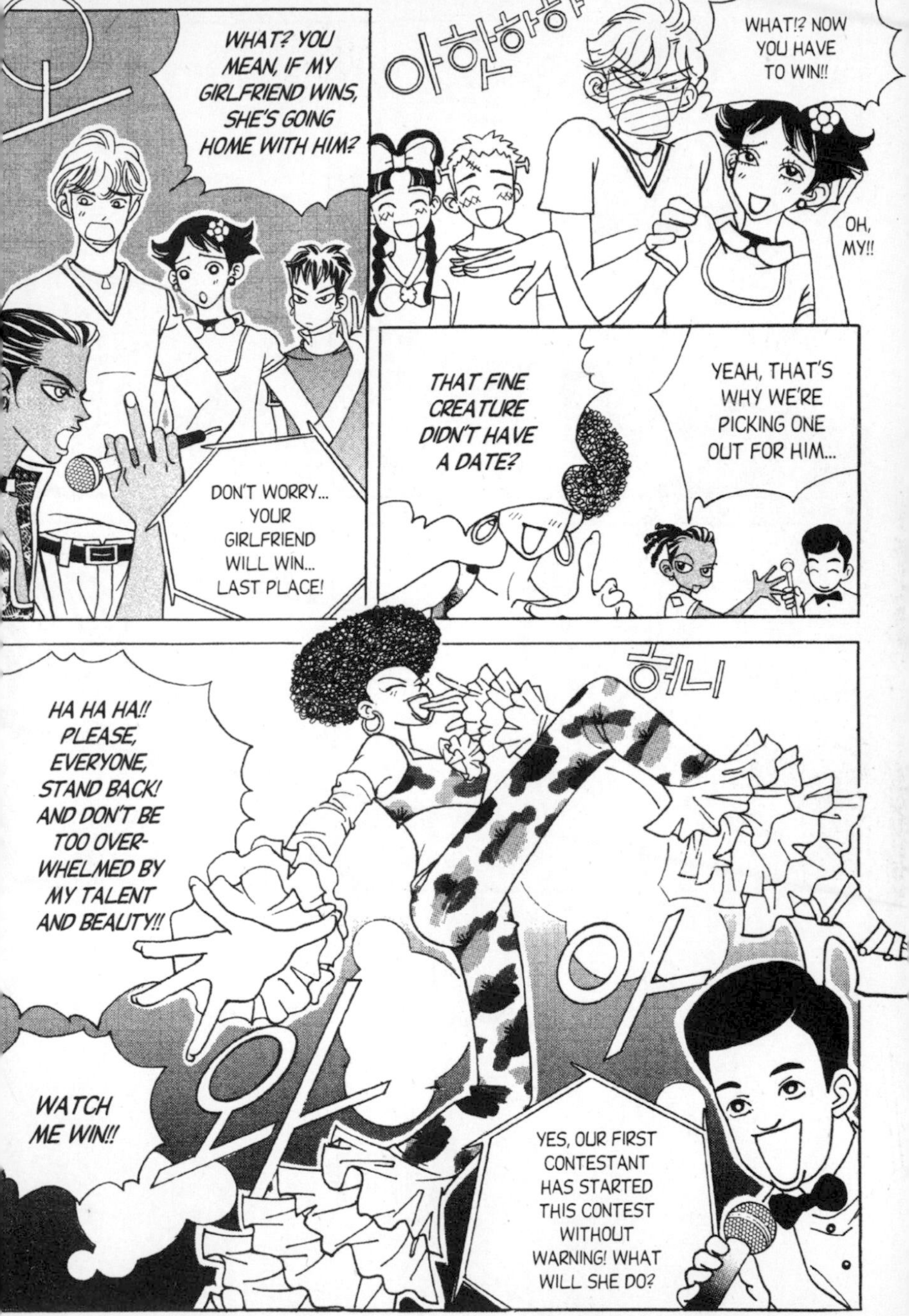
오
WHAT? YOU MEAN, IF MY GIRLFRIEND WINS, SHE'S GOING HOME WITH HIM?
DON'T WORRY... YOUR GIRLFRIEND WILL WIN... LAST PLACE!
아핫하하
WHAT!? NOW YOU HAVE TO WIN!!
OH, MY!!
THAT FINE CREATURE DIDN'T HAVE A DATE?
YEAH, THAT'S WHY WE'RE PICKING ONE OUT FOR HIM...
HA HA HA!! PLEASE, EVERYONE, STAND BACK! AND DON'T BE TOO OVER-WHELMED BY MY TALENT AND BEAUTY!!
허니
WATCH ME WIN!!
YES, OUR FIRST CONTESTANT HAS STARTED THIS CONTEST WITHOUT WARNING! WHAT WILL SHE DO?

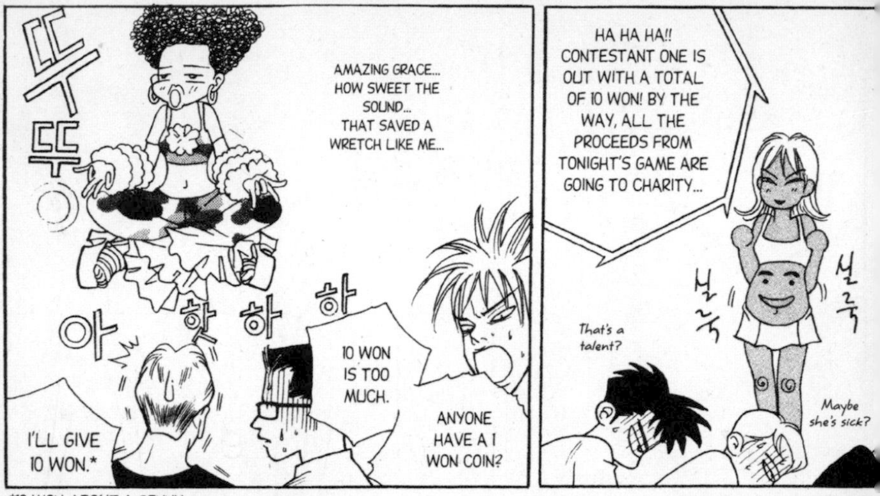
뚜 뚜
AMAZING GRACE... HOW SWEET THE SOUND... THAT SAVED A WRETCH LIKE ME...
아 핫 하 하
I'LL GIVE 10 WON.*
10 WON IS TOO MUCH.
ANYONE HAVE A 1 WON COIN?
HA HA HA!! CONTESTANT ONE IS OUT WITH A TOTAL OF 10 WON! BY THE WAY, ALL THE PROCEEDS FROM TONIGHT'S GAME ARE GOING TO CHARITY...
실룩 실룩
That's a talent?
Maybe she's sick?

*10 WON=ABOUT A PENNY

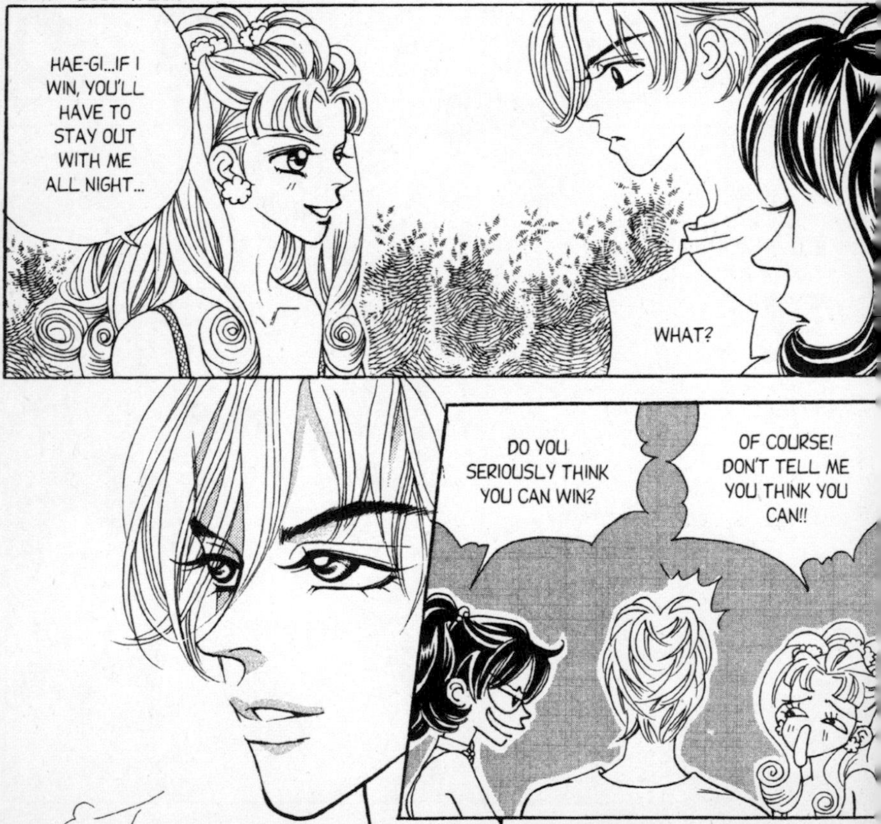
HAE-GI...IF I WIN, YOU'LL HAVE TO STAY OUT WITH ME ALL NIGHT...
WHAT?
DO YOU SERIOUSLY THINK YOU CAN WIN?
OF COURSE! DON'T TELL ME YOU THINK YOU CAN!!

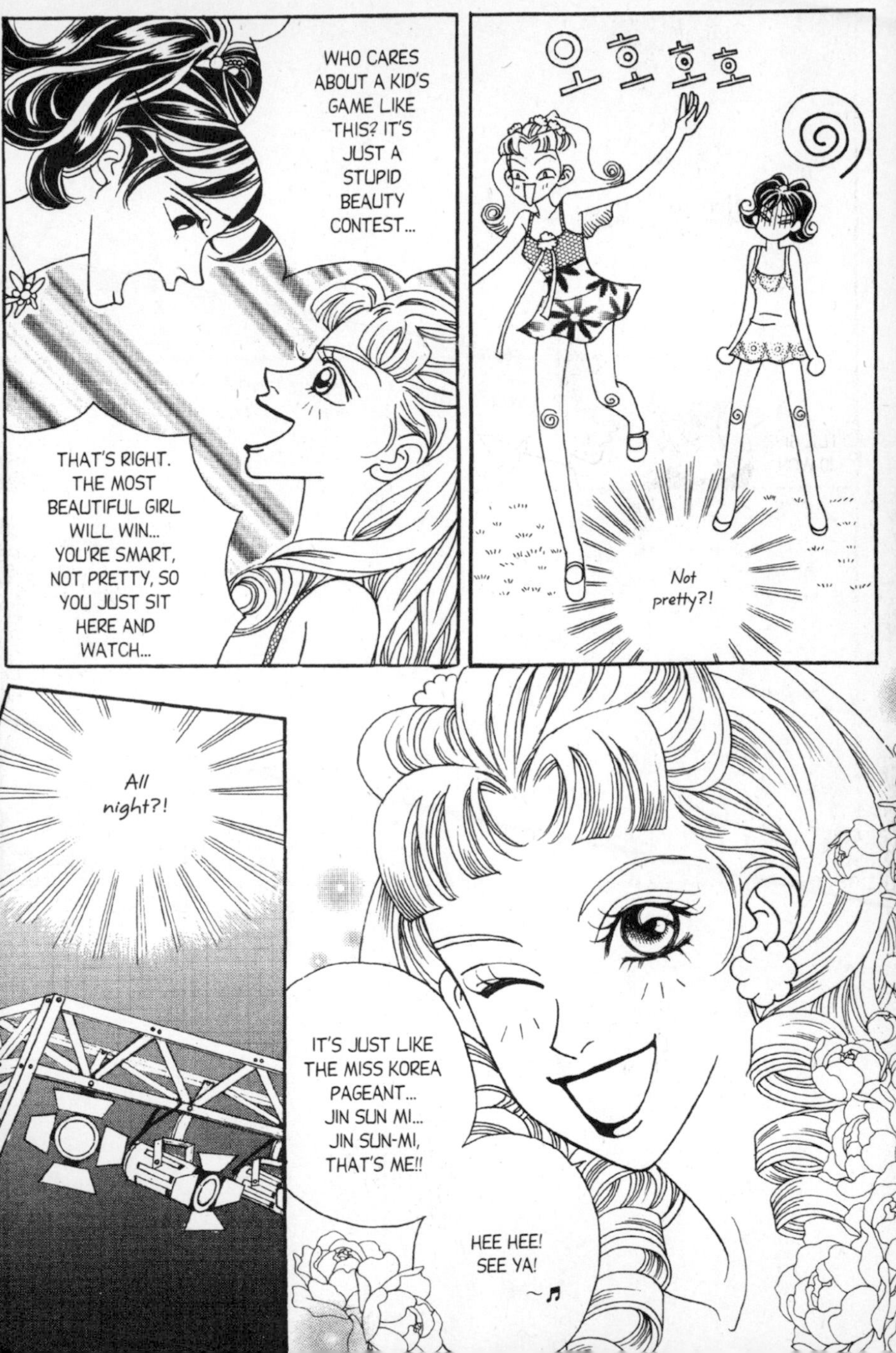
WHO CARES ABOUT A KID'S GAME LIKE THIS? IT'S JUST A STUPID BEAUTY CONTEST...
THAT'S RIGHT. THE MOST BEAUTIFUL GIRL WILL WIN... YOU'RE SMART, NOT PRETTY, SO YOU JUST SIT HERE AND WATCH...
오호호호
Not pretty?!
All night?!
IT'S JUST LIKE THE MISS KOREA PAGEANT... JIN SUN MI... JIN SUN-MI, THAT'S ME!!
HEE HEE! SEE YA!
~♫

NOTE: IN THE MISS KOREA PAGEANT, JIN=1ST PLACE, SUN=2ND AND MI=3RD. SO JIN SUN MI MEANS "1ST, 2ND, AND 3RD"

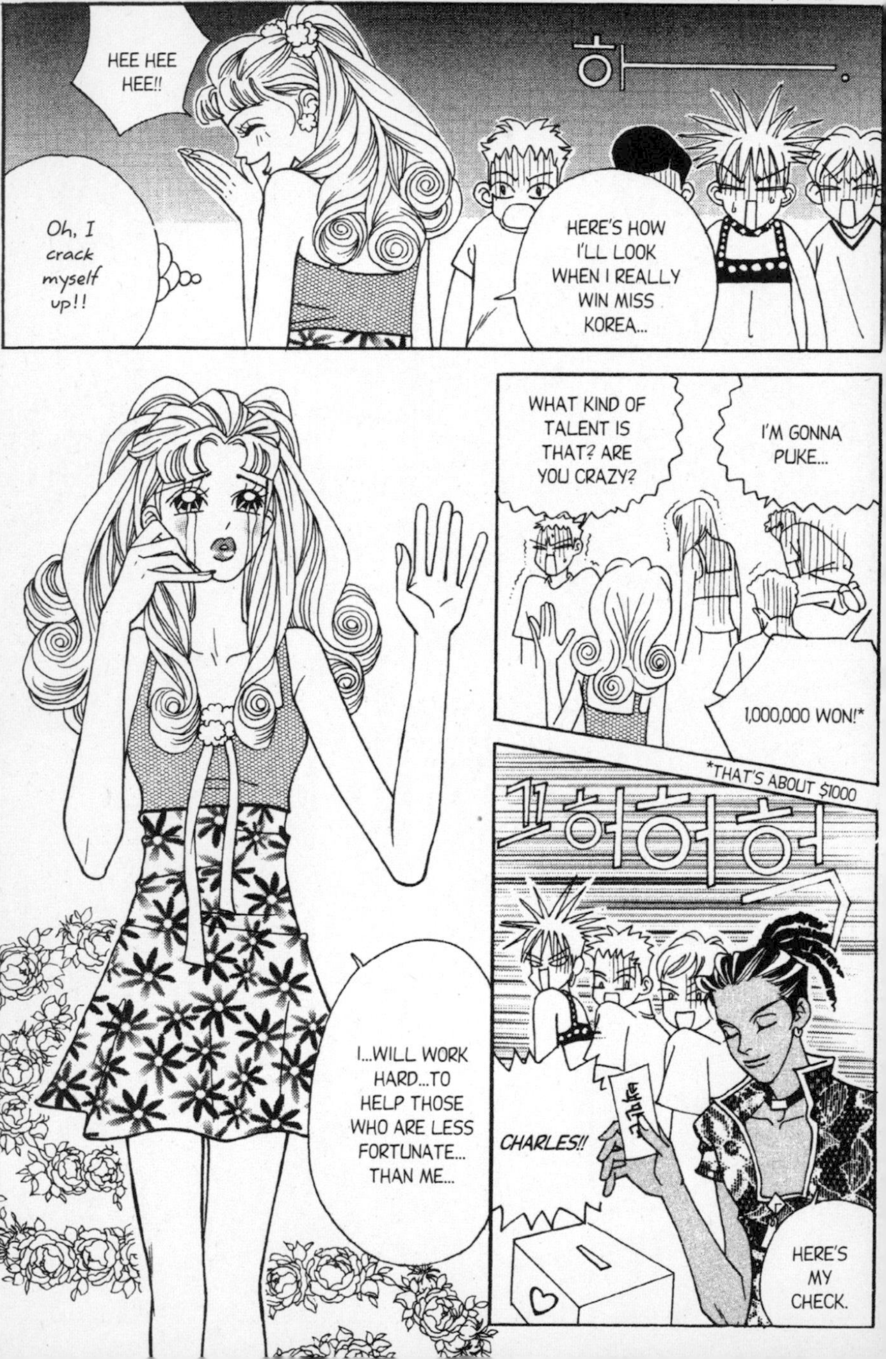
HEE HEE HEE!!
Oh, I crack myself up!!
하
HERE'S HOW I'LL LOOK WHEN I REALLY WIN MISS KOREA...
I...WILL WORK HARD...TO HELP THOSE WHO ARE LESS FORTUNATE... THAN ME...
WHAT KIND OF TALENT IS THAT? ARE YOU CRAZY?
I'M GONNA PUKE...
1,000,000 WON!*
*THAT'S ABOUT $1000
CHARLES!!
HERE'S MY CHECK.

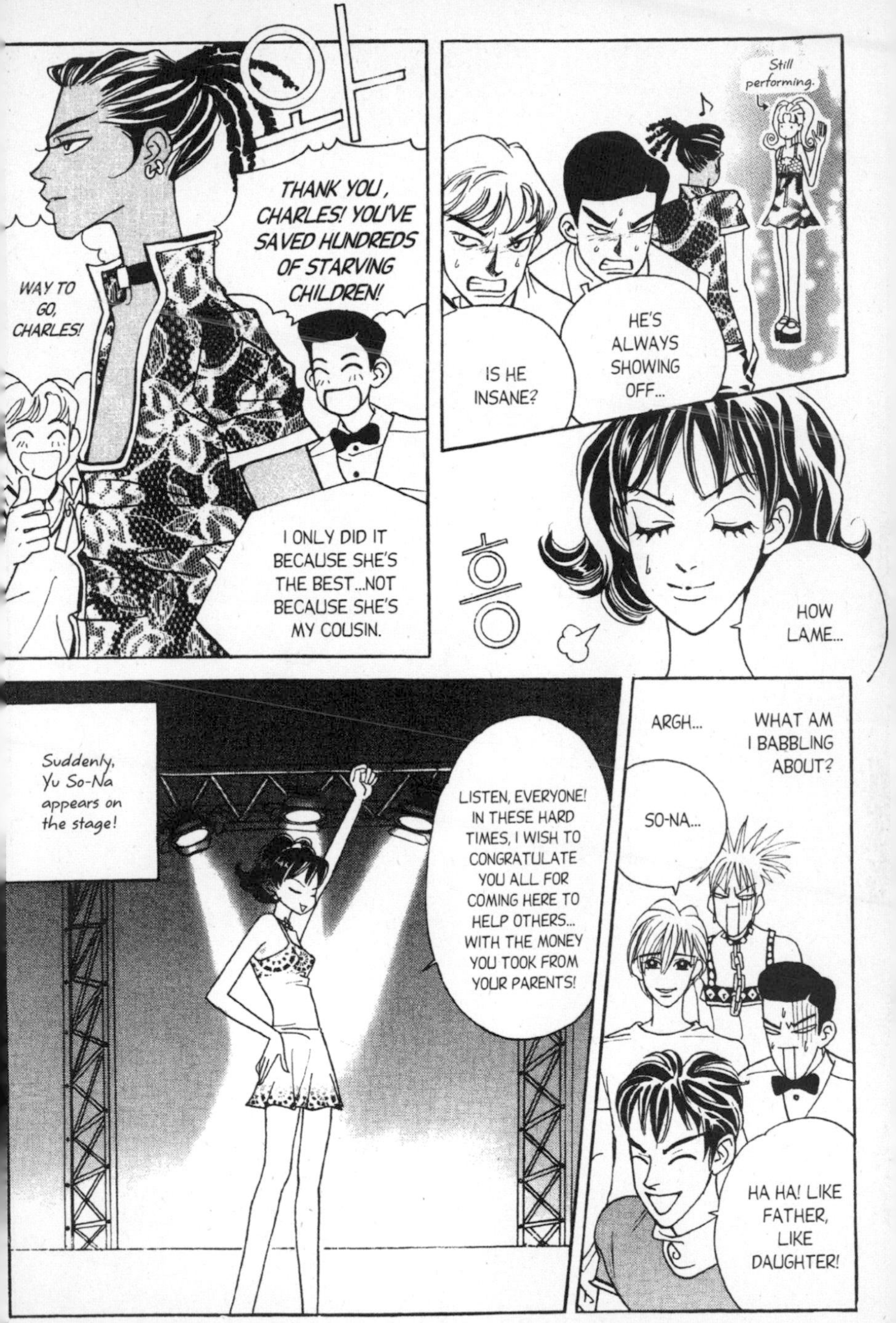
와
THANK YOU, CHARLES! YOU'VE SAVED HUNDREDS OF STARVING CHILDREN!
WAY TO GO, CHARLES!
I ONLY DID IT BECAUSE SHE'S THE BEST...NOT BECAUSE SHE'S MY COUSIN.
Still performing.
IS HE INSANE?
HE'S ALWAYS SHOWING OFF...
흥
HOW LAME...
Suddenly, Yu So-Na appears on the stage!
LISTEN, EVERYONE! IN THESE HARD TIMES, I WISH TO CONGRATULATE YOU ALL FOR COMING HERE TO HELP OTHERS... WITH THE MONEY YOU TOOK FROM YOUR PARENTS!
ARGH...
WHAT AM I BABBLING ABOUT?
SO-NA...
HA HA! LIKE FATHER, LIKE DAUGHTER!

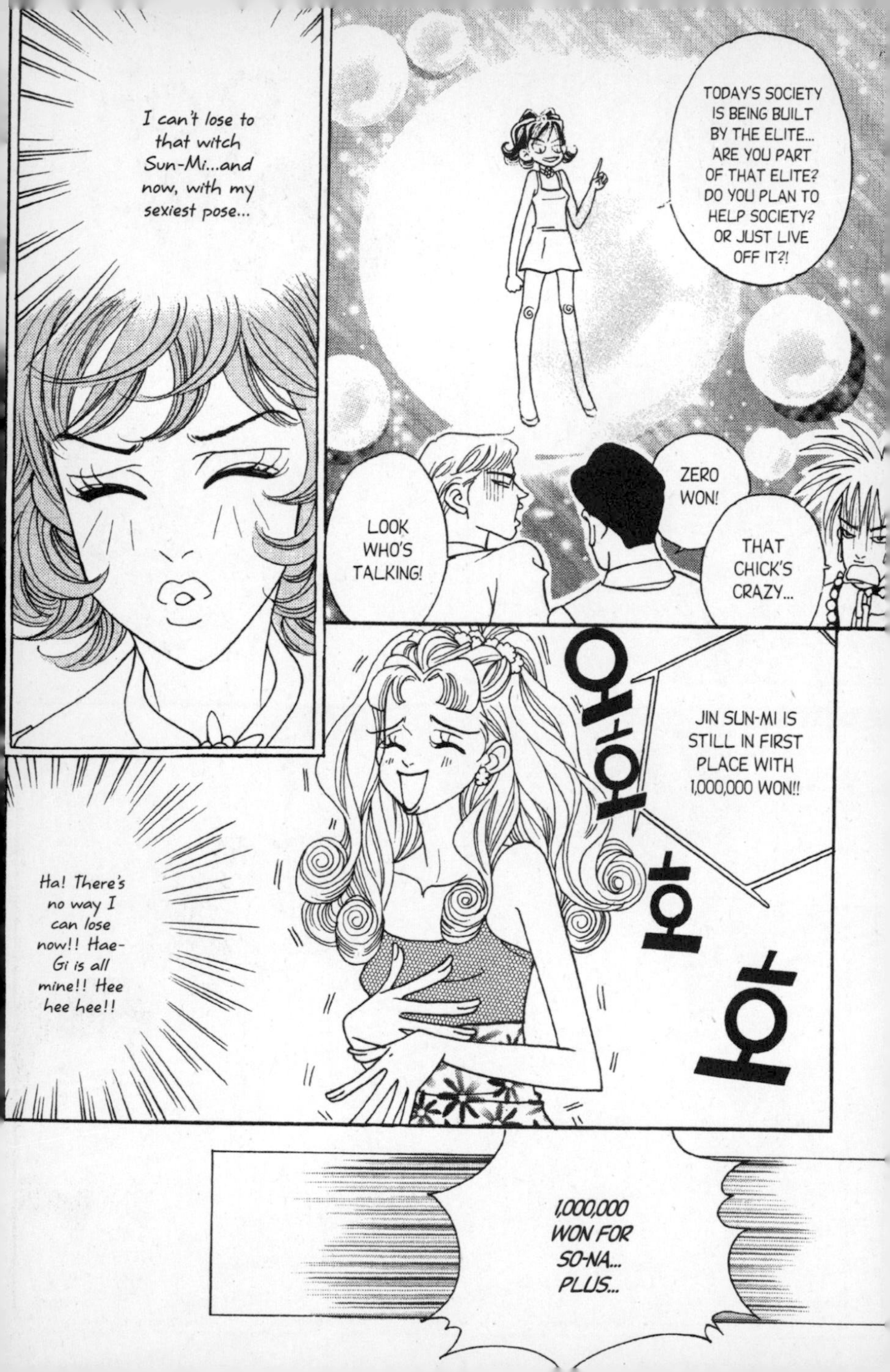
I can't lose to that witch Sun-Mi...and now, with my sexiest pose...
TODAY'S SOCIETY IS BEING BUILT BY THE ELITE... ARE YOU PART OF THAT ELITE? DO YOU PLAN TO HELP SOCIETY? OR JUST LIVE OFF IT?!
LOOK WHO'S TALKING!
ZERO WON!
THAT CHICK'S CRAZY...
Ha! There's no way I can lose now!! Hae-Gi is all mine!! Hee hee hee!!
JIN SUN-MI IS STILL IN FIRST PLACE WITH 1,000,000 WON!!
1,000,000 WON FOR SO-NA... PLUS...

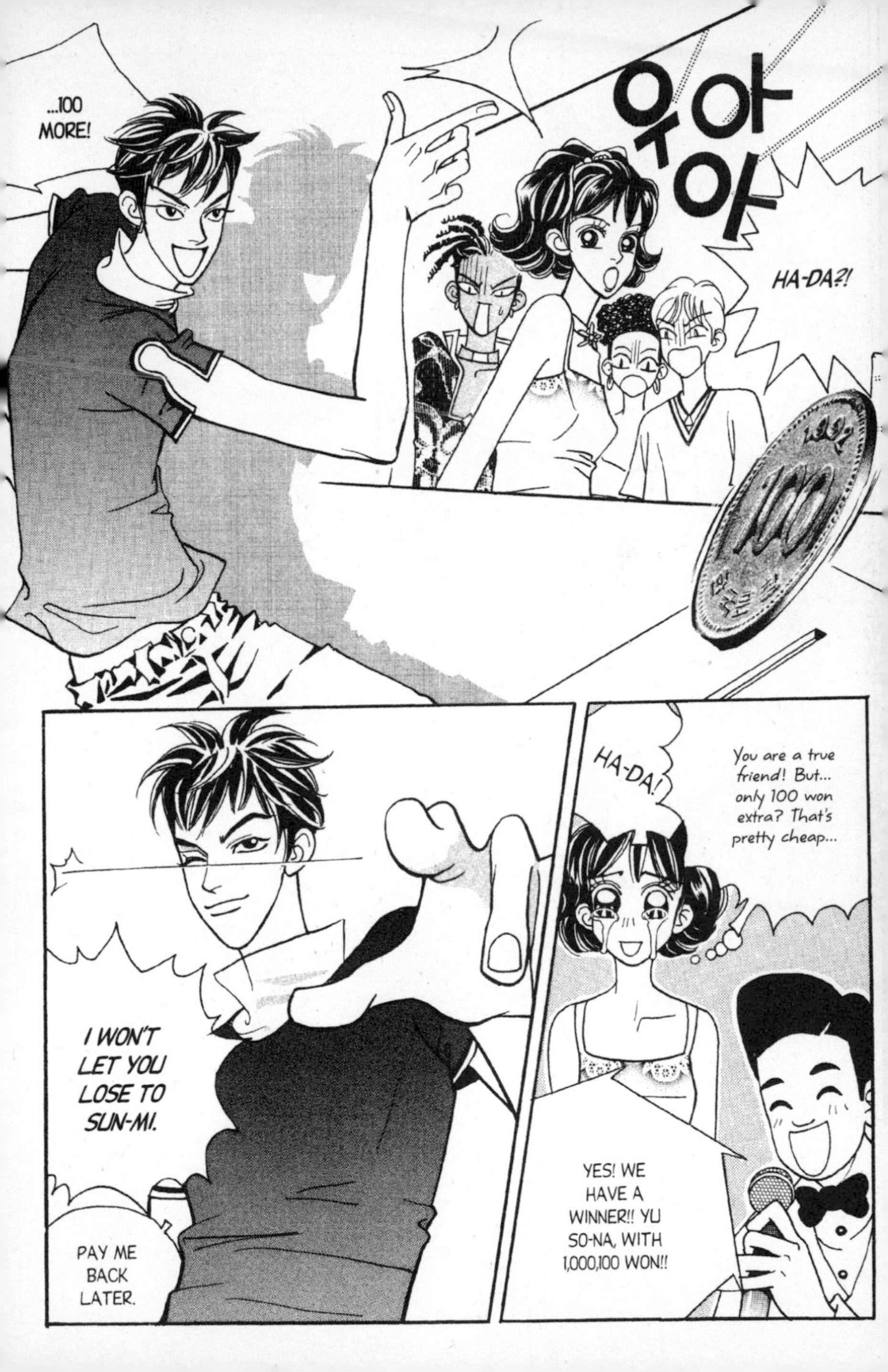

...100 MORE!
HA-DA?!
I WON'T LET YOU LOSE TO SUN-MI.
PAY ME BACK LATER.
HA-DA!
You are a true friend! But... only 100 won extra? That's pretty cheap...
YES! WE HAVE A WINNER!! YU SO-NA, WITH 1,000,100 WON!!

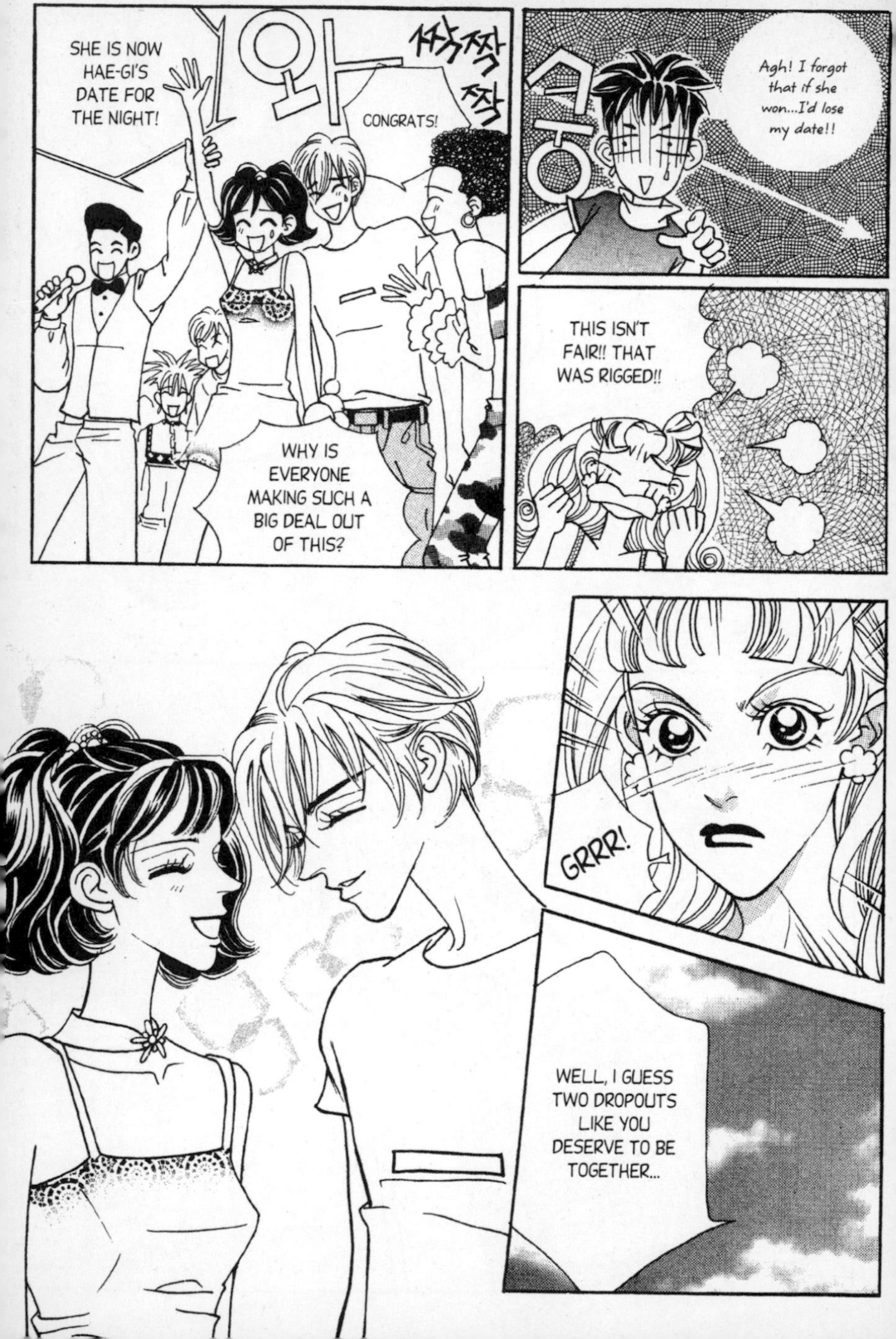

SHE IS NOW HAE-GI'S DATE FOR THE NIGHT!
와
짝짝 짝
CONGRATS!
WHY IS EVERYONE MAKING SUCH A BIG DEAL OUT OF THIS?
Agh! I forgot that if she won...I'd lose my date!!
THIS ISN'T FAIR!! THAT WAS RIGGED!!
GRRR!
WELL, I GUESS TWO DROPOUTS LIKE YOU DESERVE TO BE TOGETHER...

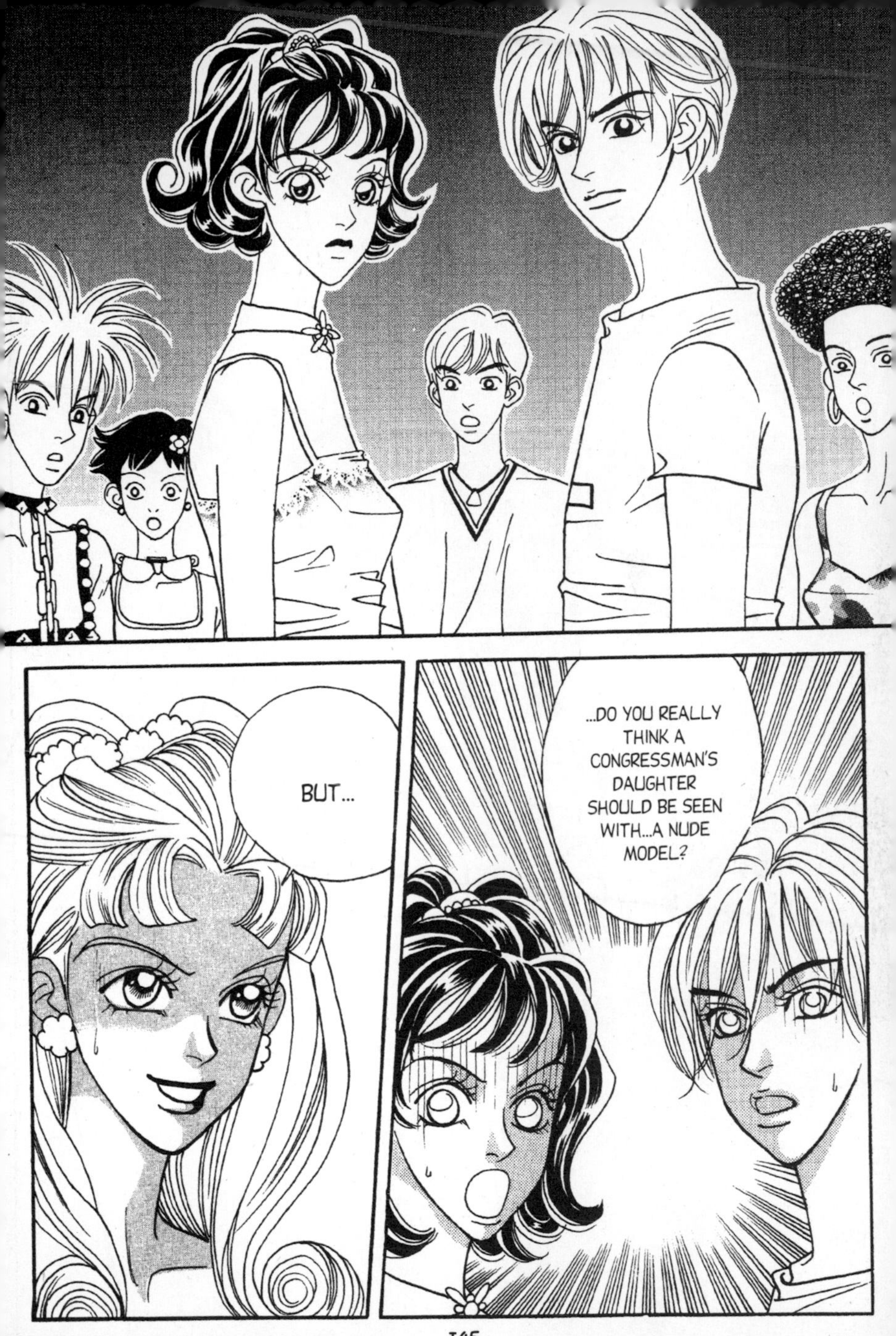
BUT...
...DO YOU REALLY THINK A CONGRESSMAN'S DAUGHTER SHOULD BE SEEN WITH...A NUDE MODEL?

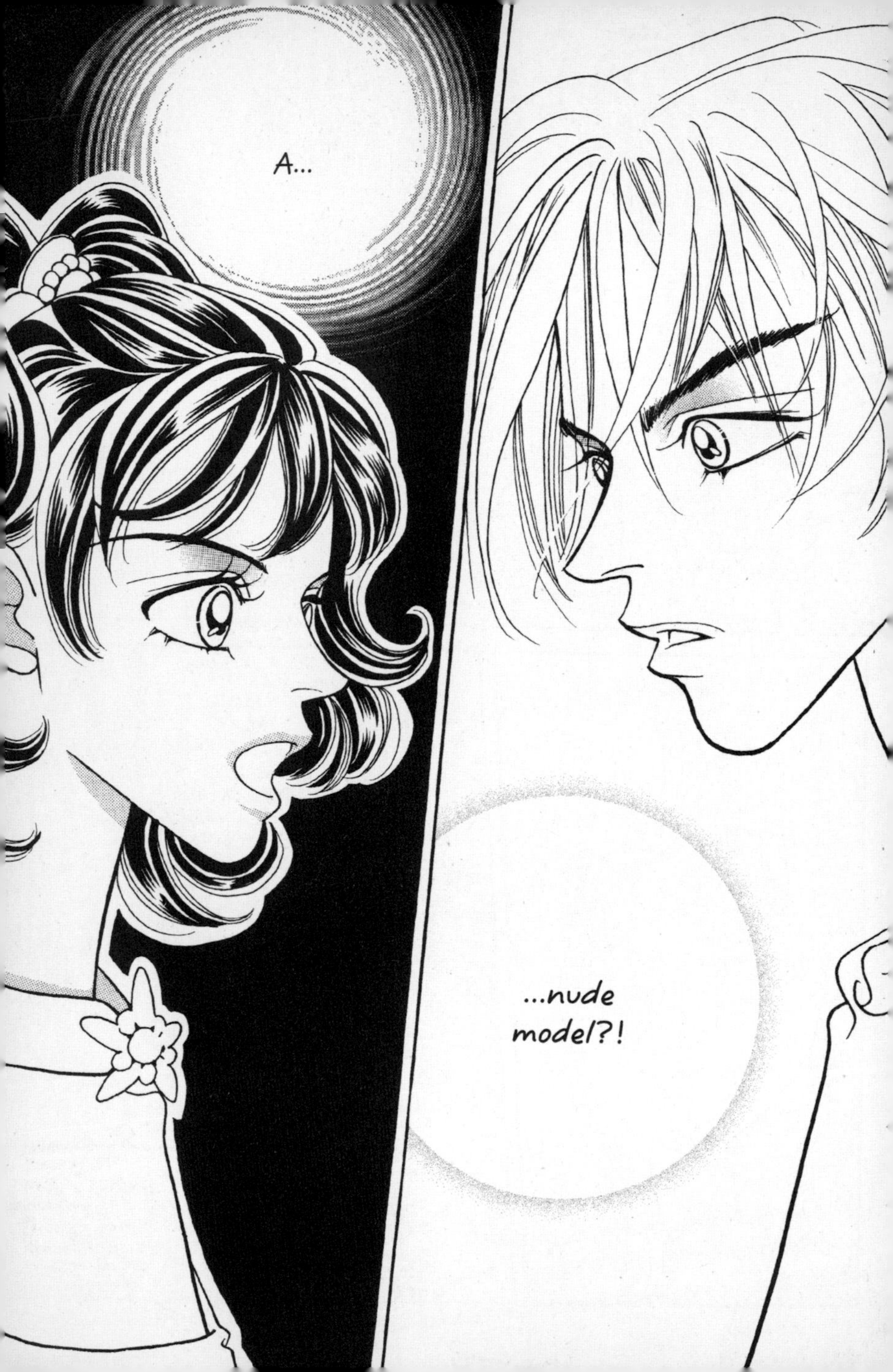
A...
...nude model?!

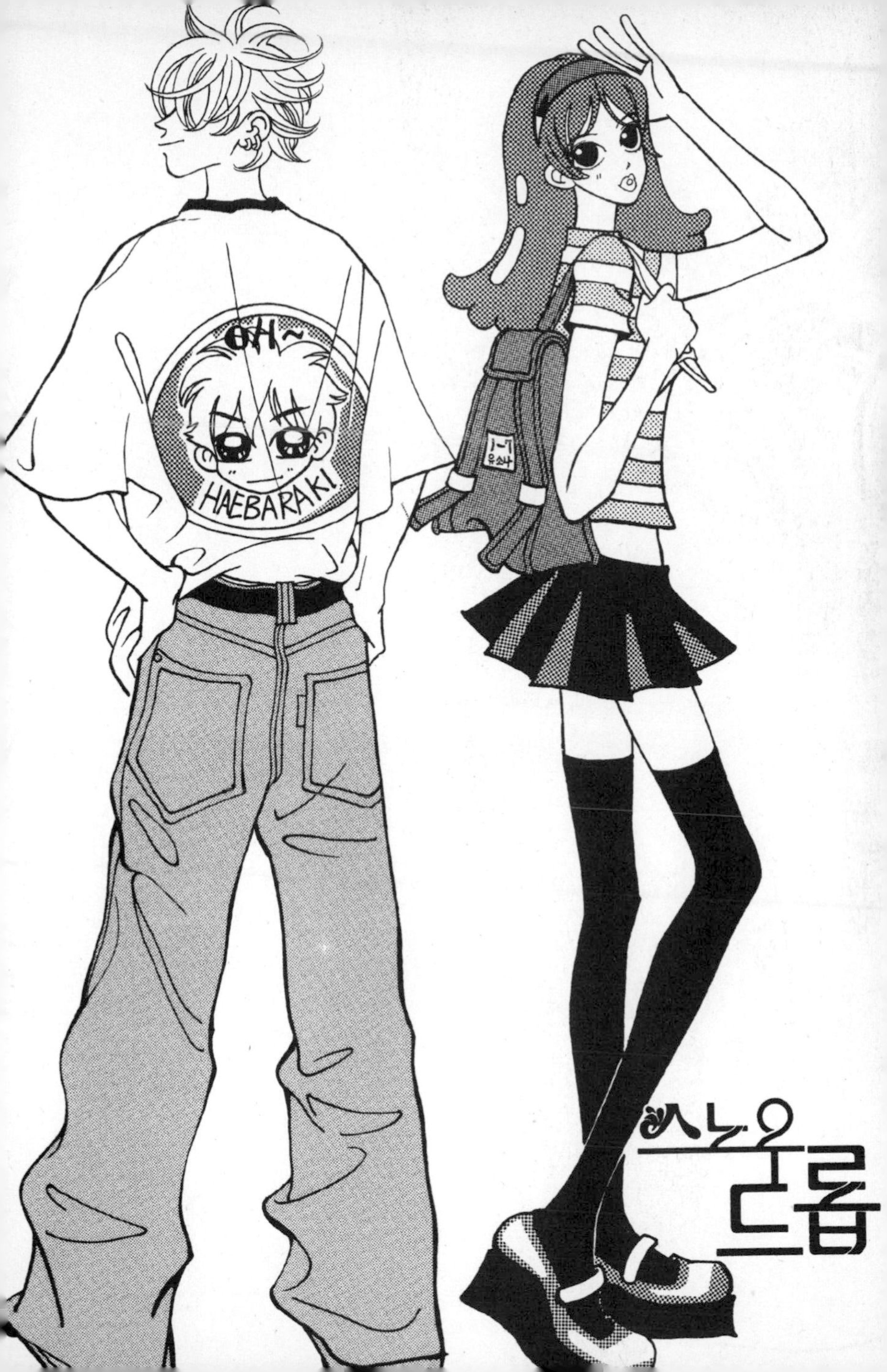
애~
HAEBARAKI
1-7
유소나
스노우
드롭

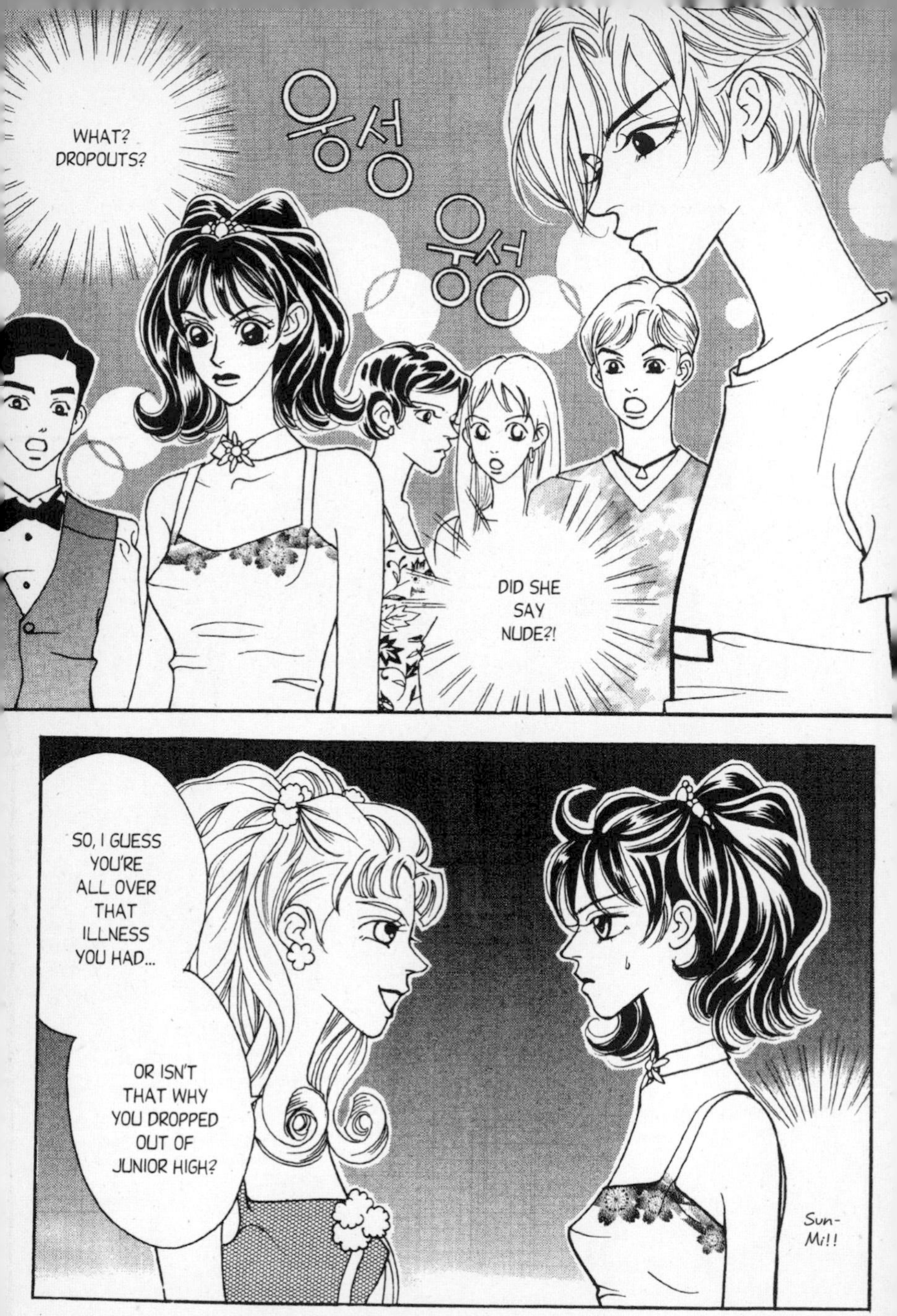
WHAT? DROPOUTS?
웅성
웅성
DID SHE SAY NUDE?!
SO, I GUESS YOU'RE ALL OVER THAT ILLNESS YOU HAD...
OR ISN'T THAT WHY YOU DROPPED OUT OF JUNIOR HIGH?
Sun-Mi!!

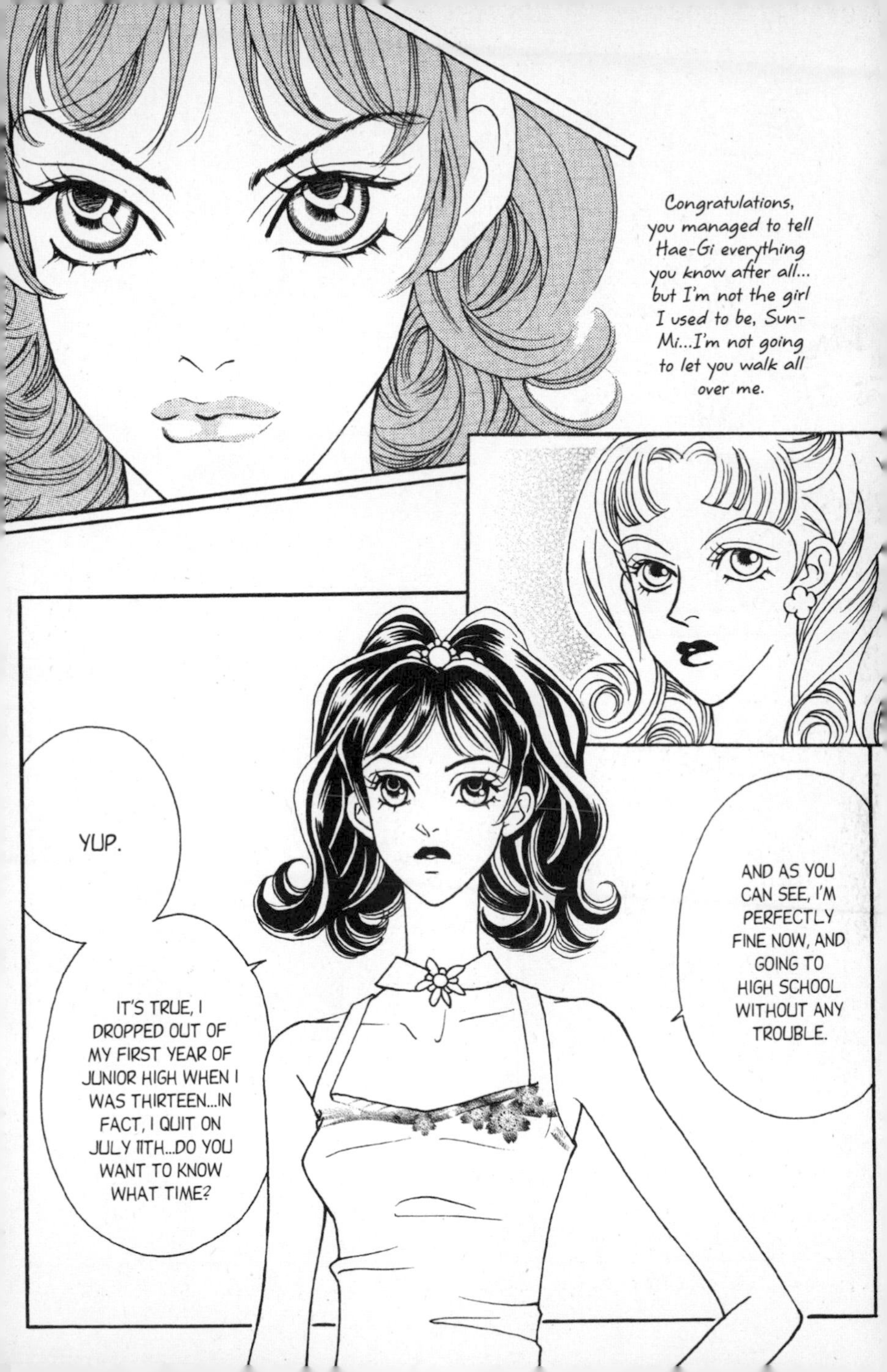
Congratulations, you managed to tell Hae-Gi everything you know after all... but I'm not the girl I used to be, Sun-Mi...I'm not going to let you walk all over me.
YUP.
IT'S TRUE, I DROPPED OUT OF MY FIRST YEAR OF JUNIOR HIGH WHEN I WAS THIRTEEN...IN FACT, I QUIT ON JULY 11TH...DO YOU WANT TO KNOW WHAT TIME?
AND AS YOU CAN SEE, I'M PERFECTLY FINE NOW, AND GOING TO HIGH SCHOOL WITHOUT ANY TROUBLE.

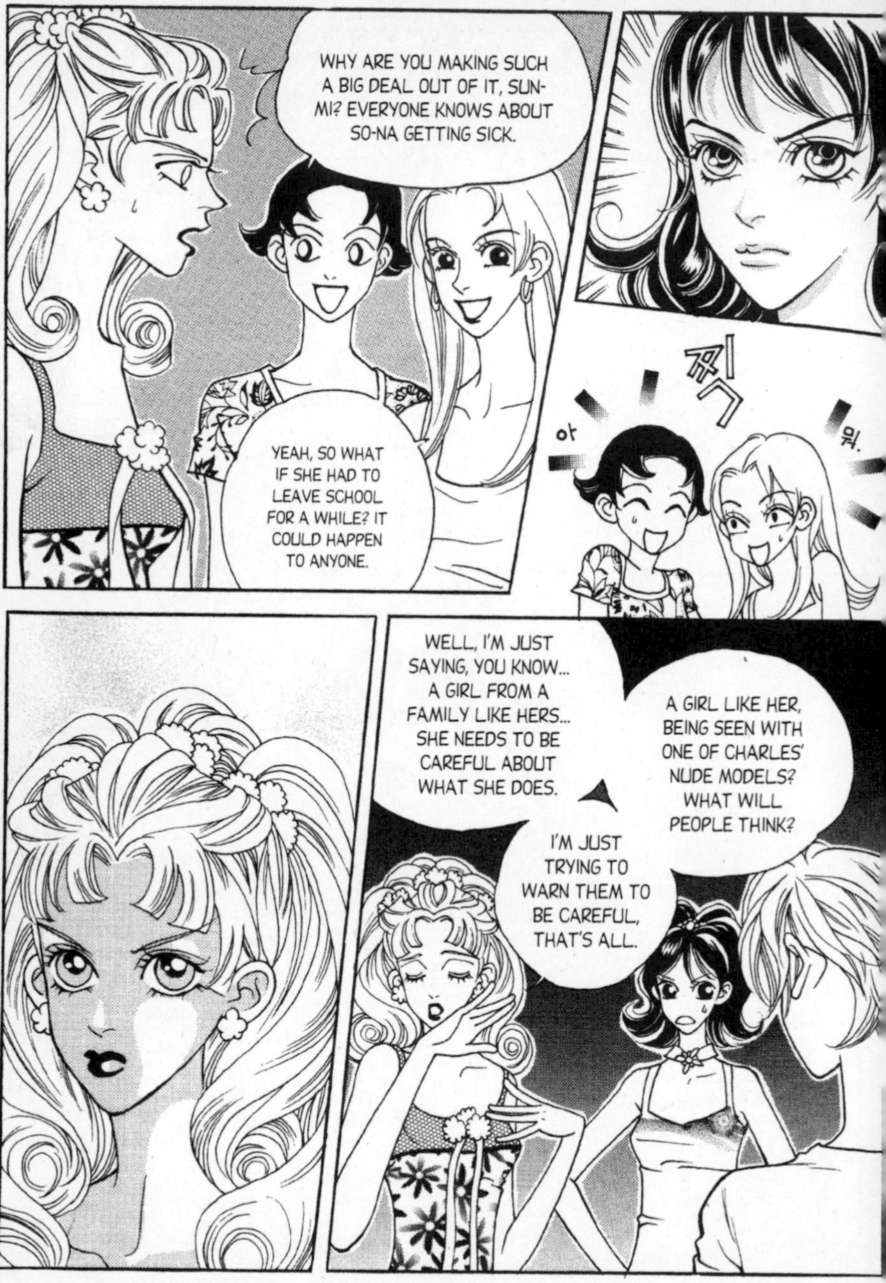
WHY ARE YOU MAKING SUCH A BIG DEAL OUT OF IT, SUN-MI? EVERYONE KNOWS ABOUT SO-NA GETTING SICK.
YEAH, SO WHAT IF SHE HAD TO LEAVE SCHOOL FOR A WHILE? IT COULD HAPPEN TO ANYONE.
아
뭐.
WELL, I'M JUST SAYING, YOU KNOW... A GIRL FROM A FAMILY LIKE HERS... SHE NEEDS TO BE CAREFUL ABOUT WHAT SHE DOES.
A GIRL LIKE HER, BEING SEEN WITH ONE OF CHARLES' NUDE MODELS? WHAT WILL PEOPLE THINK?
I'M JUST TRYING TO WARN THEM TO BE CAREFUL, THAT'S ALL.

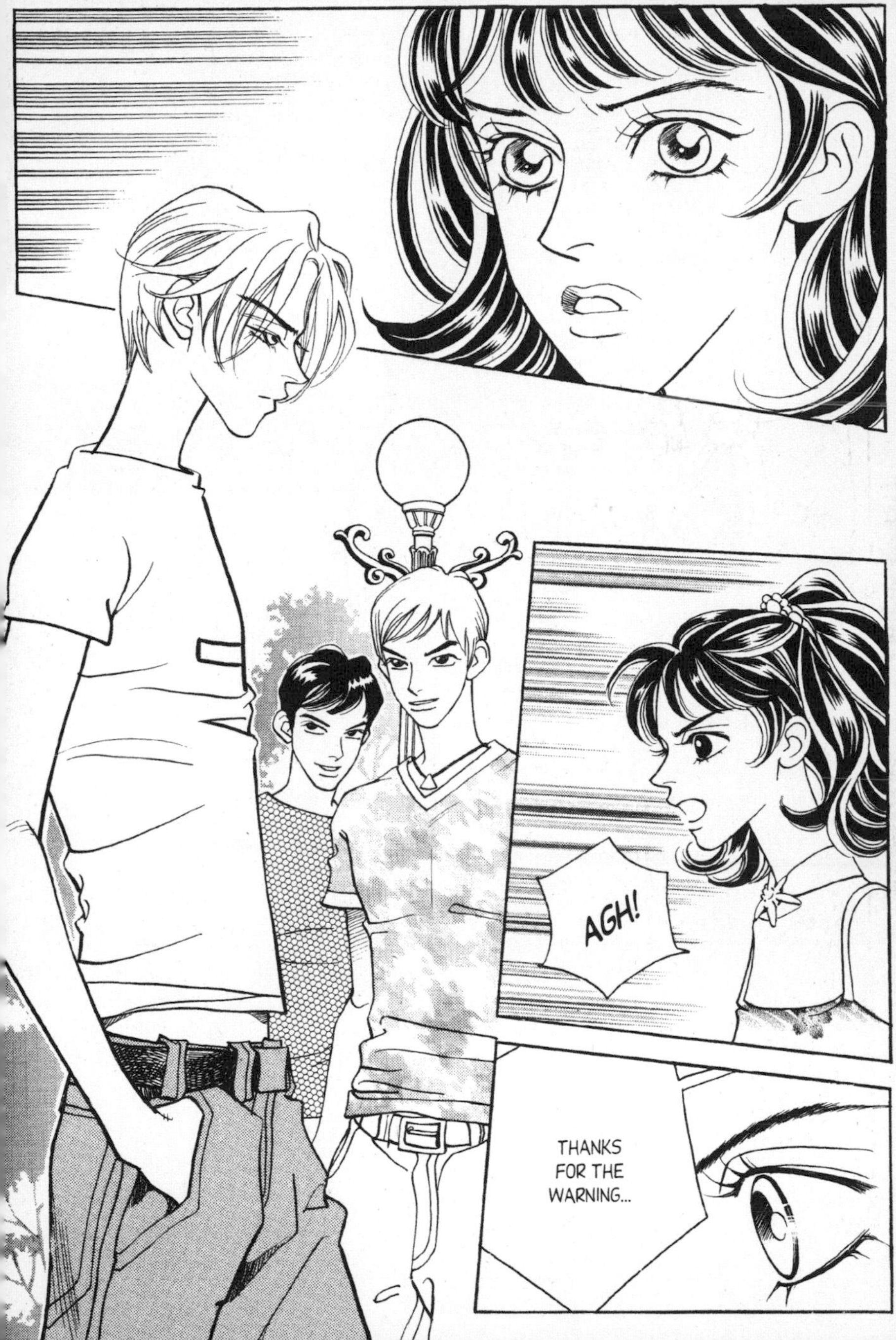
AGH!
THANKS FOR THE WARNING...

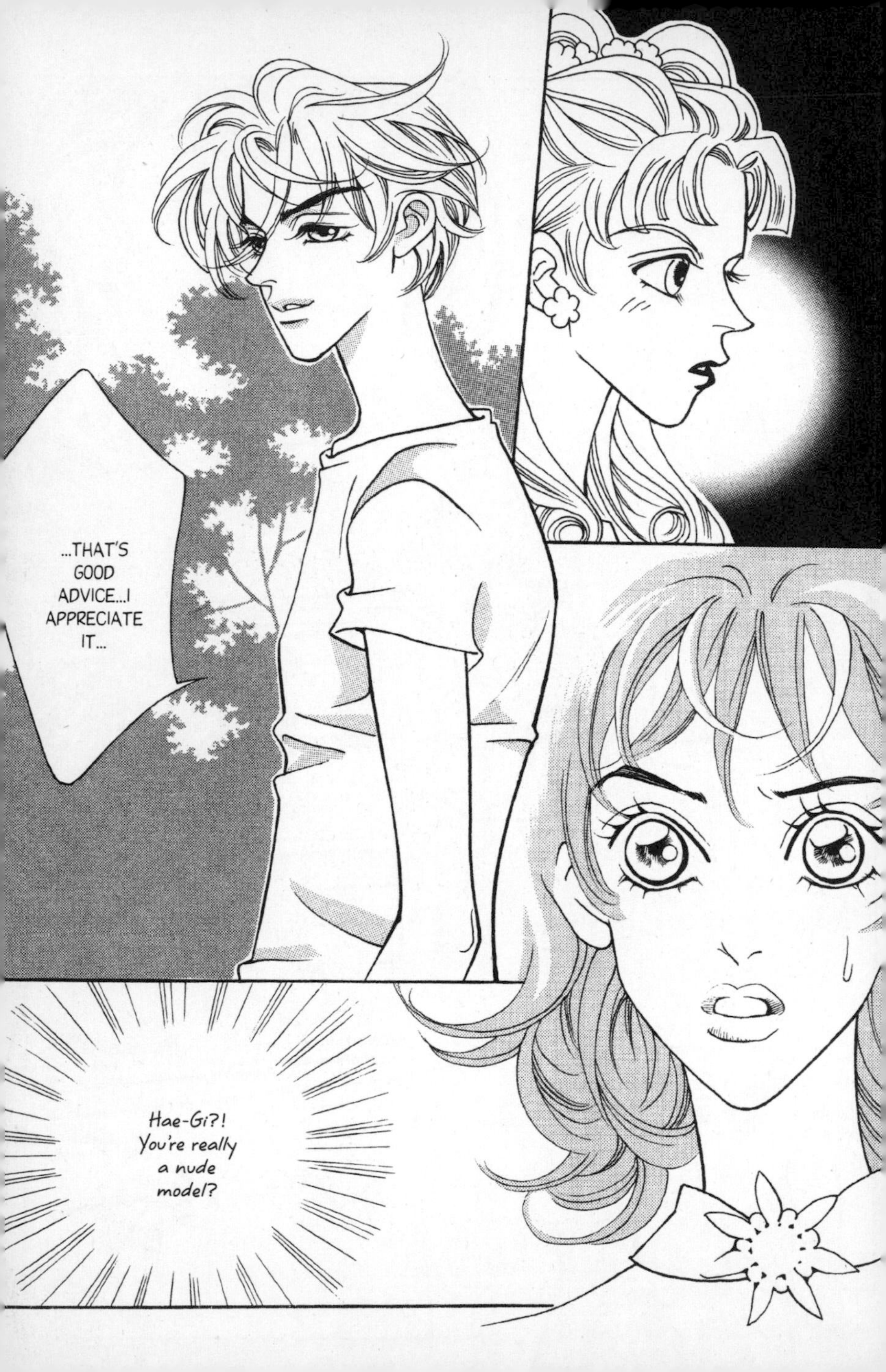
...THAT'S GOOD ADVICE...I APPRECIATE IT...
Hae-Gi?! You're really a nude model?

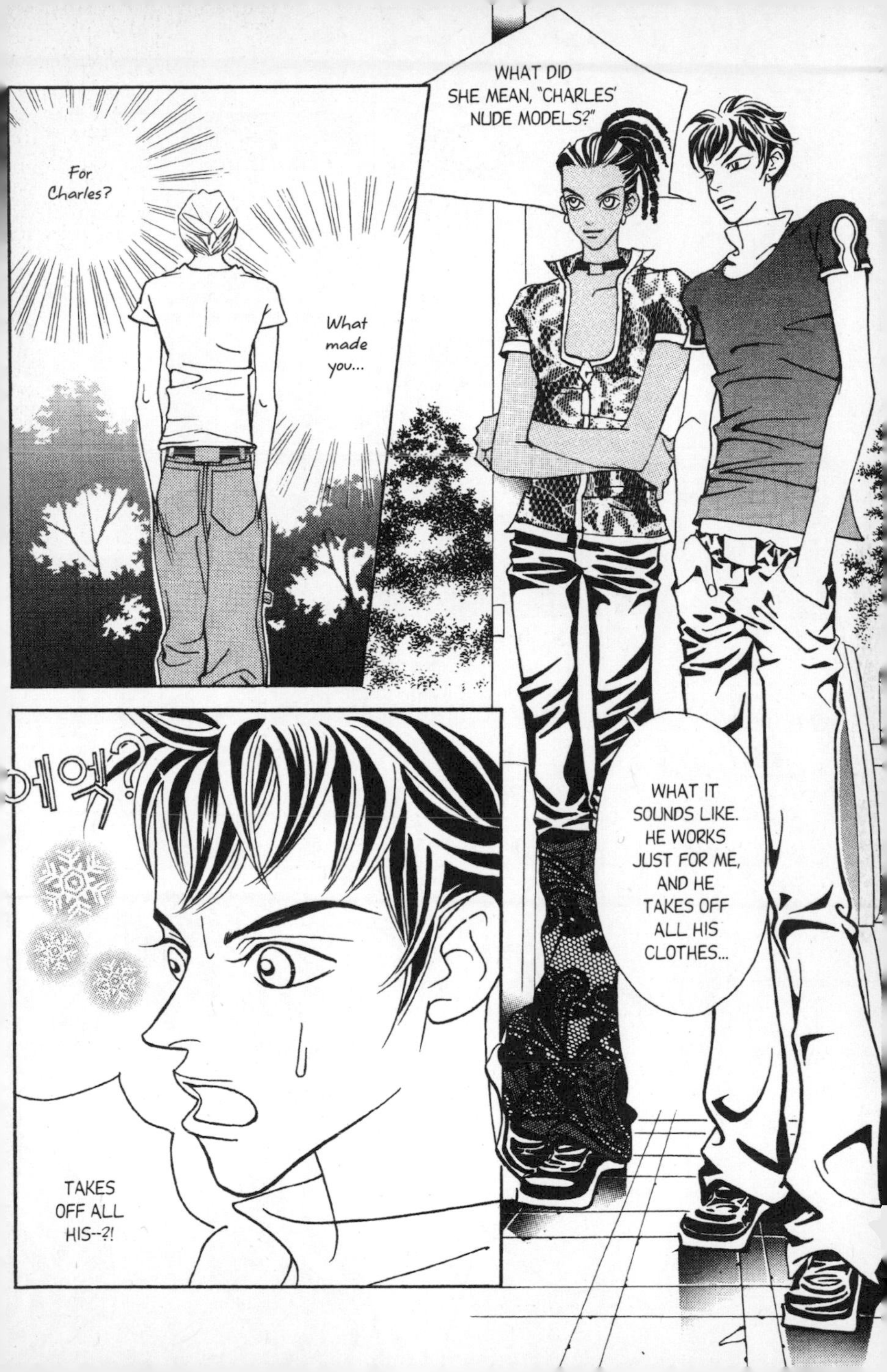
For Charles?
What made you...
WHAT DID SHE MEAN, "CHARLES' NUDE MODELS?"
WHAT IT SOUNDS LIKE. HE WORKS JUST FOR ME, AND HE TAKES OFF ALL HIS CLOTHES...
에엣?
TAKES OFF ALL HIS--?!

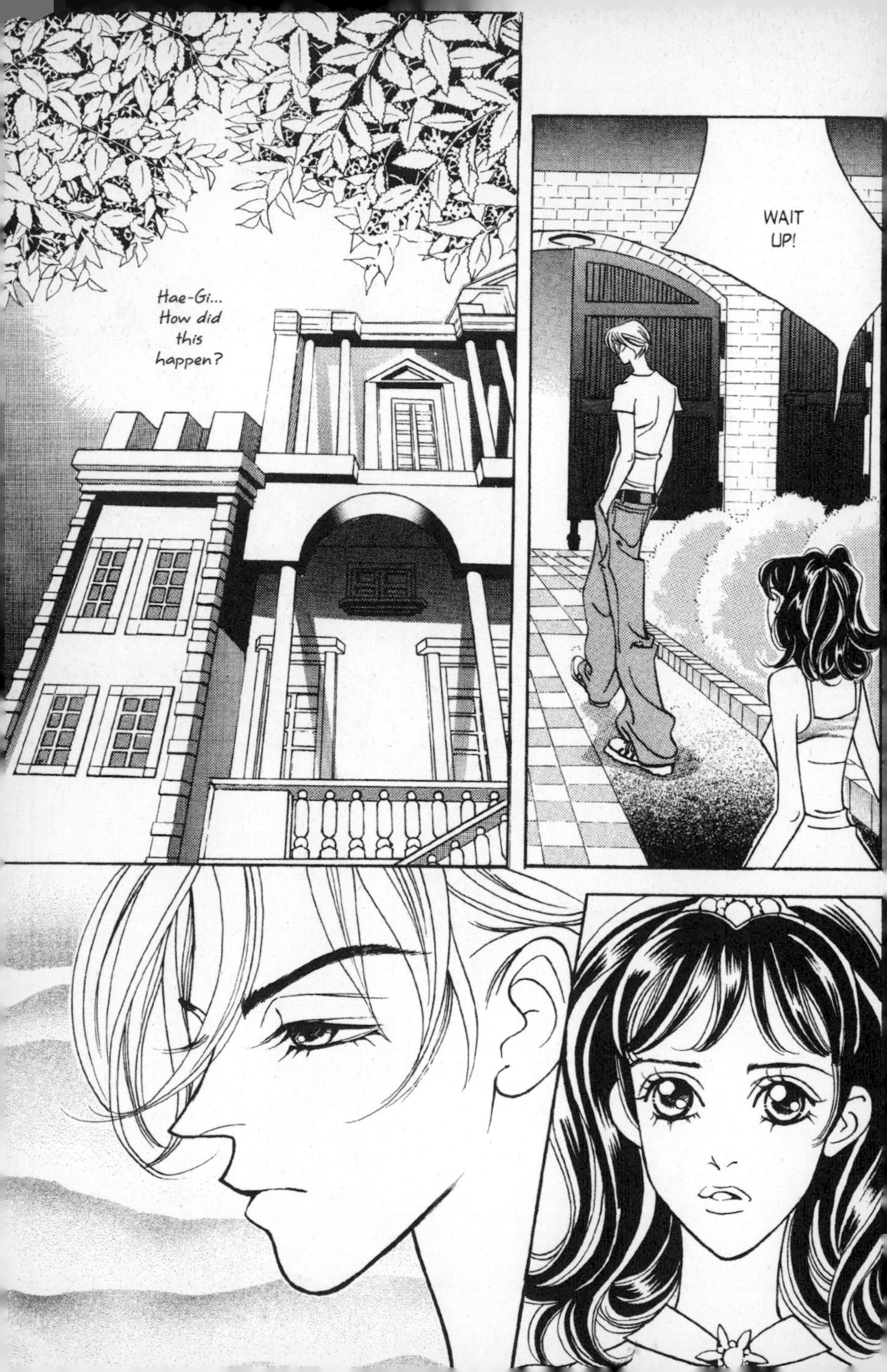
Hae-Gi... How did this happen?
WAIT UP!

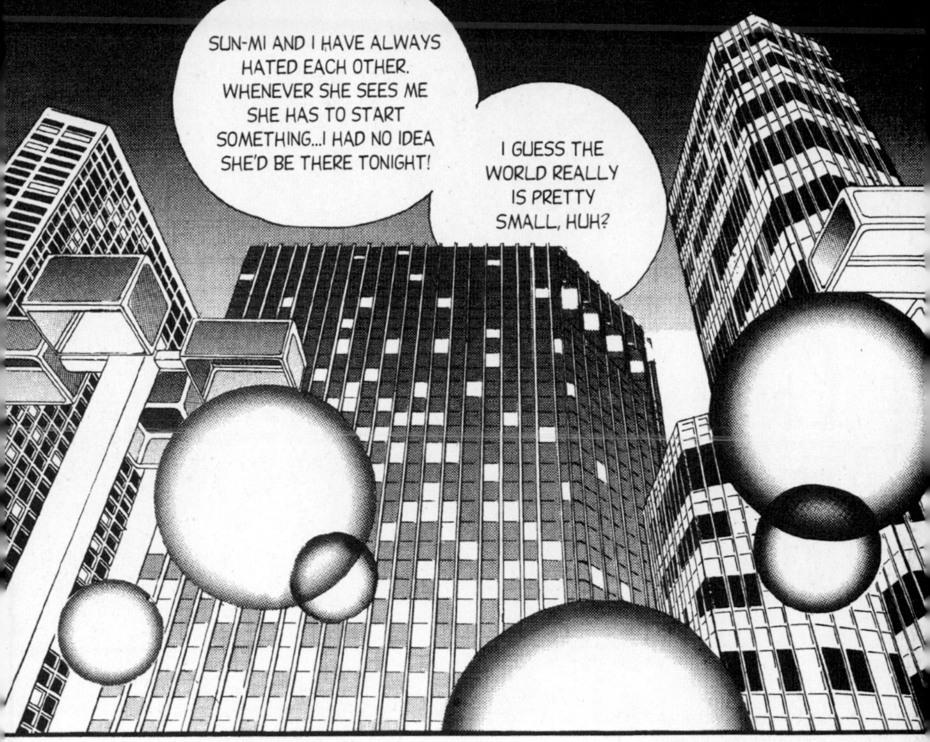
SUN-MI AND I HAVE ALWAYS HATED EACH OTHER. WHENEVER SHE SEES ME SHE HAS TO START SOMETHING...I HAD NO IDEA SHE'D BE THERE TONIGHT!
I GUESS THE WORLD REALLY IS PRETTY SMALL, HUH?

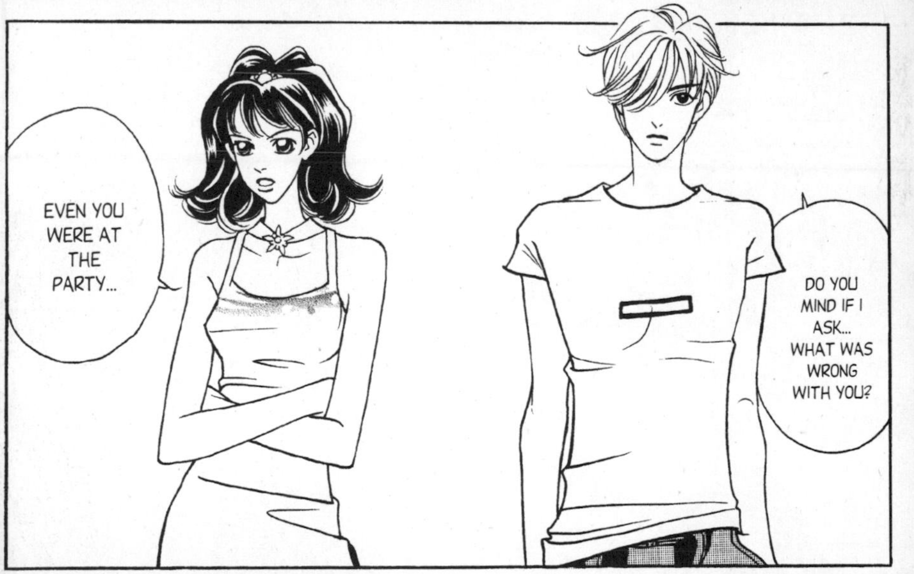
EVEN YOU WERE AT THE PARTY...
DO YOU MIND IF I ASK... WHAT WAS WRONG WITH YOU?

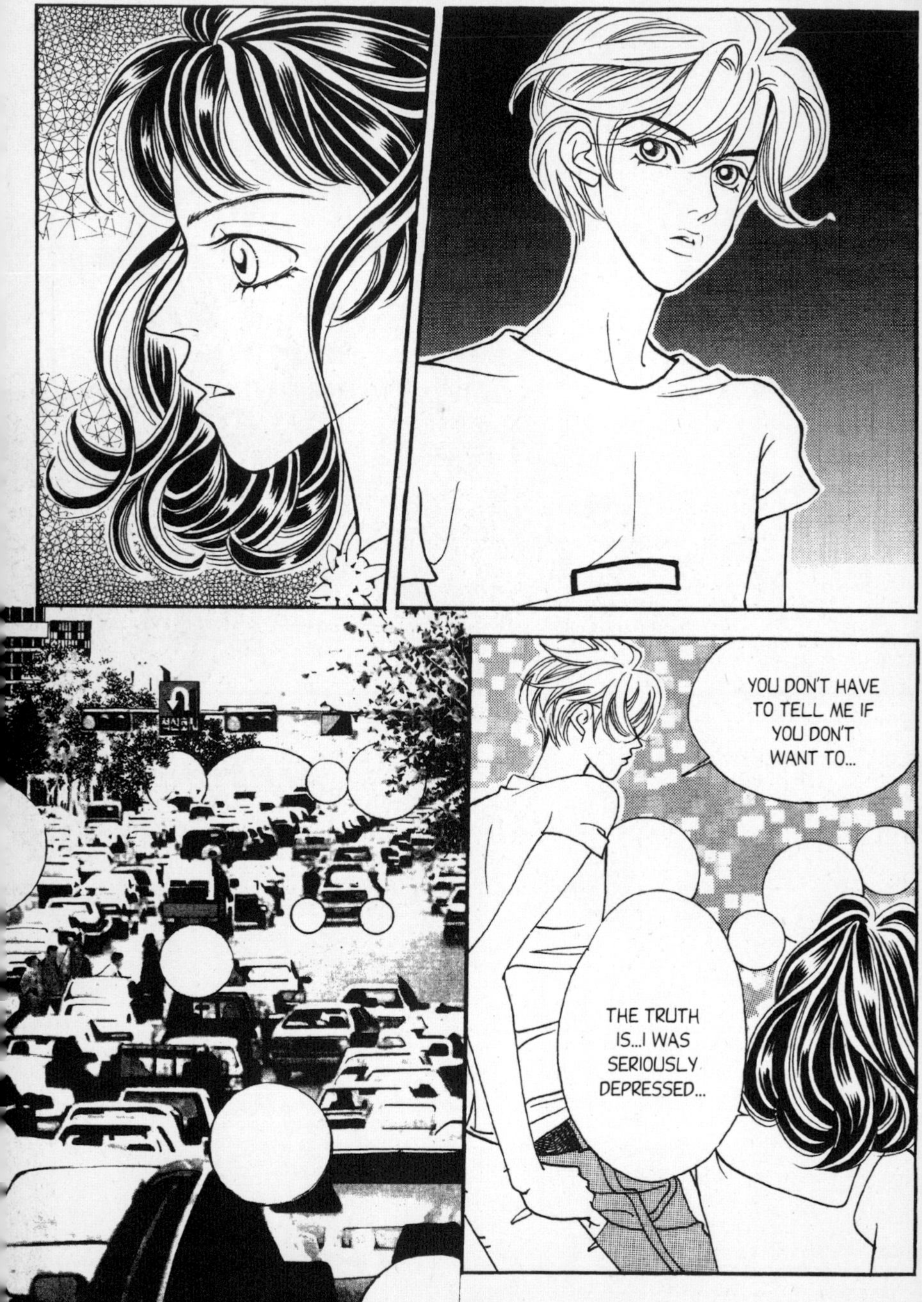
YOU DON'T HAVE TO TELL ME IF YOU DON'T WANT TO...
THE TRUTH IS...I WAS SERIOUSLY DEPRESSED...

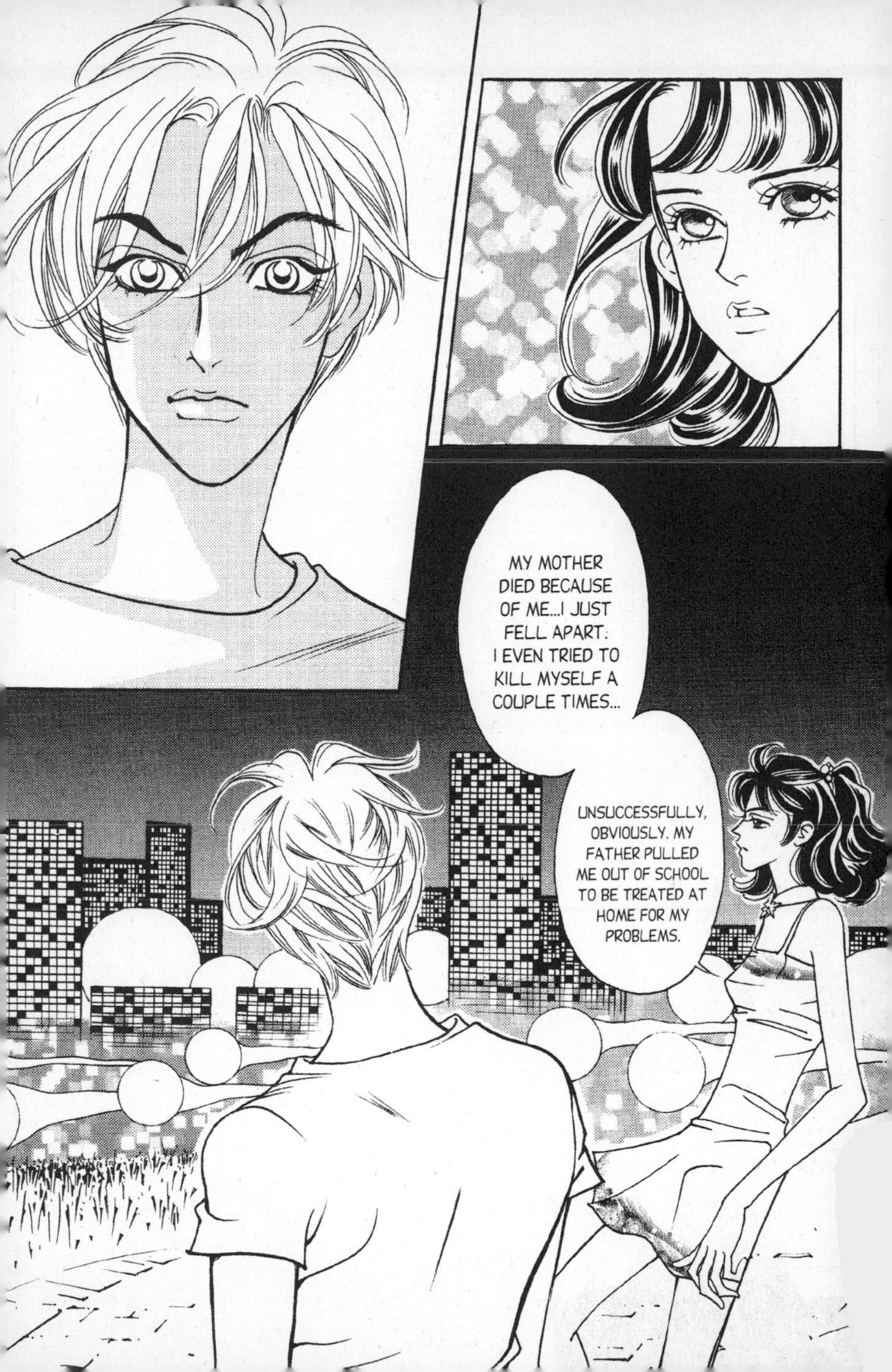
MY MOTHER DIED BECAUSE OF ME...I JUST FELL APART. I EVEN TRIED TO KILL MYSELF A COUPLE TIMES...
UNSUCCESSFULLY, OBVIOUSLY. MY FATHER PULLED ME OUT OF SCHOOL TO BE TREATED AT HOME FOR MY PROBLEMS.

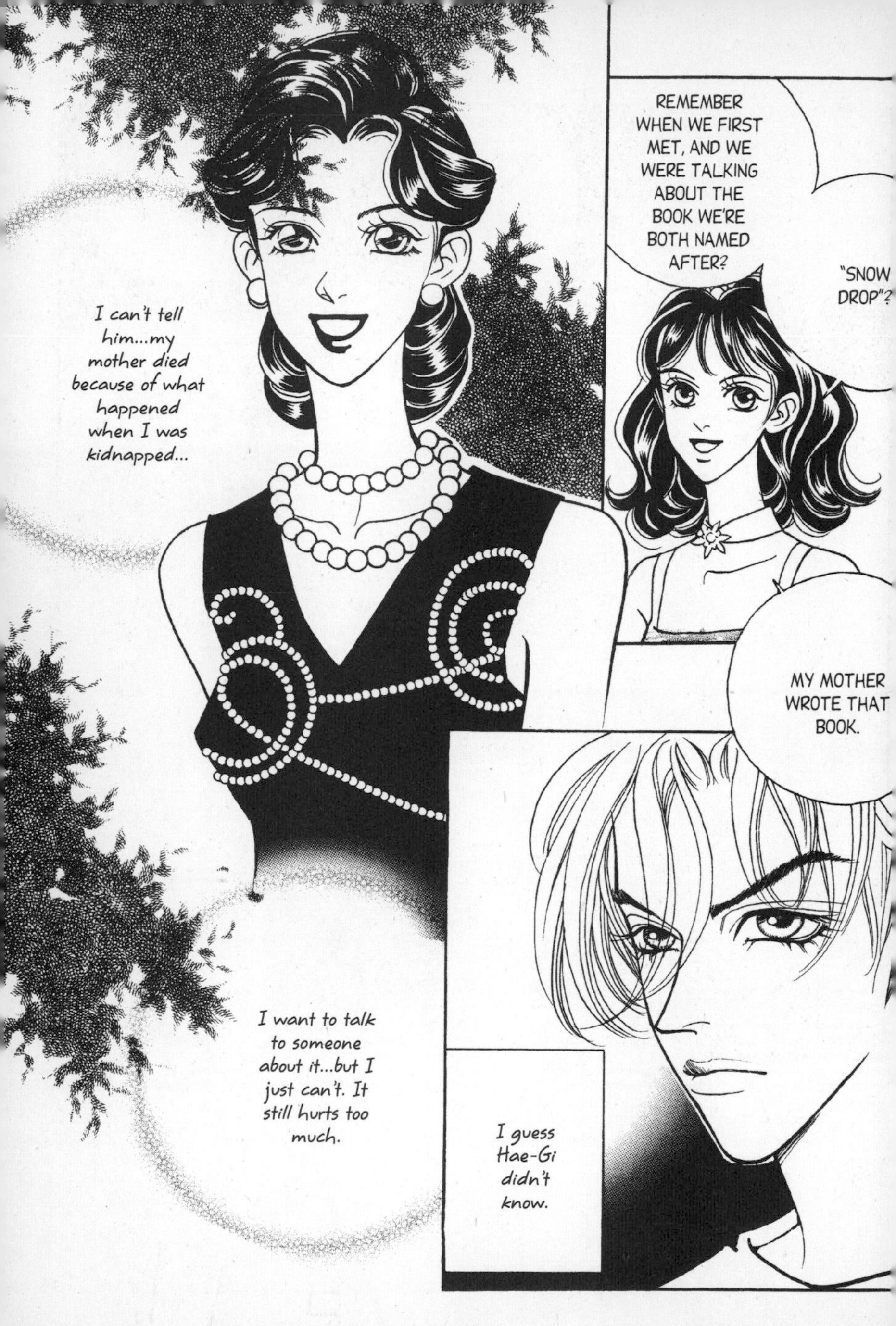
I can't tell him...my mother died because of what happened when I was kidnapped...
I want to talk to someone about it...but I just can't. It still hurts too much.
REMEMBER WHEN WE FIRST MET, AND WE WERE TALKING ABOUT THE BOOK WE'RE BOTH NAMED AFTER?
"SNOW DROP"?
MY MOTHER WROTE THAT BOOK.
I guess Hae-Gi didn't know.

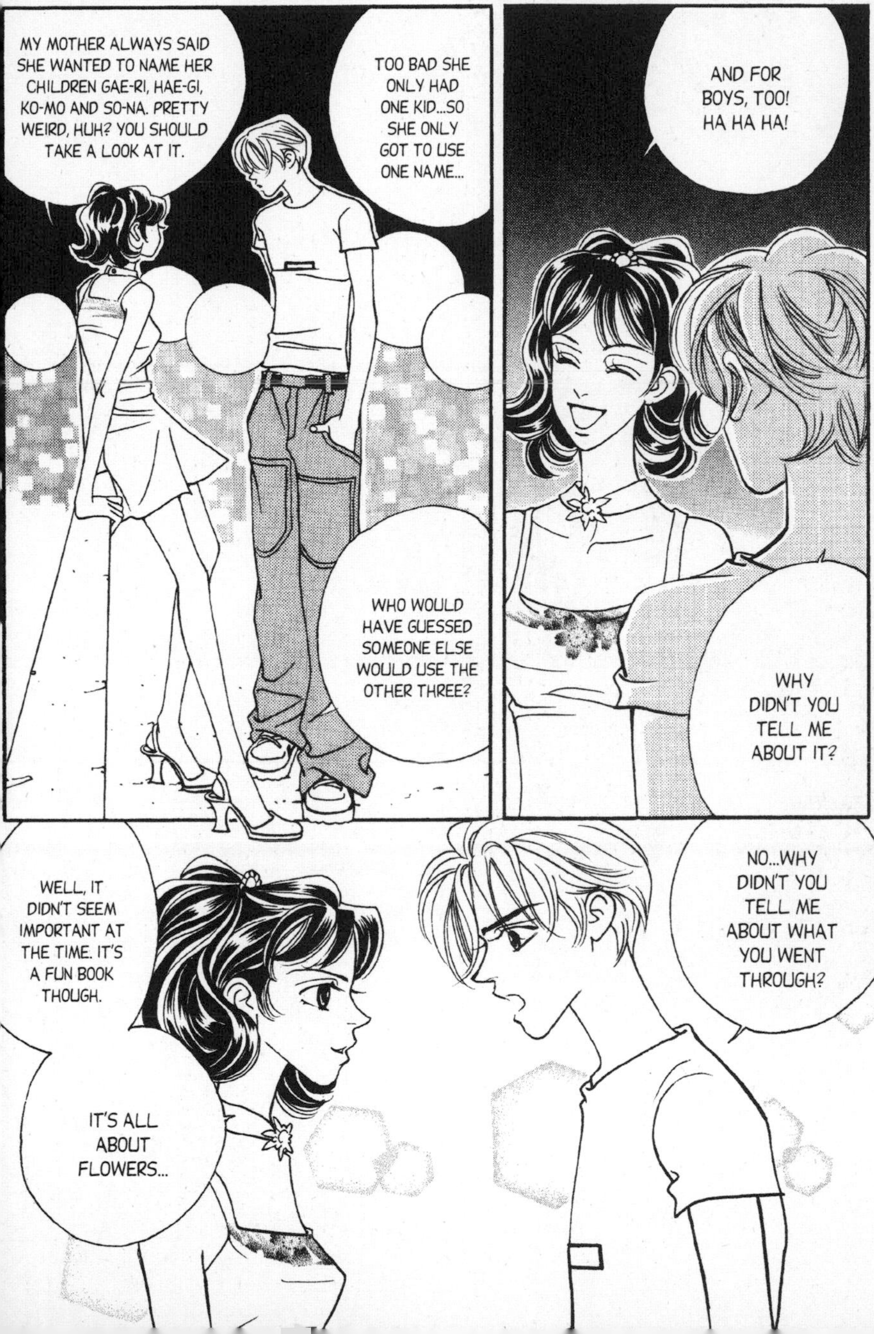
MY MOTHER ALWAYS SAID SHE WANTED TO NAME HER CHILDREN GAE-RI, HAE-GI, KO-MO AND SO-NA. PRETTY WEIRD, HUH? YOU SHOULD TAKE A LOOK AT IT.
TOO BAD SHE ONLY HAD ONE KID...SO SHE ONLY GOT TO USE ONE NAME...
WHO WOULD HAVE GUESSED SOMEONE ELSE WOULD USE THE OTHER THREE?
AND FOR BOYS, TOO! HA HA HA!
WHY DIDN'T YOU TELL ME ABOUT IT?
WELL, IT DIDN'T SEEM IMPORTANT AT THE TIME. IT'S A FUN BOOK THOUGH.
IT'S ALL ABOUT FLOWERS...
NO...WHY DIDN'T YOU TELL ME ABOUT WHAT YOU WENT THROUGH?

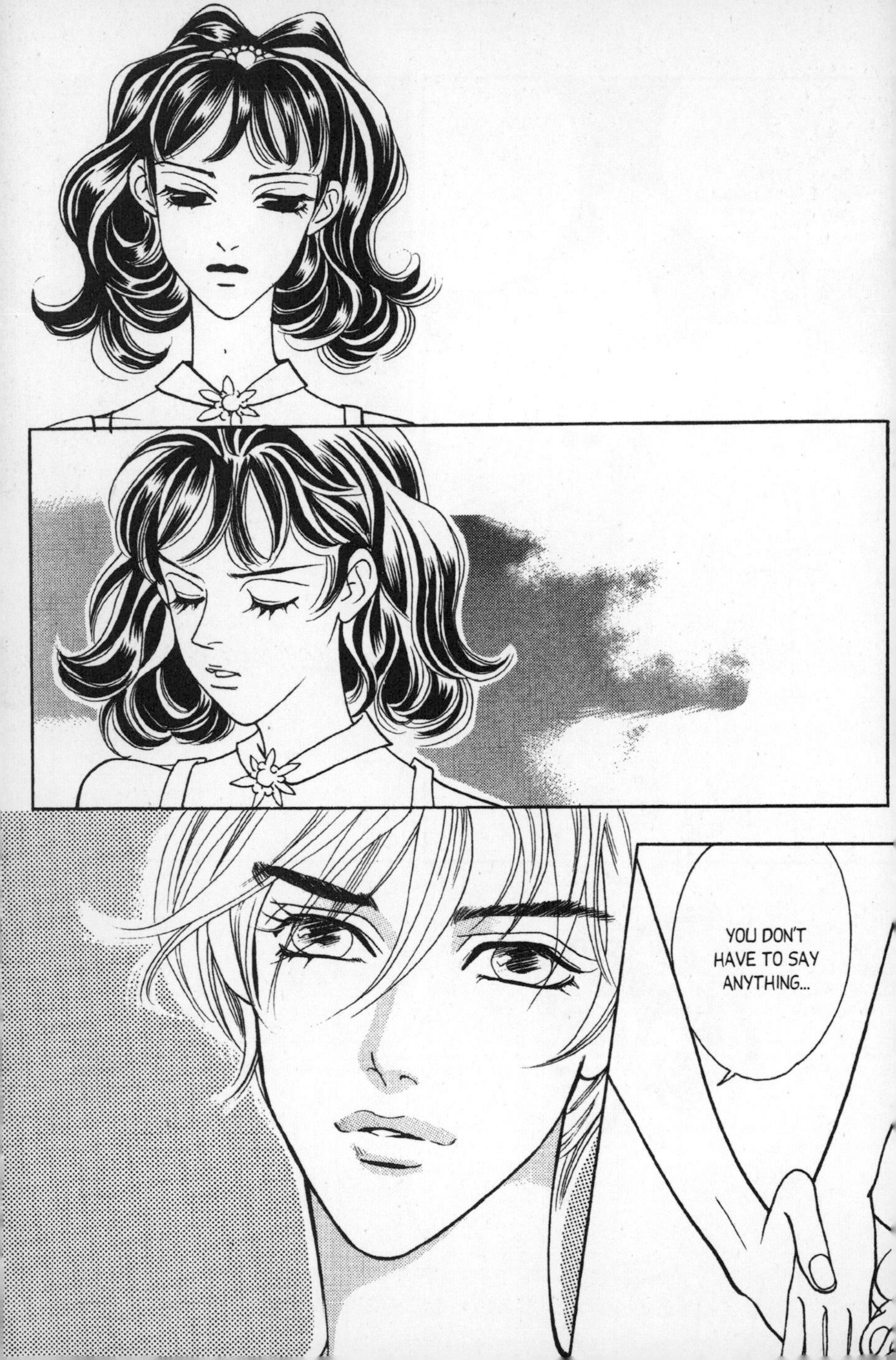
YOU DON'T HAVE TO SAY ANYTHING...

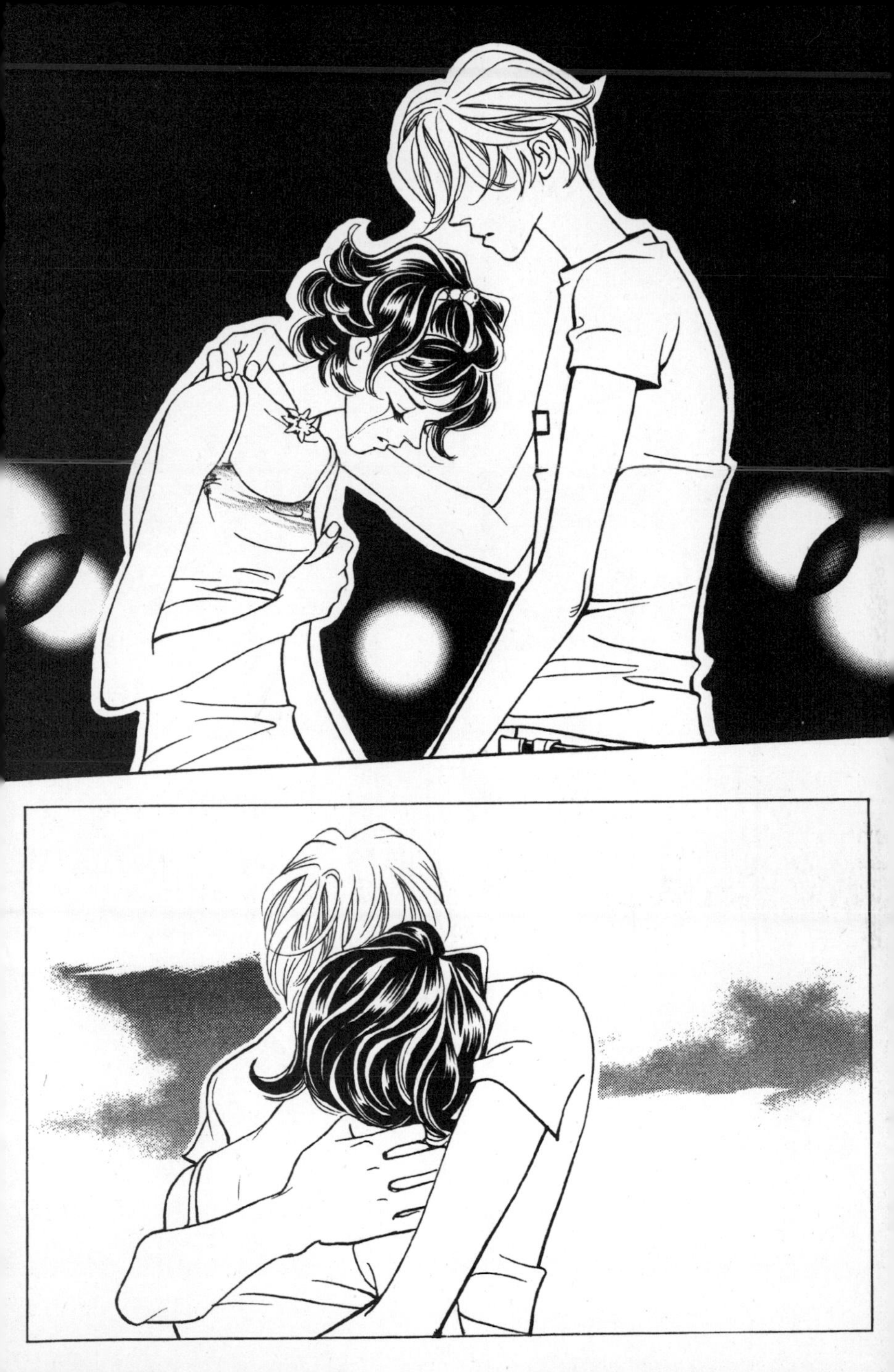

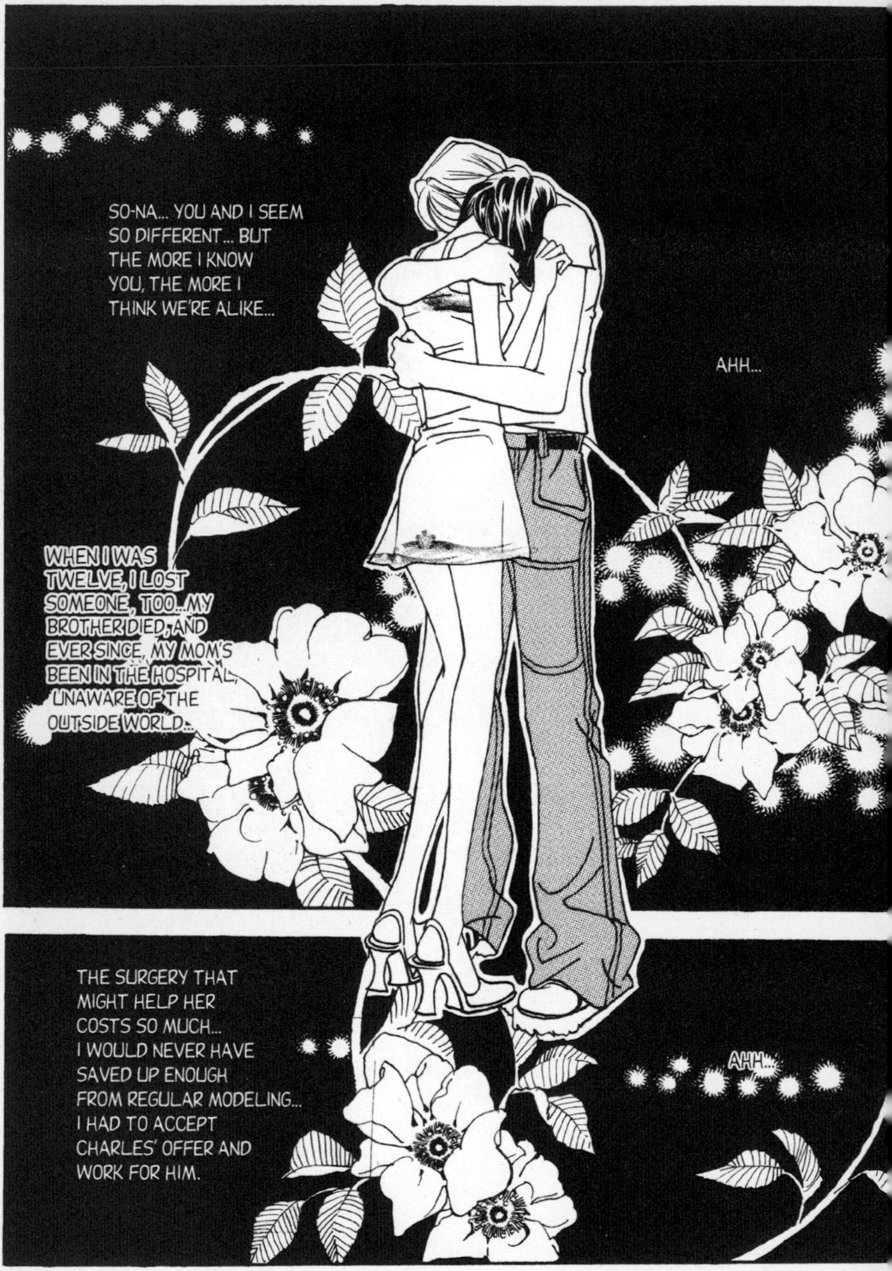
SO-NA... YOU AND I SEEM SO DIFFERENT... BUT THE MORE I KNOW YOU, THE MORE I THINK WE'RE ALIKE...
AHH...
WHEN I WAS TWELVE, I LOST SOMEONE, TOO...MY BROTHER DIED, AND EVER SINCE, MY MOM'S BEEN IN THE HOSPITAL, UNAWARE OF THE OUTSIDE WORLD...
THE SURGERY THAT MIGHT HELP HER COSTS SO MUCH... I WOULD NEVER HAVE SAVED UP ENOUGH FROM REGULAR MODELING... I HAD TO ACCEPT CHARLES' OFFER AND WORK FOR HIM.
AHH...

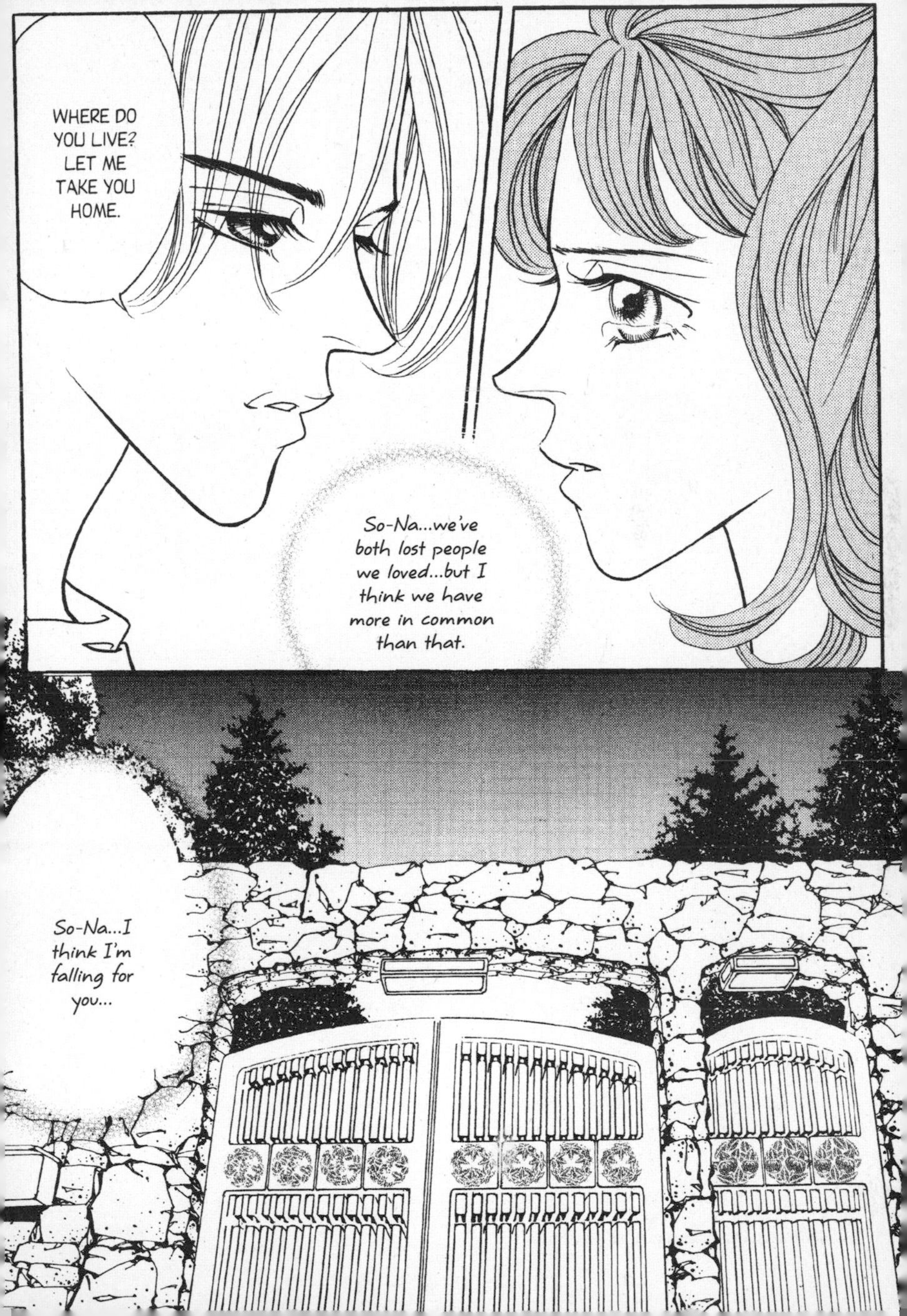
WHERE DO YOU LIVE? LET ME TAKE YOU HOME.
So-Na...we've both lost people we loved...but I think we have more in common than that.
So-Na...I think I'm falling for you...

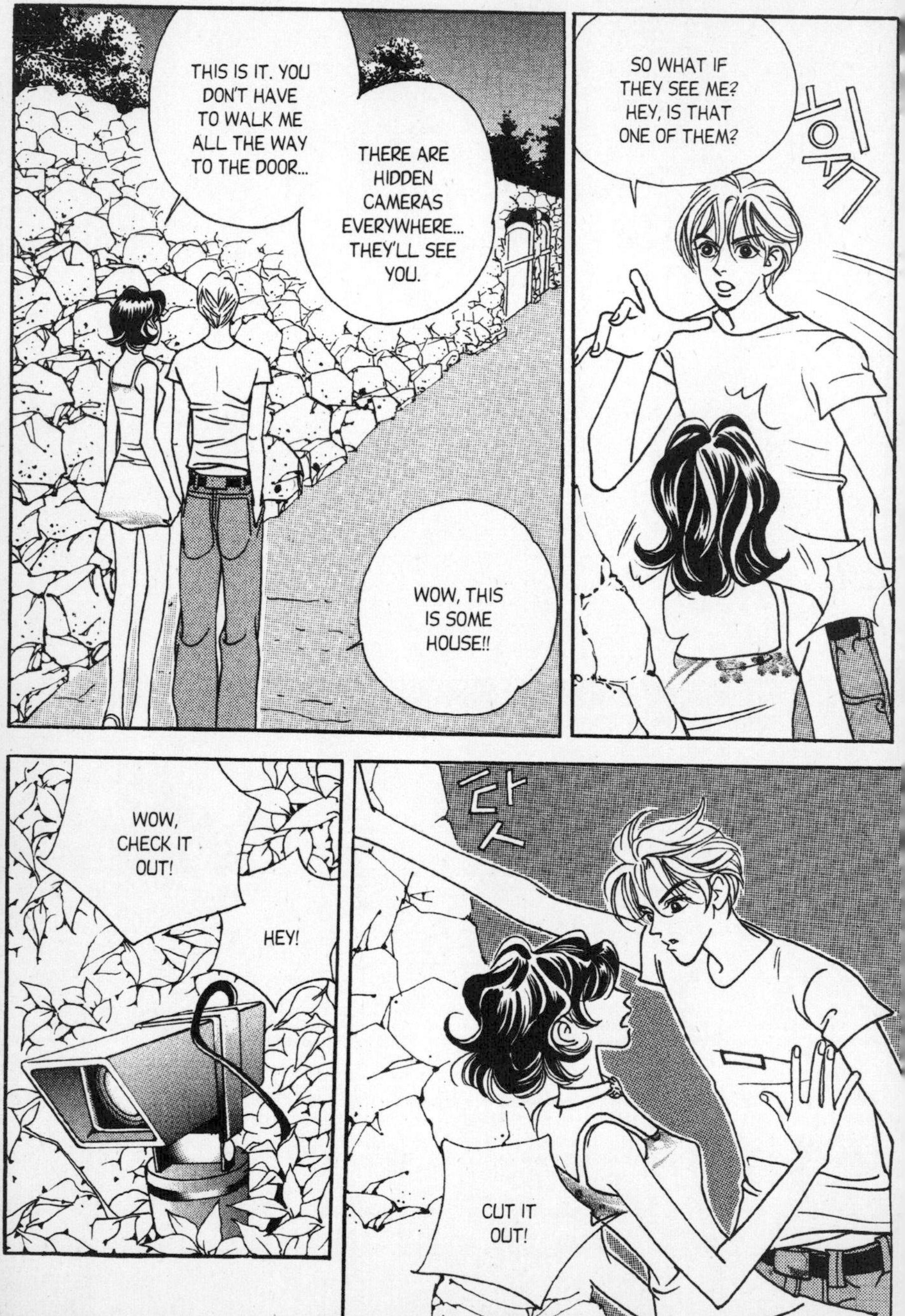
THIS IS IT. YOU DON'T HAVE TO WALK ME ALL THE WAY TO THE DOOR...
THERE ARE HIDDEN CAMERAS EVERYWHERE... THEY'LL SEE YOU.
WOW, THIS IS SOME HOUSE!!
SO WHAT IF THEY SEE ME? HEY, IS THAT ONE OF THEM?
WOW, CHECK IT OUT!
HEY!
CUT IT OUT!

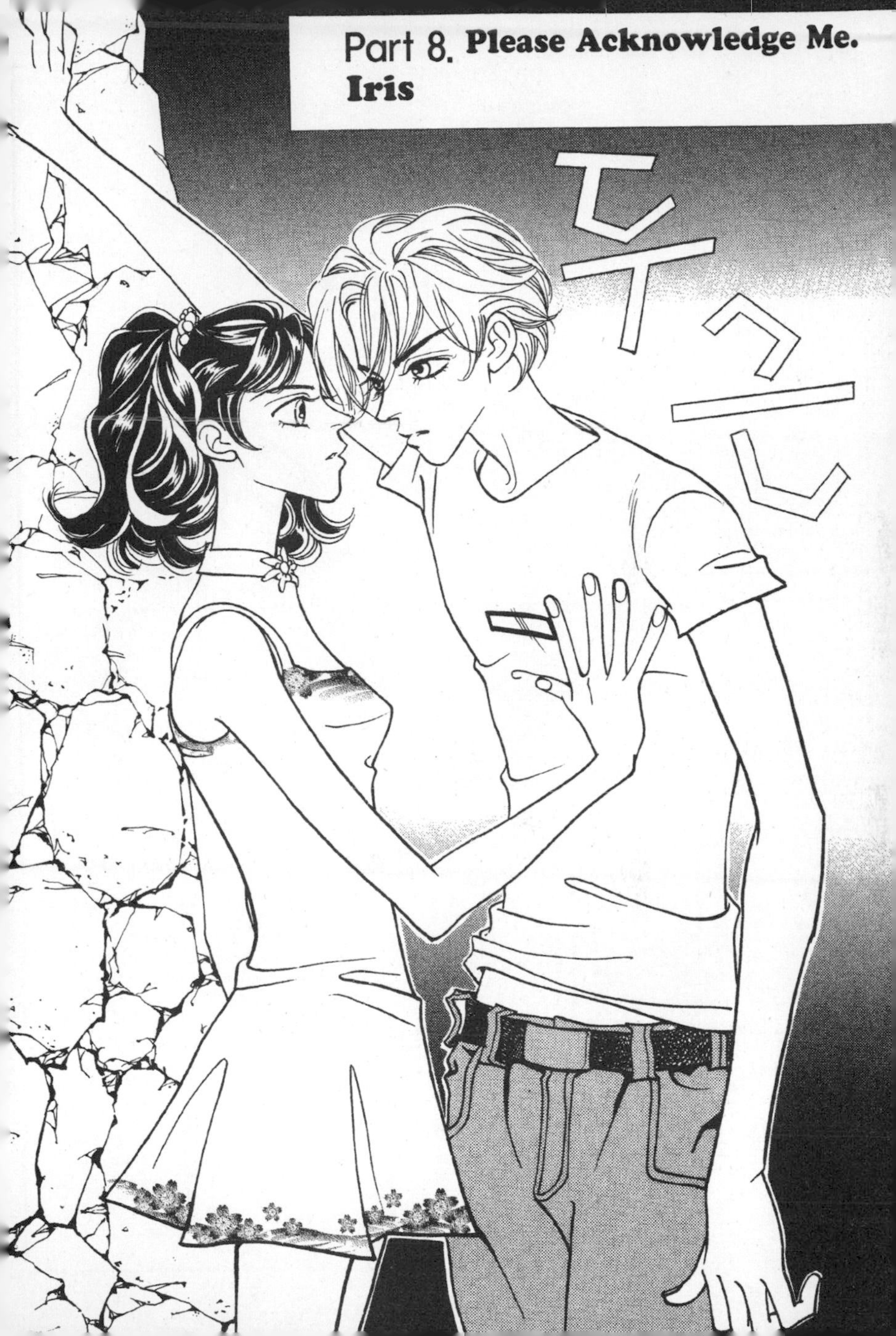
Part 8. Please Acknowledge Me.
Iris

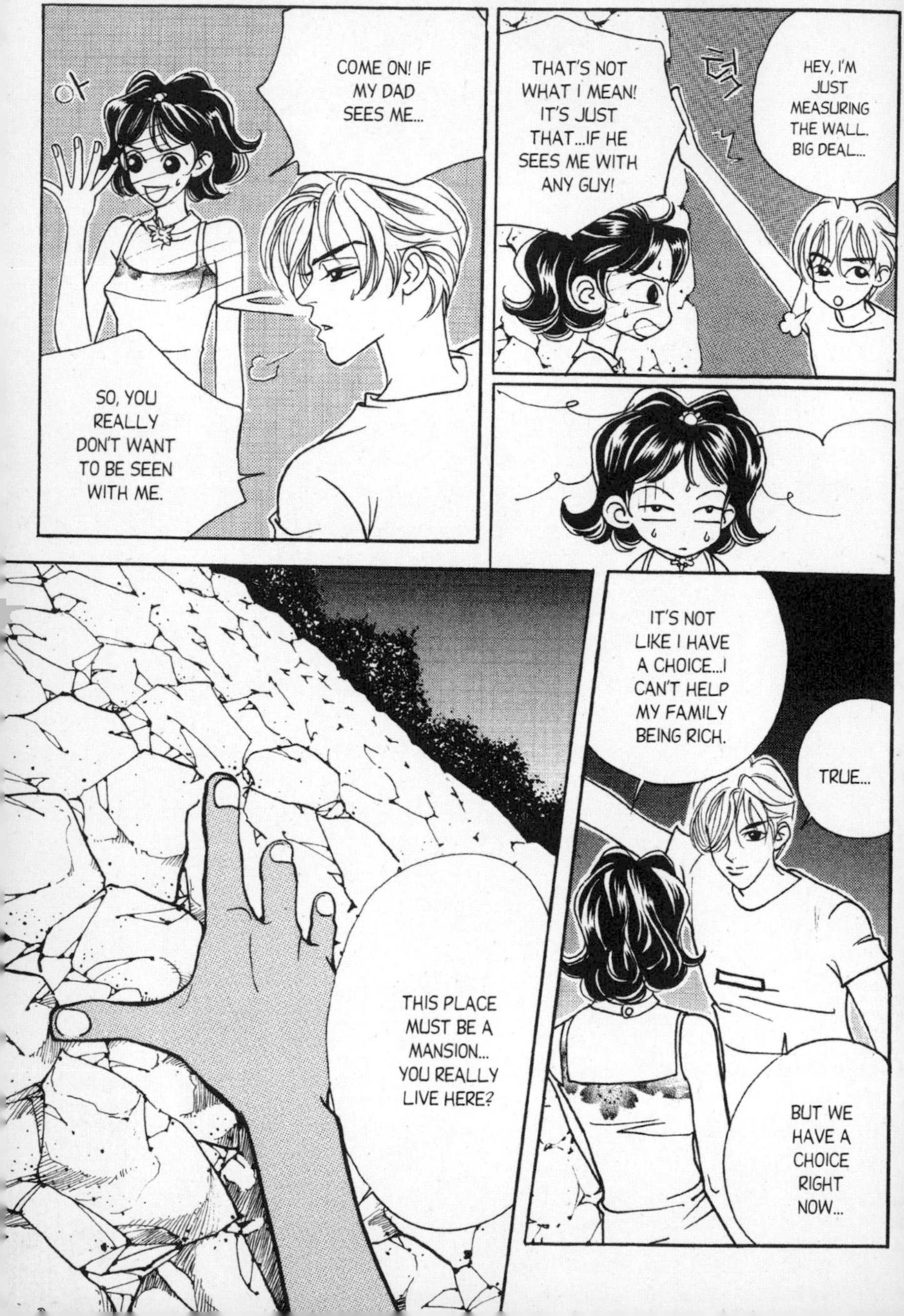
COME ON! IF MY DAD SEES ME...
SO, YOU REALLY DON'T WANT TO BE SEEN WITH ME.
THAT'S NOT WHAT I MEAN! IT'S JUST THAT...IF HE SEES ME WITH ANY GUY!
HEY, I'M JUST MEASURING THE WALL. BIG DEAL...
THIS PLACE MUST BE A MANSION... YOU REALLY LIVE HERE?
IT'S NOT LIKE I HAVE A CHOICE...I CAN'T HELP MY FAMILY BEING RICH.
TRUE...
BUT WE HAVE A CHOICE RIGHT NOW...

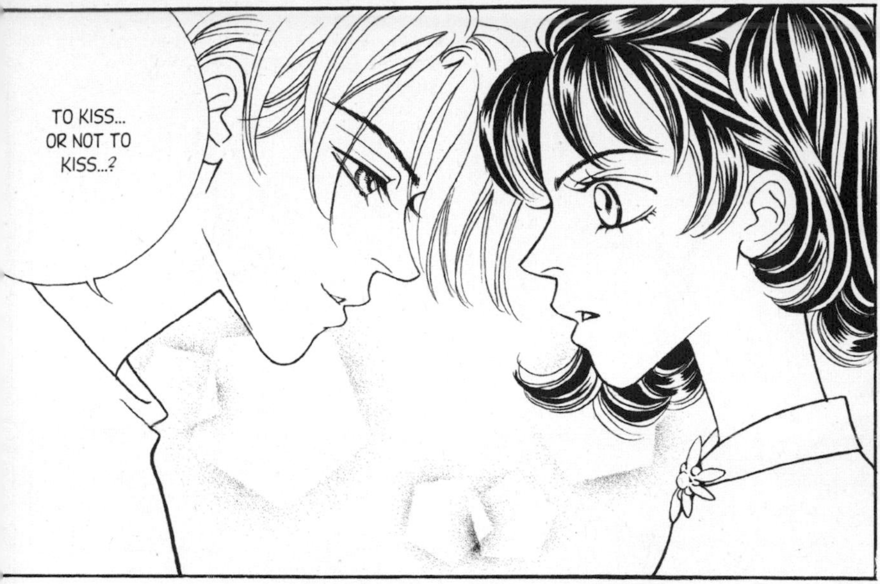
TO KISS... OR NOT TO KISS...?
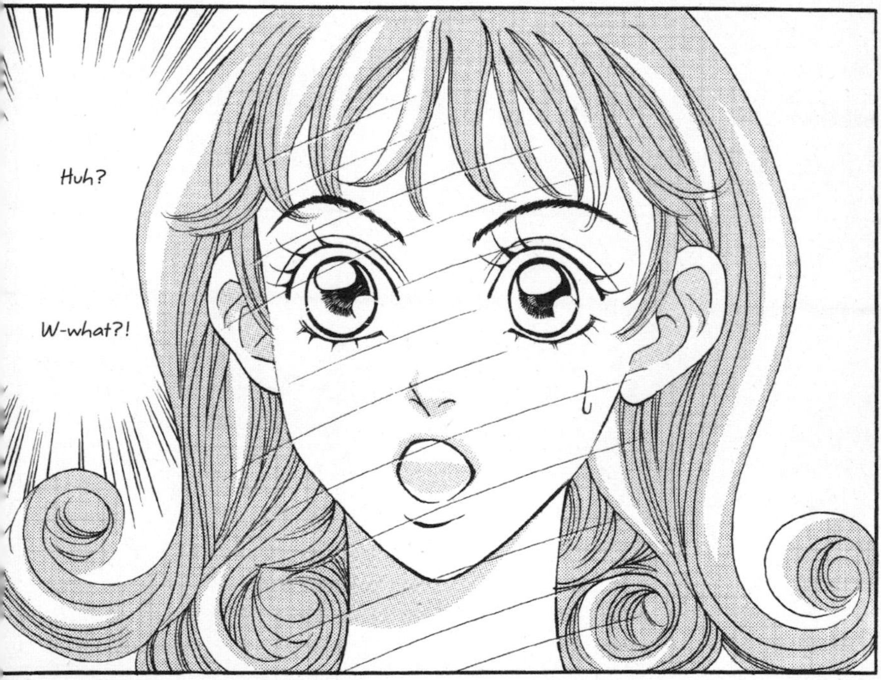
Huh?
W-what?!

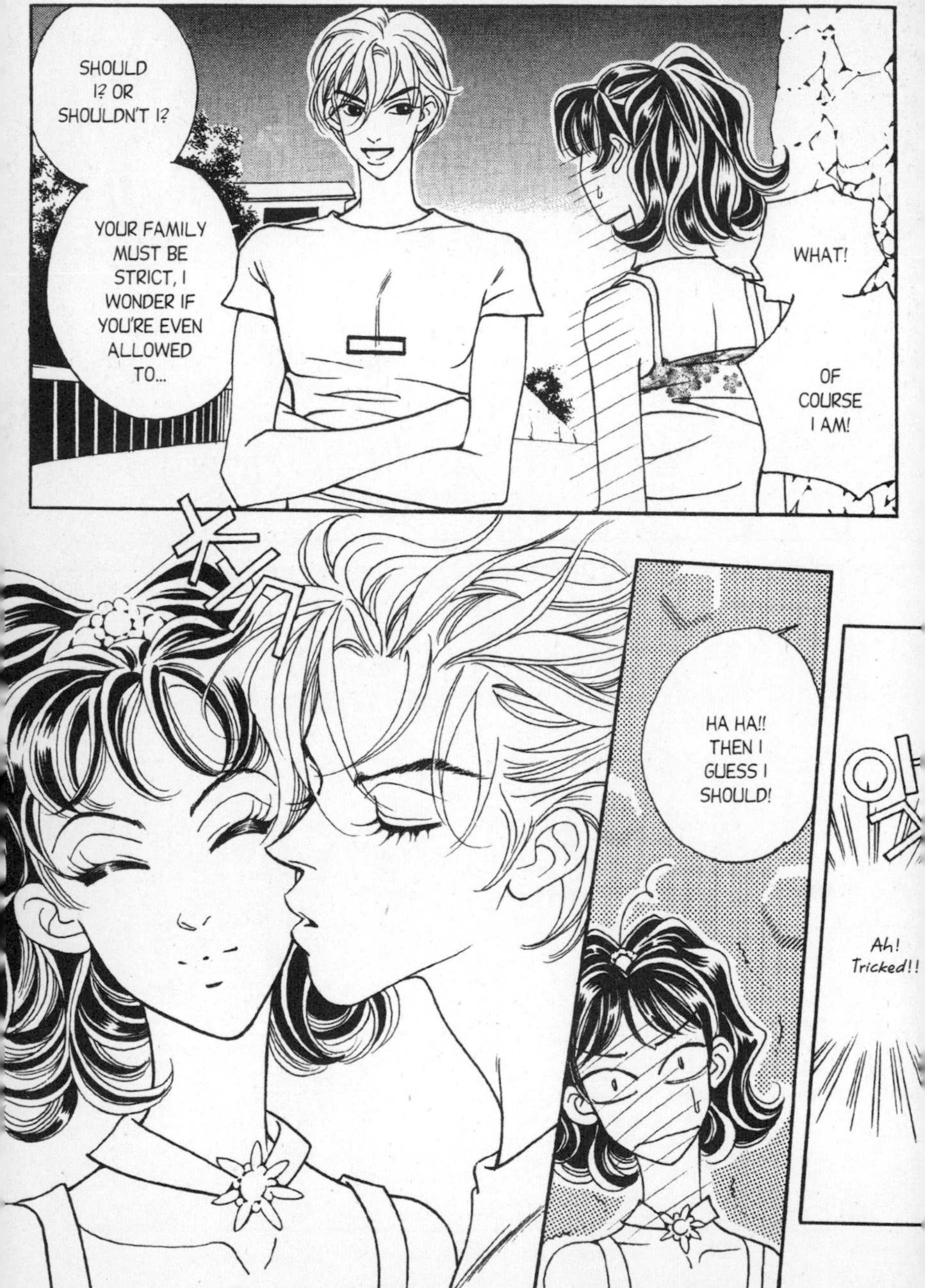
SHOULD I? OR SHOULDN'T I?
YOUR FAMILY MUST BE STRICT, I WONDER IF YOU'RE EVEN ALLOWED TO...
WHAT!
OF COURSE I AM!
HA HA!! THEN I GUESS I SHOULD!
Ah! Tricked!!

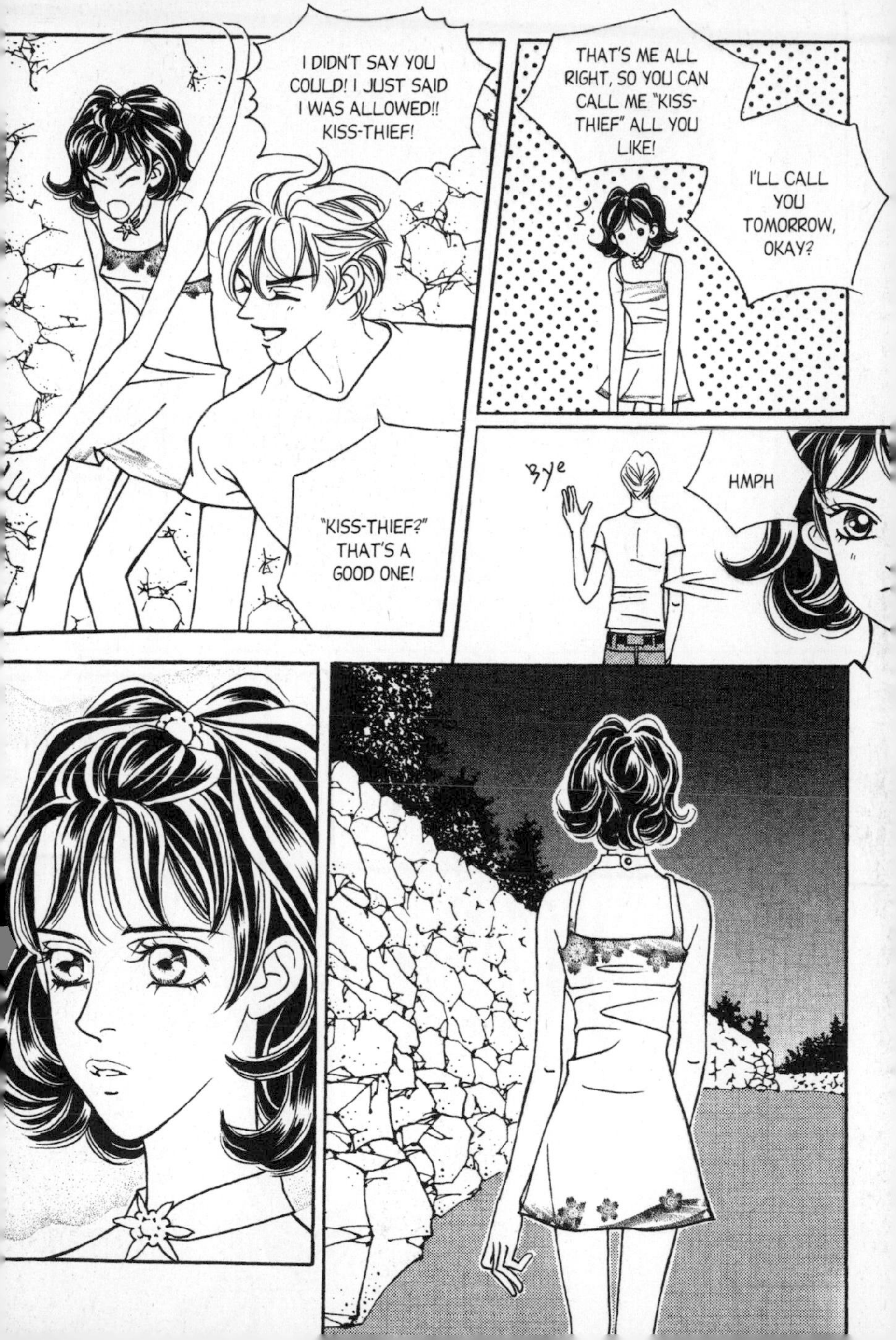
I DIDN'T SAY YOU COULD! I JUST SAID I WAS ALLOWED!! KISS-THIEF!
"KISS-THIEF?" THAT'S A GOOD ONE!
THAT'S ME ALL RIGHT, SO YOU CAN CALL ME "KISS-THIEF" ALL YOU LIKE!
I'LL CALL YOU TOMORROW, OKAY?
Bye
HMPH

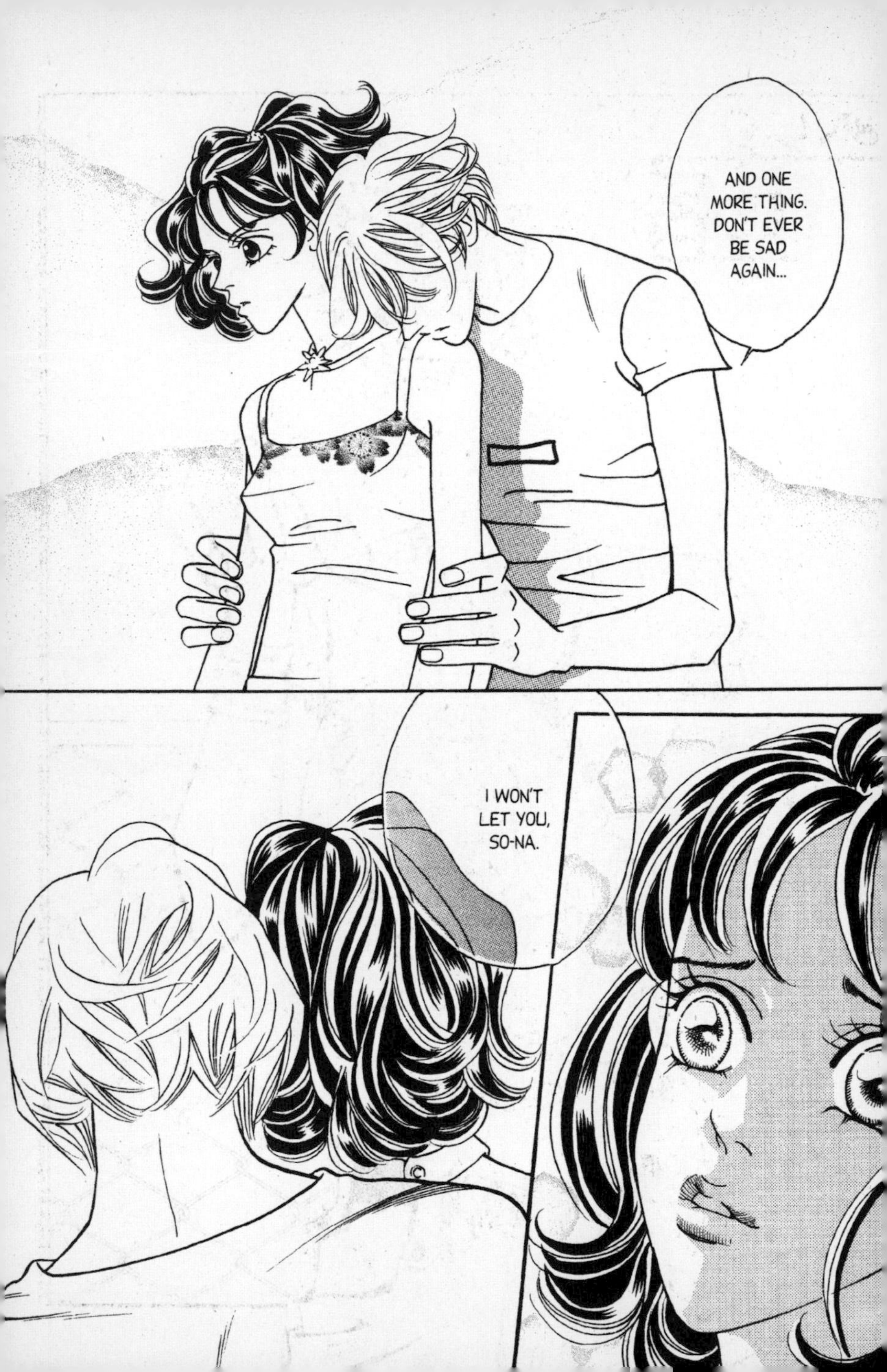
AND ONE MORE THING. DON'T EVER BE SAD AGAIN...
I WON'T LET YOU, SO-NA.

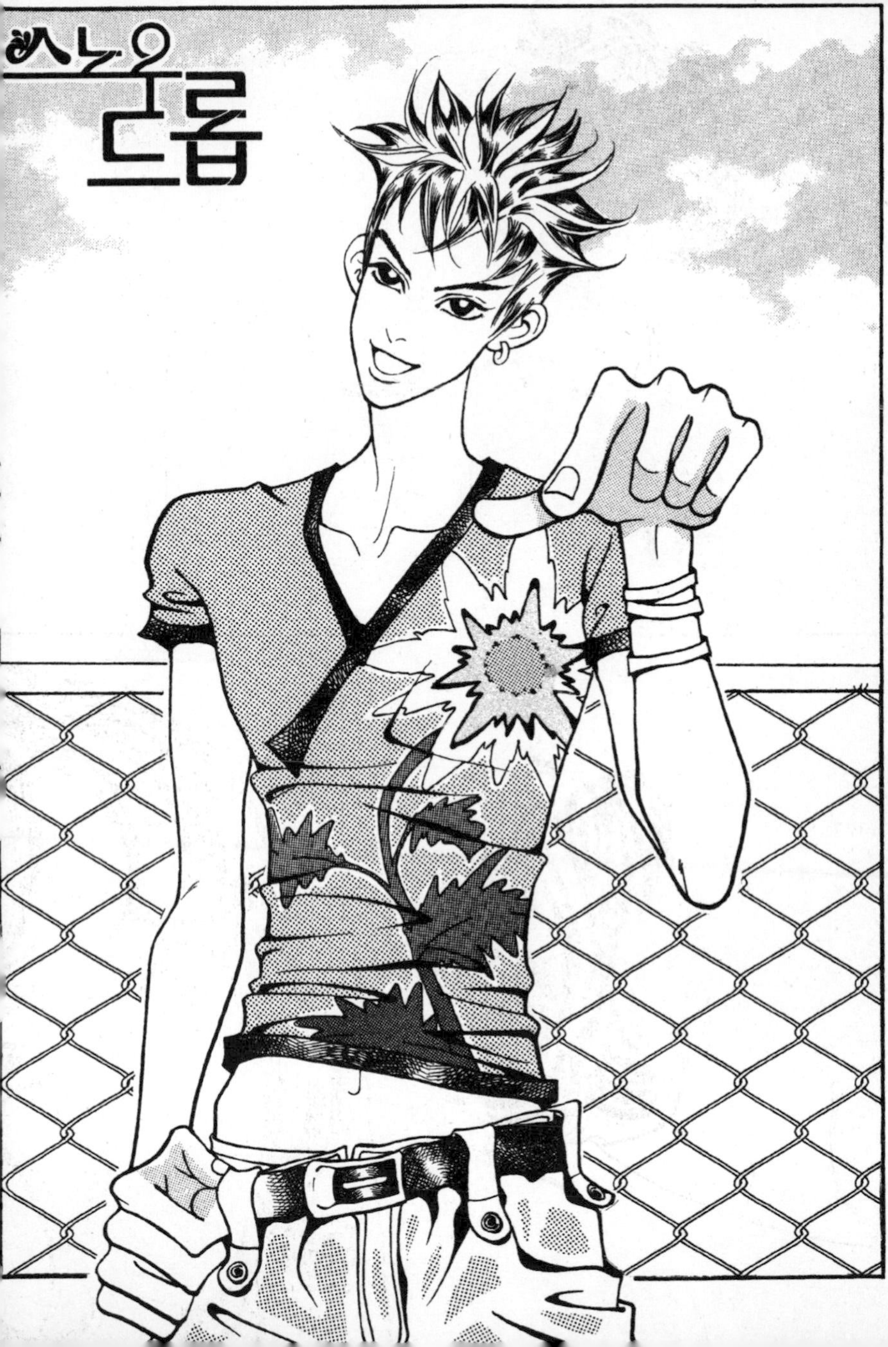
스노우 드롭

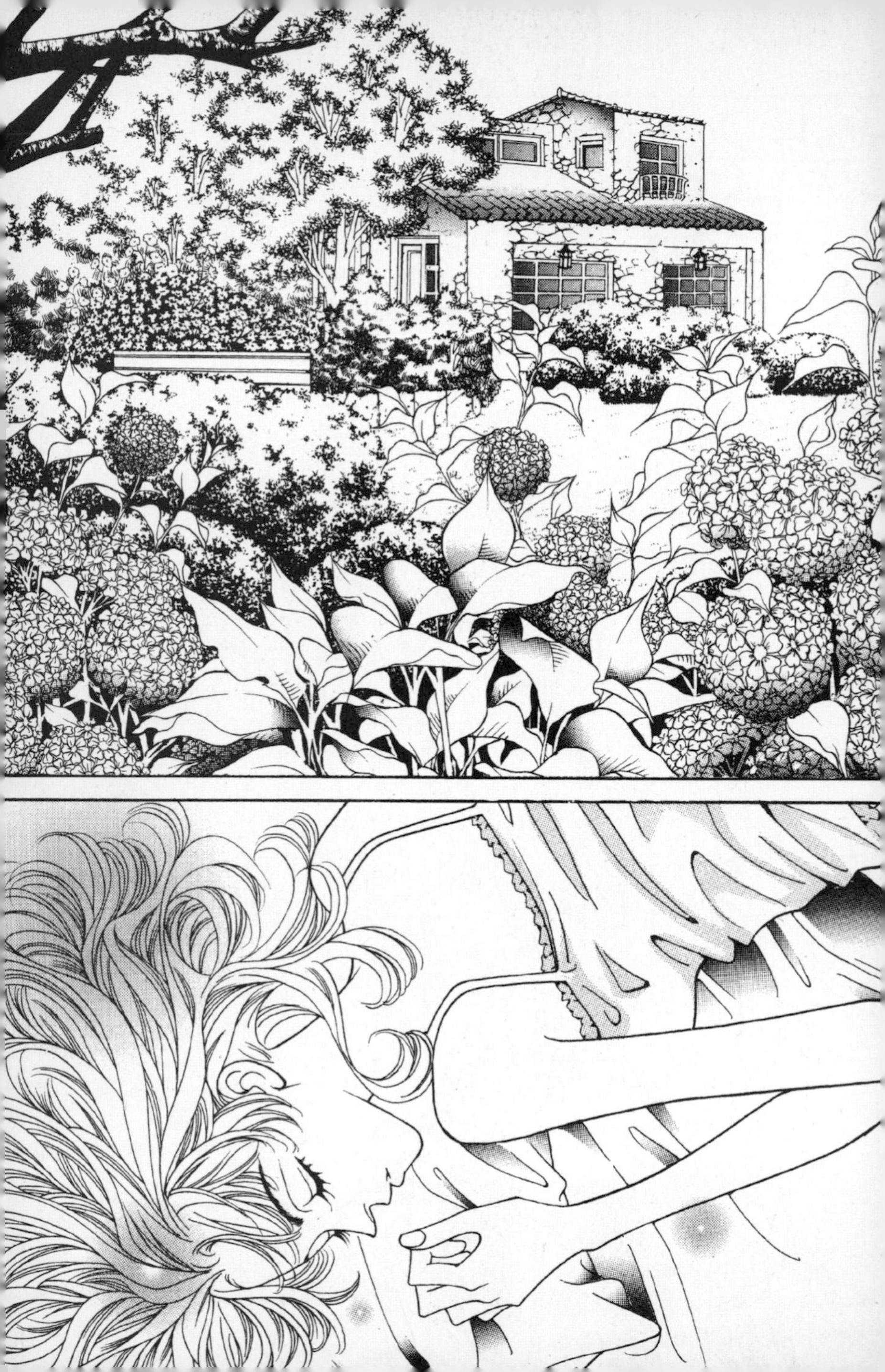

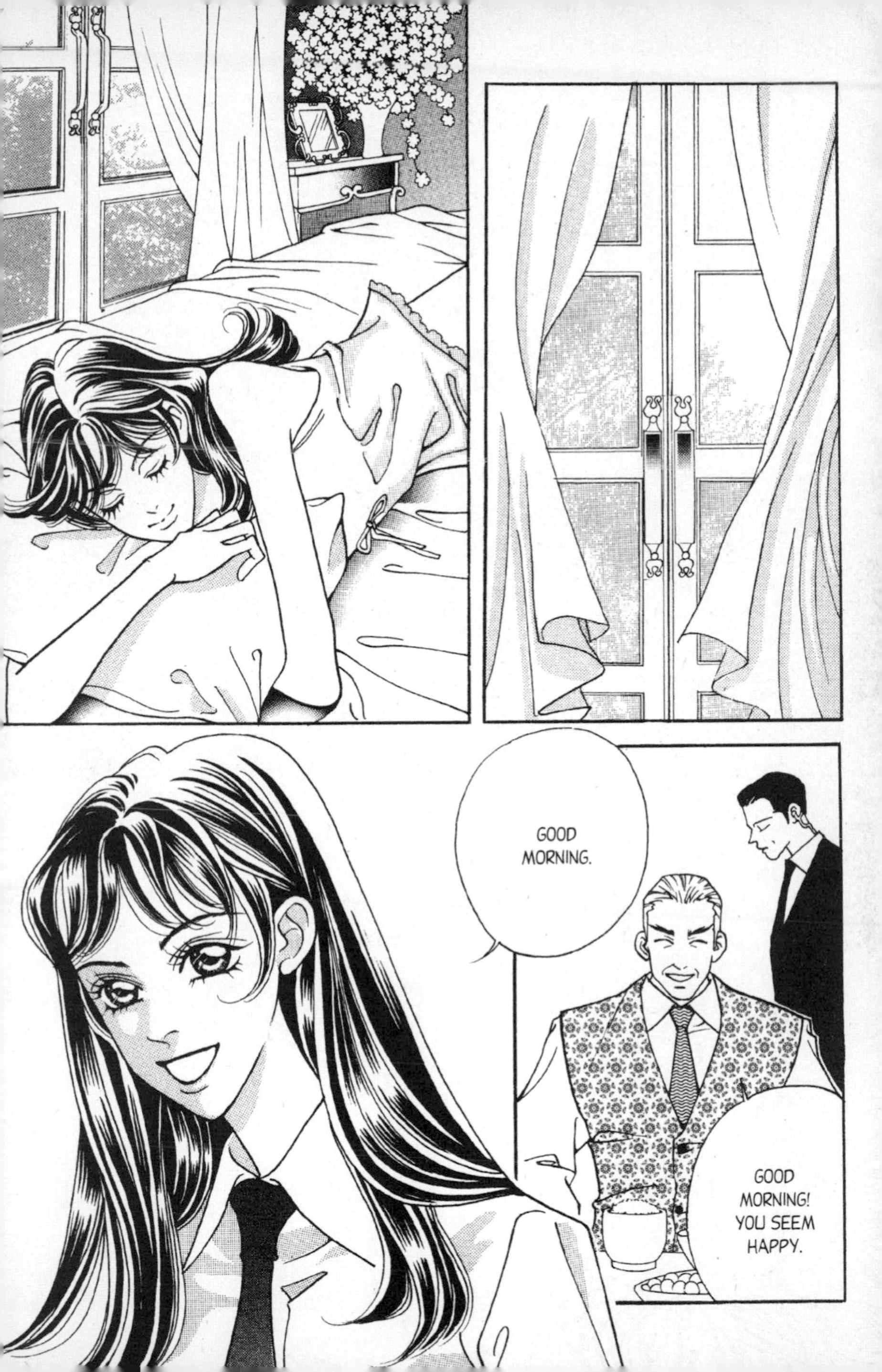
GOOD MORNING.
GOOD MORNING! YOU SEEM HAPPY.

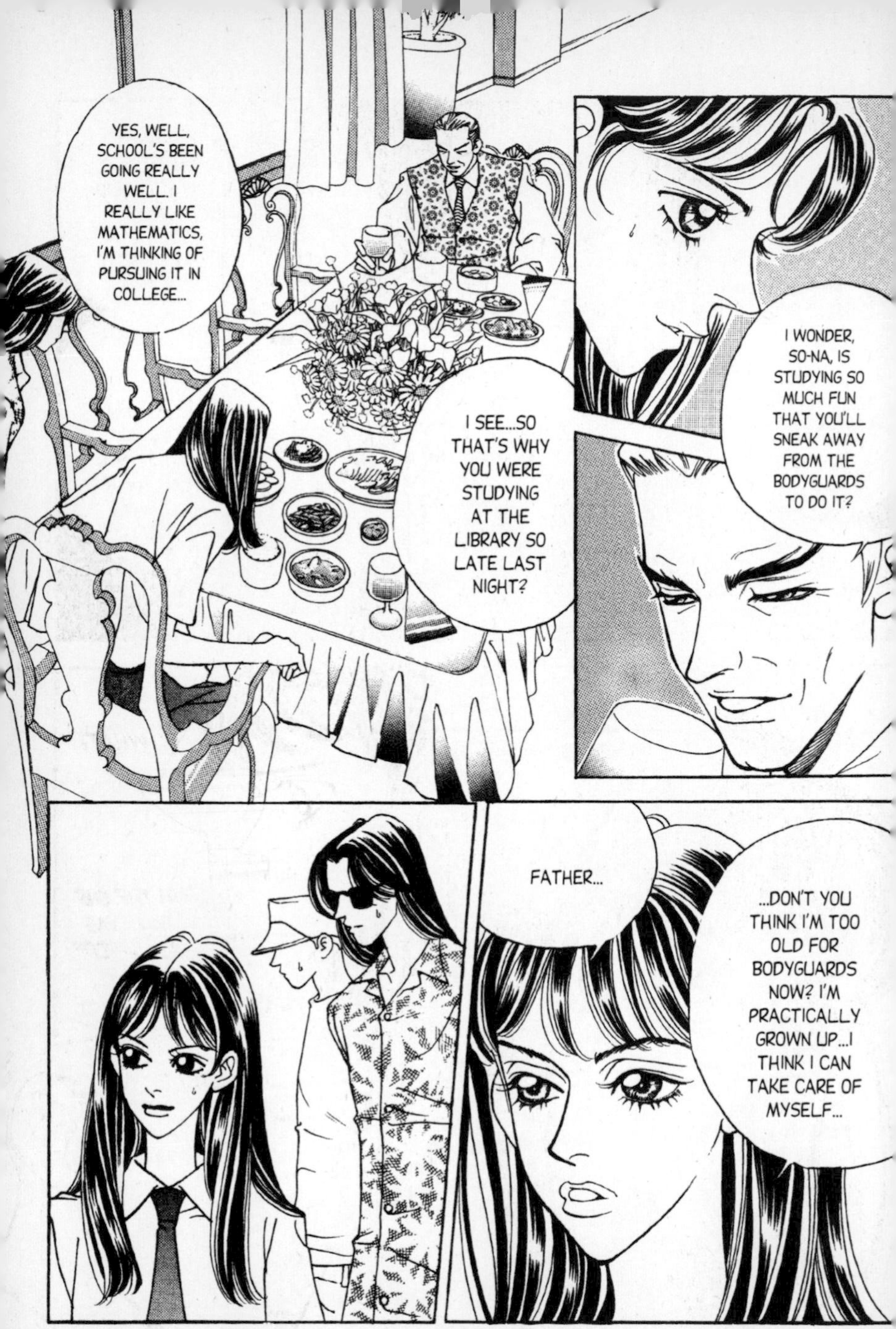
YES, WELL, SCHOOL'S BEEN GOING REALLY WELL. I REALLY LIKE MATHEMATICS, I'M THINKING OF PURSUING IT IN COLLEGE...
I SEE...SO THAT'S WHY YOU WERE STUDYING AT THE LIBRARY SO LATE LAST NIGHT?
I WONDER, SO-NA, IS STUDYING SO MUCH FUN THAT YOU'LL SNEAK AWAY FROM THE BODYGUARDS TO DO IT?
FATHER...
...DON'T YOU THINK I'M TOO OLD FOR BODYGUARDS NOW? I'M PRACTICALLY GROWN UP...I THINK I CAN TAKE CARE OF MYSELF...

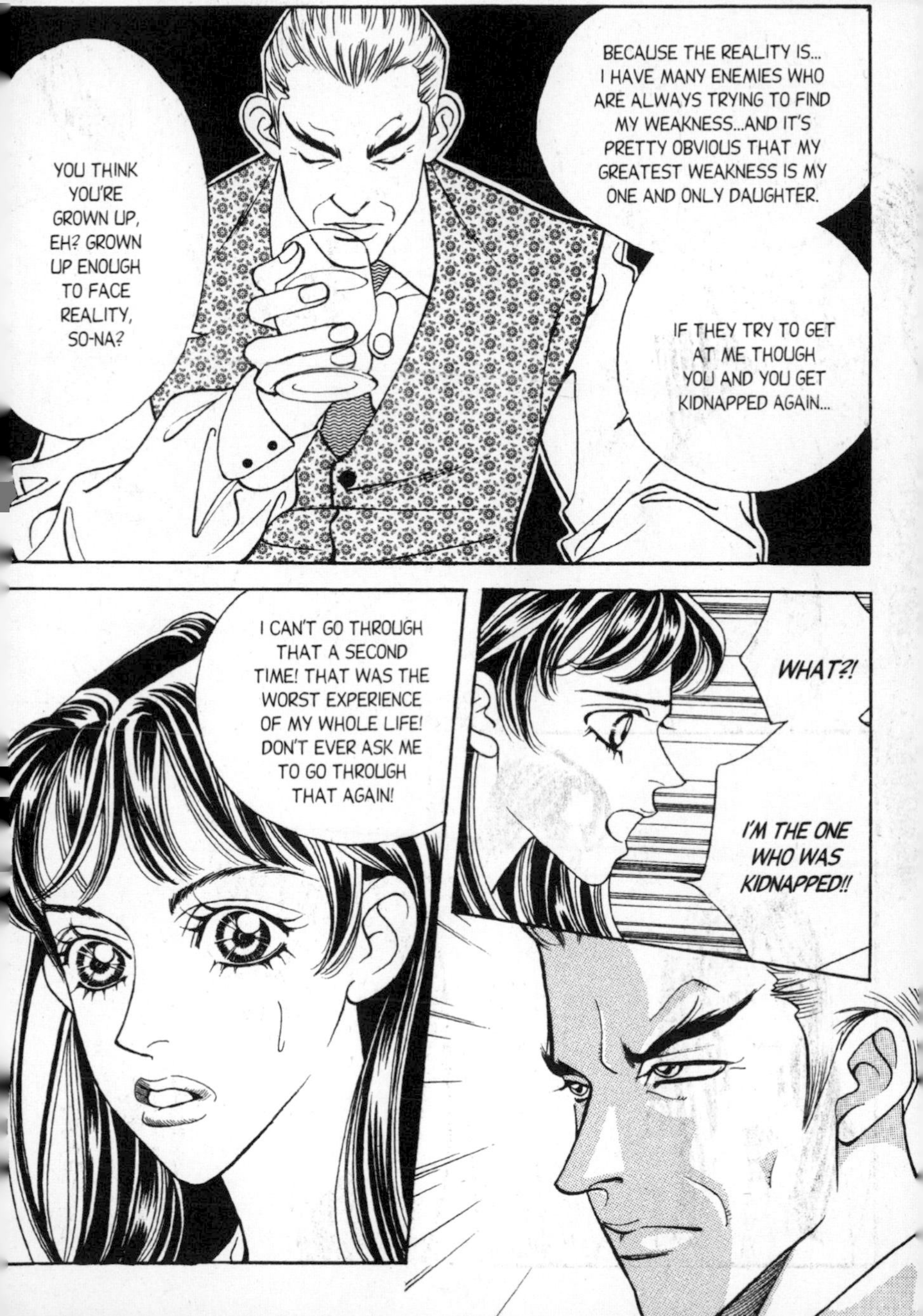
YOU THINK YOU'RE GROWN UP, EH? GROWN UP ENOUGH TO FACE REALITY, SO-NA?
BECAUSE THE REALITY IS... I HAVE MANY ENEMIES WHO ARE ALWAYS TRYING TO FIND MY WEAKNESS...AND IT'S PRETTY OBVIOUS THAT MY GREATEST WEAKNESS IS MY ONE AND ONLY DAUGHTER.
IF THEY TRY TO GET AT ME THOUGH YOU AND YOU GET KIDNAPPED AGAIN...
I CAN'T GO THROUGH THAT A SECOND TIME! THAT WAS THE WORST EXPERIENCE OF MY WHOLE LIFE! DON'T EVER ASK ME TO GO THROUGH THAT AGAIN!
WHAT?!
I'M THE ONE WHO WAS KIDNAPPED!!

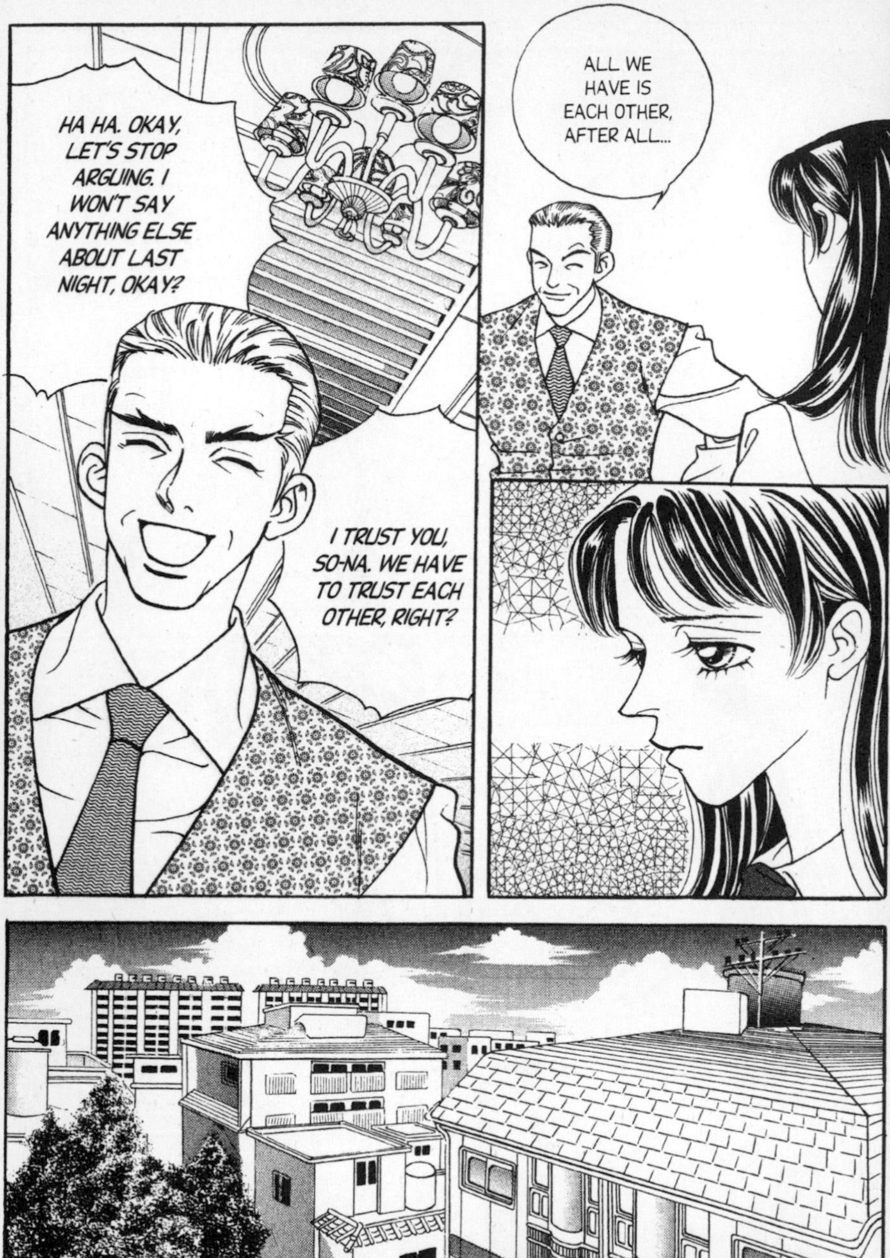

HA HA. OKAY, LET'S STOP ARGUING. I WON'T SAY ANYTHING ELSE ABOUT LAST NIGHT, OKAY?
I TRUST YOU, SO-NA. WE HAVE TO TRUST EACH OTHER, RIGHT?
ALL WE HAVE IS EACH OTHER, AFTER ALL...

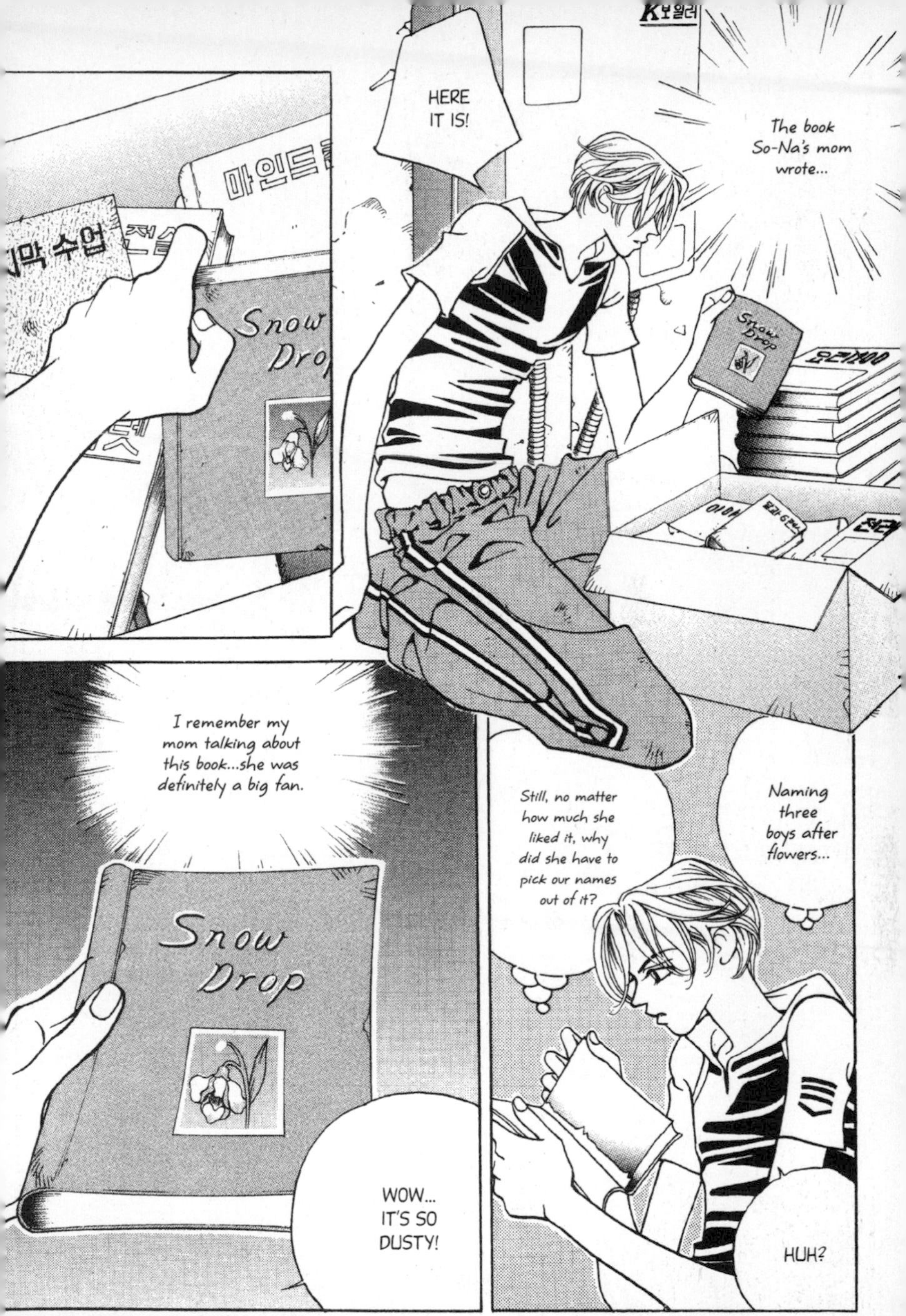
Snow Drop
HERE IT IS!
The book So-Na's mom wrote...
I remember my mom talking about this book...she was definitely a big fan.
WOW... IT'S SO DUSTY!
Still, no matter how much she liked it, why did she have to pick our names out of it?
Naming three boys after flowers...
HUH?

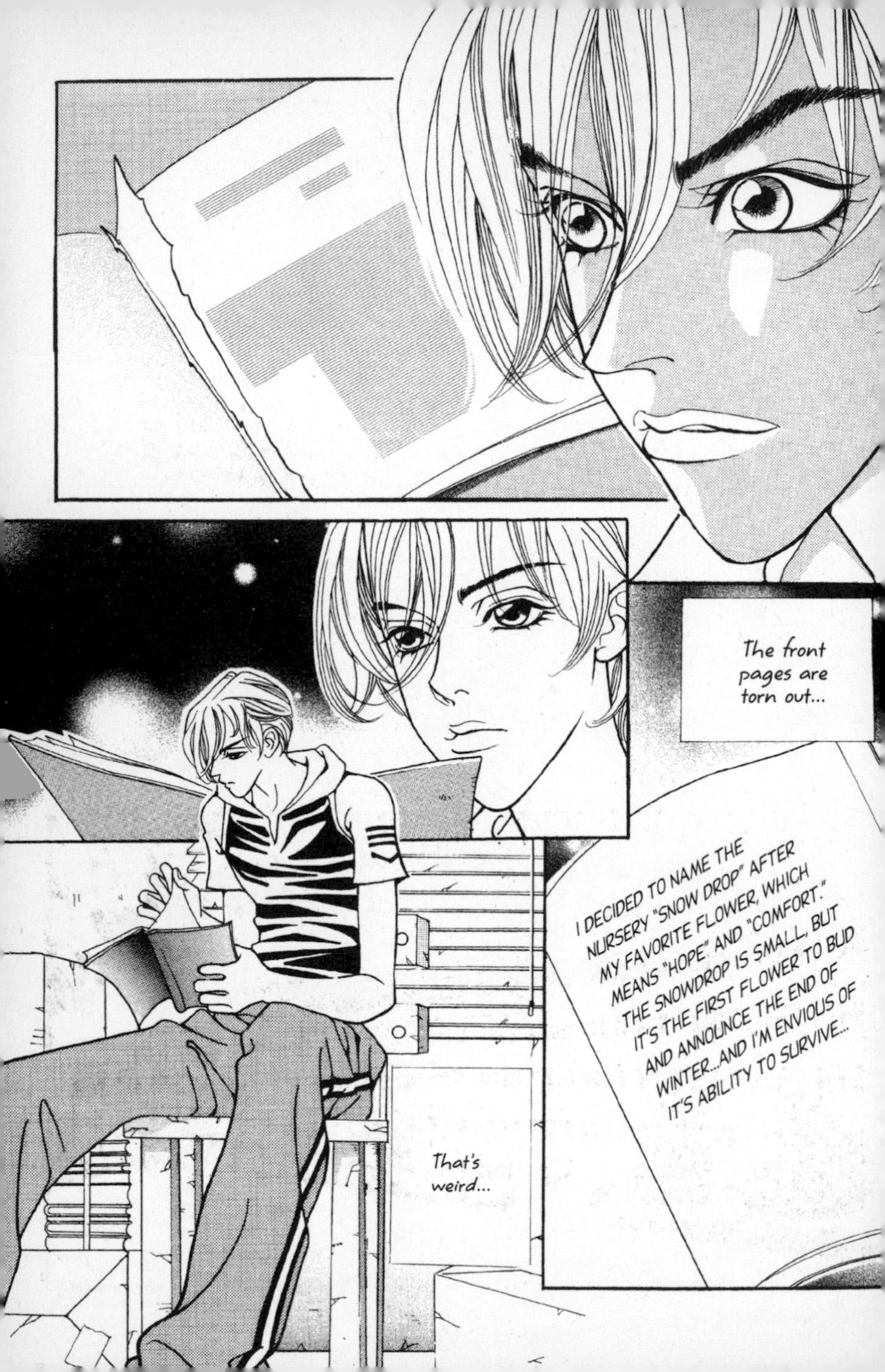
The front pages are torn out...
That's weird...
I DECIDED TO NAME THE NURSERY "SNOW DROP" AFTER MY FAVORITE FLOWER, WHICH MEANS "HOPE" AND "COMFORT." THE SNOWDROP IS SMALL, BUT IT'S THE FIRST FLOWER TO BUD AND ANNOUNCE THE END OF WINTER...AND I'M ENVIOUS OF IT'S ABILITY TO SURVIVE...

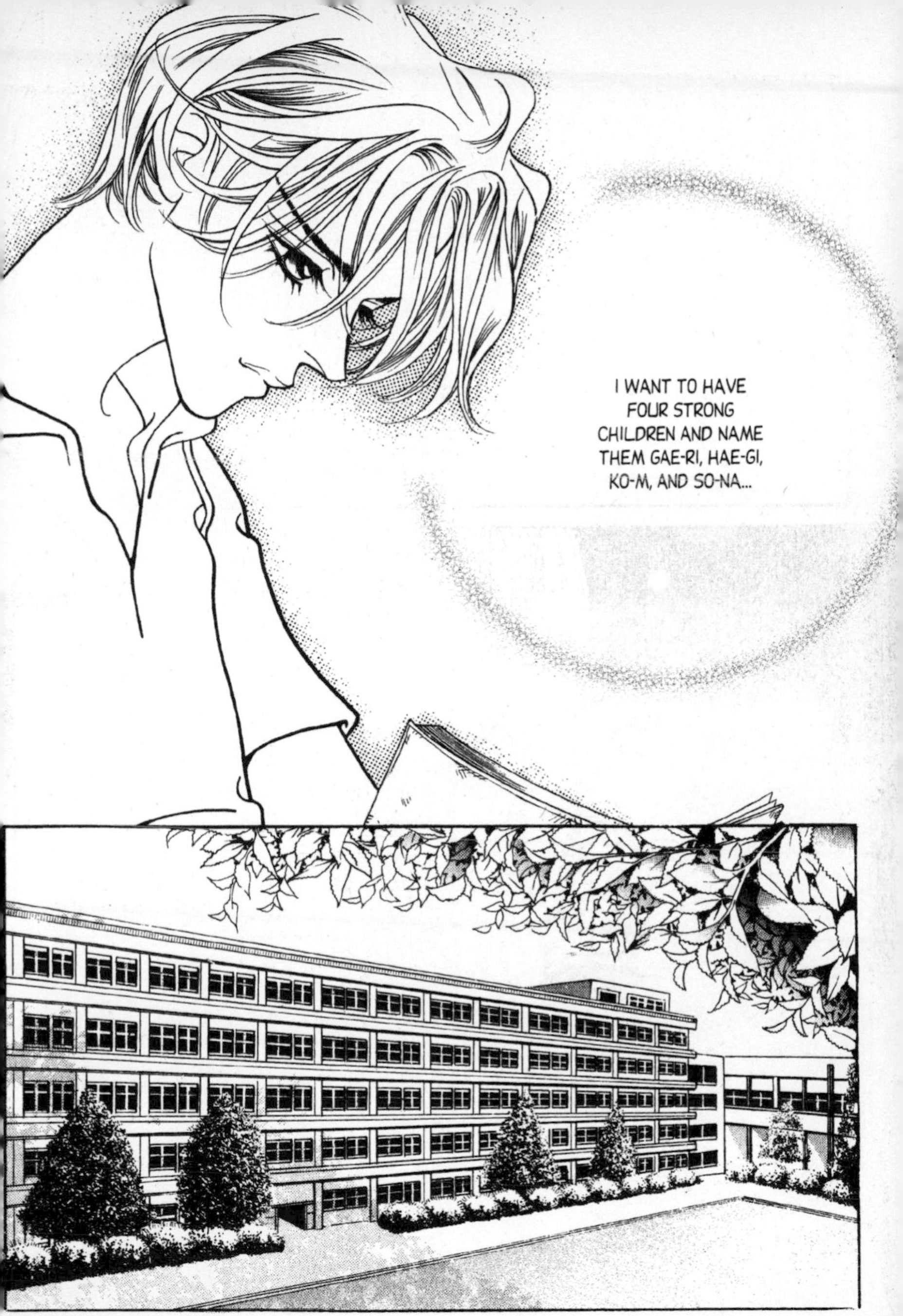
I WANT TO HAVE FOUR STRONG CHILDREN AND NAME THEM GAE-RI, HAE-GI, KO-M, AND SO-NA...

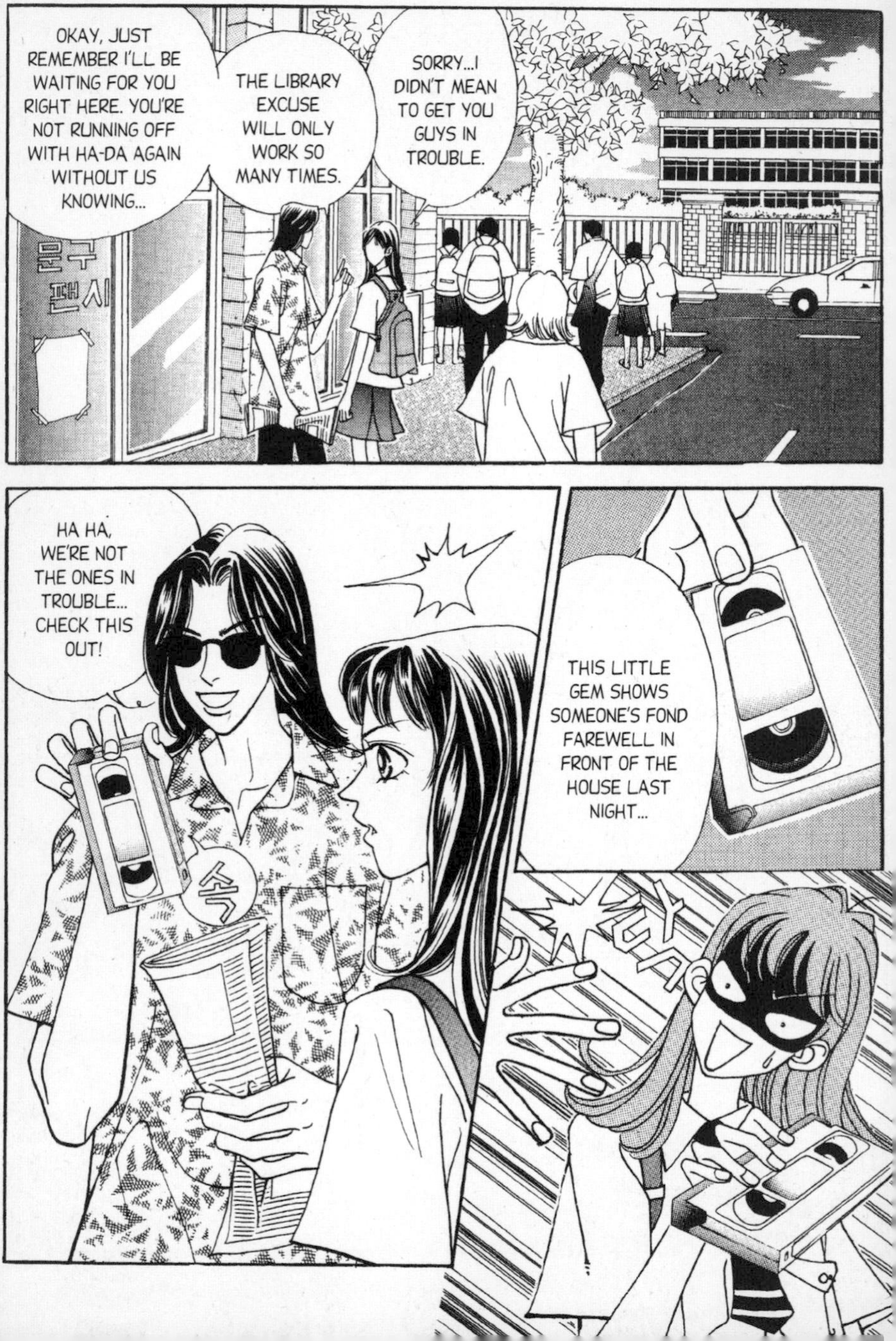
OKAY, JUST REMEMBER I'LL BE WAITING FOR YOU RIGHT HERE. YOU'RE NOT RUNNING OFF WITH HA-DA AGAIN WITHOUT US KNOWING...
THE LIBRARY EXCUSE WILL ONLY WORK SO MANY TIMES.
SORRY...I DIDN'T MEAN TO GET YOU GUYS IN TROUBLE.
HA HA, WE'RE NOT THE ONES IN TROUBLE... CHECK THIS OUT!
THIS LITTLE GEM SHOWS SOMEONE'S FOND FAREWELL IN FRONT OF THE HOUSE LAST NIGHT...

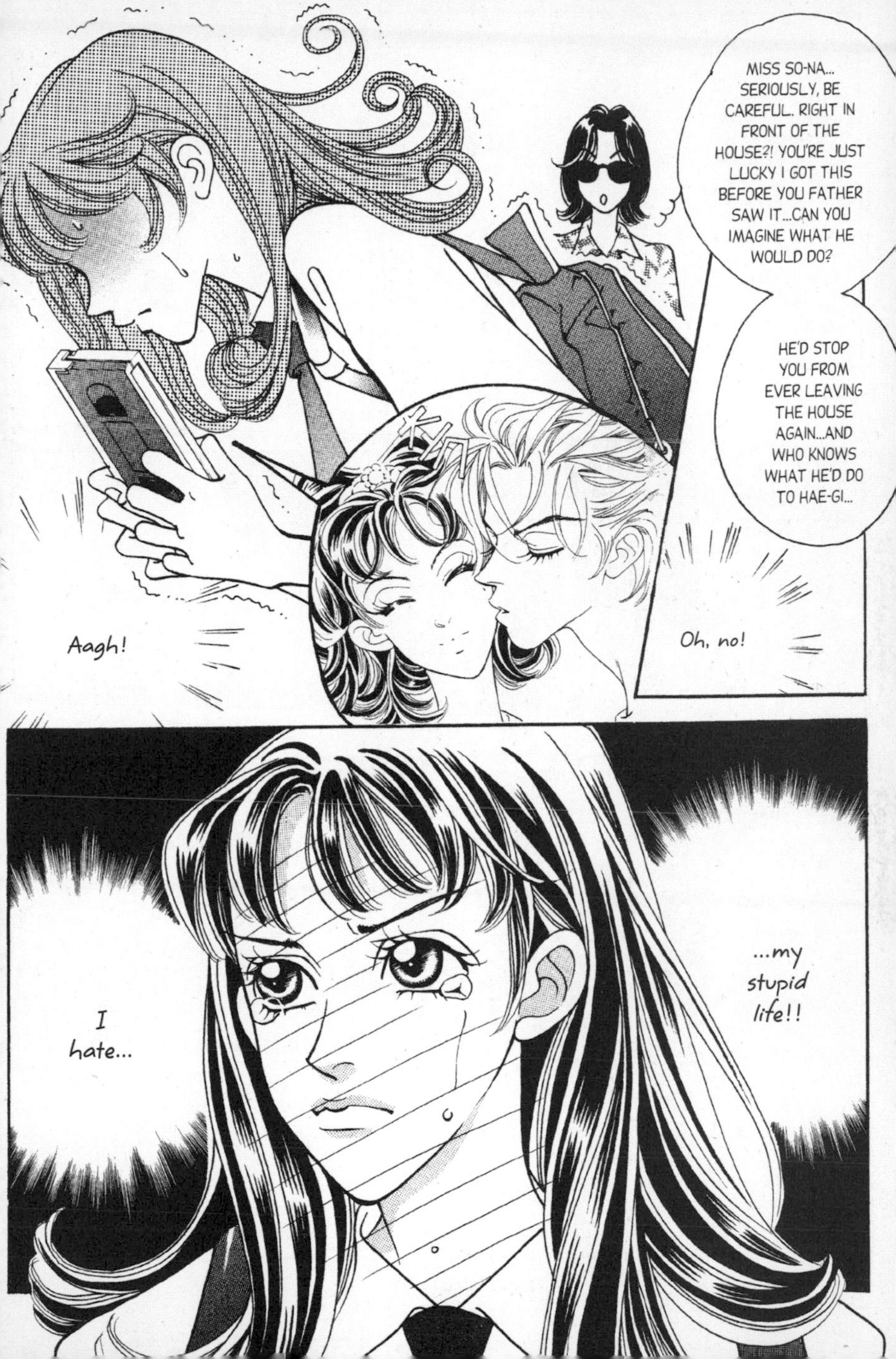
Aagh!
MISS SO-NA... SERIOUSLY, BE CAREFUL. RIGHT IN FRONT OF THE HOUSE?! YOU'RE JUST LUCKY I GOT THIS BEFORE YOU FATHER SAW IT...CAN YOU IMAGINE WHAT HE WOULD DO?
HE'D STOP YOU FROM EVER LEAVING THE HOUSE AGAIN...AND WHO KNOWS WHAT HE'D DO TO HAE-GI...
Oh, no!
I hate...
...my stupid life!!

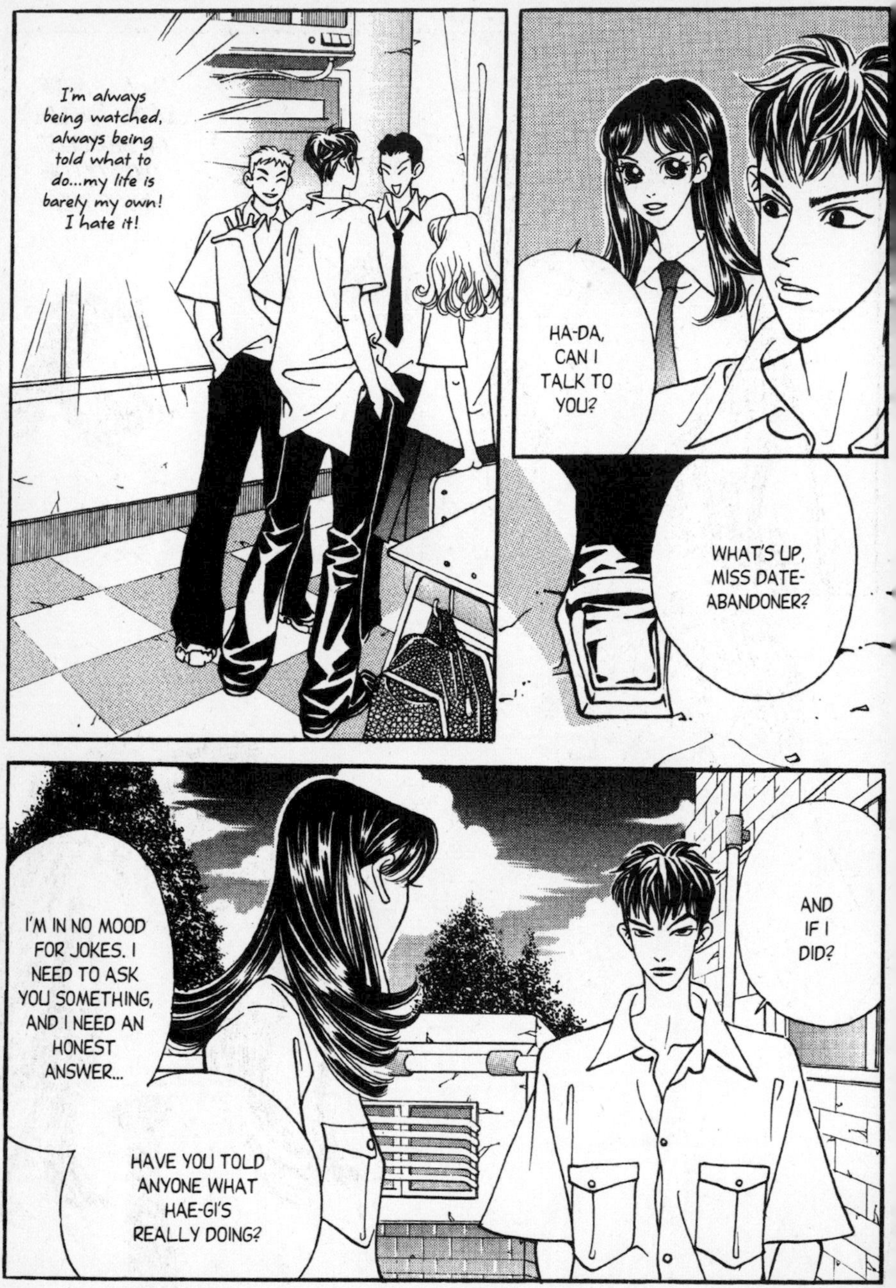
I'm always being watched, always being told what to do...my life is barely my own! I hate it!
HA-DA, CAN I TALK TO YOU?
WHAT'S UP, MISS DATE-ABANDONER?
I'M IN NO MOOD FOR JOKES. I NEED TO ASK YOU SOMETHING, AND I NEED AN HONEST ANSWER...
HAVE YOU TOLD ANYONE WHAT HAE-GI'S REALLY DOING?
AND IF I DID?

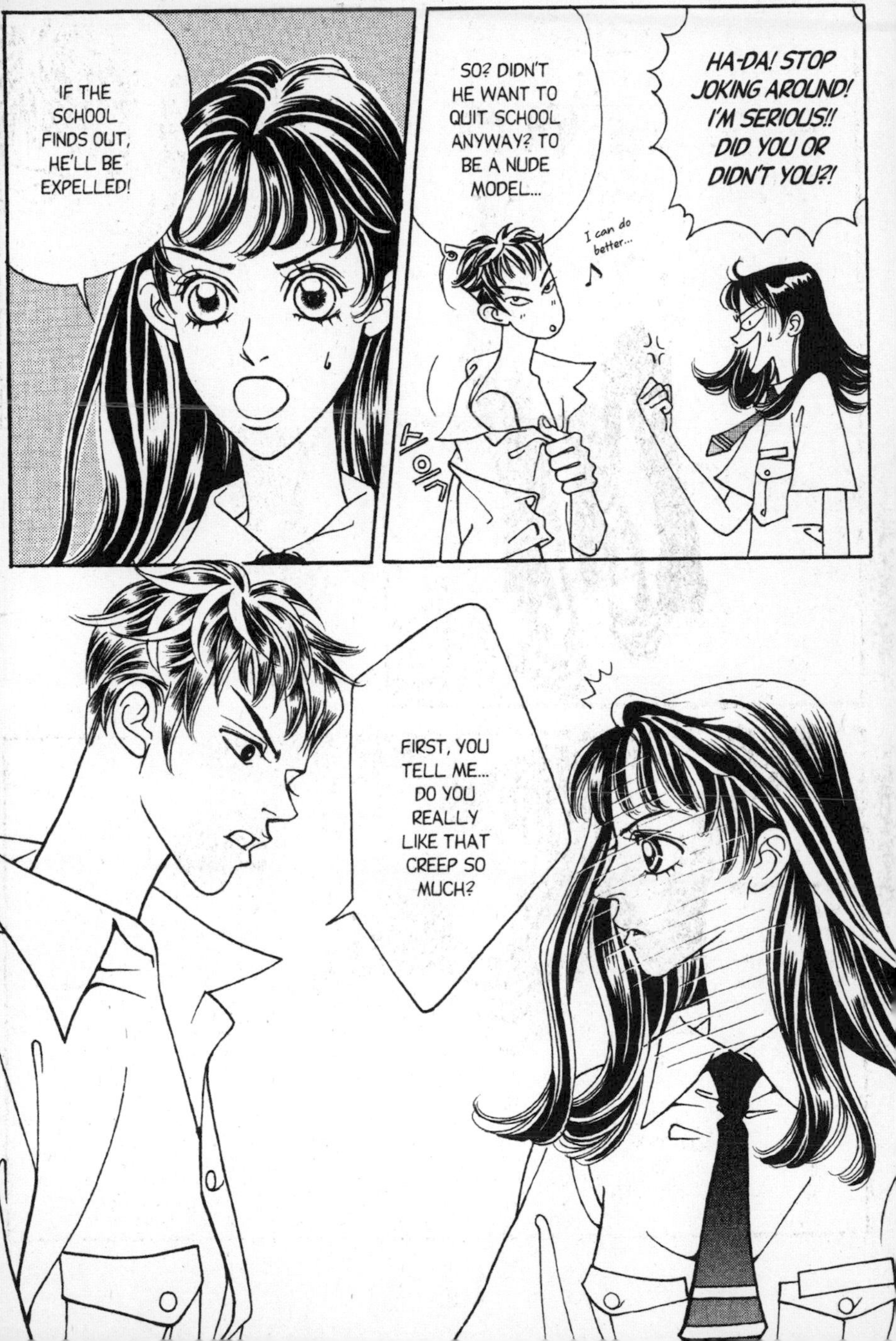
IF THE SCHOOL FINDS OUT, HE'LL BE EXPELLED!
SO? DIDN'T HE WANT TO QUIT SCHOOL ANYWAY? TO BE A NUDE MODEL...
I can do better...
HA-DA! STOP JOKING AROUND! I'M SERIOUS!! DID YOU OR DIDN'T YOU?!
FIRST, YOU TELL ME... DO YOU REALLY LIKE THAT CREEP SO MUCH?

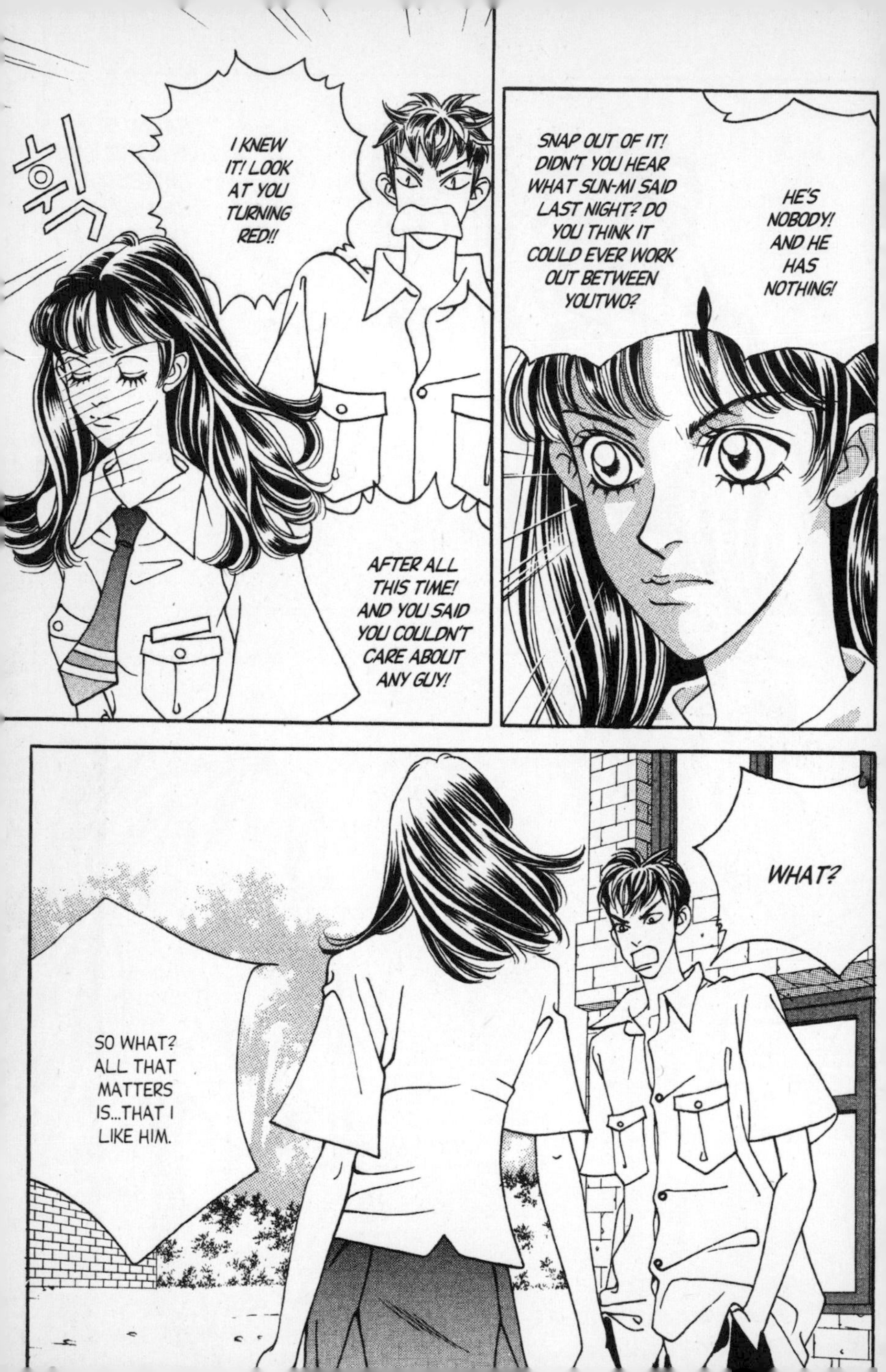
I KNEW IT! LOOK AT YOU TURNING RED!!
AFTER ALL THIS TIME! AND YOU SAID YOU COULDN'T CARE ABOUT ANY GUY!
SNAP OUT OF IT! DIDN'T YOU HEAR WHAT SUN-MI SAID LAST NIGHT? DO YOU THINK IT COULD EVER WORK OUT BETWEEN YOUTWO?
HE'S NOBODY! AND HE HAS NOTHING!
SO WHAT? ALL THAT MATTERS IS...THAT I LIKE HIM.
WHAT?

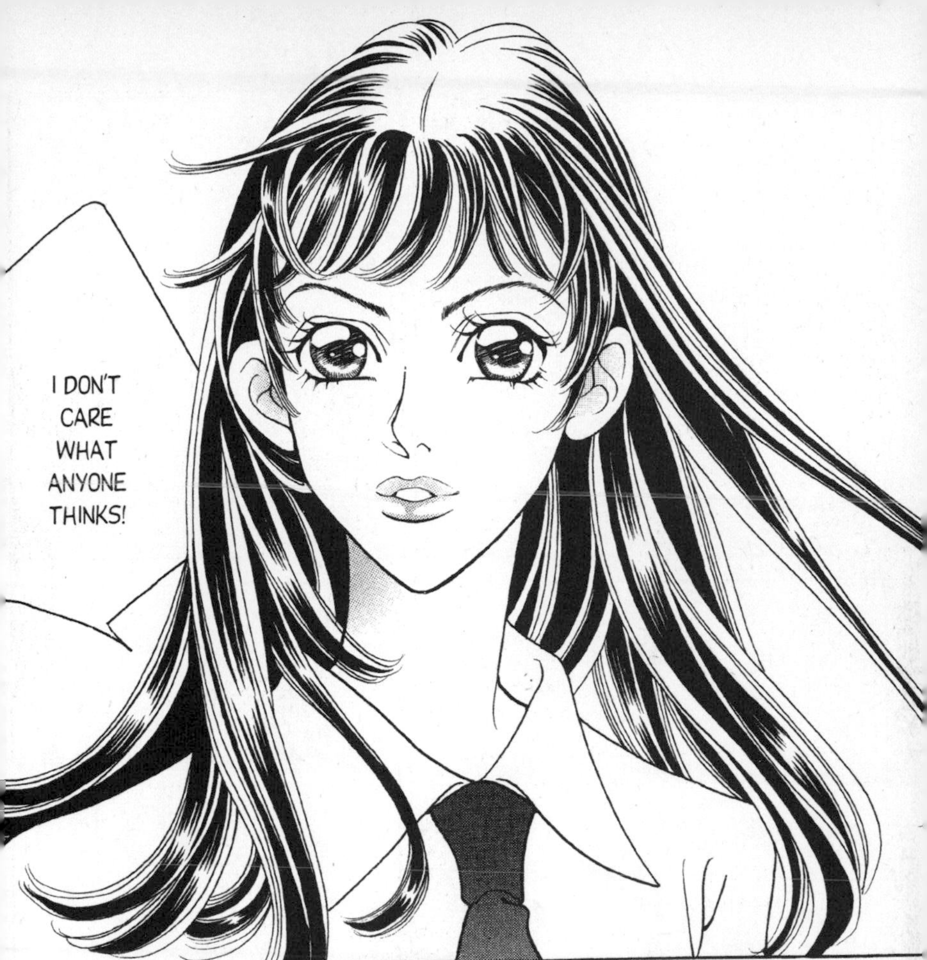
I DON'T CARE WHAT ANYONE THINKS!
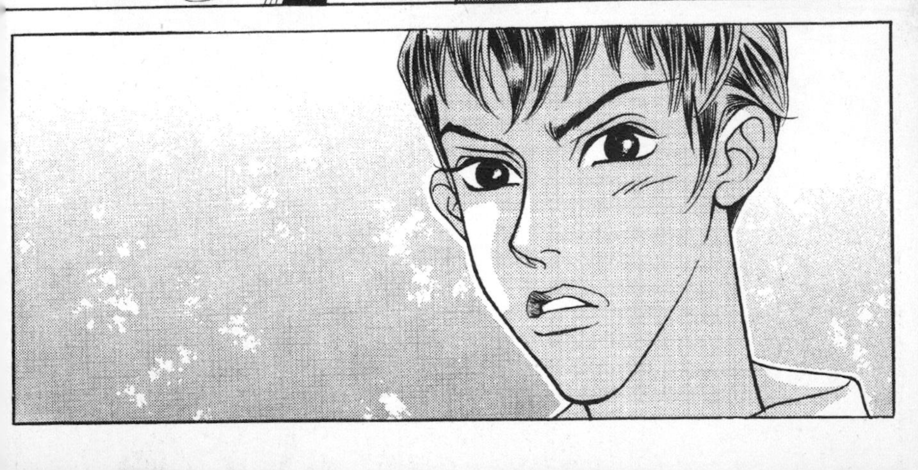

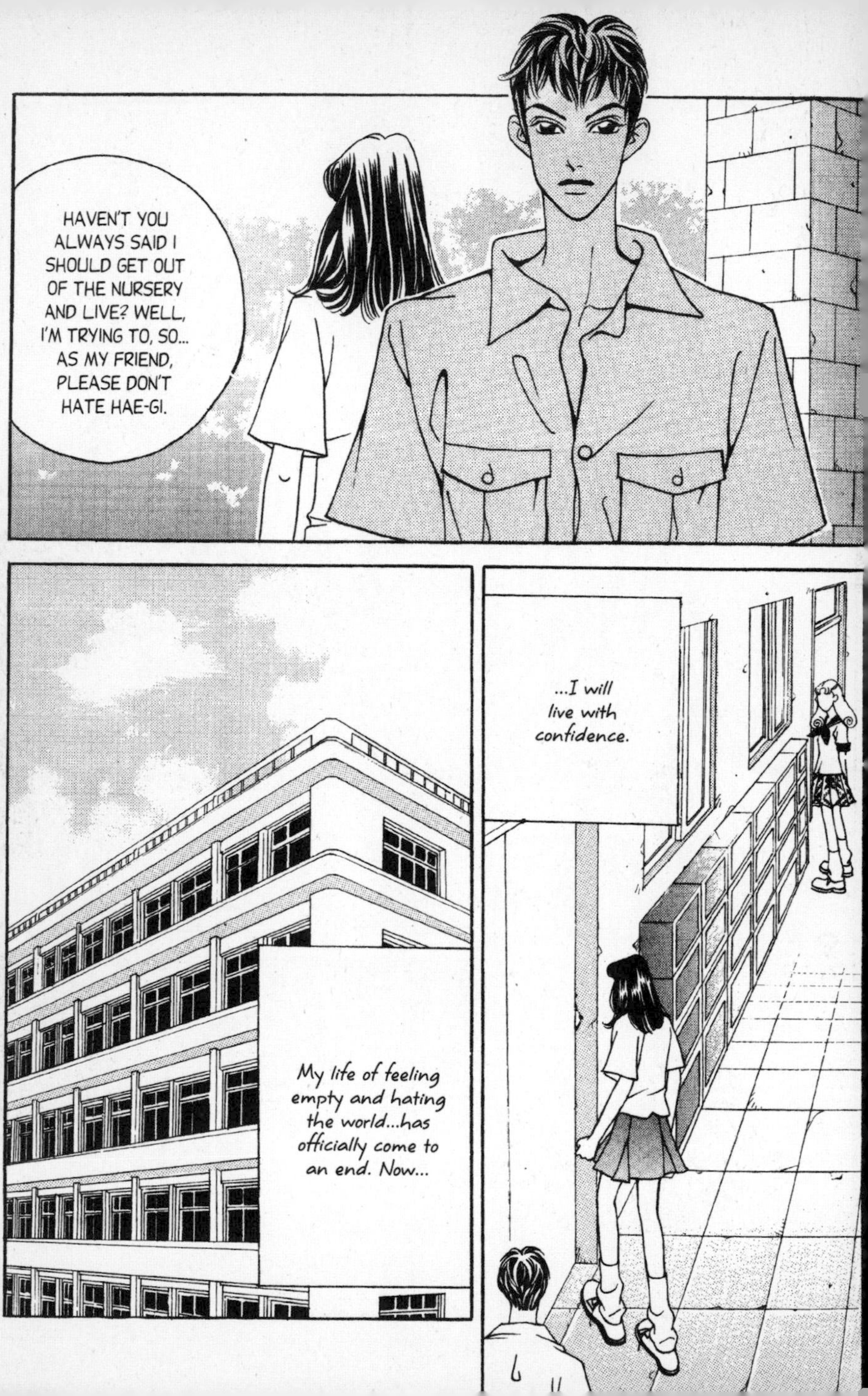
HAVEN'T YOU ALWAYS SAID I SHOULD GET OUT OF THE NURSERY AND LIVE? WELL, I'M TRYING TO, SO... AS MY FRIEND, PLEASE DON'T HATE HAE-GI.
My life of feeling empty and hating the world...has officially come to an end. Now...
...I will live with confidence.

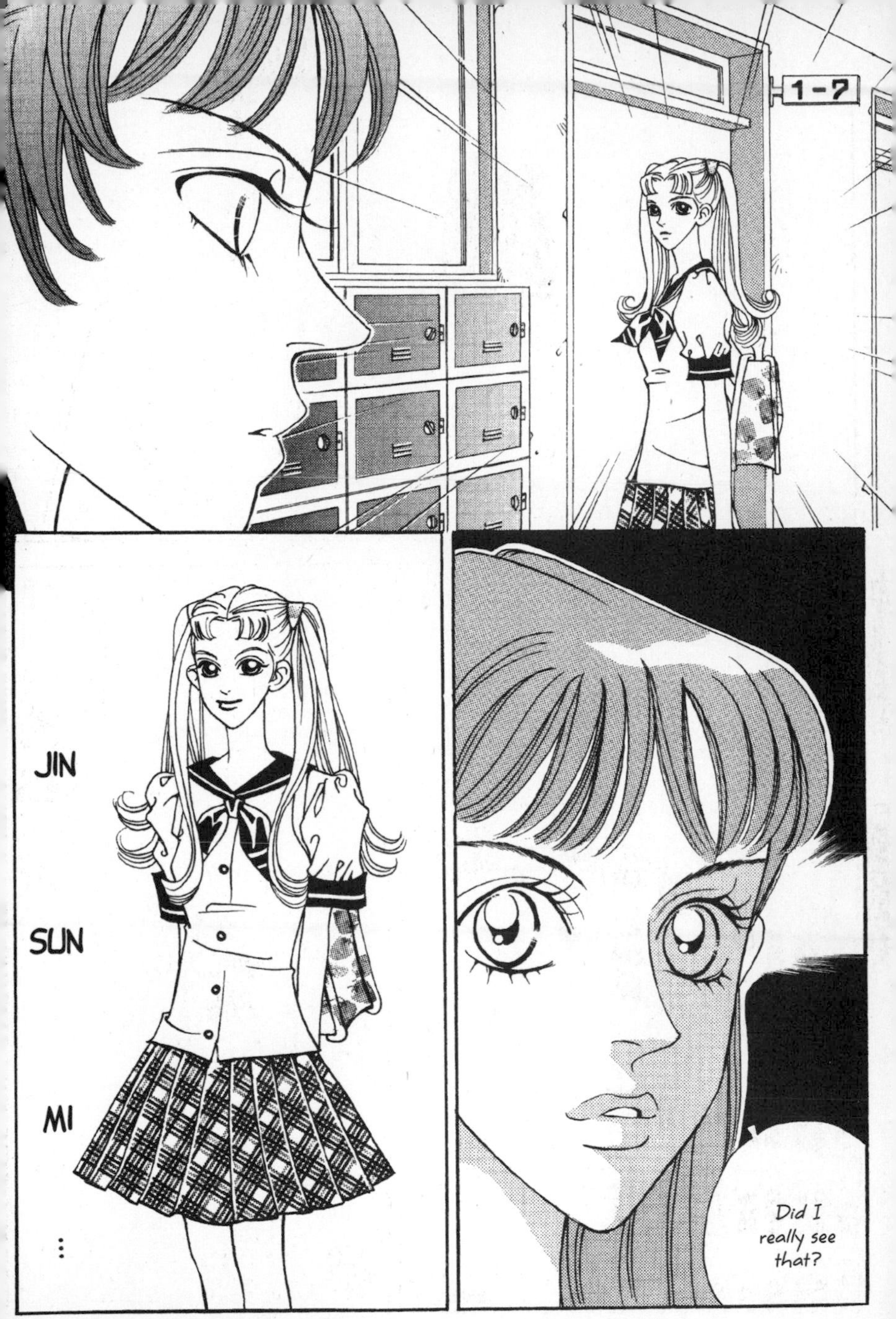
1-7
JIN
SUN
MI
...
Did I really see that?

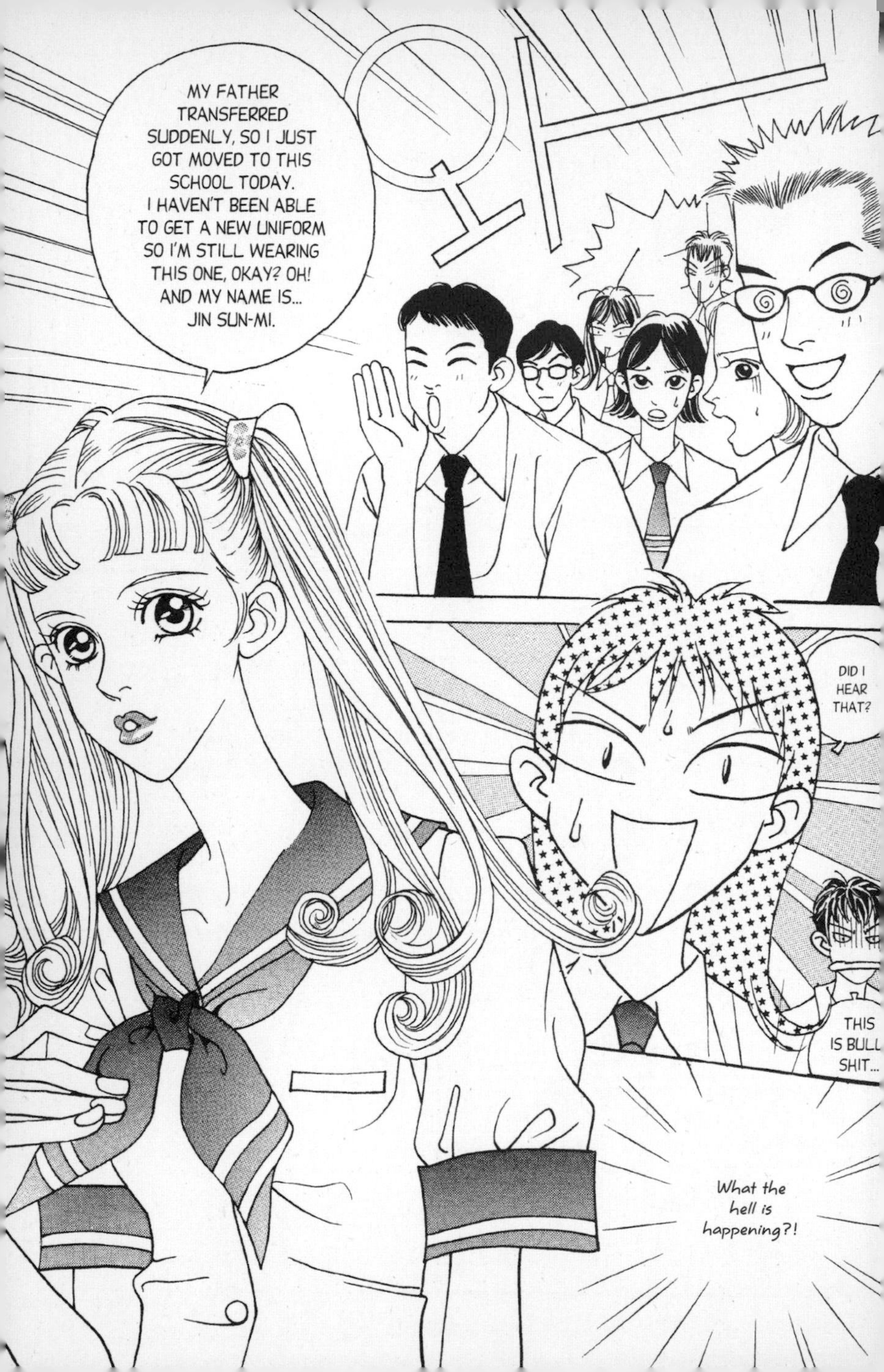
MY FATHER TRANSFERRED SUDDENLY, SO I JUST GOT MOVED TO THIS SCHOOL TODAY. I HAVEN'T BEEN ABLE TO GET A NEW UNIFORM SO I'M STILL WEARING THIS ONE, OKAY? OH! AND MY NAME IS... JIN SUN-MI.
DID I HEAR THAT?
THIS IS BULL SHIT...
What the hell is happening?!

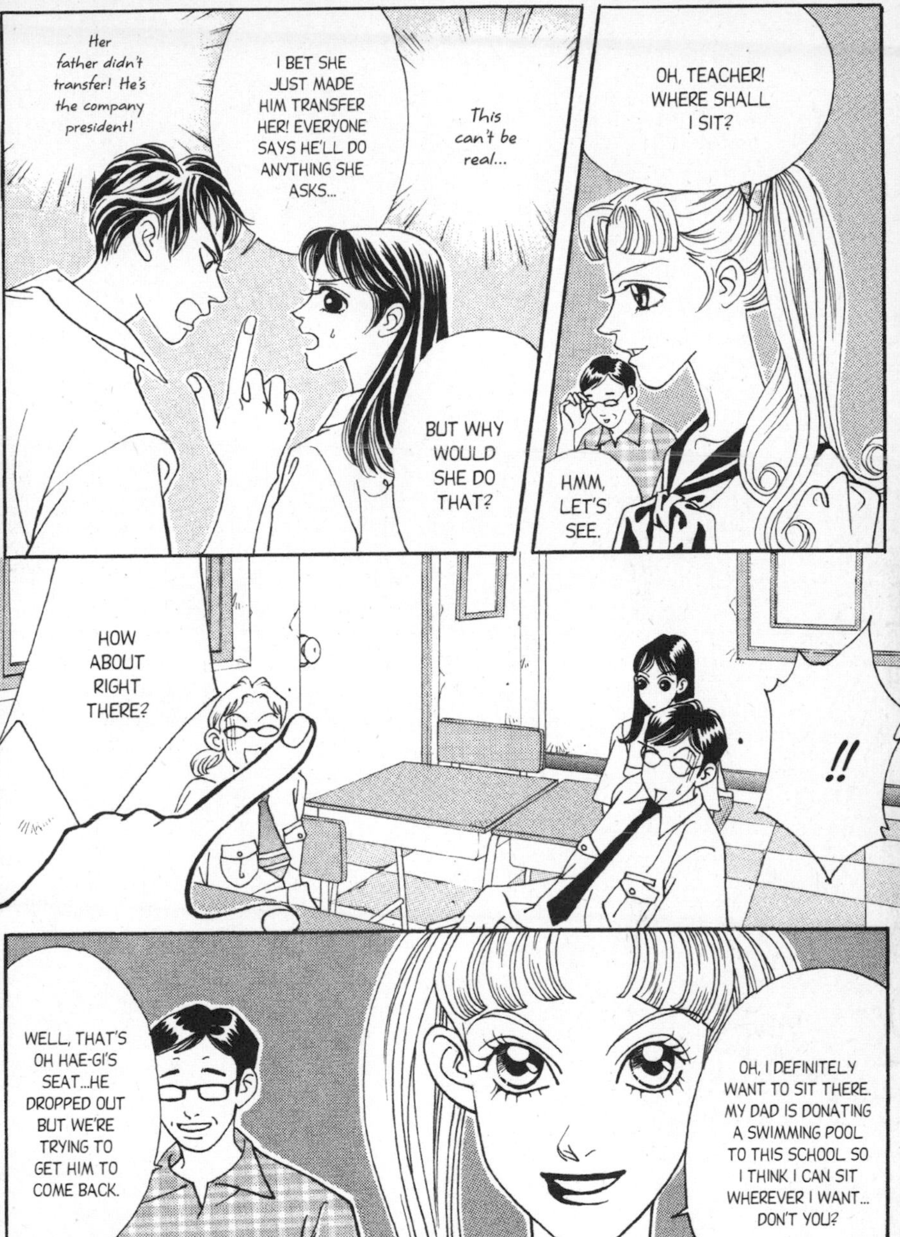
Her father didn't transfer! He's the company president!
I BET SHE JUST MADE HIM TRANSFER HER! EVERYONE SAYS HE'LL DO ANYTHING SHE ASKS...
This can't be real...
BUT WHY WOULD SHE DO THAT?
OH, TEACHER! WHERE SHALL I SIT?
HMM, LET'S SEE.
HOW ABOUT RIGHT THERE?
!!
WELL, THAT'S OH HAE-GI'S SEAT...HE DROPPED OUT BUT WE'RE TRYING TO GET HIM TO COME BACK.
OH, I DEFINITELY WANT TO SIT THERE. MY DAD IS DONATING A SWIMMING POOL TO THIS SCHOOL. SO I THINK I CAN SIT WHEREVER I WANT... DON'T YOU?

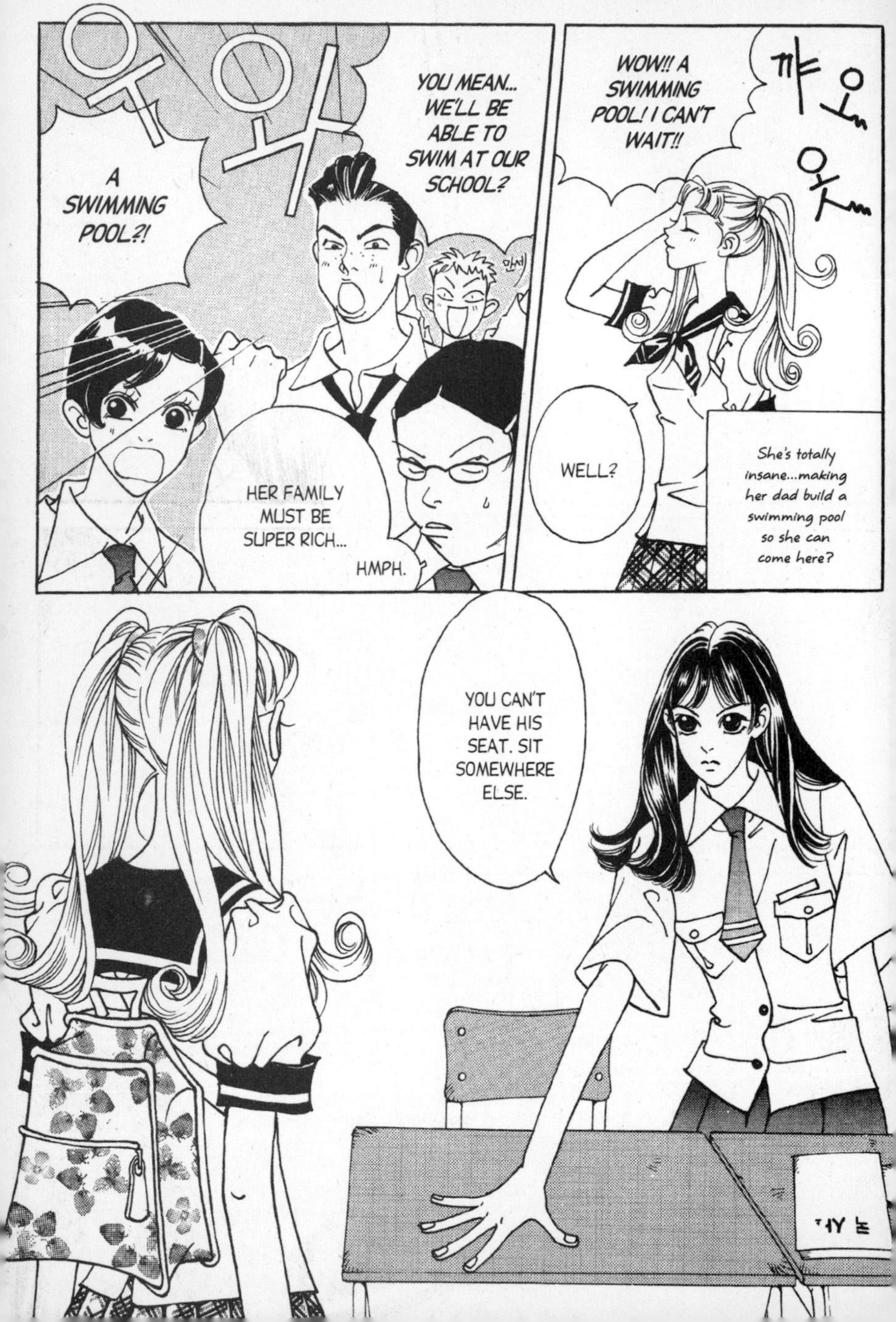
A SWIMMING POOL?!
YOU MEAN... WE'LL BE ABLE TO SWIM AT OUR SCHOOL?
만세
HER FAMILY MUST BE SUPER RICH...
HMPH.
WOW!! A SWIMMING POOL! I CAN'T WAIT!!
WELL?
She's totally insane...making her dad build a swimming pool so she can come here?
YOU CAN'T HAVE HIS SEAT. SIT SOMEWHERE ELSE.

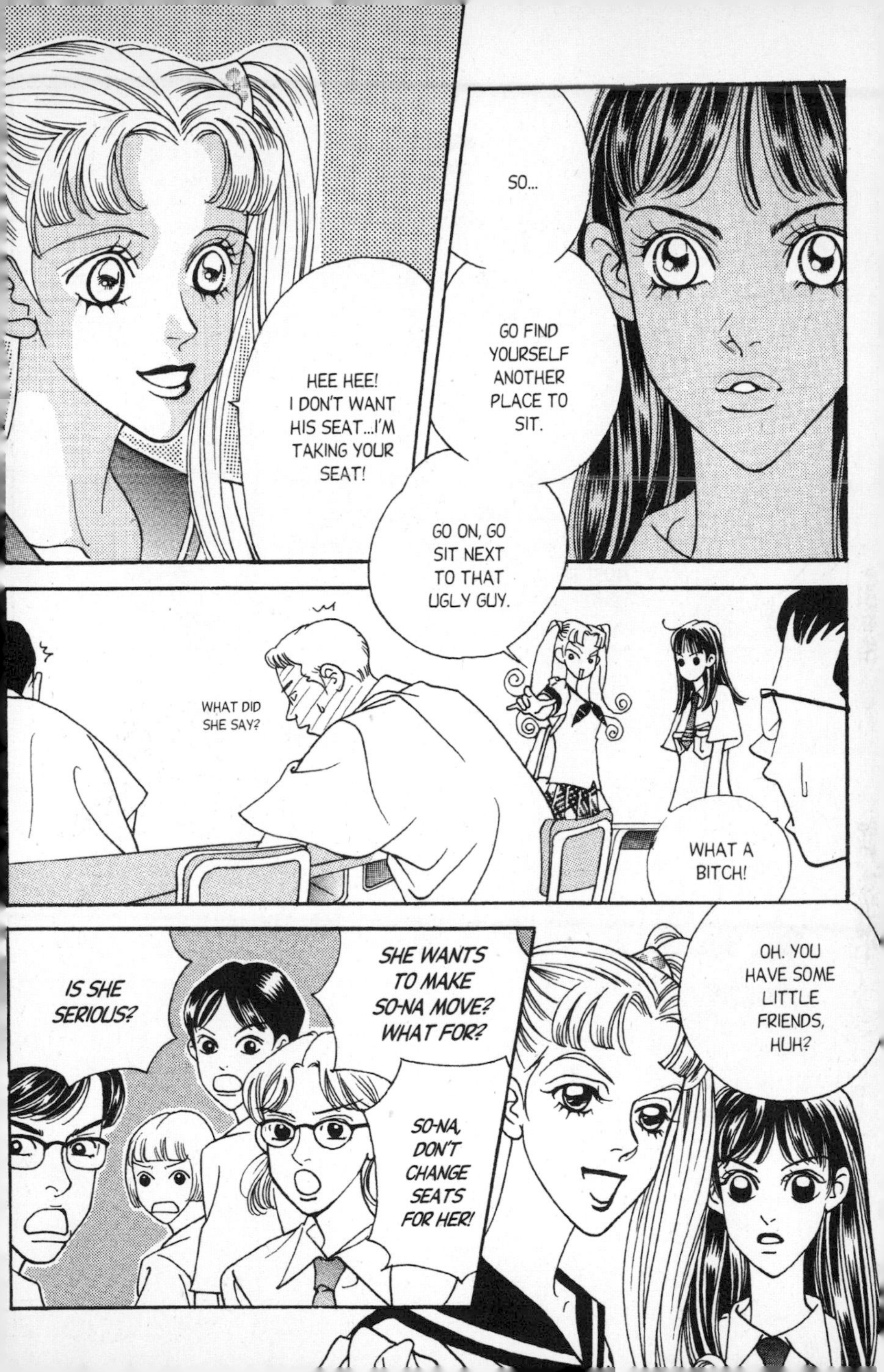
HEE HEE! I DON'T WANT HIS SEAT...I'M TAKING YOUR SEAT!
SO...
GO FIND YOURSELF ANOTHER PLACE TO SIT.
GO ON, GO SIT NEXT TO THAT UGLY GUY.
WHAT DID SHE SAY?
WHAT A BITCH!
IS SHE SERIOUS?
SHE WANTS TO MAKE SO-NA MOVE? WHAT FOR?
SO-NA, DON'T CHANGE SEATS FOR HER!
OH. YOU HAVE SOME LITTLE FRIENDS, HUH?

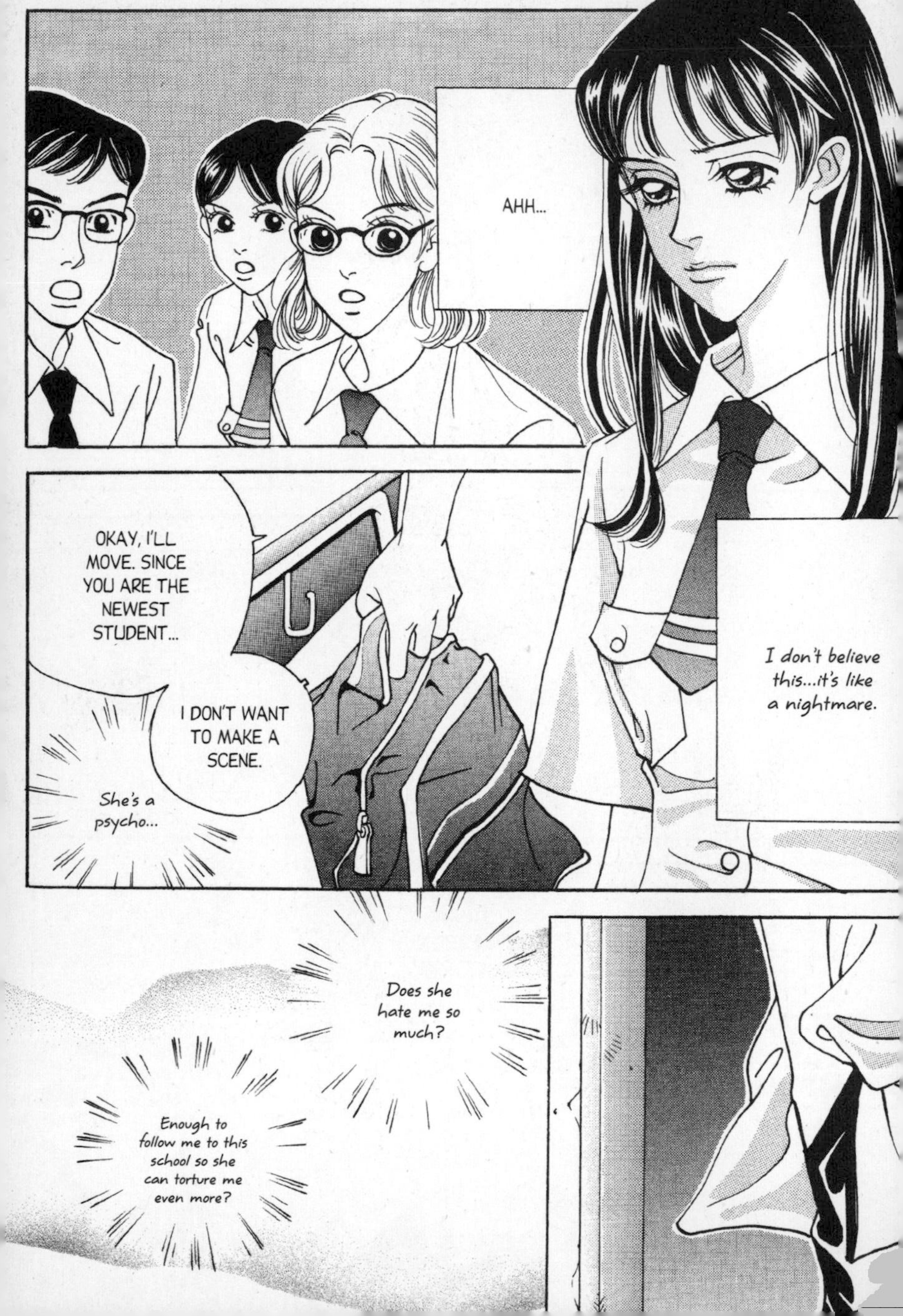
AHH...
OKAY, I'LL MOVE. SINCE YOU ARE THE NEWEST STUDENT...
I DON'T WANT TO MAKE A SCENE.
She's a psycho...
I don't believe this...it's like a nightmare.
Does she hate me so much?
Enough to follow me to this school so she can torture me even more?

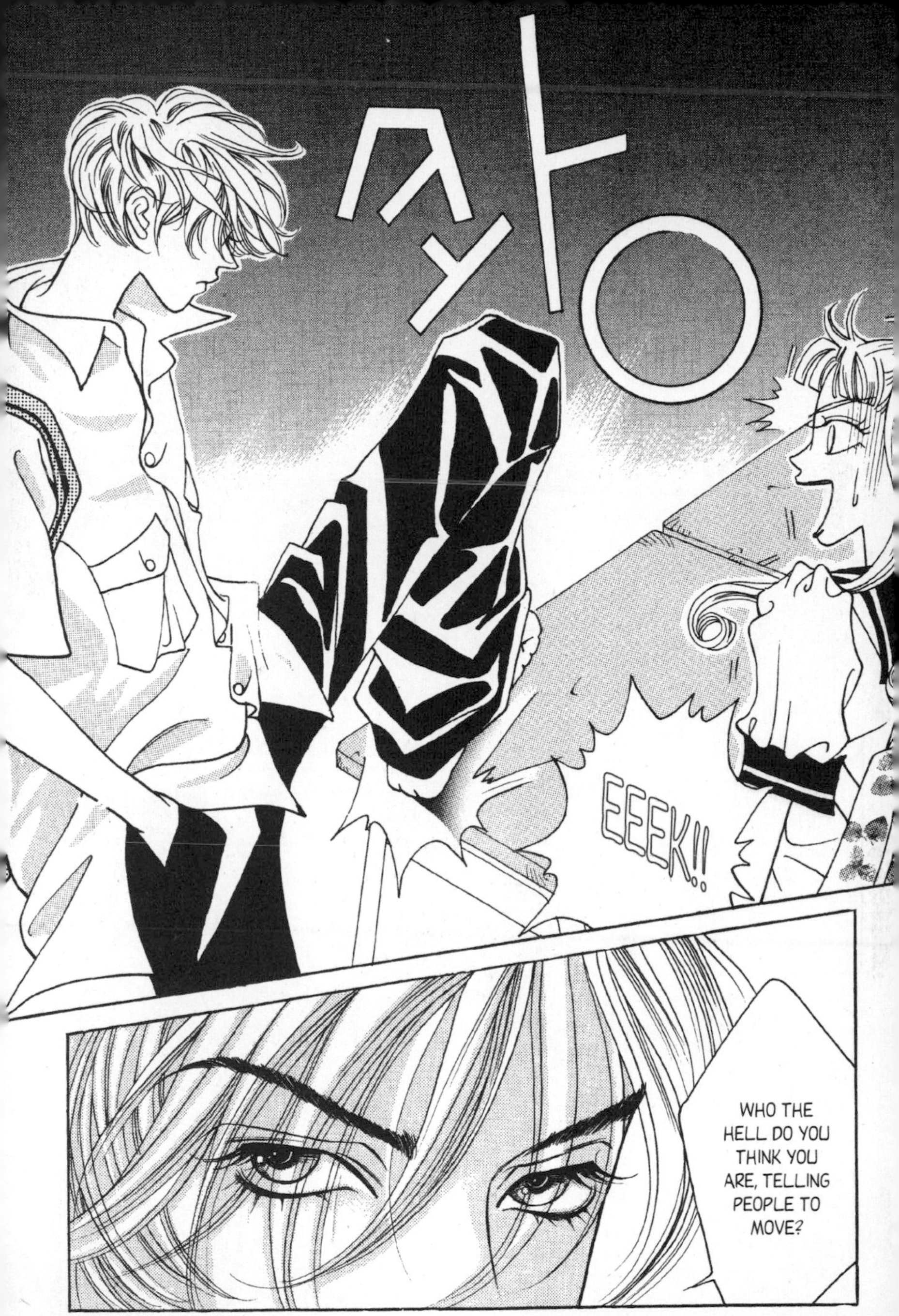
EEEK!!
WHO THE HELL DO YOU THINK YOU ARE, TELLING PEOPLE TO MOVE?

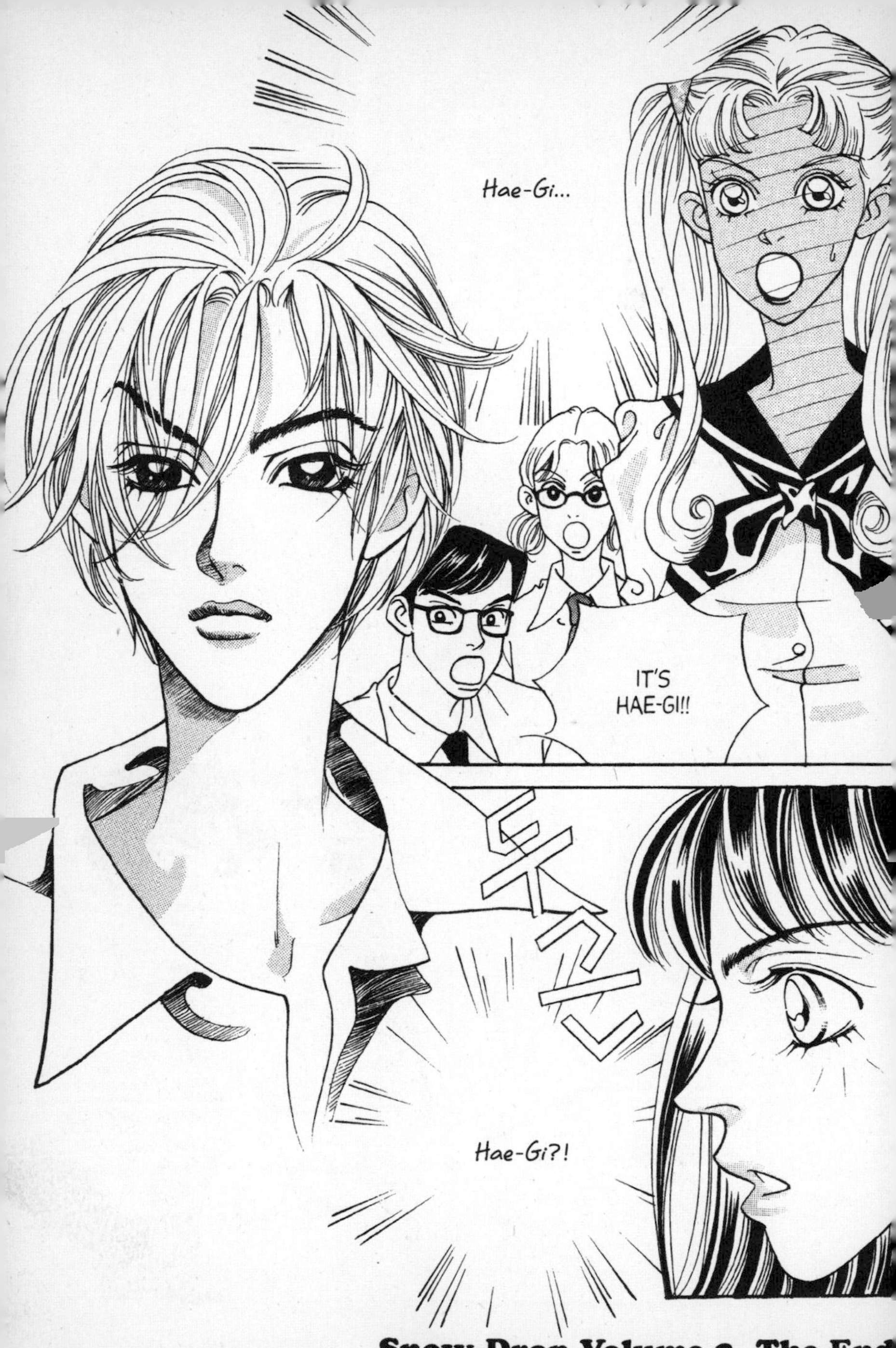
Hae-Gi...
IT'S HAE-GI!!
Hae-Gi?!

Snow Drop Volume 2 The End

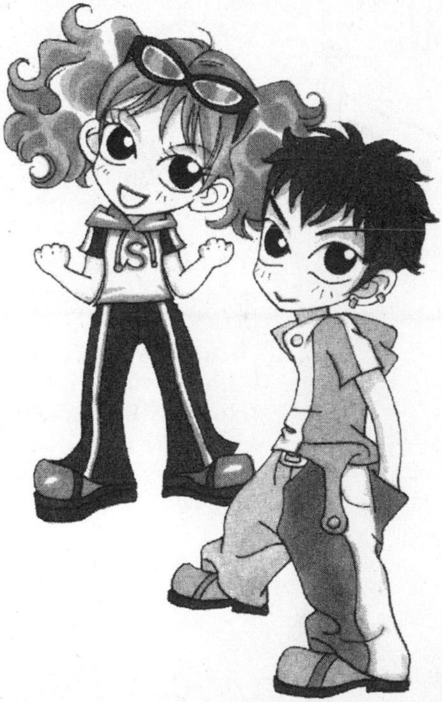
S

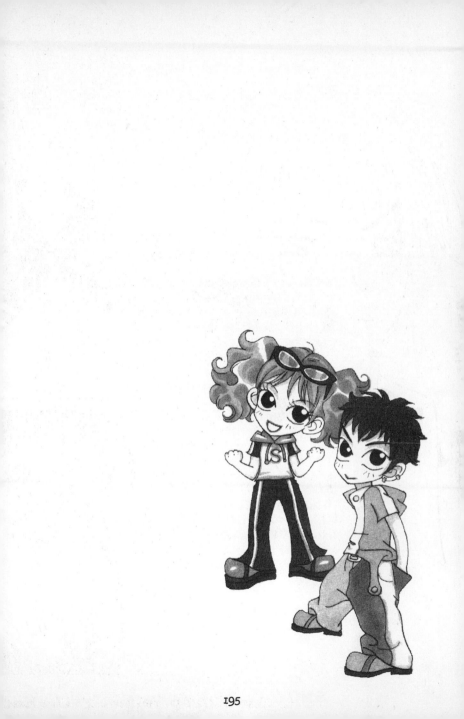

Coming in May...

Volume Three

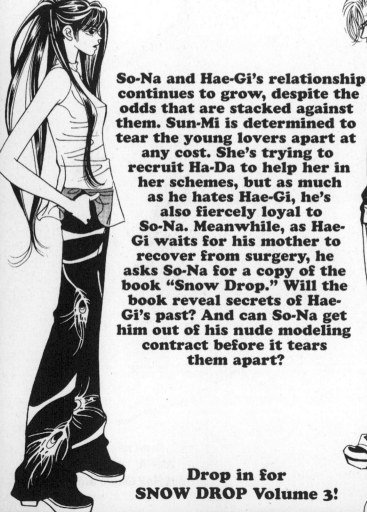

So-Na and Hae-Gi's relationship continues to grow, despite the odds that are stacked against them. Sun-Mi is determined to tear the young lovers apart at any cost. She's trying to recruit Ha-Da to help her in her schemes, but as much as he hates Hae-Gi, he's also fiercely loyal to So-Na. Meanwhile, as Hae-Gi waits for his mother to recover from surgery, he asks So-Na for a copy of the book "Snow Drop." Will the book reveal secrets of Hae-Gi's past? And can So-Na get him out of his nude modeling contract before it tears them apart?

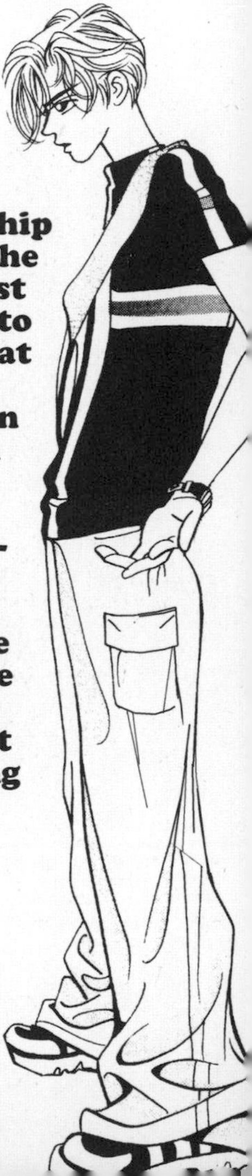

**Drop in for
SNOW DROP Volume 3!**

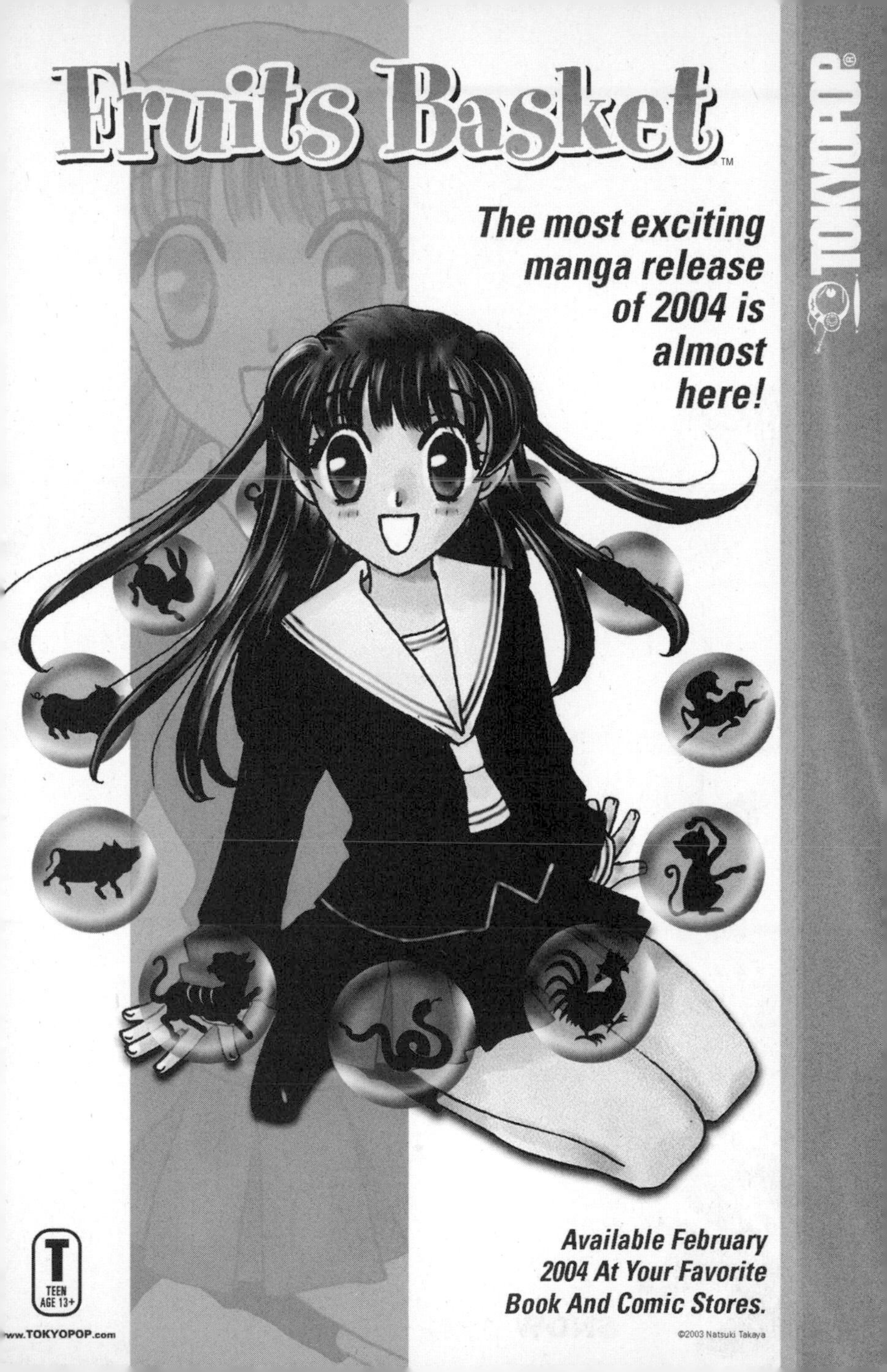
Fruits Basket™
The most exciting manga release of 2004 is almost here!
TOKYOPOP®
T TEEN AGE 13+
Available February 2004 At Your Favorite Book And Comic Stores.
ww.TOKYOPOP.com
©2003 Natsuki Takaya

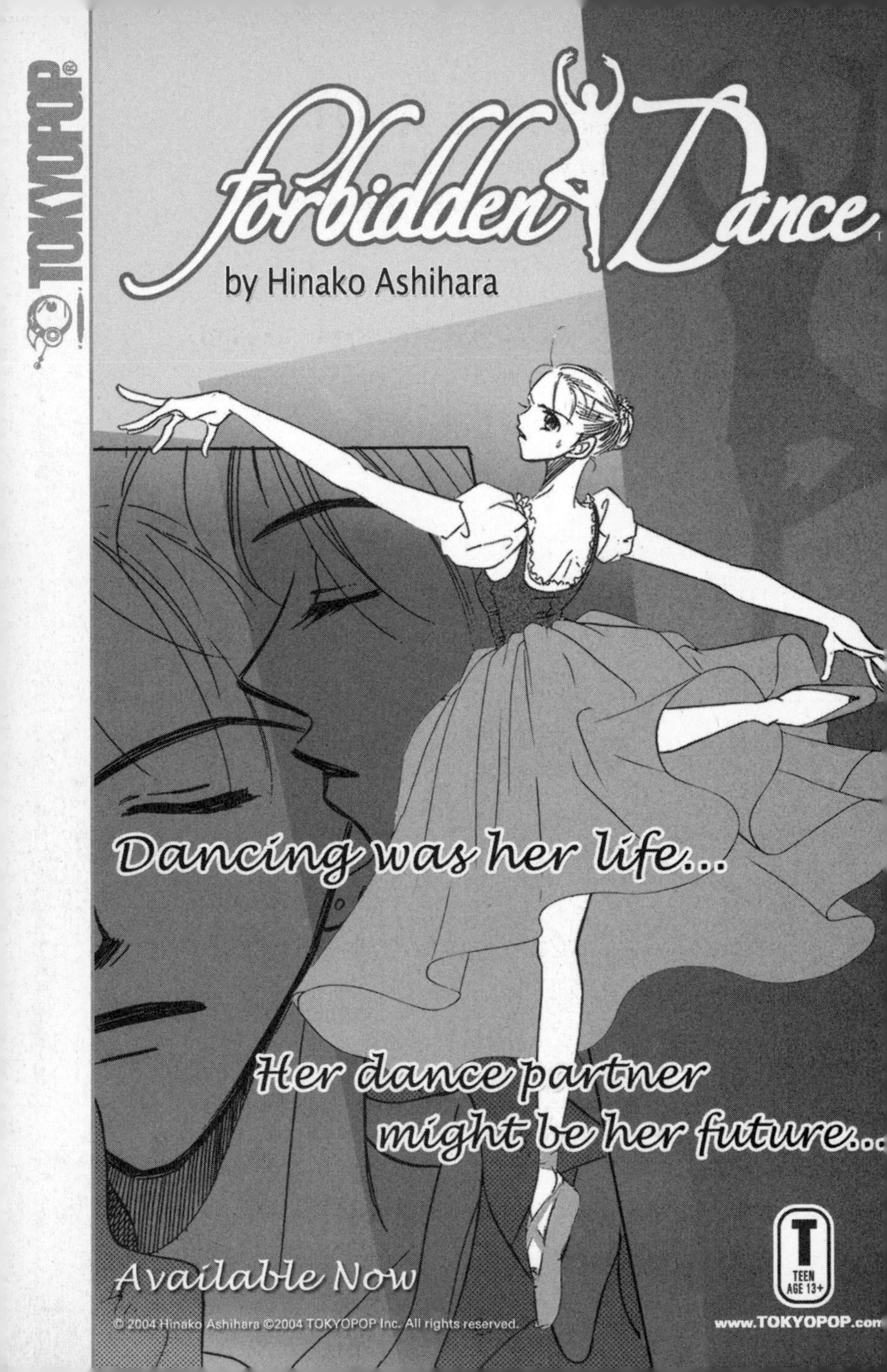

TOKYOPOP
Forbidden Dance
by Hinako Ashihara
Dancing was her life...
Her dance partner
might be her future...
Available Now
T
TEEN
AGE 13+
© 2004 Hinako Ashihara ©2004 TOKYOPOP Inc. All rights reserved.
www.TOKYOPOP.com

kare kano

his and her circumstances

Story by Masami Tsuda

Life Was A Popularity Contest For Yukino.
Somebody Is About To Steal Her Crown.

Available Now At Your Favorite Book And Comic Stores!

Rank	Name	Class	Points
1	???		
2	???		
3	Tomohiko Ta	B	
4	Takumi S	A	
5	Mieko Ta	E	
6	Nijo Watana	C	
7	Akemi Imafuku		
8	Mizue Ta aka		
9	Yuki Honj		
10	Reiko Yoko		
11	Hiroki Sato		
12	Akira Oshima		
13	Eri Yugawa		
14	Aiko Yama		
15	Shogo Ka		
16	Masami H		
17	Mizuho On		

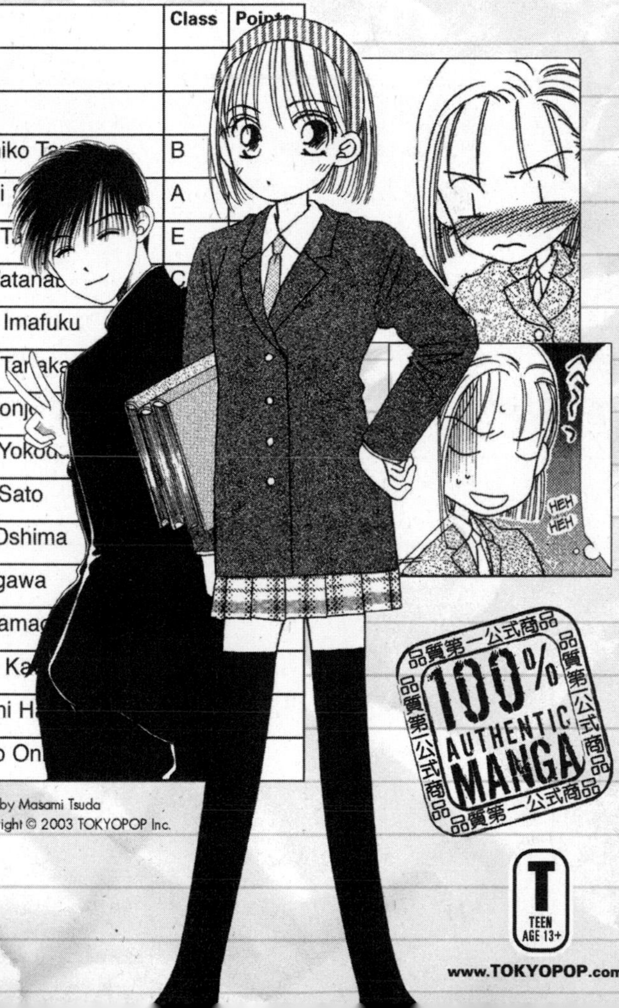
HEH
HEH
品質第一公式商品
100%
AUTHENTIC
MANGA

T
TEEN
AGE 13+

www.TOKYOPOP.com

TOKYOPOP®

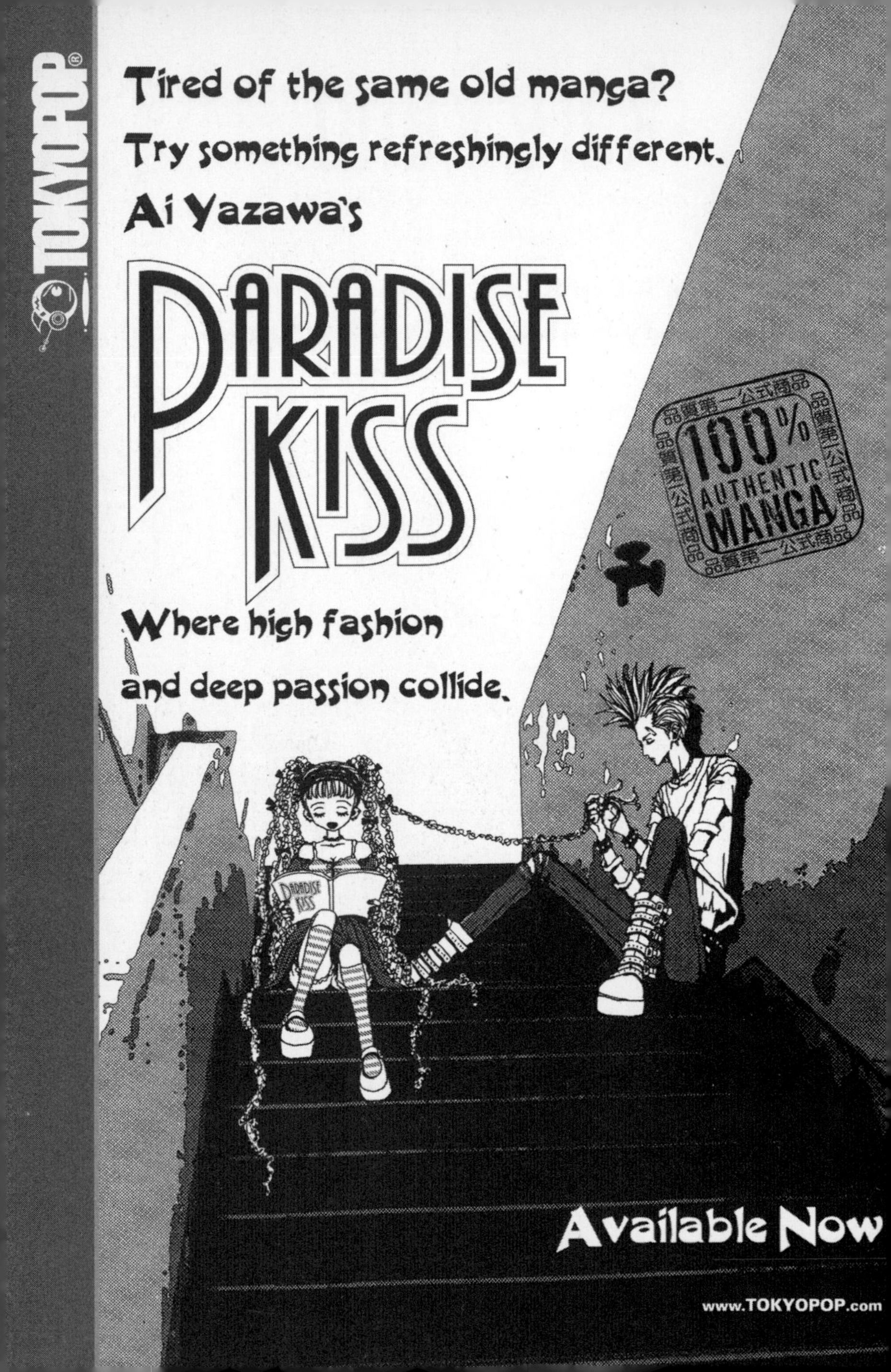
TOKYOPOP
Tired of the same old manga?
Try something refreshingly different.
Ai Yazawa's
PARADISE KISS
100% AUTHENTIC MANGA
Where high fashion
and deep passion collide.
Available Now
www.TOKYOPOP.com